B
Nel

Bradford
Nelson: the essential hero

DATE DUE

MAR. 1 8 1986		
MAR. 8 1989		
MAR. 1 6 1989		
GAYLORD		PRINTED IN U.S.A.

Nelson
THE ESSENTIAL HERO

Nelson

THE ESSENTIAL HERO

ERNLE BRADFORD

B
Nel

Harcourt Brace Jovanovich
New York and London

Printed in the United States of America

Library of Congress Cataloging in Publication Data

Bradford, Ernle Dusgate Selby.
Nelson: the essential hero.

Includes index.
1. Nelson, Horatio Nelson. Viscount, 1758-1805.
2. Admirals—Great Britain—Biography. 3. Great Britain. Navy—Biography.
DA87.1.N4B66   940.2′7′0924 [B]   77-73114
ISBN 0-15-112240-7

First American edition

B C D E

For my son
HUGH ERNLE

Contents

CONTENTS

List of illustrations and diagrams

Acknowledgements

The Author and Publishers wish to thank the National Maritime Museum, London, for their kind permission to reproduce the illustrations of plates 1, 2, 3, 4, 5, 7, 8, 9, 11, 13, 14 and 15, and the National Maritime Museum – Greenwich Hospital Collection – for plates 6, 10 and 12.

The lyf so short, the craft so long to lerne,
Th' assay so hard, so sharp the conquerynge.

Chaucer : *The Parlement of Foules*

CHAPTER ONE

Norfolk Boy

THE LAND where he was born is strange. Exposed to the North Sea, lighted by the curious water-skies that linger over the Wash and the Fens, Norfolk stands aloof from its neighbouring counties. Although the windmills which helped to grind the corn and drain the Fens have disappeared, Norfolk has changed little from the days when Nelson knew it as a boy. It has largely resisted the encroachments of the twentieth century. Above all, the dominant wind remains the same, the piercing cold easterly. It is its opposite, the westerly wind, which governs the climate of England, which brings the weather of the Atlantic, the great rolling seas that eat the coasts of Cornwall and Devon, the louring clouds that signal an advancing depression, and the rain-dropping nimbus with its darting offshoots of eddying wind that tear up trees. The westerly throws at the island those roaring Channel seas that have drowned many a hope. But the easterly is the bitterest wind that assails England's shores. It lashes into the great bight of the Wash and drives the North Sea fishermen ashore on that graveyard coast. At the same time, when in gentler mood, it brings the pale blue skies of East Anglia, and the shifting cloud-shapes that Constable recorded. It dominates the county, the home of the North Folk – descendants of those raiders who crossed from Germany in the fifth century and worked their way inland along the rivers, after they had secured their coastal bases behind them. Norfolk is a land of farmers built by sailors.

He was born on a fine autumn day, 29 September 1758, to the wife of the Rector of Burnham Thorpe, a village on the edge of the great salt marshes that fringe the Wash. He was the sixth child and the fifth son, although two elder brothers had died in infancy. His father, the Reverend Edmund Nelson, was himself the son of a clergyman, and had been educated at Caius College, Cambridge. On both sides the family was well-born, something not necessarily to be expected of a country clergyman in that day and age, when the old term 'hedge priest' might still be applied to many of them (especially in northern England), and when livings could often be £50 a year or less. But the Reverend Edmund came from a family who at one time had been considerable landowners (something that counted in the Norfolk of then, and now), and he had married well. His wife was a Miss Suckling, daughter of a late prebendary of Westminster, and was the great-niece of Sir Robert Walpole, who had been Prime Minister of England for twenty-one years. Sir Robert had represented the important Norfolk sea-port and market town of King's Lynn in Parliament until he was raised to the peerage as the Earl of Orford. It was from the Walpole family that the name Horatio derived, although the second bearer of the name, Horace of Strawberry Hill fame (who has also been called 'the best letter-writer in the English language'), preferred to be called Horace, 'an English name for an Englishman'. It would seem that the young Nelson felt rather similarly, for at the age of eleven, as one of the witnesses to a marriage, he signed himself in the registry at Burnham as Horace. His father altered the signature to 'Horatio', thus giving clear evidence of the fact that he had no wish to erase the eminent connection with the Walpoles. Indeed, at a later date, when the third Earl of Orford died, he instructed one of his daughters to put her family into mourning – as he had done his – since her great-grandmother and Sir Robert had been brother and sister.

A formal world, then, and a world where social relationships played a great part, was the one in which the young Horatio grew up. It was also, of course, overshadowed by the Church and by a quiet, loving father who might well have been the model for Goldsmith's Vicar of Wakefield : '[He] unites in himself the three greatest characters on earth; he is a priest, an husbandman, and a father of a family. . . . Such as are fond of high life will turn with disdain from the simplicity of his country fireside; such as mistake ribaldry for humour will find no wit in his harmless conversation; and such as have been taught to deride religion will laugh at one whose chief stores of comfort are drawn from futurity.' As the Reverend Edmund himself wrote in one of his letters describing life at Burnham Thorpe : 'Variety, the Great Idoll, has no shrine here.'

Of Nelson's mother we know little except, as her son was to recall in later years, that she 'hated the French'. She died when he was nine years old, having given birth to eleven children, three of whom died in infancy. The Nelsons were poor, and the rector contemplated a widower's life with the quiet resignation that seems to have marked his character. Yet he faced what was clearly going to be a difficult future with the courage that he derived from his genuine faith and a strict sense of discipline, both qualities which Nelson was to inherit. (The Reverend Edmund, for instance, would not tolerate any slovenly behaviour and believed that, when one is seated, the spine should be kept upright and not allowed to touch the back of the chair.) As well as seven older children, he had a nine-month-old baby to look after. Nurse Blackett, later to become the wife of a Mr High, landlord of the Old Ship at Brancaster, undoubtedly played a large part in the life of the family from now on. There were two menservants, and maids from the village would have come in to help with the house. This, an old L-shaped building, formed out of two cottages, was pulled down a few years before Nelson's death. But contemporary pictures of the hero's birthplace have left us with an image of an unpretentious two-storeyed building with red tiles, sleeping under an East Anglian sky. It was a home of a type such as is still to be found all over this part of the world. Together with the house went some thirty acres of land, through which ran a clear swift stream. Nelson grew up a countryman, and many times throughout his career he hankered for the peace and quiet that he had known as a boy. Burnham Thorpe's parish church of All Saints was over a mile from the Parsonage. Despite some restoration, it still survives much as he must have known it, with its weathered old font, and its mid-thirteenth-century pillars supporting the nave. The most distinctive additions are the large rood and lectern both made out of oak taken from H.M.S. *Victory*. It is peaceful here, part of an unchanging England, a far call from the London where he lies. On a summer's day, away from the roads, the eternal face of the countryside presents itself as it did to Nelson, and to his father, who spoke lovingly of his 'charming open lawns and fields'.

School was soon to claim the growing boy. He went to three in all, the High School at Norwich, a school at Downham Market, and another at North Walsham. Here his presence is recalled by a brick into which are incised the initials H.N. Like all schoolboys, he wished to make his mark, though this first evidence of his desire to be remembered is touching and prophetic. His education was simple but sound – all the better for that. As G. M. Trevelyan wrote of the period : 'There was no large half-educated class, and therefore the intellectual and literary standard of our ancestors was in some respects higher than our own. . . . The modern as well as the ancient classics held a much greater place in the national consciousness than today. Shakespeare and Milton were familiar to almost all who could read and write.' A Prussian pastor, who visited England in 1782, described one aspect of the world that Nelson knew in his Norfolk boyhood: 'Those living hedges which in England, more than in any other country, form the boundaries of the green cornfields, and give to the whole distant country, the appearance of a large and majestic garden. . . .' On the subject of education, he confirms that 'the English national authors are in all hands. My landlady, who is a taylor's widow, reads her Milton; and tells me that her late husband first fell in love with her because she read Milton with such proper emphasis.'

As in the case of all famous men, legends abound about Nelson's youth but, as the main source of these was his own family, they cannot entirely be discounted. The earliest describes how, as a small child, he was staying with his grandmother at Hilborough and wandered off bird's-nesting with another boy. When he had been lost for hours, with darkness approaching, alarm was felt in the house and people were sent out to look for him. He was found alone sitting beside a stream which was too wide for him to cross and brought back to his grandmother, who said to him: 'I wonder, child, that hunger and fear did not drive you home.' 'Fear', replied the boy, 'never came near me.' Whether one takes this as apocryphal, or as no more than a child's ignorance of what was meant by the word 'fear', the fact remains that in later life Nelson was not one of those blindly ignorant 'heroes' who rush into situations without being aware of danger. As he himself remarked: 'The brave man feels an anxiety *circa praecordia* as he enters the battle.'

Another anecdote concerns his time at school in North Walsham, where the headmaster 'Classic Jones' was noted for his generous use of the birch. Some fine pears growing in the garden aroused the natural greed of all the boys, but they were afraid of 'so keen a flogger' and left them carefully alone. Only Nelson, lowered down from the dormitory window at night on knotted sheets, would venture into Classic Jones's garden. Returning with the longed-for pears, he distributed them among the other boys, keeping none for himself for, as he said: 'I only took them because every other boy was afraid.' Next morning the large sum of five guineas was offered as a reward for anyone who would identify the thief, 'but young Nelson was too much beloved for any boy to betray him'. It is difficult not to dislike the element of sanctimonious priggishness implicit in such stories, but due allowance must be made for the fact that they were written in the early nineteenth century to embellish a national hero.

A story which his elder brother William was to tell of him with admiration in later years describes how he and Horatio were sent out on their ponies by their father one winter's day to make their way to school. When the snow, driven whirling by the North Sea wind, falls on that part of Norfolk it piles high in great drifts, obscures the guide-lines of the hedges, and even today can leave villages cut off from one another for days at a time. In the eighteenth century, when it was only man and horse or, as in this case, boy and pony, roads could quickly become impassable, as the two young Nelsons now found out. Returning home, they told their father of the snow conditions, but he urged them to make one more try. If it was dangerous, then they should return, he said, but it was left to their honour not to come back without good reason. Off they set again and, after going some distance, William came to the conclusion that they should abandon the attempt. Horatio would not hear of it. 'Remember, brother, it was left to our honour.'

If the rest of the family were to live lives of quiet undistinction, so that we know of them only because of Horatio's subsequent fame, they were typical in many ways of hundreds of similar families living in eighteenth-century England. Maurice, who was five years older than Horatio, became a clerk in the Navy Office; then there was Susannah, three years older than himself, who married a Thomas Bolton of Suffolk; and William, closest to him in boyhood and only a year older, who ultimately took Holy Orders like his father. A younger sister, Anne, died in her twenties; Edmund, four years younger, died before he was thirty. Another younger brother, Suckling, good-natured but indolent, also took Holy Orders, became his father's curate, and died in his thirties. The youngest, Catherine, a favourite of Nelson's, who was nine months old when her mother died, was to marry George Matcham, a man of some substance but little purpose, and bear him a large family. Prior to this, at a time when it looked as if his father might die and Catherine be left homeless, Nelson wrote from abroad that if this occurred he would 'immediately come to England and most probably fix in some place that might be most for poor Kitty's advantage. My small income shall always be at her service, and she shall never want a protector and a sincere friend while I exist.' He was, in fact, prepared to give up his career in order to see that his young sister was properly cared for. In the eighteenth century the family bond and family obligations, especially among country people like the Nelsons, were very close and real.

The winters in East Anglia are harsh, long and cold. It was the custom of the Reverend Edmund Nelson, whenever he could, to travel across to the famous West Country spa of Bath during the winter to take the waters, enjoy the warmer climate, and – though he was well used to the quiet monotony of his Norfolk parsonage – to see a little of the great outside world. As he wrote in a letter, with his habitual self-disparagement, he had little to offer 'except a willingness to make my family comfortable when near me and not unmindful of me when at a distance, and as it has fallen to my Lott to take upon me the care and affection of double parent, they will Hereafter excuse where I have fallen short and the task has been too Hard'.

It was perhaps not without some relief that the Reverend Edmund received a letter while he was in Bath in the winter of 1770, written by his son William. It was not on his own behalf that he wrote but on that of young Horatio. The two boys had read in a local newspaper that their uncle Captain Maurice Suckling had been appointed in command of the *Raisonable*, a warship of 64 guns, which had been recommissioned in view of an impending war with Spain. Horatio's request that his father ask Captain Suckling if he would take the boy aboard his new command was met by Suckling with the jovial, if cynical, response : 'What has poor Horatio done, who is so weak, that he, above all the rest, should be sent to rough it out at sea? But let him come and the first time we go into action a cannon-ball may knock off his head, and provide for him at once.' Suckling was to become Comptroller of the Navy as well as M.P. for Portsmouth, and was to prove a good friend to the young Nelson, but he was certainly under no illusions about the latter's physique. All the Nelson boys appear to have been sickly, and Nelson was small-boned, undersized and, on the face of it, the least likely to survive in a world that called for almost superhuman qualities of strength and endurance. All his life, in fact, quite apart from his wounds, he was to suffer from ill-health.

At the age of twelve years and three months, Nelson was rated on the books of the *Raisonable* as midshipman. There was no examination – he had on the face of it no qualifications – but there was nothing unusual in this. His uncle was the Captain, and that was enough. He had in any case chosen his own destiny, and, though he must have been quite ignorant of what life was like aboard a man-of-war, something deep in his nature had made this choice. (He might in due course have opted for Holy Orders which, some aspects of his character reveal, might equally well have suited him.) In any case, he was to do one more term at school, for the *Raisonable* had not yet finished her refit. It was not until March 1771 that a small, bewildered boy saw London for the first time and heard the deep murmur of the capital, lying under its greasy cowl of sea-coal.

His father, who had accompanied him up from King's Lynn, saw him aboard the stage-coach bound for Chatham. For the first time in his life Horatio was completely separated from family, in a world of strangers, and destined for a world about which he knew little except what he had gleaned from gossip or newspaper reports, as they filtered into the quiet drawing-rooms and parlours of Norfolk. He was to have an early foretaste of the harsh life that awaited him, for he was not expected by anyone, and his uncle was not aboard his ship – to which he was finally directed by a kindly officer who found a young boy with a soft Norfolk burr inquiring the whereabouts of the *Raisonable*. Given some refreshment and sent on his way, Nelson later recalled how he spent all the first night pacing the deck. He smelled for the first time the damp oak, the tarred rigging, and heard the wind stir over the great dockyard that had been founded by Henry VIII in the early days of England's naval expansion. It was not until the following morning that someone inquired his name and took pity on him – probably taking him below and giving him a plate of burgoo, the rough porridge with which day aboard ship more often than not began. In the early light, as he looked around the unfamiliar scene, he may well have admired a first-rate of 100 guns lying nearby. Launched only six years before, she was untried and held in reserve. On her stern in yellow letters twelve inches high was proclaimed her name : VICTORY.

Captain Suckling, who had already distinguished himself in 1757 in an action against heavy odds off the West Indies, was recognised as a distinguished sea officer and one who ran a tight ship. It is possible that his young nephew escaped some of the rigours of the midshipmen's mess, but somewhat unlikely. In that iron age it was generally accepted that, as life aboard was almost equally unpleasant for all, the young ones had better start where the going was as rough as anything they were ever likely to encounter. Many years afterwards, in his *Reminiscences* (1843), Lieutenant George Parsons recalled how he dined when a midshipman aboard the *Foudroyant* with Lord Nelson, on the anniversary of the Battle of St Vincent :

'His Lordship, after taking a bumper in honour of the glorious victory of the year ninety-seven, addressed me in a bland tone –

"You entered the service at a very early age, to have been in the action off St Vincent?"

"Eleven years, my lord."

"Much too young," muttered his Lordship.'

And now, only a year and a few months older himself, Horatio was to learn the realities of the sea-life as it was first encountered by aspirants to rank, fame and fortune – which only a minute handful ever achieved.

CHAPTER TWO

Ships and Men

A 64-GUN SHIP like the *Raisonable*, which was Nelson's first introduction to the world that he was to serve for the rest of his life, was similar in her construction to all the other ships he was to know – whether frigates, or schooners, or even giant first-rates like the *Victory*. In many respects they had changed little over the centuries, and a sailor of Drake's time, though he would have at first been confused by the size of the vessels and the multiplicity of their standing and running rigging, would quite soon have felt himself at home. Oak was the heart of these ships, much of it grown in the great royal forests like the New Forest in Hampshire and the Forest of Dean in Gloucestershire. In theory it should never have been used until it had been properly seasoned, being left for at least a year after cutting. But during the Napoleonic Wars especially, with the immense expansion of the fleet, it was inevitable that green oak should come into use – as well as Baltic oak, which was never as good as the native product. A ship like the *Raisonable* would have required nearly two thousand trees for her construction.

The principal shipbuilding yards of the country were at Chatham, Deptford, Plymouth, and Woolwich, and it was here that the ships were designed in large 'mould-lofts' by master-shipwrights, who drew out the plans at full size on the floor of the great sheds, the side elevations similarly being drawn on the high walls. Once the design was approved, and the timber ordered, the first step was to lay down the keel. This, unlike most of the rest of the vessel, was of elm, often sheathed with a false keel, also of elm, to protect the backbone of the vessel in the event of her grounding. Built in the open air, the smaller vessels were usually constructed on slips so that they could be run down to the water's edge upon completion. Very large ships like the first-rates, on the other hand, were more often than not built in dry docks so that in due course they could simply be floated out, by letting in the sea through sluices.

Since the terms will constantly occur in the story of Nelson's life,
it must be explained that a first-rate like the *Victory*, mounting 100
guns and more, was 186 feet long on the waterline, with an extreme
breadth of 52 feet, a draught of about 21 feet, and a tonnage of
approximately 2,200. A second-rate would be 170 feet long with
equivalently diminishing proportions, a third-rate 160 feet, a fourth-
rate 144 feet, and so on down to the small brigs and schooners that
were used as maids-of-all-work. First-, second- and third-rates formed
the Navy's battle fleet, and were generally referred to as ships-of-the-
line, or line-of-battle ships, since they fought in line-ahead formation.
All other ships, from those mounting 50 to 60 guns down to the fast,
relatively lightly armed frigates, were known as 'below the line'.

Quite apart from fire – the greatest hazard whether in battle or
through negligence – the main enemy of the wooden ship was the
teredo worm, *Teredo navalis*, which had been well known to mariners
since ancient times (metal sheathing to protect the hulls under water
having been used by both Greeks and Romans). This marine borer
enters the hull quite inconspicuously, then proceeds to tunnel its way
along the wood so that in due course, with hundreds of these marine
molluscs quietly eating away, a plank which to outward appearance
looks perfectly sound is no more than an empty honeycomb. More
common in warm waters than in northern climates, it had nevertheless
been brought back to such an extent by foreign-going vessels over the
centuries that no part or port of Europe was safe from its menace. At
one time lead sheathing had been used in large vessels, but this was
extremely expensive, as well as weighty, and it had finally been discovered that the best all-round protection was provided by thin sheets
of copper nailed over heavy brown paper, which had been plastered
on to the hull with pitch. A further advantage of copper was that it
not only kept out the worm but also made it more difficult for
barnacles and other marine growths to adhere to the ship's bottom.
In days when even a fast ship like a frigate might make no more than
nine knots under good sailing-conditions, a good clean copper bottom
was highly important. Heavy marine growth could take two knots or
so off a ship's speed.

After the final operation of sheathing the ship and launching her,
she was then towed out to what was called a sheer hulk, usually an
old man-of-war which had had her two upper decks removed and
sheer-legs and other lifting gear sited on what had once been her
lower gun-deck. The operation of masting the new vessel now began.
The masts, a stock of which was kept at all the dockyards, were of fir
and were preserved until needed in a mast-pond of brine. Except in

small vessels where one fir might serve as a mast, the masts of all ships of any size were built out of two or more lengths of fir which were bound together with iron hoops. Once completed, the mast was heaved up on the sheer-legs and then lowered into the ship, the heel of the mast being stepped into immensely strong sockets at the bottom of the ship. The timbers which formed these lay across the keelson, the inner part of the keel. Once the fore, main and mizzen masts were in position, the master-riggers and their mates took over, setting up the lower and bowsprit rigging first and then sending aloft the top-masts and the rigging to support them. There was no wire rope in those days, so all the complexity of the standing rigging depended on hemp rope, heavily tarred on the outside to protect it against wind and weather. After this the fir yards, on which the ship's motive power – her square-sails – depended, were sent aloft and 'crossed' on their respective masts.

Ships like the *Raisonable*, as well as her much larger sisters, would have appeared heavy and unwieldy to the eyes of sailors of the later nineteenth century, when the clipper ship – that perfection of nautical design – had been evolved. But the purpose of the man-of-war was to serve as a floating platform for guns, and as such, when her vast areas of canvas were spread and she surged down the seaways of the world, there has probably never been a more beautiful or imposing sight in the whole history of man the navigator. The guns – it was to serve these that all the men worked, and it was to bring them into the best position to batter in the sides of the enemy that the skills of men, officers, captains and admirals were directed. It was in the sight, smell, service and thunder of them that all these men lived and died. The famous broadside of which one hears so much in history – and sub-sequent fiction – did not mean that all the guns on one side were fired at the very same moment. Strong though the ship's planking, ribs and main timbers were, the whole structure would have hardly withstood the immense recoil and concussion for any length of time. The normal practice was what was known as 'ripple firing', in which the guns were fired consecutively from the forward end of the ship to the stern. Then, as each gun had fired, was run back, scoured out (to remove any burning scraps left in barrel), reloaded and run out again, the whole process was repeated. An efficient gun's crew could get off three rounds in little more than two minutes.

The guns had changed little since Elizabethan days although, like the ships themselves, they had become heavier and more powerful. The advantages of breech-loading had long been understood, but there had not been sufficient technological advance to construct an efficient breech that could withstand the concussion of the explosion. In Nelson's navy the guns were muzzle-loaders. They were almost all of iron (a very few were still of bronze), the metal itself being cast as a solid block and then bored smooth. They were known by the weight of ball they fired : i.e. 12 pound, 18, 24, and 32; 42-pounders had been tried in the larger vessels but they had been generally found too cumbrous to handle, and the 32-pounder was the standard major gun in the first-rates of the time. A 32-pound gun, weighing 2 tons, was $8\frac{1}{2}$ feet long, and was manned by a crew of fifteen men. This included the boys (or, on occasion, women who were aboard) employed in bringing up the powder from the magazines. Gunpowder was the only propellant, and the maximum range was about 2,500 yards. Really effective range was a good deal less, and the whole process of a naval engagement consisted in battering the enemy into submission, principally by bringing down his masts and yards so that he could no longer navigate or even maintain steerage-way. Chain-shot, two balls or half-balls connected by a link of chain, was used against rigging, while grapeshot and canister-shot were used for anti-personnel purposes.

Of whatever size the gun, the process of firing remained the same. First of all the powder had to be brought up from the main magazines, sited deep in the ship (a first-rate like the *Victory*, for instance, carried 35 tons of powder in her magazine) where it was taken to a ready-use magazine, measured into flannel bags and then transported to the guns. A gun which had just been fired would be cleaned out with a corkscrew-like instrument, known as the worm, which would then be followed by the sponge. The bag of powder was next inserted, followed by the shot itself, each of which was driven down the muzzle by the rammer. Sometimes two rounds of shot were put in the gun (double-shotting), and in all cases a wad was tamped down to keep everything in place. While this operation was going on, the gunner cleaned out (rimed) the vent, piercing the cartridge bag after doing so, and then inserted a quill filled with fine powder into the vent itself. The gun, having been run out by means of tackles, was then trimmed right or left by handspikes, a rough-and-ready method that had not changed over the centuries. Since, in the gunnery of that period, everything depended upon the ship's heading – which was where the handling of the ship was so important – there was very little that the gunner could do in the way of laying his weapons. He had, in any case, no more than a very simple sight on the muzzle, the dispart, which was brought into line with a notch on the breech, much in the style of a sporting gun. Apart from being able to manoeuvre the muzzle left or right through the gun-port, he could also elevate or depress it slightly by the same primitive means of handspikes, and a wooden wedge known as a quoin which was tamped in under the breech. When the order was given to fire – and this depended very largely upon the roll of the ship – the gunner ignited the fine powder in the quill either by a slow match or by a flint-lock. The latter, indeed, was one of the very few innovations in gunnery since Elizabethan times, and had been introduced into the Navy in 1755.

An intelligent youth could have made himself familiar with the basic theory and practice of gunnery in a few weeks, but only a real action could have taught him exactly what gunfire achieved. (And Nelson was not to see this for many years.) First of all, ship-to-ship engagements then were quite unlike those since the invention of explosive shot: the solid round-shot was almost incapable of holing the opposing vessel and thus sinking her. The damage was done by the gradual weakening of her structure (as round after round was poured into her sides), and above all by dismasting her. Whereas a naval action in the Second World War – long before the introduction of rockets and nuclear devices – could be over in a matter of minutes, in the eighteenth and indeed nineteenth centuries the engagement could last for many hours. No comparison comes more quickly to mind than the spectacle of a boxing-match, particularly of the old bare-knuckle breed (which was one of the favourite sports of Nelson's England), where one heavyweight stands up against another and both slug it out until one of them falls unconscious to the ground, or even on some occasions both of them together. At Trafalgar, for instance, only one vessel was sunk by gunfire, all the rest being disabled and reduced to such a condition that they could neither sail nor fight. Although the upper-deck personnel were quite often cut down (as Nelson himself was to be) by marksmen sent aloft into the rigging, as well as by cannon-balls, chain-shot or other anti-personnel shot such as grape, the major part of the injuries received by the crew were due to wood splinters. These, screaming out of the ship's sides, or whining across the deck, inflicted ghastly jagged wounds which, more often than not, could only be coped with by amputation of leg or arm. Stomach or other internal wounds were almost invariably fatal.

Sailing yachtsmen, who can appreciate the difficulties of bringing even a small boat in or out of harbour under sail alone (which few enough do in these days of auxiliary engines), will have some small idea of what it meant to handle a line-of-battle ship under nothing but canvas. To tack a ship, for instance, required an immense amount of manpower, coupled with a feeling for wind, weather and sea that few modern seamen can ever comprehend. William Falconer in his masterly *Marine Dictionary* (1780) devotes two pages to this operation. One extract will show what all sailors and embryo officers like young Nelson had to acquire by practice rather than theory – and then to embody in their frames like the instinctive knowledge of a bird:

. . . the first effort to turn the ship in tacking is communicated by the helm, which is then put to the lee-side. This circumstance being announced by the pilot, or commanding officer, who then calls out *Helm's a-lee*, the head-sails are immediately made to shiver in the wind, by casting loose their *sheets* or *bowlines.* The pilot then calls out, *Up tacks and sheets*, which is executed by loosening all the ropes which confine the corners of the lower sails, in order that they may be more readily shifted to the other side. When the ship has turned her head directly to windward . . . the pilot gives the order to turn about the sails on the main and mizen masts, by the exclamation, *Haul main-sail, haul!* The bowlines and braces are then instantly cast off on one side, and as expeditiously drawn in on the other side, so as to wheel the yards about their masts: the lower corner of the mainsail is, by means of it's tack, pulled down to it's station at the chestree [crosstree] and all the after-sails are, at the same time, adjusted to stand upon the other board. Finally, when the ship has fallen off five or six points [one point equals 11° 15′ in a circle] the pilot cries, *Haul of all!* or, *Let go, and haul!* Then the sails on the fore-mast are wheeled about by their braces: and as the ship has then a tendency to fall-off, she is checked by the effort of the helm, which for that purpose is put *hard-a-lee*. The fore-tack, or the lower corner of the fore-sail, being fixed in it's place, the bowlines are hauled; and the other sails, which have been neglected in the hurry of tacking, are properly arranged to the wind; which exercise is called trimming the sails.

It neither sounds, nor was, simple and to do it efficiently required great skill and expertise.

As for the men who formed the human machinery that drove these ships – so beautiful to the eye and yet so harsh to the bodies that served them – they will have numbered about five hundred aboard a vessel like the *Raisonable*. The well-known saying of Dr Johnson must be quoted once again: 'No man will be a sailor who has contrivance enough to get him in jail; for being in a ship is being in jail, with the chance of being drowned.' This was true enough in its way, but it must always be borne in mind that the condition of the farm labourer or the town dweller in the late eighteenth century was one of almost unimaginable squalor and brutality. Nelson was later to grow familiar with the conditions of the countryman, and was to do all that he could to alleviate the poverty of the labourers in his own area. But, even as the boy that he then was, he would have seen that the sailors aboard fared better than a great many landsmen. One of the most illuminating books to be written during this period was *Nautical Economy; or Forecastle Recollections of Events during the last War. Dedicated to the Tars of Old England by a Sailor politely called by the officers of the Navy Jack Nasty-Face*. Now 'Jack', as his title suggests and indeed as the contents of the book reveal, was no lover of the Navy, but his description of the food aboard compares very favourably with the practically starvation diet of a Norfolk farm labourer of the same period. 'Breakfast usually consists of burgoo, made of coarse oatmeal and water; others will have Scotch coffee, which is burnt bread boiled in some water, and sweetened with sugar.' At noon, 'the pleasantest part of the day . . . every man and boy is allowed a pint, that is, one gill of rum and water, to which is added lemon acid, sweetened with sugar'. Salt beef, or pork with pease pudding, provided the main dish. The evening meal consisted of 'half a pint of wine, or a pint of grog (rum diluted with water), to each man, with biscuit, and cheese or butter'.

Between decks the conditions of life were primitive and rough, but when it is remembered that even large cities at that time had no effective form of sewage disposal, and that most families lived in homes with but a single room, the necessities of discipline and some form of essential cleanliness in a ship meant that the sailor was often better off than the working man ashore. Much has been made of the harshness of naval discipline, and indeed no one could possibly defend it with a clear conscience. At the same time it must always be remembered that the general conditions of life everywhere were such that pain was a constant feature of existence : there was no recourse to anaesthetic when it came to an operation; most people had rotten teeth; a high percentage suffered from venereal disease and tuberculosis; and childbirth in itself always entailed a great degree of risk. Life was indeed 'nasty, brutish and short', and to say of the Navy that it consisted solely of 'rum, sodomy and the lash' is about as true as to judge the activities of human beings today solely by the gossip columns of the popular press. Even 'Jack', while rightly condemning most of the disciplinary practices of the Navy, had to admit that some humanitarian captains did exist :

Out of a fleet of nine sail of the line I was with, there were only two Captains thus distinguished [for their humanity]. They kept order on board without resorting to the frequent and unnecessary call upon the Boatswain and his cat, adopted by the other seven; and what was the consequence? Those two ships beat us in reefing and furling; for they were not in fear and dread, well knowing that they would not be punished without a real and just cause. . . .

Although he was always a strict disciplinarian, it was to be to the distinction of Nelson and many of the generation of officers who grew up with him that they were largely of the new persuasion. The French Revolution, against which they were to fight so hard, and which Nelson as a conservatively-minded man detested, nevertheless laid its impress even upon the men who were so largely to contribute to the downfall of French imperialistic dreams. It was hard for the old breed to comprehend, but gradually it was realised that even sailors had rights – and that an efficient ship was a happy one where recourse to the cat-o'-nine-tails was minimal.

CHAPTER THREE

Midshipman to Lieutenant

THE opening of Nelson's career was inconspicuous. The war between England and Spain, centring around a dispute over the Falkland Islands, was averted, and the *Raisonable* was paid off. Nelson had served aboard her five months and a day. It was little enough, but sufficient to give him a close acquaintanceship with the life of a midshipman in the Royal Navy. Being under the age of fifteen he came in the category of the 'youngsters', those who slung their hammocks in the gun-room, coming under the supervision and jurisdiction of the gunner. The latter ranked with the boatswain and purser as a warrant officer, and was usually appointed after having spent at least twelve months' service as a petty officer. In his charge were the provisioning, supply, and maintenance in a constant state of readiness of all the ordnance of the ship. He was, then, in a position of considerable authority and it was men such as he who, providing the link between the officers and the men, were the backbone of the Royal Navy. From a man who had 'come up through the hawse-pipe' the youths could learn more about the total operation of a ship, from sailing her to handling her in action, than they could have done in any system of special instruction ashore. From the moment that Horatio Nelson stepped into the gun-room he was part and parcel of the vessel in a way which few modern seamen in their highly complex and specialised skills can ever be.

The midshipmen were instructed every forenoon by a certificated schoolmaster in coastal and celestial navigation and in trigonometry. The 'schooly' also kept a strict eye on their behaviour and morals, reporting regularly to the captain on the character and potentialities of his charges. More often than not the schoolmaster was also the ship's chaplain. When at sea, the boys were assembled on the upper deck to take the sun's meridian altitude at noon with their quadrants. The quadrant, used for taking sun, moon and star altitudes, had been known in simple form since the thirteenth century, when it had been used by the Portuguese navigators during their epic voyages of discovery. By Nelson's time it had become a highly reliable precision instrument and was generally, but wrongly, believed to be a British invention. (Edmund Stone in an appendix to his book on navigational instruments published in 1758 categorically stated that 'The first of these instruments . . . was invented long ago by Sir Isaac Newton'.) They were then sent below to work out the latitude, combining this with a dead-reckoning of the ship's position. Nelson would soon have found out that, whether at sea or in port, there was little rest. If they were at sea they were employed on the watches to learn an officer's duties, while at the same time they were expected to mix with the men in all operations of sail-changing, either on deck at the braces, or aloft furling canvas. In the mornings one of their duties was to see that the sailors' hammocks were properly lashed and stowed and, in general, to supervise all the operations of the ship. In harbour, as well as at sea, they were kept permanently busy as messengers by the First Lieutenant and one of their primary duties was boat service. If it was a hard life, it was a healthy one, and Nelson undoubtedly benefited from it.

It is unlikely, since he was a 'youngster' and aboard a ship commanded by his uncle, that Nelson saw much of the seamier or more squalid side of life as it was lived in the 'olders' ' mess, where those who had reached the age of fifteen and had been rated as midshipmen lived under conditions that have often been described, though by few better than Frederick Chamier in his *Life of a Sailor* (1833):

Cups were used instead of glasses. The soup tureen, a heavy lumbering piece of block tin, pounded into shape, was, for want of a ladle, emptied with an ever-lasting tea cup; the forks were wiped on the table cloth by the persons about to use them, who, to save eating more than was requisite of actual dirt, always plunged them through the table cloth to clean between the prongs. . . . The rest of the furniture was not much cleaner; now and then an empty bottle served as a candlestick; and I have known both a shoe and a quadrant-case used as a soup plate. . . . [The midshipman] dressed and undressed in public; the basin was invariably of pewter; and the wet towels, dirty head-brush etc., were, after use, deposited in his chest. A hammock served as a bed, and so closely were we all stowed in war, that the side of one hammock always touched that of another; fourteen inches being declared quite sufficient space for one tired midshipman.

What Captain Chamier omits to say in his depressing account of the midshipman's life is that a hammock was far more comfortable than a bunk or a bed in a seaway and, whatever else may have been amiss in the midshipmen's quarters, hammocks were eminently practical. (They remained in use in the Royal Navy and the United States Navy until after the Second World War.)

On the *Raisonable*'s paying off, Captain Suckling was transferred to the 74-gun *Triumph*, guardship at the Nore, that famous sandbank at the mouth of the Thames. It was a dull routine job, and one which offered practically no chance for a young man to learn about the sea-life, or indeed about anything very much except sailing and handling the ship's boats. Maurice Suckling very wisely decided that his nephew needed sea-experience, and something in the youth's bearing and capabilities as shown during his brief time in *Raisonable* must have convinced him that it was worth giving him a real chance to prove himself. Nelson had been entered in the books of the *Triumph* as 'captain's servant', a normal custom of the time whereby captains could take young relatives along to sea with them – and designed most probably to ensure that they could keep a strict eye on them. It was in this capacity that Maurice Suckling recommended Horatio to John Rathbone, master of a West Indiaman, running from the Bahamas and the Antilles all the way through the sunny, sugar-cane islands as far as Venezuela. Nelson saw real sea-time for the first time aboard a merchantman, and the experience was to have a lasting effect upon him.

The little he had seen of naval life in the *Raisonable* had probably shocked a sensitive youth, fresh from the quiet of Norfolk and from the age-old decencies of church and family life at Burnham. His own words written from Port Mahon in 1799, twenty-eight years later, show that the impressions made by the Merchant Service after his initial experience of the Royal Navy still had not faded:

I was sent in a West India ship belonging to the house of Hibbert Purrier Horton, with Mr John Rathbone, who had formerly been in the *Dreadnought* with Captain Suckling. From this voyage I returned to the *Triumph* at Chatham, in July 1772, and if I did not improve my Education, I returned a practical seaman, with a horror of the Royal Navy, and with a saying then constant with the seamen, '*Aft the most honour forward the better man*'. It was many weeks before I got in the least reconciled to a Man-of-War, so deep was the prejudice rooted; and what pains were taken to instill this erroneous principle in a young mind!

'Erroneous principle' Nelson may well have been able to term it all those years and triumphs later, but it is clear how deeply it had sunk in that he should recall it in the very short space of his autobiography.

So now he saw the chops of the Channel for the first time, felt the long Atlantic surge as the merchantman ran down with the north-east trade winds boosting her canvas. With all sail set, she made that sparkling passage which puts Europe behind, and suddenly one day hauls up out of a seemingly limitless skyline the wind-broomed islands of the West. The youth who had known nothing but the simplicities of the English countryside, and then that brief spell aboard the *Raisonable* in 'Chatty Chatham', encountered the brilliant Caribbean seas, flying-fish weather, the eternal green of the tropics, and an entire new world. The discipline, though stringent aboard a merchant-man, had none of the harshness of a man-of-war. Captain Rathbone was kind to the young man, and life, which had seemed to close upon him with the harsh thud of a gun-port coming down, opened in a flower of islands. His fresh eyes registered black faces; immaculately dressed white planters; longshoremen of all types; bum-boats piled with unfamiliar fruit; lean dark bodies diving for small coins or buttons; orchids and tobacco; the rich plantation-lands that gave Europe its sugar, and the local boats carved from a single tree-trunk that crested under thin sails over the flashing Trade Wind seas. After a year, when he returned to rejoin the *Triumph*, he had a memory of this world that he would never lose. He might have echoed their great discoverer who, all those centuries before on his first voyage westward, had written : 'It is like April in Andalusia. Nothing is missing except the nightingales. . . . How great a pleasure is the taste of the mornings !'

Captain Suckling, seeing perhaps in this sun-tanned young nephew a spirit of antagonism towards the Navy (Nelson could never conceal his feelings), came to the wise decision to give him as much practical boat-work as possible. This was something that got a youngster out into the cold fresh air and gave him a feeling of independence as well as responsibility. Nelson applied himself to his navigation, and was then allowed to put it into practice in the *Triumph*'s cutter, and later in her decked long-boat. This experience was to serve him in good stead, for it was to some extent on account of his proven abilities in command of small boats that he secured his next, and so far most important, step forward in his career. Both cutters and long-boats were equipped for sailing as well as rowing, the cutter being the general maid-of-all-work used for carrying stores, provisions and passengers. The long-boat, on the other hand, was the largest boat carried aboard a man-of-war and was often decked, or at least half-decked, and sometimes used for sending boarding parties aboard enemy merchantmen, for cutting out smugglers, and for landing troops in shore actions. A young man in command of a ship's boat learned in microcosm, as it were, all the niceties of sailing, of pilotage, and of the ever necessary use of lead and line in shoal waters.

In 1773, Nelson, who was nearly fifteen, heard the story that was exciting everyone in the naval service – an expedition to the Arctic was being fitted out. Two bomb-vessels, chosen because of the massive strength built into them to allow for the recoil of the heavy guns in their bows, had been selected and were already being provisioned and further strengthened against ice. (Two-masted, with main and mizzen, a bomb-ketch of this type was between 100 and 250 tons, and was designed for engaging fortresses. Falconer in his *Marine Dictionary* credits them with having been a French invention and first used in the bombardment of Algiers, adding 'till then it had been judged impracticable to bombard a place from the sea'.) One of the two ketches was the *Racehorse*, Captain Constantine Phipps, and the other the *Carcass*, Captain Skeffington Lutwidge. Nelson at no time in his life was one to hang back when there was a chance of prefer-ment. He had already shown his determination in that original letter which he had made William write to their father and now, having chosen his career, he was equally determined that he should get ahead in it. With peace heavy on the waters there was little or no chance of advancement for anyone in the Service, let alone young midship-men. The only thing on the horizon at that moment was this Arctic expedition, and young Horatio would move hell and high water to make sure that he at any rate was considered, even if not taken. The very fact that the proclaimed order of the day was 'no boys' spurred him on even further.

As always in rules and regulations there was a loophole, for although boys were not required, as being of 'no use', the captains themselves might take some personal servants. Captain Lutwidge was accordingly badgered by Horatio Nelson (Maurice Suckling without any doubt lending a private word, not only about his nephew's enthusiasm but also his ability as a small-boat handler). '. . . Nothing could prevent my using every interest to go with Captain Lutwidge in the *Carcass*; and, as I fancied I was to fill a man's place, I begged I might be his cockswain : which, finding my ardent desire for going with him, Captain Lutwidge complied with, and has continued the strictest friendship to this moment.' Nelson not only knew how to be persuasive but, as events would prove, to show such spirit and evidence of his capabilities that no senior officer from whom he sought preferment regretted his choice.

The expedition, designed to explore the possibilities of a north-east passage into the South Seas, as well as to promote the interests of science, was not very memorable in itself. The ships penetrated to within ten degrees of the Pole, but were stopped by ice. In scientific terms, the most useful advance was found in an ingenious machine which turned seawater into fresh – something which forestalled the condensers of later days after the Age of Sail had yielded to that of Steam. For Nelson as for his companions, however, the experience must have been vivid and memorable. They moved through waters that few men had known, and saw off the gloomy coast of west Spitsbergen the dazzling sheen of the giant glaciers. From time to time with a horrendous crash huge sections fell away and burst into the sea, while all the time the ice-blink, the frost-smoke and the water-skies spoke of the world where Captain Pell had vanished two centuries before, attempting to unravel its secrets.

From Spitsbergen, where seal abounded and where they saw blue whales, the ships moved on over a greasy sea to the north of Novaya Zemlya. Fog was often with them now and they kept one another informed of their position by firing signal guns. The two pilots, who were masters of Greenland traders and had been specially picked for the voyage, were constantly aloft conning the ships through pack ice – difficult enough nowadays, but fantastically so under canvas and with light, errant winds. Finally they were embayed, two stalwart bomb-ketches, the ice glistening in their rigging, while the ships' companies, as if unaware of their very real danger, played like schoolboys over the frozen fields.

It was during this period that an incident occurred which, though always recorded by Nelson biographers, cannot be omitted for a very good reason. It indicates an aspect of Nelson's character which has often been misconstrued – and generally in his favour. Here it is in the words of Clarke and M'Arthur, his first biographers:

Among the gentlemen on the quarter-deck of the *Carcass*, who were not rated midshipmen, there was, besides young Nelson, a daring shipmate of his, to whom he had become attached. One night, during the mid-watch, it was concerted between them that they should steal together from the ship, and endeavour to obtain a bear's skin. The clearness of the nights in those high latitudes rendered the accomplishment of this object extremely difficult:

they, however, seem to have taken advantage of the haze of an approaching fog, and thus to have escaped unnoticed. Nelson in high spirits led the way over the frightful chasms in the ice, armed with a rusty musket. It was not, however, long before the adventurers were missed by those on board; and, as the fog had come on very thick, the anxiety of Captain Lutwidge and his officers was very great. Between three and four in the morning the mist somewhat dispersed, and the hunters were discovered at a considerable distance, attacking a large bear. The signal was instantly made for their return; but it was in vain that Nelson's companion urged him to obey it. He was at this time divided by a chasm in the ice from his shaggy antagonist, which probably saved his life; for the musket had flashed in the pan, and their ammunition was expended. 'Never mind,' exclaimed Horatio, 'do but let me get a blow at this devil with the butt-end of my musket, and we shall have him.' His companion, finding that entreaty was in vain, regained the ship. The captain, seeing the young man's danger, ordered a gun to be fired to terrify the enraged animal. This had the desired effect; but Nelson was obliged to return without his bear, somewhat agitated with the apprehension of the consequences of this adventure. Captain Lutwidge, though he could not but admire so daring a disposition, reprimanded him rather sternly for such rashness, and for conduct so unworthy of the situation he occupied; and desired to know what motive he could have for hunting a bear? Being thought by his captain to have acted in a manner unworthy of his situation, made a deep impression on the high-minded cockswain; who, pouting his lip, as he was wont to do when agitated, replied, 'Sir, I wished to kill the bear, that I might carry its skin to my father.'

This tale is often told with admiration as evidence of Nelson's daring and courage, but it was evidence of more than that. Nelson was, like many another boy, high-spirited, thoughtless and brave. But he is shown here as acting in disobedience of the orders of an officer infinitely senior to himself while in pursuit of an immediate ambition. It also makes clear that, when on fire with this ambition, he was capable of recklessness – something that was to cost him dearly many years later at Tenerife. Something else about his character is also revealed – that deep love of home and of his family, for the picture that inspired him to disobedience was of a snow-white polar-bear skin shining out against the sombre browns of wood and leather in his father's study.

The two bomb-ketches having finally extricated themselves from
the ice, more by luck than anything else (for the wind shifted favourably into the north-north-east), returned to England in the autumn of
1773 and paid off. In a time of inactivity for the Navy Nelson might
well have found himself, along with so many others, relegated once
again to such tedious duties as aboard the guardship at the Nore, but
he was lucky in two things – his uncle's influence and the fact that a
squadron was fitting out for the East Indies station. The squadron
was under the command of Commodore Sir Edward Hughes in the
Salisbury, and under him was Captain George Farmer in the 20-gun
frigate *Seahorse.* Farmer had served with Maurice Suckling as a midshipman, so it was natural enough for one old friend to help another
over the matter of finding a berth for his nephew. Nelson was lucky
not only in Suckling's influence but in the spheres to which that
influence managed to send him. Having experienced the West Indies
and the Caribbean world, he had known the Polar ice and was now
to see the East from which Britain and so much of Europe drew its
wealth and its luxuries. He was lucky also in his captain, George
Farmer, a strict disciplinarian, and in the master, Mr Surridge, who
unlike so many others took a real interest in teaching the youngsters
their duties and was also a first-class celestial navigator. Years later
Nelson was to say of him that he was 'a very clever man and we
constantly took lunar observations' : these, the most difficult of all
astronomical observations in the days before the predigested tables of
today, involved a considerable knowledge of trigonometry. George
Farmer later went on to meet a heroic death in battle against a
French frigate in 1779 when, his own ship having been set afire, he
refused to leave her after all the ship's company had done so, and
went down sitting on the anchor flukes after a last exhortation to his
men, 'Conquer or die!' Apart from the influence of these two officers,
Nelson was also lucky in having with him Thomas Troubridge who
was his own age but who had entered the Navy two years later than
him, having been educated at St Paul's School. Troubridge was to
be one of Nelson's lifelong friends, one of those who formed the 'Band
of Brothers' who during the long struggle with Napoleon helped give
England the mastery of the seas.

A frigate like the *Seahorse* fulfilled much the same functions as a
destroyer in twentieth-century navies. She acted as the eyes of the
fleet and was built for swift sailing and easy manoeuvrability, being,
as a contemporary writer described her, 'a light nimble ship'.
Originally the term 'frigate' had been applied to fast, undecked
vessels – propelled by oars as well as sails – and used throughout the

Mediterranean. It was the French, however, who had first applied the word to full-rigged, three-masted vessels, carrying between 20 and 40 guns, used for cruising and scouting purposes. They had come into their own during the Seven Years War (1756–1763) and were to play an immensely important part in the Napoleonic Wars, when on more than one occasion Nelson was to regret their scarcity or, indeed, their absence. When communications were entirely visual, and the sighting of an enemy fleet depended on these fast outriders of fleet or convoy, the frigate enjoyed a position of importance out of all proportion to its actual firepower. For a young officer, to serve in a frigate was to learn all the niceties of sailing and to enjoy in the ease of her handling and the speed of her advance the greatest delights of sail.

After calling at Funchal in Madeira, where there was already a British community established, mostly engaged in the wine trade, the *Seahorse* sailed down via the remote islands of Amsterdam and St Paul. They were in the Tropic of Capricorn, the ship scudding before the steady wind and the long swell, in rough but exhilarating sailor's weather. Nelson's health must have improved during his few years in the Navy for Mr Surridge, the master, who had taken a fancy to his keen and intelligent pupil, later recalled that he was 'a boy with a rather florid countenance, rather stout and athletic'. The colouring was undoubtedly due to the long days of wind and sun, for Nelson had a fair skin, but his physical build can only be attributed to the healthy life and exercise of recent years. Rated midshipman on the master's recommending him to Captain Farmer, Nelson for the first time knew the exhilaration of being allowed to tack the ship in fair weather under the keen eyes of the officer of the watch. The memory of that first moment of being in authority, of seeing the sheets hauled, the great sails fly, thunder and then come to rest, as the *Seahorse* drew away on her new tack, will have stayed with him for ever.

After altering course northward for India, with Madras the first port of call, they made for the Hoogly River, then Madras again, and from there on to Bombay. Nelson was now in the world from which England drew so much of her wealth, and it was ships like the one in which he sailed which made the transport of that wealth secure and possible. One could but wish that a Conrad had been aboard to depict the Bombay scene as it was then, or at Bushire which they reached on 25 May. For nearly two years he was in the East, learning the sailor's trade, becoming familiar with the pattern of a world that was the far side of the moon to quiet Burnham, and indulging no doubt like any young man on 'runs ashore' into hot foreign ports, where the very unfamiliarity of everything bred an indifference to conventional rules of behaviour. Many years later in Naples he confided to a lady that he had once sat down for an evening of cards with a cheerful party in the East Indies, and had come away £300 better off. Reflecting next morning, probably with a headache, that if matters had gone differently he might have been ruined, he resolved never to play again. It was a resolve from which even Emma Hamilton in that far distant future could hardly break him.

He saw many places; among them the thriving town and naval station of Trincomalee, where the pearls from Tambalagam were beyond a midshipman's pocket, but not the observation that it was 'the finest harbour in the world'. He did not escape from the East unscathed, and in the December of 1775 he was struck down by a 'malignant disorder'. He was for a time semi-paralysed and very nearly died, indeed would most probably have done so if the surgeon of the *Salisbury* had not advised an immediate return home on the first available ship. In March 1776 a cadaverous, fair-haired midshipman climbed haltingly up the gangway of the frigate *Dolphin*. He was taken under the care of her captain, James Pigot, who showed him such attention that Nelson was convinced that, but for him, he would long since have been dead. The illness was almost certainly malaria, at that time one of the greatest scourges of the East India station, from the after-effects of which he was to suffer nearly all his life. From now on, whether from this or other and later fevers, from wounds and manifold injuries, he would nearly always live with pain.

The *Dolphin* was six months on the return voyage, six months during which he slowly began to rebuild his health, watching the light move across the deckhead in the cabin where he lay, sunrise and sunset, and the dark of night broken only by a lamp's pale glow if a visitor looked in on him. He heard the pound and scuffle of bare feet on the upper deck, the shouts and orders, the cries of blocks and tackles, and then felt the change of angle as his body sagged from one side to the other when the frigate came about and headed off on her new tack. Often he had fevers and the clinging sweat that went with them, delirium even, and on one occasion a vision which he was later convinced proved the turning point in his life. He had been in a deep trough of depression, a dark night of the soul where everything seemed against him – his illness, his lack of real influence, and the insurmountable obstacles that seemed to lie in his way. 'I could discover no means of reaching the object of my ambition. After a long and gloomy reverie, in which I almost wished myself overboard, a sudden glow of patriotism was kindled within me, and presented my king and country as my patron. My mind exulted in the idea. "Well then," I exclaimed, "I will be a hero, and confiding in Providence, I will brave every danger." ' As he was often to tell Captain Hardy in later years, he saw suspended before him a 'radiant orb' ever urging him onwards. He was not quite eighteen.

CHAPTER FOUR

Lieutenant

THE midshipman who had lain so sick and despondent in his bunk during the long voyage home was to find that his star was indeed with him. During his absence, Captain Suckling had been appointed Comptroller of the Navy. Since this office entailed control of all naval shipbuilding, repairs, and manning of the fleet, it was in many respects a position almost comparable to that of the First Lord of the Admiralty. Despite much that has been said to the contrary, Nelson's advancement – at least in his early days – can be largely ascribed to influence. True, if he had not shown himself competent and zealous not even influence would have prevailed, but he had much to thank his dead mother for having come from the Sucklings (with the shadow of the Walpoles at their backs).

Two days after the *Dolphin* paid off at Woolwich, on 24 September 1776, the convalescent midshipman was ordered by Admiral Sir James Douglas, who was in command at Portsmouth, to report aboard the 64-gun *Worcester* as acting lieutenant. Captain Mark Robinson, who was in command, received his new officer with enthusiasm and was pleased to find out on their first voyage down to Gibraltar that young Nelson was competent to take the deck and be in charge of the watch. There can be no doubt that those two years in the East Indies had taught him a great deal.

The *Worcester* was employed on convoy duties, the War of American Independence having broken out the year before and, although France had not yet declared herself ranged with the revolutionary colonists, there could be no doubt in anybody's mind that she would do so in the very near future – in which case every British merchantman at sea would be at hazard. As Admiral Lord Charles Beresford commented: 'A weapon was being silently and steadily forged to strike the British Empire down. The French dockyards were reorganised till Brest had 3,000 shipwrights against our insignificant

800 at Portsmouth. Line-of-battle ships were built with astounding celerity, till the *Pégase* was laid down, launched, and actually at sea within eighty days.' France, recovered from the disasters of the Seven Years War, was determined to attack her old antagonist as soon as opportunity offered. And the revolt of the colonists provided it. It was not only in the rapid construction of new ships that the French excelled, but in the training of their officers and men. Furthermore, they produced the most beautifully proportioned, fastest and best-armed ships in the world. It is significant that so many of the most famous 'British' men-of-war were, in fact, ships captured from the French.

While Nelson was at sea on convoy-duty, bound for Gibraltar, the shipyards of Spain were almost as busy as those of France. Mindful of old wars and unavenged defeats, the Spaniards were fighting to close the gap of sea-power. They succeeded to such an extent that by 1779 they could muster 62 line-of-battle ships. Unlike the French, however, they did not understand that, however well-built, strong and well-armed a vessel, all is to no avail unless the officers and men are of the same calibre. As Nelson was to note in later years, 'the Don' could build fine ships, but he did not know how to handle them. The officers were chosen from the nobility and the men from peasant servitude. Neither were suitable for the sea. Nelson was never to hate the Spaniards as he hated the French. One suspects that he felt some sympathy with them: they were monarchists, something which he respected; their officers knew how to die like gentlemen; and, in the final analysis, they were to become little more than the dupes of Napoleon's imperial ambitions. (The position of Spain relative to that of France in the Napoleonic Wars was somewhat akin to that of Italy and Germany in the Second World War.)

On his first visit, sent ashore by the commanding officer with despatches and letters, Nelson admired the great fortress-rock of Gibraltar, symbol of Britain's hold over the sea-lanes of the world. He came to know its story: how Admiral Sir George Rooke, in command of a small Anglo-Dutch fleet, had stormed the Rock and seized it from the Spaniards in 1705. Ever since then, having endured its 'Great Siege' by the combined French and Spanish forces which began in 1779 and lasted for three years, seven months and twelve days – the longest continuous siege in history – it had become a corner-stone of Empire. The phrase 'as solid as the Rock of Gibraltar' had passed into the language. Over his head, as the young acting lieutenant went ashore, the muzzles of guns protruded everywhere from the galleries cut in the great limestone mass, and the British flag waved over them in the wind. The Spaniards could never forgive, nor forget, that encroachment upon their land. It dominated the straits, facing towards Mount Ceuta on the Moroccan coast, only fourteen miles away. Nelson would most probably have known, however sketchy his knowledge of the classics, that the two of them had represented to the ancients the Pillars of Hercules. This was the end of voyaging for early Mediterranean men who, peering fearfully at the great ocean beyond, had decided that they marked the limits of the world.

Nelson recorded that he 'was at sea with convoys till April 2nd 1777', so he knew a hard winter and the kind of weather that the Bay of Biscay can throw at sailors, seas which will founder even the stoutest ships. It was a good training ground, and one to which he would often return, and where he would learn the ominous swell that presages rising winds and storm, and how to handle a ship when they came. Did the hairs on his neck bristle, did a shadow cross his path as he first set foot upon the Rock? It was to 'this dark corner of the world', as he once referred to it in later years, that his body was brought ashore from H.M.S. *Victory* on 28 October 1805. But now as he looked about him, recovered in health and happily conscious of the dignity of his acting rank, he would have seen in the naval, military and marines' uniforms happy evidence of that far hand of Empire which he himself had represented in the Arctic, and which he had seen in all its formality in the sun-drenched West Indies. As a seaman he would have remarked on one occasion or another when the east wind, or Levanter, was blowing out of the Mediterranean the ashen tail of the Levanter cloud as the humid air spun up off the sheer eastern face of the Rock, lifting to a thousand feet and more, and then condensed into a cloud that trailed away westerly darkening all Gibraltar and the Bay of Algeciras beyond. He stood at the mouth of the Mediterranean and looked inward from the great ocean at the wrinkled, ancient sea. He would have learned from experience, as well as from instruction, of the two- to three-knot current that flows steadily into the Mediterranean as the Atlantic makes good the inland sea's water-loss due to evaporation. He was at the gateway of the world where he would make his name, and cause the flag of his country to fly above all others.

Early in April 1777, the *Worcester* was paid off at Portsmouth and Nelson found himself facing the first major hurdle in his professional career: his examination for lieutenant. By now he had the necessary qualifications to prove that he had been at sea for more than six years (he had, to be exact, done six years, three months, one week and six days since he had first joined the *Raisonable* in Chatham). His certificates showed him to be over twenty years of age, whereas he was five months under his nineteenth birthday – a fact which must have been well enough known to Comptroller Suckling, who was on the board that examined him. Clarke and M'Arthur say that the latter purposely concealed his relationship from the other examining captains :

When his nephew had recovered from his first confusion [at finding his uncle present at the Navy Board interview], his answers were prompt and satisfactory, and indicated the talents he so eminently possessed. The examination ended in a manner very honourable to him; upon which his uncle threw off his reserve, and rising from his seat, introduced his nephew. The examining Captains expressed their surprise at his not having informed them of this before. 'No,' replied the independent Comptroller, 'I did not wish the younker to be favoured, I felt convinced that he would pass a good examination; and you see, gentlemen, I have not been disappointed.'

The first known extant letter from Nelson follows upon this important event, and is addressed to his brother William, at Christ's Church College, Cambridge :

My father arrived in town on Friday evening in tolerable good health; my sister and brother are both well, and desire their love to you. I suppose you have not heard of my arrival in England yet, but we arrived on Thursday week. . . . I passed my Degree as Master of Arts on the 9th instant [that is, passed the Lieutenant's examination], and received my commission on the following day for a fine Frigate of 32 guns. So I am now left in the world to shift for myself, which I hope I shall do, so as to bring credit to myself and friends.

His manner is formal, his mood elated, but it would be some years before the acquired diction and style of the age would mellow into the 'personal' Nelson, one whose emotions leaped out from the thicket of convention.

He was lucky in his ship, the *Lowestoffe*, for his captain was William Locker, who had served under Admiral Hawke in the last war and had been wounded in an action with a French privateer, as a result of which he walked with a limp. He was in every sense a very fine example of a sea-officer, who had not let the Navy or anything else deprive him of a sense of humour and love of learning. Nelson was to come to regard him as a father, while he himself was treated like a son. But first of all, before his 'fine Frigate' took to the sea, spread her sails and headed west for the Caribbean, Nelson had to learn the other side of the coin that was entailed by the privilege of being a lieutenant.

One side is easily exemplified by the portrait for which he sat to the Swiss-born Royal Academician John Francis Rigaud, a competent craftsman of his time, who made his living out of just such 'delineations' of aspiring officers and middle-class civilians. Nowadays the camera would have captured Nelson's likeness on passing out from Dartmouth, perhaps, and the portrait have been mounted in a silver frame in some family home for parents to point at proudly and say, 'That is my son.' The Rigaud portrait was commissioned by Nelson, undoubtedly with a view to giving it to his father. But it was not completed before he sailed for the West Indies, and in the end, with the rank changed to that of a captain, was given by Nelson to Captain Locker in 1781. The obverse of the coin, which probably was partly responsible for Nelson's being unable to complete the sittings in 1777, was that the duties of a lieutenant could also entail being in charge of the press-gang. Since the First Lieutenant, who would normally have undertaken this charge, was away on leave it fell to the young Horatio to lead the party which combed the docks, the brothels, and sailors' taverns to complete the complement. The ill-famed press-gang was made necessary through the lack of volunteers, and an insufficiency of those who had automatically been sent aboard under the terms of the Vagrancy Act. This Act laid down that 'all disreputable persons' were liable for impressment into the fleet, as were fishermen, sailors and watermen. A rendezvous for pressed men had been opened near the Tower of London, and it was from here that Nelson and his party sallied forth to comb suitable areas to complete the crew. On such excursions the press-gang went armed only with cudgels and belaying pins, although the officer and senior ratings would usually carry cutlasses – 'more for their majesty to astonish the enemy' than for use, though used they would be if there were any real attempt made to rescue their victims.

The composition of the Navy's lower deck was mongrel. Captain Marryat refers to a ship which was manned by the men of nineteen nations, for anyone taken in these encounters was liable for impressment. John Masefield, who had served under sail and had heard from the old hands authentic tales of the way it was in their fathers' days, wrote in 1905 : 'Tailors, little tradesmen, street loafers, all were fair game. They were taken to the boats and shipped aboard, and cracked across the heads with a cudgel if they protested.' Imprisoned below under the guard of marine sentries, they were examined in due course by the surgeon and the senior officer aboard, and only those who could prove that they were entitled to exemption – apprentices, for instance, or merchant seamen who were already signed aboard a ship – were spared from impressment. The rest were entered on the muster book; names, physical descriptions, and such identifying marks as tattoos being duly recorded, so that, in the event of any of them deserting, their records were lodged with the ship and their particulars could be sent to the Admiralty. It was on one of these cold wet nights along the Thames foreshore that Nelson, while out on a duty that can only have seemed demoralising to anyone of his nature, was suddenly taken ill. Most probably it was a recurring bout of his malaria, though one may suspect that some psychosomatic cause was at the root of it. He had to be carried back to the rendezvous by a strong young midshipman named Bromwich, who later rose to lieutenant and served under Nelson for a number of years.

The French, more intelligent than their ancient enemies, although they did resort to such rough-and-ready methods for manning their ships when times were hard, generally tried to attract suitable men to the marine in a practical way. Fishermen and merchant-seamen were given training aboard naval vessels and a bonus for such services in time of peace. The fact that during the Napoleonic Wars the quality of their seamen, and indeed of their officers, was generally speaking lower than that of the British was largely due to the effects of the Revolution, which had decimated the ranks of the officer class. It was also caused by the absurd idea that *liberté, égalité, fraternité* could prevail aboard any ship at sea – let alone a man-of-war – and to the fact that the best gunners were recruited for the army to serve Napoleon's ambitions in the sphere in which he was supreme, the land.

In July 1777, after another sparkling passage of the North Atlantic, although this time in a frigate on convoy-duty with eighteen merchant-men to protect, Nelson renewed his acquaintance with the Caribbean on the Jamaica station. 'Always lay a Frenchman close, and you will beat him' was one of Captain Locker's laconic injunctions to his young officer (one he would never forget), and it was probably with this in mind that Nelson's 'active' nature prompted him to seek something more adventurous than a frigate on station duty. He was given command of a schooner, the *Little Lucy*, a tender to the *Lowestoffe* and named after Locker's first-born child. He had earned this early command. On the *Lowestoffe*'s second cruise out of Port Royal in November she came up with an American privateer. The weather was

bad, a heavy sea running, and when the time came to board the prize
the First Lieutenant, whose prerogative it was to lead the boarding
party, was an unconscionably long time below putting on his sword.
The ship's boat lying alongside was in danger of filling and the irate
Locker bawled down : 'Have I no officer who can board the prize?'
The Master of the *Lowestoffe* was making his way to the gangway
when Nelson turned him back with the words, 'It is my turn now.'
The boat reached the American vessel which was lying half water-
logged, having practically driven herself under in her efforts to escape.
Nelson and his men – like many a lifeboat's crew in later years – had
the harrowing experience of going in on a roller, clean over the deck,
and out on the other side. Finally they got aboard and the prize was
taken, but in the thick weather and spindrift-seas they lost contact
with the *Lowestoffe*. Yet, despite everything, the young lieutenant
managed to get his prize safe back to port. In 'Daddy' Locker's eyes
his protégé had proved himself worthy of the trust that was now to
put him in charge of the *Little Lucy*.

His first command. . . . He, who would order great fleets in action,
when cumulus clouds of sails covered the horizon, now knew the
instant joy of having beneath his feet a schooner whose every rope
and pitch-line of deck, tarred lanyard, wooden dead-eye, and square
foot of sail came within his immediate vision and control. How well
he remembered it ! 'In this vessel I made myself a complete pilot for
all the passages through the Islands situated on the north side of
Hispaniola.' The words ring back to Drake. Though centuries separated the two men there was something very similar about them. Both
were the sons of clergymen, both first learned the trade of the sea
in small boats on the east coast, and saw in their country's enemy
an almost personal foe whom they detested. Drake in his staunch
Protestantism had seen Philip II as anti-Christ, and Nelson was
to regard Napoleon as the embodiment of evil in the shape of
revolutionary, atheist France.

In 1778 Sir Peter Parker arrived in Jamaica as Commander-in-
Chief. Nelson was warmly recommended to him by Captain Locker,
with the result that Sir Peter took Nelson into his flagship *Bristol* as
Third Lieutenant. Within the year he had risen to be First Lieutenant,
and on 8 December 1778 he was promoted to be Commander of the
brig *Badger*. War with France had begun, the West Indies station was
already an active one in view of the American Revolution, and
Nelson's rise – though rapid – was somewhat predictable, particularly
in view of the fact that not only Captain Locker, but also the new
Commander-in-Chief and his formidable wife Lady Parker, had all

taken to Horatio. Influence counted, but it is clear that there was a great deal more to it than that. His last promotion in this year occurred after Maurice Suckling had died – leaving a will in which all his nephews were to inherit five hundred pounds, and his nieces one thousand. The rich and childless Comptroller had been a kind promoter of the young Nelson; had indeed launched him in no mean way on a career in which he was to repay his uncle a thousandfold. But his influence died with him, and it was to Admiral Parker's credit that he promoted Nelson entirely on his own judgement.

Nelson's first job in command was to 'protect the Mosquito shore and the Bay of Honduras, from the depredations of the American privateers'. One letter from this period of his life tells us more about the young man, his enthusiasm, his affection for friends and his dedication to his calling than a ream of words. Captain Locker had fallen ill, as did most who spent much time in the West Indies, where everything from yellow fever to malaria, manchineel poisoning and the pox had played havoc with European man ever since Columbus had first stumbled upon this outwardly smiling sea. 'A bloody war and a sickly season' had long been the toast amongst those who aspired to promotion among the offshore islands of the New World.

Nelson's letter to Locker was dated aboard the *Badger* 30 April 1779:

> I hope with all my heart you are much better than when I left you, and that you will not be obliged to go home on account of your health. I wish sincerely it was in my power in some measure to show some small return for the many favours I have received, but I am sure you do not think me ungrateful. If you come on the North Side [of Jamaica], and I hear of it, I will come in. I know you will be pleased with this little earnest of success, but we have had a great deal of plague with her. [He had captured the 80-ton *La Prudente*.] Two days before we could find the French papers, at last found them in an old shoe. There is a polacre [a three-masted merchantman without topmasts] coming this way; I hope we shall fall in her way. I wish I could give a good character of Mr Capper; he is a drunkard; I need say no more. We shall part whenever we can get Mate of a Merchant ship. George Cruger behaves very well. If you have heard from Mrs Locker, I sincerely hope she and all the family are in good health; and that you and they may continue so, and enjoy every blessing of this life.

Some years later, a fellow captain, envious of the charm (though it was a great deal more than that) with which Nelson seemed able to captivate his senior officers, wrote to him : 'You did just as you pleased in Lord Hood's time, the same in Admiral Hotham's, and now again with Sir John Jervis; it makes no difference to you who is Commander-in-chief'. So now, with Captain Locker returned sick to England, with Maurice Suckling dead, Nelson continued to advance as steadily as if both these old friends and protectors had been there to help him.

Sir Peter Parker and his lady took to Nelson as if he were their own son, and Lady Parker's regard (like that of many other admirals' wives over the centuries) meant almost more than her husband's on the station he commanded. On 11 June 1779, Nelson was appointed to the frigate *Hinchinbrooke* of 32 guns. He was now a post-captain, that is to say rated capable of being in charge of a ship of over 20 guns. The frigate's previous captain had been killed by a random shot. Nelson was, in the phrase, 'made'. That is to say, no junior officer could be passed over him, and he had only to stay alive and commit no grave misdemeanour, and nothing could prevent him in due course from rising to flag rank. 'I got my rank', he wrote, 'by a shot killing a Post-Captain, and I most sincerely hope I shall, when I go, go out of the World the same way.' He was still under twenty-one.

At the same time as promoting Nelson to the *Hinchinbrooke* Admiral Parker also moved Lieutenant Cuthbert Collingwood, who had followed in Nelson's footsteps in the *Lowestoffe*, into the command of the *Badger*. Two lifelong friends went up the ladder together, both chosen for their commands by the same man, and both to share in the glory of Trafalgar, when together they led into action the two columns of the British fleet. Collingwood was ultimately to die worn out by the exigencies of the Mediterranean command, which had so nearly crippled his chief, and Admiral Parker, aged eighty-two, was to be present as chief mourner at Nelson's funeral. The destinies of the three men were strangely linked.

CHAPTER FIVE

Post-Captain

THE summer of 1779 saw the arrival in Hispaniola of the French admiral, Count d'Estaing, and it was naturally assumed that an attack on Jamaica was in the offing. Since he had with him 22 ships-of-the-line, as well as many transports (said to be carrying 20,000 troops) there was great alarm in the colony, especially when it was estimated that they could raise no more than 7,000 troops for their defence. Nelson was busily involved in all this activity. He had been appointed to take charge of the principal battery of Port Royal, which defended Kingston and Spanish Town and was therefore the key to the island. D'Estaing, however, was not destined for Jamaica but Savannah, where he met with failure and returned to France. Nelson had gained some experience in the positioning and handling of shore-batteries, but otherwise had profited little from this brief period ashore, and was correspondingly relieved when his ship, which had been away on cruise, arrived back at Port Royal. He was off at once, eager to enjoy his first major command, and hopeful of prize money. He was not to be disappointed in this, for the *Hinchinbrooke* took several small prizes, netting Nelson about £800. (Collingwood in Nelson's old position aboard the *Lowestoffe* did even better, for his ship managed to capture a number of Spanish treasure ships lying in the Bay of Honduras.) The whole of this period of Nelson's life, even the places involved, although two centuries later, still has an Elizabethan ring about it. His next major task was to be one that would have appealed to Drake.

In January 1780 an ambitious scheme was evolved by the head-quarters staff at Port Royal who, like many planners before and since, could read their maps and estimate the benefits to be obtained by success, but could not in any degree envisage the climate and the territory where what looked so easy on paper would prove almost impossible in practice. The object of the expedition seemed logical in

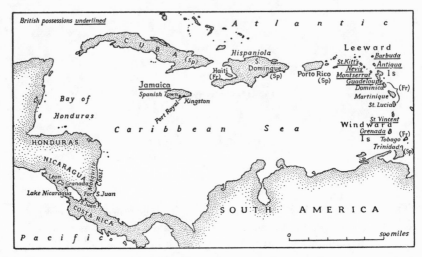

The West Indies in 1780

the extreme: land a force at the mouth of the San Juan river, proceed up it, capture Fort San Juan, and thus obtain control of Lake Nicaragua. Holding Lake Nicaragua, 'the inland Gibraltar of Spanish America', they would then have the route open before them all the way to the Pacific. They would seize the cities of Granada and Leon, which were reported to be fabulously wealthy, and, having reached the Pacific, would have succeeded in cutting America in half. The dream which inspired Governor Dalling at Port Royal was as ambitious as anything that was later to beckon Napoleon: none other than the establishment of a new empire in the southern part of America, which would more than equal the one that the British were on the verge of losing in the north.

Unfortunately neither sufficient men nor matériel were available for so ambitious a project; even more serious was the ignorance of the real nature of the terrain through which this task force was to proceed. The Governor of Jamaica could spare little more than 500 men and the expedition arrived on the Mosquito coast in the unhealthy rainy season. The Indians upon whom they had been relying to supply river transport and guides, believing that they had come to take them as slaves to Jamaica, disappeared on their arrival. Nelson, who had been detailed to escort the soldiers in the *Hinchinbrooke* and to provide a naval shore party, volunteered to command the small contingent of sailors and marines. He described how 'I quitted my ship, carried troops in boats one hundred miles up a river, which none but the

Spaniards since the time of the buccaneers had ever ascended . . .
boarded (if I may be allowed the expression) an outpost of the
Enemy, situated on an Island in the river; that I made batteries,
and afterwards fought them, and was a principal cause of our
success'.

Nelson was never prone to self-effacement, and all through his life
would sound his own trumpet whenever he saw fit to do so. The fact
is that the attitude of mock modesty, of 'not I, but so-and-so deserves
the praise', so often associated with the British, is a comparatively
new phenomenon. It originated in the days of the nineteenth-century
Empire and later, when 'good form' (based perhaps on the muscular
Christianity of Dr Arnold, Thring and their counterparts) decreed
that a man should be brave, but self-effacing. No such idea prevailed
in the eighteenth century, when all sang their own praises, knowing
full well that in the hard fight for promotion, influence and power
precious few other people would do it for them. Nelson, in fact, here
as elsewhere, need hardly have bothered. His words are well confirmed
by Major Polson, who was in command of the soldiers: 'A light-
haired boy came to me in a little frigate,' he wrote. 'In two or three
days he displayed himself, and afterwards he directed all the operations.' In the official despatch he recorded that 'He [Nelson] was the
first on every service whether by night or day. I want words to express
what I owe to that gentleman.'

Toiling upstream through dense rotting vegetation, the sun
obscured by the thick growth over their heads, the soldiers and the
small party of sailors and marines were exposed to the deadly 'Yellow
Jack', yellow fever, which haunted that graveyard coast. It was bad
enough to be aboard a ship lying off for, as Nelson later wrote to his
friend Dr Benjamin Mosely in a note to the latter's *Treatise on
Tropical Diseases*: 'In the *Hinchinbrooke*, with a complement of two
hundred men, eighty-seven took to their beds in one night.' In his
final estimate, 'very few, not more than ten survived of that ship's
crew'. How much worse then was it for the men ashore, wearing
uniforms quite unsuited to the tropics, with few medical skills (though
they had a doctor with them), and no real knowledge of what risks
they ran. They were to be faced by the back-breaking toil of hauling
their boats through shallows – only to be met further upstream by
boulder-strewn banks and waterfalls. It is surprising, a tribute to their
leaders and to their own resilience, that they ever reached Fort San
Juan at all.

It was only after seventeen days of nightmare, in the course of
which Nelson, sword in hand, led a frontal assault on a small fortified

island which lay in their way, that the bedraggled, exhausted and, in many cases, dying troops finally reached their objective. Nelson, his spirit unquenched even though the seeds of disease must already have been active in his body, was all for an immediate assault. In this his instinct was correct, for the Spanish garrison, demoralised by their station and no doubt many of them as ill as the attackers, would hardly have put up much of a fight. Such, however, was not the way of the eighteenth-century military. They had been instructed and trained in the formal and 'scientific' methods of the age : the formal siege which, though usually suitable in the terrain of Europe, was quite out of place in South America.

Napoleon would undoubtedly have acted as Nelson would have done, but lesser minds must always abide by the book of rules. While perceiving the folly of the method, Nelson nevertheless acted properly in his subordinate position and followed the instructions of the military. He was ever first in the batteries as the slow zig-zag of trenches crept nearer to the fort, and, as Major Polson reported, 'there was scarce a gun but what was pointed by him or Lieutenant Despard'. The fort finally fell on 24 April, but Nelson was not present to witness its capture, for he had been recalled to Jamaica to take command of the 44-gun *Janus*. In his first experience of field action he had shown his usual enthusiasm and initiative; he had learned something about co-operating with the Army which would serve him in good stead years later in Corsica. He had also learned that, whether ashore or afloat, the book of rules should be thrown away whenever it was considered necessary by the man on the spot. By carrying out, under unsuitable conditions, the slow formal siege tactics that they had been taught, the expeditionary force had run into the rainy season, when the torrential downpour prevented any further activity and disease flourished even faster than before. The San Juan expedition was a failure, very few returned, and those who did were ravaged by yellow fever.

One of the sufferers was Nelson, who was carried ashore in Jamaica and was never well enough to take command of the *Janus*. In the *Lowestoffe* he had endured a recurrence of his malaria as well as suffering from manchineel poisoning. The latter was one of the minor hazards of the West Indies, but unpleasant enough in itself, as Columbus's sailors had found all those years ago. The corrosive poison of the leaves, or the fruit, acted upon the central nervous system – something which the Carib Indians had long known, since they tipped their arrows with its juicy sap. Now he was suffering from yellow fever, which was transmitted by several types of forest mosquitoes. A

modern clinical diagnosis describes many of the symptoms from which
Nelson was to suffer during his recuperation, 'headache, backache,
fever, prostration, vomiting, and jaundice', and goes on to say, 'there
is no specific treatment for yellow fever. Provision should be made for
good nursing, quiet surroundings, alkaline water and fruit juices to
drink . . .'.

All these Nelson was to find ashore in Jamaica, and there can be
no doubt that, if he had stayed longer at San Juan and had not been
recalled, he would almost certainly have died. On 30 August 1780,
he formally applied to Admiral Parker: 'Having been in a very bad
state of health for these several months, so bad as to be unable to
attend my duties on board the *Janus*, and the faculty having informed
me that I cannot recover in this climate, I am therefore to request
that you will be pleased to permit me to go to England for the
re-establishment of my health.' Lady Parker (who had spent long
hours nursing the young officer) and her husband Sir Peter were as
sad to see him go as if they were indeed losing a son. They would
not forget him. It says something for the medical care he received
that neither then nor on later occasions did Nelson succumb to his
illnesses or his wounds. Somewhat ungenerously he was to write to the
Duke of Clarence in 1794: 'One plan I pursue, never to employ a
doctor, nature does all for me and Providence will protect me.'
Perhaps . . . But Haslar Naval Hospital in Portsmouth had opened its
doors some four and a half years before he was born, and records
show that he was looked after at various times during his life by some
twenty-five doctors.

Returned to England aboard the *Lion*, whose Captain 'Billy Blue'
Cornwallis looked after him with as much care as had Captain Pigot
in the *Dolphin*, Nelson paid a brief visit to Captain Locker and other
friends in London, and then made his way to Bath in the autumn of
1780. Unlike most of the other visitors he was not in search of high
play, romance, or even specifically those curative waters which had
made the city a spa since Roman times. He was in search of a climate
that would not be too intolerable for a sick man just returned from the
West Indies. From Bath, recuperating slowly and having to be 'carried
to and from bed with the most excruciating tortures', he wrote to
Captain Locker describing how he had almost lost the use of his left
arm, while at a later date, returned to London, he wrote to his brother
William: 'I have entirely lost the use of my left arm, and very nearly
of my left leg and thigh, and am at present under the care of a
Mr Adair, an eminent surgeon in London.' The interesting point
about these two letters is that, whereas the one to Locker is dated

15 February 1781, that to his brother is dated 7 May. Either Nelson had had a relapse, or had been putting a good face on his condition for Locker's benefit, just in case there was any chance of a new command in the offing.

In every respect his life to date might have been paralleled by that of many another naval officer, except perhaps for his quick rise to post-captain. Many were taken ill with fevers – many recovered – but few, though, so readily impressed the senior officers with whom they came in contact that there was lurking within them some especial spark which one day, given luck or opportunity, would set them apart from other men. His life continued humdrum, although he did get his new appointment: this time to a 28-gun frigate, the *Albemarle*, in which he spent the winter of '81 on convoy duty to the Baltic and back. It was a far call from his last station, but the cold of the North Sea and the Baltic – about which he complained – most probably did his health a great deal more good than if he had been returned to the West Indies or sent out to the East. Ordered once more on convoy duty, this time to Quebec, he wrote bitterly : 'I want so much to get off this d—d voyage. Mr Adair has told me that if I was sent to a cold damp climate it would make me worse than ever.'

Nelson's illnesses were real enough, and no less than fourteen different occasions have been recorded on which he suffered among other things from malaria, pains in his chest and lungs, 'rheumatic fever' and severe physical breakdown accompanied by mental depression. All this was quite apart from the later wounds, and the seasickness which he mentioned on numerous occasions ('Heavy sea, sick to death – this sea-sickness I shall never get over' – as late as August 1801). He was to undergo more operations than any other flag-officer. Yet despite all this, his slight frame, driven by the wind of a desire for fame – or rather a passionate search after 'Honour' – was to carry him through where many an apparently stronger constitution yielded. The fact is, as his correspondence bears out, that Nelson was something of a hypochondriac. His sickly childhood, his damaged health in youth, were to give him a constant concern about his health that the more robust never possess. As an old Norfolk saying has it : 'A creaking gate lasts for ever.'

A bad passage across the Atlantic, not so surprising in spring, when the north-westerlies hurl themselves across in what can sometimes seem not a succession of gales but a permanent one, found Nelson with part of his convoy at the unattractive gate of Britain's senior colony. He thought little of it – 'this disagreeable place' he said of St John's – but had to admit that 'the voyage agrees better with me than I expected'. The tone of his letters throughout all this period is dull and almost rancorous : not so surprising when one considers that his services in the West Indies, which had nearly cost him his life, would in modern times have earned him something like a year ashore on sick leave. Possibly he should never have been passed fit for the *Albemarle*, but the fact was that he could not afford to be 'on the beach' so long as there was a war, a chance of action and of prize money. Promotion he could not of course expect to see for many years, since he had already advanced as far as any sea-officer could do by the age of twenty-three.

It was in Canada, in Quebec, that Nelson first shook off the illnesses that had been plaguing him, and here also that he first fell in love. Everything in his letters to date would suggest that he was not only sexually inexperienced – somewhat rare for that time – but that he had never been in any way emotionally moved. His experiences among the midshipmen with their free-and-easy sex lives, his knowledge of Chatham and Portsmouth, of the sailors and their women (who were quite often carried at sea aboard the larger vessels), had most certainly given the son of the parsonage a distinct distaste not for the opposite sex, but for carnality as such. Nelson's attitude towards women would seem to have been that simple one which, until recent times, was held by many Englishmen of his type and class. There were two categories of women : superior beings who were placed on a pedestal, of a more sensitive order than men, and destined to be wives and mothers; and whores, strumpets, drabs and doxies, with whom officers and men took their sexual pleasure when ashore. It was not for many years that he was to find out that there was, as it were, a kind of 'halfway house', women who could grace an assembly or a dinner party and also be sensual and active lovers. His first love was almost inevitably of the romantic kind. Nelson was indeed a great romantic, although not in the sense that Lord Byron was to show himself – whose outward trappings of romanticism cloaked an inherent cynicism that reflected the attitudes of the eighteenth century rather than those of the nineteenth. Nelson was at no time in his life capable of cynicism.

The object of his affection was Mary Simpson, the sixteen-year-old daughter of a gentleman named 'Sandy' Simpson, of Scottish descent and a great friend of a man who was to play a large part in Nelson's life, Alexander Davison, another northcountryman. When ordered to escort a convoy of troops to New York, Nelson, with all the passionate enthusiasm of an ingenuous young man very much in love for the first time, was prepared to leave his ship, resign his commission and lay his heart at the feet of this 'fair Diana'. Fortunately for him, the practical Davison convinced him of the total folly of such an action and sent a chastened young captain back to his ship and his convoy. The violence of Nelson's affections, within six years to be submerged in marriage, would not be in evidence again for a long time. For a brief moment one has glimpsed the tip of a berg that may wreck a ship, then it vanishes beneath the ice-smoke of a northern sea. But the hidden acres remain, one day to emerge under the influence of a warm and indolent climate.

On 11 November 1782, the *Albemarle* and her convoy came to anchor just off Sandy Hook lighthouse. Nelson, who earlier at Quebec had bemoaned the duty ('a very *pretty job* at this late season of the year, for our sails are at this moment frozen to the yards'), could congratulate himself on one of those routine, thankless tasks which comprise ninety per cent of war, brought to a successful conclusion. At the same time, he eyed with envy a squadron from the West Indies fleet that lay at anchor inside New York harbour. It had taken part in Rodney's successful action – the Battle of the Saints – on 12 April that year, and was under the command of the awe-inspiring Lord Hood. It was among them that he longed to be, not on this station which his own commander-in-chief recommended to him as 'a good station for prize money' – a remark which elicited from Nelson, 'Yes, but the West Indies is the station for honour.' Although in later years Nelson was careful about his rights over prize money, meticulous, some might even say on occasions grasping, yet it was always a secondary concern with him. That 'radiant orb' had beckoned him on to honour, not necessarily to fortune. As ever, he was not one to let an opportunity slip by, and on a cold November day, not long after Nelson had come to anchor, the midshipman on watch aboard Hood's flagship the *Barfleur* saw a ship's barge with a captain aboard drawing towards him. The side was manned, and he awaited with all the natural unease of an ordinary midshipman the presence on deck of one of those gods who could make you or break you. But this was no ordinary midshipman, though he was treated with only a little more consideration than the others, but Prince William Henry, son of George III, the future Duke of Clarence, ultimately to become William IV, 'The Sailor King'.

Years later, when Trafalgar had been fought, and when Clarke and M'Arthur were compiling Nelson's life, William IV vividly recalled that first meeting. Even allowing in some respects for the benefit of hindsight, his recollection of young Captain Nelson is signed with a visual authenticity :

I was then a midshipman aboard the *Barfleur*, lying in the narrows off Staten Island, and had the watch on deck, when Captain Nelson of the *Albemarle*, came in his barge alongside, who appeared to be the merest boy of a captain I ever beheld; and his dress was worthy of attention. He had on a full-laced uniform; his lank unpowdered hair was tied in a stiff Hessian tail, of an extraordinary length; the old-fashioned flaps of his waistcoat added to the general quaintness of his figure, and produced an appearance which particularly attracted my notice; for I had never seen anything like it before, nor could I imagine who he was, nor what he came about. My doubts were, however, removed when Lord Hood introduced me to him. There was something irresistibly pleasing in his address and conversation; and an enthusiasm, when speaking on professional subjects, that showed he was no common being.

Nelson, for his part, was careful to express his warm attachment to his king and to the honour of the Navy. This was far from being the natural lip-service that might be expected from an ambitious officer. Throughout his life Nelson time and again showed that his devotion was wholeheartedly given to his monarch as well as to the naval service and his country. The key that unlocks him is his genuine simplicity. Now, aboard the *Barfleur*, he saw in the Prince a fine youngster and – as did many at the time – one who might well prove a useful, as well as powerful, addition to the Navy. He was to comment approvingly that the Prince would prove to be a 'disciplinarian and a strong one', little knowing that authority and the exercise of discipline would go to his head and that he would become a singularly unattractive officer, whose later career was marked by a niggling attention to detail and a punctilious regard for his own importance. But that was in the future and, while Nelson approved the midshipman, the latter saw in the young, unfashionably dressed captain something of that strange combination of fire and charm which was always to surround Nelson with a halo of friends and admirers. Prince William's regard for him remained unaltered over the years and he was to keep all the letters that Nelson wrote to him. But the Prince's friendship was not always the happiest thing to have bestowed on one, once his true character had been revealed by that infallible assessor of men and ships – the sea.

CHAPTER SIX

Captain with Problems

TRANSFERRED from Admiral Digby's fleet, the *Albemarle* under her young captain (whose appearance certainly suggested that he needed the prize money which he had spurned by asking to serve under Hood's flag) sailed for the West Indies on 22 November. But Nelson's hopes of participating in some striking action – and it must be remembered that up to date he had had no experience of a real naval engagement – were thwarted. While Hood and his squadron cruised back and forth off Cape François at the western end of Haiti, hoping to catch the French fleet which was bound from Boston for the Caribbean, the latter escaped them by sliding through the Mona Passage to the east of the island and making for Curaçao. It was an uneventful and frustrating period in Nelson's life, and even an attempt to recapture Turk's Island from the French proved abortive. Peace was on the horizon, and in 1783 the treaty was signed which stripped Great Britain of the United States as well as of far-off Minorca, a Balearic Island that was to figure later in Nelson's Mediterranean years.

Admiral Lord Charles Beresford, writing at the turn of the century, in the full flower of the British Empire, commented on the events of 1783 : 'The nation had lost no honour. It had fought with stubborn tenacity a hopeless fight. The Navy, though mismanaged and without great leaders, had held its own.' This was true enough in its way, but it had lost a great deal of national pride and had been humbled not only by its former colonists but by those ancient enemies, the French. It was this that rankled and, though Nelson makes no mention of it in his correspondence of the time, his hatred of the French – largely, it is true, reinforced by their later Revolutionary excesses – very probably stemmed from his awareness that it was they who had contributed so greatly to the loss of Britain's American empire. He could hardly have been aware that the industrial revolution was to make good all this and more; that Pitt's star was rising on the horizon; that India which had been saved by Warren Hastings was to become the jewel in the imperial crown; and that, far to the south, the one-time *terra incognita* of Australia was receiving its first settlement in New South Wales. But for the moment, contemplating an uncertain future, it must have looked to any aspiring sea-officer that a career in the Navy no longer held out much promise. Peace on half-pay, even with a command, was something that a post-captain without private means could hardly afford.

Once more he put the West Indies behind him but, though low in spirit, he was vigorous in health. Ordered home, as was the rest of the fleet under Lord Hood, Nelson saw the familiar outline of Portsmouth harbour rise before him, but this time bristling with the masts and spars of inactive ships. His own was to join them, and on 26 June 1783 he learned that the *Albemarle* was to be paid off within a week. It was not a happy moment to be an officer, particularly one as conscientious as he was. He showed now, as he was always to do, that the welfare of the men who had served under him was near to his heart. This was the gentleness, the *rapport* with his seamen, which, so rare in his age, was to make him that most exceptional of beings – a commander who was not only respected by the rank and file, but also truly loved. The reason for it comes over clearly in a letter which he wrote to Captain Locker from London on 12 July:

My time, ever since I arrived in Town, has been taken up in attempting to get the wages due to my *good fellows*, for various Ships they have served in the war. The disgust of the Seamen to the Navy is all owing to the infernal plan of turning them over from Ship to Ship, so that Men cannot be attached to their officers, or the Officers care two-pence about them.

My ship was paid off last week; and in such a manner that must flatter any Officer, in particular in these turbulent times. The whole Ship's company offered, if I could get a Ship, to enter for her immediately.

This was indeed a remarkable tribute to her captain, for the rapidity of paying off ships, coupled with the inefficiency in calculating for how long and in what ships the men had served, had already led to near-mutiny in a number of vessels at Spithead. What Nelson knew by sympathy and instinct, what indeed Drake had known centuries before – that the man before the mast had his rights every whit as much as the gentlemen aft – was not to be understood by the

Admiralty until serious trouble had forced their unwilling eyes to
contemplate the reality of the sailor's life. Something else which must
have pleased Nelson was that Lord Hood, far from forgetting a junior
officer who had shown at Sandy Hook a desire to follow the call of
action and honour rather than cruise and prize money, took him to
Court and presented him to the King. The latter was delighted to
meet a friend of Prince William's and invited Nelson down to Windsor
Castle to take leave of the prince, who was about to set out on a
Continental tour. There were many captains in the Navy, few though
as young as Nelson, and Lord Hood's approbation coupled with his
king's seal of approval meant much not only to Nelson himself but
to others who judged a man's star by his appearance at Court.
George III, a moralising family man and staunch upholder of the
old ways, was somehow equated in Nelson's heart with his own
father. It was with genuine satisfaction that he wrote to his friend
Hercules Ross, a merchant from Jamaica: 'I have closed the war
without a fortune : but I trust, and, from the attention that has been
paid to me, believe there is not a speck on my character. True honour,
I hope, predominates in my mind far above riches.' Coming from
another pen the words might sound sanctimonious, but in Nelson's
case they ring true.

In October 1783 he applied to the Admiralty for six months' leave
of absence in order that he might visit France 'on my private
occasions'. The desire to see the country of his recent enemies was
natural enough; important too was the acquisition of the French
language, still that of refined society, and very useful to a naval officer
who might one day be required to interrogate prisoners, or to read
the papers and documents found aboard captured ships. One suspects
that the latter was of more interest to Nelson than the beauties of the
language (which he never did acquire). His first letter to William
Locker, written from St Omer, presents a familiar picture of an
insular naval officer whose standards of shore life had largely been
set by Augustan London or parochial Burnham. Nelson could not
agree with Sterne that 'they order things better in France', although
he was familiar with *Sentimental Journey* and with Hogarth's
engravings, as his letter makes clear : '. . . At half-past ten we were
in Monsieur Grandsire's house at Calais. His mother kept it when
Hogarth wrote [sic] his *Gate of Calais*. Sterne's *Sentimental Journey*
is the best description I can give of our tour.' He travelled with an
old shipmate from the *Lowestoffe*, James Macnamara, who could
speak some French and who was to be his mentor on their tour.
Nelson remained resolutely unimpressed by France, and was equally

disapproving of most of the English whom he met there. Although he was to comment favourably on the food, 'partridges two-pence halfpenny a couple, pheasants and woodcock in proportion', most other things including the travelling arrangements compared unfavourably with England.

They told us we travelled *en poste*, but I am sure we did not get on more than four miles an hour. I was highly diverted looking what a curious figure the postillions in their jack boots, and their rats of horses made together. Their chaises have no springs, and the roads generally paved like London streets; therefore you will naturally suppose we were pretty well shook-together by the time we had travelled two posts and a-half, which is fifteen miles, to Marquise.

The inns were no better : 'We were shown into a room with two straw beds, and, with great difficulty, they mustered up clean sheets; and gave us two pigeons for supper, upon a dirty cloth, and woodenhandled knives – *O what a transition from happy England.*'

Arrived at St Omer, which 'Mac' had suggested as a suitable base for the prosecution of their studies, Nelson was happier not only because they lodged with a pleasant family but because there were two attractive young daughters present. He remained disapproving, however, of the way in which so many of his countrymen adopted French manners and even sartorial habits. 'Two noble Captains are here – Ball and Shepard, you do not know, I believe, either of them; they wear fine epaulettes, for which I think them great coxcombs : they have not visited me. I shall not, be assured, court their acquaintance.' The voice of the provincial is unmistakable, and no doubt Ball and Shepard hardly considered the drably dressed captain worthy of their attention. It is amusing to reflect that only two years later epaulettes were ordered to be worn as part of British naval uniform, while Alexander Ball was later to become a rear-admiral, a baronet, one of Nelson's closest friends, and first Governor of Malta. His equally over-dressed friend James Shepard became a vice-admiral. But by that time Nelson himself would have come to other conclusions about the pleasures of decorations and fine clothing.

At St Omer he once again fell in love, this time with one of two daughters of a visiting English clergyman. The eldest daughter captivated the impressionable tow-headed captain, who seems to have spent much of his time with the family – 'French goes on but slowly' –

and who was finally to declare that she was 'the most accomplished young woman my eyes ever beheld'. He even went so far as to write to his uncle William Suckling asking him if, in the event of his marriage, he would make an allowance of 'a hundred a year, until my income is increased to that sum either by employment or any other way'. His total income at that time was less than £130 per annum.

Uncle William was certainly prepared to help him – as indeed he did at the time of Nelson's marriage in 1787 – but before he could signal his readiness to do so Nelson arrived back in London. Various reasons have been suggested to account for this, among them the fact that his twenty-three-year-old sister Anne had just died at Bath. But Nelson's letters to his correspondents all differ, and to such an extent that one sees him at something of a loss to explain his sudden change of plans. It would seem most probable that the captivating Miss Andrews had rejected him : after all, a post-captain with no private fortune, on half-pay in a time of peace, was no great catch. The very fact that Nelson does not refer to her again suggests the chagrin of a rebuffed suitor. One cannot help wondering whether in later days she did not regret her decision. As for Nelson, a woman whom he found so attractive – with 'such accomplishments that, had I a million of money, I am sure I should at this moment make her an offer of them' and coming from the same background as himself – might well have made an ideal wife. It is noticeable that he never displayed such evidence of passion towards the lady who ultimately did become his wife. Meanwhile, his general air of uncertainty about his future seems reflected in his letters. He wrote to his brother William that 'London has so many charms that a man's whole time is taken up', suggesting that, as far as his pocket permitted, he was living the life of a man about town. A letter written on 31 January, however, is more revealing. The general election of 1784 had taken place, and it is clear that Nelson had for a time considered himself as a potential candidate for Parliament. In disillusionment as to the Walpole connection, he wrote to the Reverend William : 'As to your having enlisted under the banners of the Walpoles, you might as well have enlisted under those of my grandmother.' That Fox had got in instead of his hero Pitt was a bitter blow but 'Mr Pitt, depend upon it, will stand against all opposition : an honest man must always in time get the better of a *villain*; but I have done with politics; let who will get in, I shall be left out.' Nelson was lucky that the sea soon reclaimed him. A man so honest and ingenuous, so incapable of the backbiting and devious intrigue that constitutes politics, would have proved nothing but an unwitting tool or a sad disaster.

On 18 March he was appointed yet again to a 28-gun frigate, this time the *Boreas*. Miss Andrews' younger brother George went with him, so at any rate he was still on good terms with the family, even if matrimony was no longer on the cards. He hoped this time for the East Indies, but was to be disappointed. It was to be the West Indies once again, and this time not only with a lot of young midshipmen to train but, worst of all, with the wife of the Admiral commanding the Leeward Islands as a guest aboard. Lady Hughes and her daughter Rosy were to prove a sore affliction, the former eternally talkative and the latter clearly despatched as part of 'the fishing fleet' to catch herself a husband on her father's station – if she could not find one before. Nelson was in a bad temper from almost the moment they set out, and he was rightly worried at the cost (which fell on him) of looking after Lady Hughes and her daughter in the manner that their station warranted. A small ship was hardly the place for women, and to add to his general irritability he had also to take his brother, the Reverend William, who had suddenly decided that he liked the idea of a sea life.

His temper was far from improved by the fact that 'The d—d pilot, it makes me swear to think of it – ran the Ship aground, where she lay with so little water that the people could walk round her till next high water.' A dispute with a Dutch Indiaman in the Downs, who was illegally holding sixteen British seamen on board against their will, had to be settled by sending over an armed guard. The Dutch captain reported his behaviour to the Admiralty who, fortunately for Nelson, approved his side of the argument, 'a thing they are not very guilty of when there is a likelihood of a scrape'. But once at sea, Madeira-bound, the quiet routines and ordered discipline of the ship – even if his quarter-deck was cluttered up with unwanted passengers – exercised their usual calming influence. Crossed in love, disappointed in political ambition, he was happy in that element which seemed to have chosen him quite as much as he had chosen it. His enthusiasm and his pleasure in the details of command, even down to the training of the midshipmen, were recalled many years later by Lady Hughes in a letter to George Matcham, who had married Nelson's favourite sister Catherine :

As a woman, I can only be a judge of those things that I could comprehend – such as his attention to the young gentlemen who had the happiness of being on his quarter-deck. It may reasonably

be supposed that among the number of thirty, there must be timid
as well as bold; the timid he never rebuked, but always wished to
show them that he desired nothing of them that he would not
instantly do himself : and I have known him say : 'Well, Sir, I am
going a race to the masthead, and beg I may meet you there.' . . .
His Lordship never took the least notice with what alacrity it was
done, but when he met in the top, instantly began speaking in the
most cheerful manner, and saying how much a person was to be
pitied that could fancy there was any danger, or even anything
disagreeable in the attempt. After this excellent example, I have
seen the timid youth lead another, and rehearse his captain's words.
In like manner, he every day went into the school-room, and saw
them do their nautical business, and at twelve o'clock he was first
upon deck with his quadrant.

She also recollected how on another occasion, when the *Boreas* was
at Barbados, she and Nelson were due to call on the Governor and
Nelson asked permission to bring one of the midshipmen with them,
excusing himself by saying, 'I make it a rule to introduce them to all
the good company I can, as they have few to look up to besides
myself during the time they are at sea.' It is hardly surprising
that 'This kindness and attention made the young people adore
him. . . .'

If Nelson at the time, and certainly in recollection, pleased Lady
Hughes, the same could not be said of the effect made upon him by
her and her husband. Sir Richard Hughes was an amiable but insignificant man who had lost the sight of one eye – something which
might have inspired respect if it had been a war wound, but not when
it was known that it was due to an accident in youth while chasing
a cockroach with a table fork. Nelson was later to dismiss him with
the comment, 'tolerable, but I do not like him, he bows and scrapes
too much for me', adding on closer acquaintance, 'the admiral and
all about him are great ninnies'. There can be no doubt that from the
very beginning he was unhappy on this station and, had it not been
for the presence of Cuthbert Collingwood and his brother Wilfred,
there would have been few with whom he could share his thoughts
and feelings, let alone the serious problems that were soon to confront
him. His own brother, William, was soon to leave, though not to any
great regret on Nelson's part : he was unfitted for the life of a chaplain
afloat and found, as did so many, that the languorous climate of the
West Indies did not agree with him. The eternal afternoon of the
tropics, the susurrus of the wind through the palm trees, the monotony

of the breakers on the windward side of the islands, and the dreamy slip-slop of the Caribbean on the lee, were often to prove the undoing of men raised in colder and more stimulating climates. Nelson recorded of one of his brother officers, Charles Sandys: 'I am sorry to say he goes through a regular course of claret every day.'

Antigua, crowned by a line of forts around the crater of its vast ancient volcano, and with the English Harbour – now restored as a haven for those last voyagers under sail, the private yachtsmen – provided the West Indies squadron with a fine base for refitting and maintenance work. The dockyard saw much of Nelson, as did the Commissioner and his wife. Captain John Moutray was a retired naval captain, considerably senior to Nelson, who had been appointed as Commissioner of the Navy in a civil capacity connected with the running of the Antigua dockyard. For Mrs Moutray Nelson conceived one of those sentimental and romantic passions which, while perfectly harmless in itself and recognised as such by both parties, seemed to give him a purpose for living. While the *Boreas* was repainting he was entertained at the Moutrays' house and his admiration for the lady steadily increased. Knowing that she was unattainable, and being himself on awkward terms – professionally at any rate – with Commissioner Moutray, and well aware that both she and her husband were due to return to England within a year, Nelson permitted himself a Werther-like dream of romance. As he was later to write to brother William: 'You may be certain I never passed English Harbour without a call, but alas! I am not to have much comfort. My dear, sweet friend is going home. I am really an April day; happy on her account, but truly grieved were I only to consider myself. Her equal I never saw in any country or in any situation.'

Nelson's brush with Commissioner Moutray was caused by the fact that Sir Richard Hughes had given the latter a memorandum authorising him to act as Commander-in-Chief during the absence of a senior officer, and to hoist the broad pendant of a commodore. Nelson justifiably, though perhaps somewhat punctiliously, saw this as quite incorrect, for the Commissioner, though formerly a senior post-captain, was now working in a civilian capacity. Correspondence ensued between Nelson and Sir Richard, and between Nelson and the Secretary to the Admiralty. In the end the issue was resolved when the Moutrays sailed for England, while for the future the Admiralty decided that all Commissioners of the Navy should be on full pay, and appointed to the nominal command of a ship, or 'stone frigate' as such shore-bases came to be called. But the incident in itself should have warned the indolent Sir Richard that he had a gad-fly on the station, one who was determined to see that rules and regulations should be obeyed to the letter.

It is difficult not to see in this and Nelson's subsequent actions something of an officiousness unattractive in so junior a captain. That, certainly, was how his behaviour was judged by most of the civilians and even many of the Navy in the West Indies. In the major dispute that followed over the implementation of the Navigation Act, however, one finds an officer who is so dedicated to the Service that he is prepared to sacrifice his whole career and prospects to what he judges to be the rights of the laws that he has been appointed to defend. Briefly, only British-built and British-owned ships were allowed to trade with her colonies; this meant that the Americans, who until recently had been British colonists, were now excluded, by the very fact of their independence, from the rights possessed by British citizens. No one could possibly dispute this, but the fact was that not only the inhabitants of the West Indian islands but the Americans themselves did not see things in this light. The former colonists had enjoyed a very prosperous trade with the West Indies and they could not see why they should now be disbarred just because they were now citizens of what, in effect, had become a foreign power; neither could the majority of the merchants in the islands who had long traded with their American friends and had well-established connections with them.

Nelson, long since removed from the scene of his youthful indignation and therefore no longer pressing his own case, could be quite dispassionate in the account that he gave in the 'Sketch of My Life'. Investigation has shown that his statement of the case is accurate and, though at this distance in time it seems but a storm in a teacup, the issue was very real to a junior captain who hazarded his future on the true and just interpretation of the laws. Of the West Indies, he wrote :

The Station opened a new scene to the Officers of the British Navy. The Americans, when colonists, possessed all the trade from America to our West India Islands; and, on the return of Peace, they forgot, on this occasion, they became foreigners, and of course had no right to trade in the British Colonies. Our Governors and Custom-house officials pretended, that by the Navigation Act they had a right to trade; and all the West Indians wished what was so much for their own interest.

Nelson acted according to what he saw as right, and seized many of the American trading ships, incurring so much displeasure and downright hatred in so doing that 'I was persecuted from one Island to another, that I could not leave my ship'. Admiral Hughes, when called upon for judgement, was unable or, rather, unwilling to make up his mind on the subject. He had hoped for a quiet and easy time in this station, and had little counted on having such a general commotion about his ears – and all caused by a junior post-captain. Nelson equally had his views about the Admiral:

Our Commander has not that opinion of his own sense that he ought to have. He is led by the advice of the Islanders to admit the Yankees to a Trade; at least to wink at it. He does not give himself the weight that I think an English Admiral ought to do. I, for one, am determined not to suffer the Yankees to come where my ship is; for I am sure, if once the Americans are admitted to any kind of intercourse with these Islands, the views of the Loyalists in settling Nova Scotia are entirely done away. They will become first the Carriers, and next have possession of our Islands, are we ever again embroiled in a French war. The residents of these Islands are Americans by connexion and by interest, and are inimical to Great Britain.

In all of this, Nelson was quite correct, but how explain it to the authorities thousands of miles away at home, let alone to those who had sleeping or vested interests in the trade of the West Indies?

He was lucky that he had Collingwood to stand by him, for few wanted to know him during those difficult days. It has been said of him very accurately that 'a prudent man, with an eye only to his own interests, would have avoided conflict with his superior officer: only a man absolutely fearless, and capable of setting duty above all other considerations, would have risked a quarrel which might ruin him for life'. It is true that in later life we hear much of Nelson's physical courage, but his moral courage as displayed in the West Indies, when he had no one behind him to back him up and he was in conflict with his senior officer, shows him in a dazzling light – unlit by cannon or thundering sails, or the inexorable approach of one wind-blown fleet upon another.

CHAPTER SEVEN

West Indian Marriage

THE storm clouds gathered. Sir Richard Hughes, after having his attention drawn to the Navigation Laws by Nelson and Collingwood, was finally forced to take some action. But, in accordance with his character, having first instructed all the ships under his command to enforce the Laws and regard Americans as foreigners, he yielded to circumstances, and to the friends by whom he was surrounded. On 11 January 1785 he modified his original instructions, ordering Nelson to do no more than cause foreign merchantmen to anchor near his vessel and report their arrival to the governor of the colony where he then was. Sir Richard added the rider that 'if, after such report shall have been made and received, the governor or his representative shall think proper to admit the said foreigner into the port or harbour of the island where you may be, you are *on no account to hinder or prevent such foreign vessel from going in accordingly, or to interfere any further in her subsequent proceedings* [my italics]'. This laid the way wide open for whatever governor might be concerned to interpret the Navigation Act as he thought fit. It removed the onus of enforcing it from the Navy, where it belonged.

Nelson immediately remonstrated with his commander-in-chief. He pointed out that in times of peace, such as those, the function of His Majesty's ships-of-war was to protect the commerce of the nation, which in its turn meant ensuring that foreigners did not trade in areas where they were forbidden. He pointed out that landsmen might easily be taken in by a merchant captain's saying that his ship was in distress or in need of repair but, 'in judging of their distress, no person can know better than the sea officers. The governors may be imposed upon by false declarations; we, who are on the spot, cannot.' Nelson refused to obey the amended orders for, as he wrote to Locker whose experience he valued almost as much as his friendship, 'Sir Richard Hughes was a delicate business. I must either disobey my orders, or disobey Acts of Parliament, which the admiral was disobeying. I determined upon the former, trusting to the uprightness of my intention. In short, I wrote the Admiral that I should decline obeying his orders, till I had an opportunity of seeing and talking to him, at the same time making him an apology.'

Nelson was also soon embroiled with General Shirley, the Governor of the Leeward Islands, who was as inclined to turn a blind eye to the traffic with America as was Sir Richard. In reply to Nelson's remonstrations he said sharply that 'old respectable officers of high rank, long service and of a certain life are very jealous of being dictated to in their duty by young gentlemen whose service and experience do not entitle them to it'. Nelson, according to Lieutenant Wallis of the *Boreas*, said in reply that he had the honour of being as old as the Prime Minister of England (Pitt) and 'think myself as capable of commanding one of His Majesty's ships as that Minister is of governing the State'.

Nelson's troubles increased. The islanders of Nevis, infuriated by the fact that he had seized four American vessels off their shores, raised a large sum to enable the ships' owners to sue Nelson, who could not go ashore or he would have been arrested. Significantly, Mr John Richardson Herbert, the President of the Council of Nevis, offered to become his bail if need be to the sum of ten thousand pounds – significantly because he was the uncle of a young woman in whom Nelson was to show no little interest. The conclusion of the long-drawn-out affair of the Navigation Act came from England with the news that Nelson's costs in the case would be met by the Treasury. At the same time there came, with the cruellest irony, a commendation of both the governor and the admiral for their diligence in protecting British trade in the West Indies. Nelson would scarcely have been able to savour the humour of that. . . . But he was, despite all the troubles by which he was still surrounded, now given the official seal of approval and came under the protection of the authorities at home. He remained, of course, unpopular. He was compensated by fate in his acquaintanceship with a niece of President Herbert. Herbert was a widower with one daughter, and was visited from time to time by various nieces from England who came out to find themselves husbands – and usually did. One of them, Frances Herbert Nisbet, was a young widow with a boy of five named Josiah. She was staying with friends on the island of St Kitts at the time that Nelson dined with Mr Herbert in his large house, Montpelier, on Nevis, and she first heard of Nelson – a name generally scorned and detested in the islands – in a letter from one of her cousins:

We have at last seen the Captain of the *Boreas*, of whom so much has been said. He came up, just before dinner, much heated, and was very silent; yet seemed, according to the old adage, to think the more. He declined drinking any wine; but, after dinner, when the President, as usual, gave the following toasts, 'the King', 'the Queen and Royal Family', and 'Lord Hood', this strange man regularly filled his glass, and observed that those were always bumper toasts with him; which having drank, he uniformly passed the bottle, and relapsed into his former taciturnity. It was impossible, during this visit, for any of us to make out his real character; there was such a reserve and sternness in his behaviour, with occasional sallies, though very transient, of a superior mind. Being placed by him, I endeavoured to rouse his attention by showing him all the civilities in my power; but I drew out little more than 'Yes' and 'No'. If you, Fanny, had been there, we think you would have made something of him; for you have been in the habit of attending to these odd sort of people.

'Odd sort of people' most sea captains were, for the loneliness of command turned them in upon themselves and although, like Nelson, many were friendly and even gregarious by nature, there remained always with them a kind of aloofness, difficult to define but somewhat akin to the indifference of the sea that they served. A young captain like Nelson, particularly in view of his relationship with most of the civilians whom he met – or did not meet – in the islands, was likely to be more taciturn than most.

A side of his nature which was in evidence all his life, stemming no doubt from having grown up in a large, happy family, was brought to the somewhat astonished attention of the President of Nevis a few months later. Nelson had not yet met Mrs Nisbet but, calling on Mr Herbert early one morning on his return to Nevis, he found her five-year-old son in the room into which he was shown. A short time later Mr Herbert came down to meet his visitor. . . . 'Good God!' as he later exclaimed to his household at breakfast, 'Good God! If I did not find that great little man of whom everybody is afraid, playing in the next room, under the dining-table, with Mrs Nisbet's child.' If a suitor had intended a sure way to a mother's heart he could not have been more aptly engaged. Indeed, when the two first met at dinner a few days afterwards, the young widow was at once to thank Nelson for 'the great partiality he had shown to her little boy'.

Frances Nisbet had been born a Miss Woolward, daughter of William Woolward, Senior Judge of Nevis, and her mother, who had died when Frances was young, had been President Herbert's sister. Shortly after her father's death she had married the doctor who had attended him, Josiah Nisbet, and had returned to England with her husband where he too died a year and a half later. She was left with her infant son, Josiah, little money and no property. Her uncle had provided the solution by asking her back to Nevis to help him in running his large household. She was a few months older than Nelson, born in the same year, and had been four years a widow when first they met. All the circumstances were ripe for the romance that followed; the lonely widow, the even lonelier bachelor, and the congenial atmosphere of her uncle's house, where all was elegance and comfort. Frances Nisbet, as her portraits show, was slim, with delicate features, fine dark-grey eyes and dark hair. Irresistibly she reminded Nelson of the paragon Mrs Moutray, but with the advantage in her favour that she was younger, and unmarried. She had, furthermore, all the hallmarks of well-bred distinction which appealed to him, being fluent in the tongue that had mocked him – French – and a fine needlewoman, as well as having an air of somewhat porcelain grace that could hardly fail to appeal to a sea-officer whose daily life was marked by a complete absence of femininity. His was a world of hard-case sailors and equally tough officers, nearly all of whom were fond of the bottle or of the local women, or of both. As late as the 1840s a frigate captain in the West Indies sent ashore for 300 black women, so that every man aboard might have a mistress while in port. The women were supplied from one of the plantations. Rum and venereal disease took a high toll of sailors, whether officers or men, and a naval surgeon writing in 1826 could report a number of deaths which he had recorded due to 'debauched habits'. The syphilis, which had almost certainly been endemic in the West Indies at the time of Columbus's navigations, had subsequently been reinforced by venereal diseases of European origin. A sailor's life in the Caribbean in the late eighteenth century was as beset with disease as it had been since the days of the buccaneers. The world of Montpelier was a far remove from all this. Mrs Nisbet was, in the phrase, genteel – and so was Nelson.

Their courtship was conducted in a setting that would have been familiar to Jane Austen – indeed the two main characters might well have emerged from one of her novels. Only the exotic background of Nevis presented an unfamiliar touch. Nevis, which Columbus called after the Mountain of Nieves in Spain because its summit was nearly always snow-like with grazing clouds lodged there by the trade wind, was the peak of an extinct volcano, and the brilliant green of its lower slopes shone out against the turning blue and the raked-white waves

of the Caribbean. In unusual but charming contrast to this world of
natural beauty was the small 'court', for such it almost seemed, of the
President's house, where the attachment of the shy naval officer to
the quiet young widow proceeded as if according to a well-ordered
plan. Nelson's letters reflect the courtesies and conventions of the time
but, though they display an eager desire to be married, they are
lacking in the fire and spontaneity of his reflections upon Mrs Moutray
or even upon the clergyman's daughter at St Omer. One suspects that
loneliness was very largely responsible for driving him to marriage,
as well as a feeling that he had reached the time of life when marriage
was somehow the suitable, and settling, answer to his personal
problems. As for Mrs Nisbet, a young widow with a small child, and
dependent upon her uncle, she viewed Nelson's advances with careful,
but thankful, appraisal, observing of him that he was of 'a superior
mind'. The trouble was that her suitor, as has been seen, had nothing
other than his naval pay.

Nelson proposed in August, having made up his mind to do so in
June, and having first met his future bride in March. But everything
depended on the reactions of uncle William Suckling to his nephew's
request for financial help and, above all, to the reaction of President
Herbert, who would naturally be unwilling to lose a housekeeper. His
view on the financial side of things was expressed as follows: 'Nelson,
I am proud, and I must live like myself, therefore I can't do much
in my lifetime; when I die she shall have twenty thousand pounds;
and if my daughter dies before me, she shall possess the major part of
my property. I intend going to England in 1787 and remaining there
my life; therefore, if you two can live happily together till that event
takes place, you have my consent.' Pending a definite reply from
William Suckling, and something a little more concrete from the
President, Nelson and 'Fanny' – for such she had now become in his
letters – had to settle down and wait for eighteen months, during
much of which time Nelson was inevitably away from his fiancée as
his duties called him backwards and forwards between the islands.
For a time during November 1786 he even found himself temporarily
in command of the whole station, his former adversary Sir Richard
Hughes having been appointed home, and his relief, Sir Richard
Bickerton, not having arrived.

One expects illusions from a man in love, but Nelson's letters –
whether to his fiancée, his brother William, or his uncle – are all
eminently practical, and the most evidence of passion that can be
found is couched in the copper-plate conventions of the time. Thus,
at sea off the island of Désirade on 3 March 1786, he writes:

'Separated from my dearest what pleasure can I feel? None! Be
assured all my happiness is centred with thee and where thou art not
there I am not happy. . . . I daily thank God who ordained that I
should be attached to you. He has I firmly believe intended it as a
blessing to me, and I am well convinced you will not disappoint His
beneficent intentions.' And so on. To his brother he writes: 'The dear
object you must like. Her sense, polite manners, and to you I may say,
beauty, you will much admire', while to uncle Suckling, 'Her mental
accomplishments are superior to most persons of either sex. . . . My
affection for her is fixed upon that solid basis of esteem and regard
that I trust can only increase by a longer knowledge of her.' The
sentiments were always impeccable, if uninspired, and all would seem
to have augured well for a quiet conventional marriage, reinforced in
due course by a household of healthy children.

In only one letter dating from this period of his life do we catch
a glimpse of the real Nelson, alone, and aboard his ship, and understand the monotony that made up so much of a sea-officer's life.
Boreas was refitting at English Harbour, Antigua, and something of
the indolence of the island, the sweat-soaked sailors, the smell of fresh
pitch in the seams, the distant sounds from the rope-walk, and the
clunk of the caulker's hammer, emerges. The letter was sent to Fanny
Nisbet, and was dated 'Monday (21 August) Seven in the Evening
[1786]':

As you begin to know something about Sailors, have you not often
heard that salt water and absence always wash away love? Now
I am such a heretic as not to believe that Faith; for behold, every
morning since my arrival, I have had six pails of salt water at daylight poured upon my head, and instead of finding what the Seamen
say to be true, I perceive the contrary effect; and if it goes on so
contrary to the prescription, you must see me before my fixed time.
At first, I bore absence tolerably, but now it is almost insupportable;
and by and by I expect it will be quite so. But patience is a virtue;
and I must exercise it upon this occasion whatever it costs my
feelings. I am alone in the Commanding Officer's house, while my
ship is fitting, and from sunset until bedtime I have not a human
creature to speak to; you will feel a little for me I think. I did not
use to be over-fond of sitting alone. The moment old *Boreas* is
habitable in my cabin, I shall fly to it, to avoid mosquitoes and
melancholies. Hundreds of the former are now devouring me
through my clothes. You will however find I am better [he still
suffered from recurrent fever]; though when you see me, I shall be

like an Egyptian mummy for the heat is intolerable. But I walk a
mile out at night without fatigue and all day I am housed. A quart
of goat's milk is also taken every day, and I enjoy English sleep,
always barring mosquitoes which all Frank's care with my net
cannot keep out at present. . . .

(Frank Lepée, who had been with Nelson on the Nicaraguan
expedition, was later to accompany him to Norfolk.) 'English sleep',
yes, that such as he had known at Burnham, was what he needed. He
was constantly ill in the West Indies, 'worn to a skeleton' as he wrote
to uncle Suckling in July; and several months later, to Captain Locker,
that the doctor had 'thought I was in a consumption, and quite
gave me up'.

The arrival on the station of H.M.S. *Pegasus* under the command
of Prince William Henry early in November gave him an impetus
which – even if at times awkward for a devoted royalist – prevented
him from relaxing into any form of languor, and indeed almost took
his thoughts off his impending marriage. The Prince, of whom Nelson
had expected so much (and to whose clearly apparent faults he turned
a blind eye) was to prove something of a handful, and to require a
great deal of tact in dealing with. The martinet that was latent in
the Prince had surged to the fore under the influence of command.
He was also a great gadabout and, as we learn from his medical
officer, in May 1787 Prince William was on a mercury cure 'for a
sore I had contracted in a most extraordinary manner in my pursuit
of the *Dames de Couleurs*'. Less than a year later, in February 1788,
his surgeon was to report to his senior officer Captain Elphinstone,
who had suggested a further period in the West Indies for the Prince,
that 'I cannot recommend it for his Royal Highness to return where
he has suffered so materially'. Clearly there were disadvantages in
George III's admirable (on the surface of it) idea of having his son
learn the hard trade of a sea-officer. There were nevertheless some
who approved, and Frederick the Great rationalised : 'As our young
nobility in general never learn anything, they of course are exceed-
ingly ignorant. In England one of the King's sons, wishing to interest
himself, has not scrupled to set out as a common sailor.' The phrase
which here betrays the Continental, aristocratic outlook towards the
service of the sea is 'common sailor'. But Frederick could also and
rightly comment about the England which produced the Prince, as
well as men like Nelson, that :

When you see how in this happy country the lowest and meanest
member of society testifies the interest he takes in everything of a

public nature, when you see how high and low, rich and poor, all concur in declaring their feelings and their convictions, how a carter, a common tar, a scavenger, is still a man, nay, an Englishman, – take my word for it you will feel yourself very differently affected from what you are when staring at our soldiers in their exercise in Berlin.

Nelson, concealing from Fanny any real feelings he may have had about the Prince's conduct in the islands, could write on Christmas Eve 1786 that: 'I fancy as many people were as happy to see His Royal Highness quit as they were to see him enter St John's [Antigua], for another day or two's racquet would have knocked some of the fair sex up. Three nights' dancing was too much and never Broke up till near day. . . . I will tell you much when we meet, for you never know the danger of putting too much upon paper.' Later, on 1 January 1787, he confesses that he is worn out – being Senior Captain on the Leeward Islands station was no sinecure when the Prince was about: 'I was in hopes to have been quiet all this week. Today we dine with Sir Thomas [Shirley]; tomorrow the Prince has a party; on Wednesday he gives a dinner in Saint John's to the Regiment; in the evening is a Mulatto ball; on Thursday a cockfight, dine at Colonel Crosbie's brother's and a ball, on Friday somewhere but I forget; on Saturday at Mr. Byam's the President.' One great change in his fortune, however, was that the formerly detested Captain Nelson was now seen to be the close friend and confidant of a prince of the blood royal. That made all the difference, and doors that had been studiedly closed against him ever since the troubles over the Navigation Act were now thrown open, and hats were raised in streets where formerly heads would have been averted – or where, indeed, he would once have been thrown in jail if he had been so unwise as to land.

On the other hand, the Prince brought troubles with him. There was the affair of Lieutenant Schomberg, a knowledgeable thirty-four-year-old officer who had considerable previous West Indies experience and who had been appointed First Lieutenant of the *Pegasus*, to act discreetly as mentor to his twenty-two-year-old Captain. This was something that was far from the Prince's taste, for he had a great deal of the Hanover autocrat in him, as well as a swaggering insouciance that is reminiscent of Mr Toad. The troubles aboard H.M.S. *Pegasus* were sadly brought to Nelson's notice when he received a formal letter from her First Lieutenant asking for a court-martial, as his Captain had accused him of neglect of duty. Nelson was faced with a very awkward situation. He had Schomberg put under arrest, hoping for the arrival of the new Commander-in-Chief who would relieve him of responsibility : at that moment, in any case, there were not enough senior officers available to form a court. He heard in the interim that other officers serving under the Prince were likewise on the verge of asking to be court-martialled. In the end, since no senior authority appeared on the scene to relieve him of an impossible situation, Nelson had the *Pegasus* transferred to Port Royal, Jamaica, where there was a commodore, and where the whole matter could be sorted out – or allowed to simmer down. He was later to be reproved by the Admiralty for his action, though this was little more than a formality, but by then he had yet other troubles to deal with. In the event, Schomberg, though superseded in his post, went on to become First Lieutenant in the *Barfleur* under Lord Hood (a man who certainly never tolerated incompetence or indeed anything else), and finally rose to become one of the Commissioners of the Navy Board.

Far more serious, as far as Nelson was concerned, was the case involving accusations laid by two merchants of Antigua about speculations by Crown officials in the Leeward Islands. They brought the matter to Nelson, since it was now well known that he would defend the rights of the Crown against all comers. This whole affair was to prove every whit as troublesome as the previous one had been, and dragged on for many months. In the end Nelson was finally justified and 'as the Naval Storekeeper is punished by fine and imprisonment it is to be hoped a stop will by this means be put to further embezzlement'. It never was, of course, and – given the nature of mankind – never will be. But the parson's son possessed a conscience, while the naval officer would never tolerate the greasy *mores* of landsmen, longshoremen, and civilians in general. Like most seamen he understood perfectly the simple peccadilloes of drunken sailors – though he would never tolerate indiscipline in any form – but he had no tolerance of corruption.

Quite apart from his health, always indifferent, if not bad, on this station, Nelson had found little happiness in the West Indies. He was only to revisit the area once again, and that was in the year of his death. Even then, he found (as Columbus had done centuries before him) that, in the final analysis, the islands yielded little or no luck. But, on the surface at least, his happiness was ensured on Sunday, 11 March 1787, when two twenty-eight-year-olds, Captain Horatio Nelson and Mrs Frances Nisbet, were married by the Rector of St John's in President Herbert's house, Montpelier. Prince William

Henry, who earlier had jocularly teased Nelson with the remark that it was only 'a great esteem' which Nelson felt for Mrs Nisbet, and not that thing 'which is vulgarly called love', had broken his rule of never accepting private invitations and undertaken the role of father of the bride. The couple undoubtedly felt the honour of the presence of His Royal Highness in this capacity – though for different reasons. Both perhaps also felt a little uneasy: Mrs Nisbet because the bonhomie of Prince William could hardly disguise his basic cynicism; and Nelson because he must have felt some truth in the Prince's jest. Had he not quoted the remark to Fanny, adding on his own account: 'He is right, my love is founded on esteem, the only foundation that can make the passion last'? He was correct, some would say, but the words seem a trifle cool and measured coming from so young a man.

In May 1787 the *Boreas*, having completed her tour of duty in the West Indies, sailed from the Leeward Islands bound for Portsmouth, Fanny and her son travelling independently in a West India merchant-man. Not long beforehand Nelson had written to his old friend Locker that 'no man has had more illness or trouble on a Station than I have experienced; but let me lay a balance on the other side – I am married to an amiable woman, that far makes amends for everything: indeed till I married her I never knew happiness. And I am morally certain she will continue to make me a happy man for the rest of my days.' Captain Pringle, a friend of Nelson's since his days in the *Albemarle*, voiced another opinion: 'The Navy, Sir,' he remarked sadly, 'yesterday lost one of its greatest ornaments, by Nelson's marriage. It is a national loss that such an officer should marry; had it not been for that circumstance, I foresaw Nelson would become the greatest man in the Service.'

CHAPTER EIGHT

Ashore

IT IS the silences that reveal. The whole of Nelson's life during the five years which were to follow is compressed into two brief sentences in the 'Sketch of My Life', which he gave to John M'Arthur in 1799. The first refers to the years 1787 : 'And in March, this year, I married Frances Herbert Nisbet, widow of Dr Nisbet, of the Island of Nevis; by whom I have no children.' The following sentence reads : 'The *Boreas* being paid off at Sheerness, on November the 30th, I lived at Burnham Thorpe, county of Norfolk, in the Parsonage-house.'

It is true that the Victor of the Nile writing this abbreviated sketch in Port Mahon, Minorca, was only concerned with recording the outline – and the highlights – of his naval career. But it must seem strange that the man who could later add such superficially irrelevant items as that 'his Sicilian Majesty presented me with a Sword magnificently enriched with diamonds' should dismiss his marriage so briefly. The answer is contained in the fact that by 1799, when he wrote this outline, he had met and fallen in love with Emma Hamilton, and that for him his marriage was already over. An immense sadness – a bitterness even – lifts like a wave in the brief words, 'by whom I have no children'.

If one were to judge solely by this laconic account, Horatio Nelson left the *Boreas* and immediately settled down to the quiet routine of life at Burnham Thorpe. This was far from the case, for the foreign situation was such that it looked as if war was yet again to break out between England and France, and the *Boreas* had to be revictualled for further potential service. And this time Nelson was not spared the troubles that so often attended the end of a commission, for the ship's company was eager to be paid off and to enjoy some of the pleasures of home. Desertions were frequent and the names and descriptions of the men concerned had to be forwarded to the Admiralty. Nelson himself, no more than his crew, could not enjoy the pleasures of the shore or of seeing his wife. The *Boreas* was ordered to the Nore, and it was from here that he had to make arrangements for lodging Fanny and young Josiah in London. It was an unhappy time in his life, and the fact that the *Boreas* was detailed to act as a 'receiving ship' did not appeal to an officer who, it is clear, had earlier shown a dislike of the forcible impressment of men to serve the fleet. A receiving ship was one which was detailed to board all passing vessels, whether large or small, and take from them as many of the crew as possible, without actually endangering the seagoing abilities of the ship concerned. In effect, this meant leaving the boarded vessel so short of hands that she could do little but make for the nearest port. It was not until the end of November that, the alarm of war having died down, the *Boreas* was finally paid off and Nelson was free to join his wife. It is not insignificant, however, that at one moment during this period of service, when it seemed as if war was imminent, he had written : 'If we are to have a bustle, I do not want to come on shore; I begin to think I am fonder of the sea than ever.'

In many respects, newly married though he was, it was natural that he should long above all else for sea service. Ambition drove him, a very deep love of his profession – far in excess of anything he seems to have felt for his wife – but in addition to this there was the over-riding matter of money. To support Fanny and his stepson was hardly going to be easy on half-pay. As a post-captain, he drew only a little more than one hundred pounds a year, and if it had not been for the help of William Suckling and Mr Herbert the Nelson family could have done nothing but exist in genteel poverty in the Burnham parsonage. As it was, Fanny received £100 a year from her uncle – who had retired to England as he had intended – while Nelson had a similar amount from William Suckling. It is indicative of monetary values in the England of that time that on this amount the Nelsons did in fact manage to live quite comfortably. Indeed, during the first months of their stay they managed to spend Christmas in London with Mr Herbert – as well as travelling to Exmouth and Bath. Nelson also visited Plymouth while he was in the West Country, on an invitation from Prince William. But this ability to travel and maintain a respectable appearance must be seen in the context with which, as will be seen, Nelson in due course made himself very familiar : the earnings of an East Anglian farm labourer were little more than £20 a year.

One letter, written from Bath on 27 January 1788 to William Locker, gives some indication of why he retired to the parsonage in Norfolk : 'Your kind letter I received yesterday, and am much obliged by your kind inquiries about a house. I fear we must at present give [up] all thoughts of living so near London, for Mrs Nelson's lungs are so much affected by the smoke of London, that I cannot think of placing her in that situation, however desirable. For the next summer I shall be down in Norfolk, from whence I must look forward.' The fact was that, although she was to outlive him and indeed practically all the other participants in the saga of his life by many years, Fanny seems never to have been well in England. The cold and the damp (which affected Nelson as well, 'The rain and the cold at first gave me a sore throat') proved almost intolerable to a woman who had spent most of her life in the West Indies. She suffered from rheumatism or arthritis, or both (medical records are non-existent).

Fanny appears to have become barren after bearing her one son, and seems also to have been constantly prone to what were known in those days as 'the vapours', but which would nowadays be diagnosed as some form of hysteria or psychosomatic illness. It is most unlikely that any evidence will ever come to light as to the real nature of her nervous complaints, and it is pointless at this time to speculate in Freudian or other psychoanalytical terms about Fanny Nelson's problems. All the records, including his many letters to her, show that she had in Nelson a loving and very thoughtful husband. If passion was absent, perhaps it was rejected? His earlier feelings and responses to attractive young women show him to have been a perfectly healthy normal man, capable of such an ardent response as even to consider abandoning his career for a woman he had known for only a short time. Such had never been the case with Fanny, and his responses, if warm and genuine indeed, had always been safeguarded by material considerations, and observations about those excellences of her character that would make her a good wife. As to Nelson's own sexuality and fertility, of these there can be no doubt, for his physical passion for Emma Hamilton was unbounded, and she was to bear him two children.

The final decision to stay at Burnham Thorpe with his father was prompted not only by financial considerations, by a belief (mistaken as it turned out) that the Norfolk air would suit Fanny, but by the old rector's desire to have his son and his new daughter-in-law at home with him. Now that all the other birds had flown the nest, the Reverend Edmund was lonely. As he grew older, so his health deteriorated, and the visits to Bath in the winter became more of a necessity than a mild self-indulgence. But a worse place for poor Fanny than Burnham could hardly have been chosen. It was not that there was no social life, for there was constant family visiting – to the

Matchams and Horatio's favourite sister Kitty, to the William Nelsons, and to his sister Susannah and her husband Thomas Bolton. It was all perhaps somewhat parochial after the splendours of the President's house on Nevis, but whatever Fanny felt about the limited company to be found in such Norfolk rounds it was nothing compared with the effect on her of the weather. As the local guide accurately comments: 'We stand and look right across the North Sea to the North Pole. There is nothing to break the sweep of tumbling waters, save the fields and cliffs of ice which ring it round. And well do we know all this when the Nor'Easters whistle in off our steel-grey sea every day from January to June; stiffening our backs and shutting tight our mouths.' Then the snow came – 'Hush, at High Noon as at Midnight,' commented Nelson's father – and the frail exile from the tropics was often forced to take to her bed, sometimes for days on end. She had not even the companionship of her son, Josiah, except during his holidays, for he had been sent away to boarding-school.

The rector conceived a great affection for his daughter-in-law, worried that she had so little company, observed how good a wife she made Horatio, and looked after her as she in her turn looked after him. It was a strange quiet life in winter, Nelson brooding over charts or reading Dampier's *Voyages*, which he considered the most interesting book he had ever read, or writing constantly to their Lordships to remind them of his existence, and in the hope that he would be looked on in the future with some favour. The fact of the matter was that his tour in the West Indies had not served him in good stead. It was not only that he had incurred the enmity of a number of powerful individuals through his insistence on carrying out the Navigation Act, but he had quarrelled with and disobeyed his Admiral, and had stirred up even more trouble by his action over the peculations of Crown Officials in the Leeward Islands. A further fact, which did not exactly place him in the good books of George III, was his friendship with Prince William. This, which might at one time have seemed to serve him in good stead, did him nothing but disservice with a father who was almost daily further infuriated by the scandals, scrapes and peccadillos that surrounded the Prince.

When the slow spring returned, the early green flickering on branches for so long bare, and the birds once more active on lawns or in the renewing hedgerows, Nelson became once more a Norfolk boy. It was almost as if nothing had happened during the intervening years – no visits to Indies East and West, no brilliant long Atlantic crossings, and no sweltering under tropic suns. His first biographers paint the picture:

It is extremely interesting to contemplate this great man, when
thus removed from the busy scenes in which he had borne so
distinguished a part, to the remote village of Burnham Thorpe. His
mind, though so entirely taken from its proper element, and sphere
of action, could not remain unoccupied. He was soon, therefore,
engaged, and with considerable zeal, in cultivating his father's
garden, and in learning to farm the adjoining glebe; but the former
was his principal station : he would there often spend the greater
part of the day, and dig, as it were, for the sake of being wearied.
At others, he would renew the early pastime of his childhood, and
with a simplicity that was peculiar to him, when his mind was not
employed on the great objects of professional duty, would spend
the greater part of the day amidst the woods, in taking the eggs of
various birds, which, as he obtained, he gave to Mrs Nelson, who
at his express desire always attended him. He sometimes also
employed his time, *when his eyes would admit of it* [my italics], in
reading; and particularly such periodical works of the day as he
could procure; but oftener in studying a variety of charts, and in
writing, or drawing plans.

The most interesting point here is the reference to his eyesight, for
the general belief that the wound which he later received during the
siege of Calvi was all that was wrong with his eyes is quite incorrect.
The fact was that, even by the age of thirty, he was beginning to
exhibit the sign of a pterygium growing at the inner corner of either
eye. This is a diseased condition of the conjunctiva of the eye : the
mucous membrane, which lines the inner surface of the eyeballs, being
gradually obscured by a pterygium, or 'little wing'. Eleven years later,
when the condition was far more advanced, Lord Elgin was to
comment that he 'appeared to have a film growing over both eyes',
and Thomas Trotter in 1801 remarked on 'a membranous substance
seemingly spreading fast over the pupil'.

A fact that emerges from these years is that Nelson, though happy
in the country, and often hankering after its simplicities in later life,
was never a countryman in the sense that the yeoman farmer was, let
alone the squirearchy or landed gentry. In Norfolk, for instance, that
county devoted since time immemorial to shooting and coursing, he
cut a singularly poor figure – something which he did not attempt to
disguise. It is reported that he once shot a partridge, but it would
have been difficult in those days not to have shot many partridges. . . .
'Shoot I cannot', he admitted, 'therefore I have not taken out a
license; but notwithstanding the neglect I have met with I am happy'

– the neglect, one can only assume, referred here to his country neighbours who clearly found this naval officer a poor shot and a rather
dangerous one to have around. This, at any rate, can be judged from
the fact that it was his habit to carry his gun fully cocked and to open
fire the instant a bird rose – without even troubling to bring his gun
to his shoulder. Such guests are rarely, if ever, welcome on shooting
parties.

He knew of course the famous Coke family of Holkham Hall, and
once a year in the company of his wife visited Lord Walpole in his
residence at Wolterton. But the fact was that Nelson could in no
respect be called 'county', to use that nuance by which the English
indicate those who really belong to the top echelons of the land. It is
very doubtful whether he had any ambitions to be accepted as such,
even if his means had permitted, but he was – and remained to the
end of his life – a true 'countryman', and he genuinely cared about
the condition of the labouring people among whom he lived. Although
he was a conservative, a true-blue Tory, with a complete distrust of
the reformers of the time (such as the celebrated Dr Joseph Priestley,
who campaigned for better rights and pay for labourers, and advised
them not to pay their taxes), yet he wished desperately for an improve-
ment in the condition of the working man – provided always that it
could come legally and from the top.

It was in this vein that he wrote to Prince William, now the Duke
of Clarence, in December 1792 :

> That the poor labourer should have been seduced by promises and
> hopes of better times, your Royal Highness will not wonder at,
> when I assure you that they are really in want of everything to
> make life comfortable. Part of their wants, perhaps, were unavoid-
> able from the dearness of every article of life; but much has arose
> from the neglect of the Country Gentlemen in not making the
> farmers raise their wages in some small proportion as the prices of
> necessaries increased. The enclosed paper will give your Royal
> Highness an idea of their situation. . . . I have been careful that
> no Country Gentleman should have it in his power to say, I had
> pointed out the wants of the poor greater than they really are.

The 'enclosed paper', over which Nelson must have taken a great
deal of trouble, shows that 'A Labourer in Norfolk with a wife and
three children, supposing that he is not to be one day kept from labour
in the whole year' might earn a grand total of twenty-three pounds
and one shilling per annum. Nelson carefully itemised all the necessary

expenses, compared them against the maximum earnings that could be expected, and added this conclusion : 'Not quite twopence a day for each person; and to drink nothing but water, for beer our poor labourers never taste, unless they are tempted, which is too often the case, to go to the Alehouse.'

His care and concern were what set him apart from the 'Country Gentlemen', and it was the combination of these same qualities that was to make him a rare commanding officer in a brutal century. A very accurate comment, which may explain something about Nelson in the context of these country years, is made in Ronald Blythe's *Akenfield*, which deals largely with the same area of England – but as late as the twentieth century : 'East Anglia is a nation which makes it different. They talk their heads off in the West Country and Wales but the only kind of East Anglians who will talk freely are the fishermen. You will always notice that when a village boy joins the navy he begins to talk easily. It is because the sea is free and people catch the freedom. The inland country people do not have this sense of freedom.' If Nelson had never gone to sea he might, like his neighbours, have seen nothing unusual in the poverty that surrounded him.

Digging, gardening, enduring the cold winters, aware by now that his fragile and nervous wife was unlikely ever to bear him any children, passed over from active service when it seemed that war was yet again imminent, Nelson's situation might have induced despair. He knew that in high places his name was disliked. Had not Lord Hood, when he had called on him, remarked that 'The King was impressed with an unfavourable opinion of me'? It was a remark that Nelson never forgot, for it was the ultimate wound that his king, whom he thought he had served so honourably in preserving the country's interests in the West Indies, had turned against him. Indeed, as late as December 1792, when (though he could little know it) his long exile was drawing to a close, he had written to the Duke of Clarence, who had asked what was his relationship with Lord Hood :

I can readily and truly answer. We have not for a long time had any communication with each other. Our familiar correspondence ceased on a difference of opinion. However, in consideration of our former intimacy, whenever I have gone to London, I have hitherto thought it right to leave my name at his Lordship's door. I certainly cannot look on Lord Hood as my friend; but I have the satisfaction of knowing, that I never gave his Lordship just cause to be my enemy.

Since the winter of 1791, Horatio and Fanny had been the sole
occupants of the Parsonage House, for the Reverend Edmund, whose
eyesight was failing as well as his general health, had leased a cottage
in the nearby village of Burnham Ulph which was more convenient
for him in the performance of his duties. Every spring Nelson went to
London to attend a *levée* for, even if out of favour, he must not be
forgotten; nor could he endure that the years should go by and that
he should never again meet and talk with his fellow sea-officers.
Unbelievably tranquil by modern standards, the life of the childless
couple at Burnham pursued a routine pattern that was perfectly
normal in rural England. Such it had been for centuries, and such it
was believed it would always be. No letters or diaries in English give
so perfect a picture of this life as the diary of James Woodforde, from
1776–1803 the Parson at Weston Longeville, yet another sleepy
village in Norfolk. But even here, after such entries in the winter of
1792 as 'Dinner today boiled Tongue and Turnips and a fine couple
of Ducks roasted', the outside world gradually begins to intrude. The
storm that was about to burst over the Continent, heralded by the
French occupation in November that year of the Austrian Nether-
lands, and the spread of revolutionary ideas, was felt even in distant
East Anglia: '. . . Much talking about Mobs rising in many parts of
the Kingdom especially in Norfolk and in Norwich, a great Number
of Clubs about the County and the City, who stile themselves
Resolution-Men alias Revolution-Men.' But on 8 December, the quiet
routine of Parson Woodforde, no doubt like that of the Nelsons at
Burnham Thorpe, was broken by the newspapers: 'Alarming Accounts
in the Papers, Riots daily expected in many parts of the Kingdom,
London &c. A fresh proclamation from the King on the present
affairs. . . . Every appearance at present of troublesome times being
at hand, and which chiefly are set on foot by the troubles in France.'

Five days later, the King, in a speech which almost everyone
thought admirable, and which bears all the hallmarks of Pitt's style,
sounded the grim note of warning. The days of peace would soon be
over, the pattern of life as it had been lived for centuries in Europe
would be shattered, and among the innumerable thousands who
would soon be employed in the armies and navies of the warring
powers was a comparatively obscure naval captain in Norfolk.
Referring to the current wave of unrest, the King said:

A spirit of tumult and disorder . . . has shown itself in acts of riot
and insurrection, which required the interposition of a military force
in support of the civil magistrate. The industry employed to excite

discontent on various pretexts, and in different parts of the kingdom, has appeared to proceed from a design to attempt the destruction of our happy constitution, and the subversion of all order and government; and this design has evidently been pursued in connection and concert with persons in foreign countries. So far neutrality in continental affairs has been maintained, but the French efforts to excite disturbances in other countries 'and to pursue views of conquest and aggrandizement' are causing me serious uneasiness.

He went on to say that he must therefore augment the naval and military forces for prevention and internal defence, 'being persuaded that these exertions are necessary in the present state of affairs, and are best calculated both to maintain internal tranquillity, and to render a firm and temperate conduct effectual for preserving the blessings of peace'.

Among the many ships which were destined to engage in the war that was soon to follow was the 64-gun *Agamemnon*. She was lying at Chatham, where Nelson had started his naval career.

CHAPTER NINE

The Agamemnon

THE enthusiasm with which the French Revolution had originally been greeted in some quarters in Britain did not last long. That an autocratic monarchy distinguished by extravagance and folly should be abolished was one thing, and it was not only men like Charles James Fox who rejoiced in what they saw as a new dawn on the Continent. But the execution of Louis XVI in January 1793, coupled with the atrocities unleashed in France, and the threat that they would spread across the Channel and infect those with republican beliefs in England, was quite sufficient to induce a general stiffening of resolve. There was a determination to prevent the export of any more of 'the French disease' (slang for the pox). The Paris Convention which 'promised assistance to all people who wish to recover their liberty' was not acceptable to Britons. However badly treated many of them were, they did not seek for a foreign helping hand. The subsequent actions of the Convention proved conclusively that 'every revolution contains in it something of evil'. Men like Nelson would have agreed with a speech made by Edmund Burke some nineteen years earlier: 'The only liberty I mean, is a liberty connected with order; that not only exists along with order and virtue, but which cannot exist at all without them.'

Nelson, who had either been hurriedly summoned to London, or had gone there of his own accord (knowing that in the immediate expansion of the fleet post-captains with fourteen years' seniority would hardly be neglected), wrote an ecstatic letter to Fanny on 7 January 1793:

Post nubila Phoebus – your son will explain the motto – after clouds comes sunshine. The Admiralty so smile on me that really I am as much surprised as when they frowned. Lord Chatham yesterday made many apologies for not having given me a Ship before this time, but that if I chose to take a 64-gun ship to begin with I should be appointed to one as soon as she was ready, and that I should as soon as in his power be removed into a 74.

By 26 January Lord Hood had informed him that he would be appointed to the *Agamemnon* at Chatham. She had been built at Buckler's Hard in Hampshire on the Beaulieu river, and Nelson joyfully proclaimed her as 'without exception one of the finest 64s in the Service . . . with the character of sailing most remarkably well'. Fanny did not receive the information with any great enthusiasm, and the news that war would break out at any moment can hardly have cheered her. She was always to show an anxious concern about her husband's safety that, while loving and natural, was inconsistent with her part as a sailor's wife. In any case, she had no intention of staying on in the Parsonage alone, and Nelson had to see her set up in lodgings in the market town of Swaffham before hastening to join the *Agamemnon*. A ship! To be aboard a ship again after all those years, when it had looked as if he would be forever landbound, wearing out a weary life in the dull routines of the Parsonage, without even the consolation of raising a family. . . . On 1 February, the French Republic declared war on England and Holland. Six days later Nelson joined the *Agamemnon*.

He had been in touch with his old friend Locker, who was now Commodore at Sheerness, and who helped him greatly in getting his crew together. Nelson had already done all that he could to find volunteers in Norfolk and Suffolk : 'I have sent out a lieutenant, and four mids, to get men at every sea port in Norfolk, and to forward them to Lynn and Yarmouth.' The ship's muster book, the record of her complement, soon bore many names from East Anglia and, one volunteer being worth any number of pressed men, Nelson could feel happy not only in his ship but the crew that went with it. It was his turn now to be able to help a Suckling, and he had his cousin, Maurice Suckling, as a lieutenant aboard, while Fanny's son Josiah, now twelve years old, was in the gun-room. Poor Fanny! She was now left entirely alone except for visits to the Reverend Edmund and other relatives in the area. As for Nelson, his letters are instinct with happiness. 15 March 1793 : 'If the wind is to the northward of west, we go down the river tomorrow, and are ordered to Spithead with all possible despatch, as we are wanted, Lord Hood writes me word, for immediate service; and hints, we are to go a cruise, and then to join his fleet at Gibraltar . . . therefore I am anxious to get to Spithead. . . . I never was in better health. . . . I hope you intend a new lease of your life.' (Mr Herbert, her uncle, had died, and had left provision for Fanny.) He was overjoyed with his ship, his officers and men, and the new phase of his relationship with Lord Hood. 'Spithead, April 29. We arrived at Spithead last night, and this morning, have got my orders to go to sea until the 4th of May, when I shall be at Portsmouth : Lord Hood will then be at Portsmouth. . . . We are all well.'

A rendezvous in the Channel was arranged by Hood for the ships which were to come under his command in the Mediterranean. A convoy from the West Indies had to be escorted safely home, and it was not until June that eleven sail-of-the-line, 'frigates &c.', were on their way south. The Spaniards, who had not yet been able to come to any real conclusion about French intentions in the world, were at this time willing to consider the other option – the British. It was for this reason that part of the fleet, which included the *Agamemnon*, was invited to pay a friendly visit to Cadiz : a circumstance which gave Nelson food for thought and room for comment on the ships and the men with whom, once Spain had become France's ally, England would in due course become embroiled. The Spaniards built good ships, that was something he readily conceded : 'They have four first-rates in commission at Cadiz, and very fine ships, but shockingly manned. . . . I am certain if our six barges crews, who are picked men, had got on board one of their first-rates, they would have taken her. The Dons may make fine ships, they cannot however make men.'

Yes, 'It isn't the ships, it's the men in them', and no one knew that better than this particular observer, who went on to be disgusted by 'a bull feast, for which the Spaniards are famous; and from their dexterity in attacking and killing of these animals, the ladies choose their husbands'. One sees the curl of the sensitive mouth, and hears the voice of disapproval from the parson's son. 'How women can even sit out, much more applaud, such sights, is astonishing. It even turned us sick, and we could hardly go through it : the dead mangled horses with their entrails torn out, and the bulls covered with blood, were too much.' It was play-acting – one senses his verdict – and the same English who were revolted by the spectacle would be able to take all and a great deal more, involving the destruction of themselves, their fellows and the enemy, than any Spaniard in a bull-ring. He had his judgement confirmed when, some weeks later, Lord Hood's ships rendezvoused with 24 Spanish sail-of-the-line who were supposed to be co-operating with them in the Mediterranean. A message was sent over by a Spanish frigate that they would not be able to join the British as they had so many ill on board that they must of necessity put into Cartagena. The captain of the frigate added: 'It was no wonder they were sickly, for they had been sixty days at sea.' Nelson found this quite derisory: 'This speech appeared to us ridiculous; for from the circumstance of having been longer than that time at sea, do we attribute our getting healthy. It has stamped in my mind the extent of their nautical abilities: long may they remain in their present state.'

On 27 June 1793 the *Agamemnon* sailed from Gibraltar as part of Lord Hood's fleet. It numbered nineteen sail-of-the-line, with Lord Hood wearing his flag in the *Victory*. They escorted a convoy of fifty merchantmen, while on their flanks and scouting ahead of them scudded a number of frigates. The Strait was alive with sails as, taking the inflowing current under their heavy sterns, the British entered the Mediterranean. It was to be the centre of Nelson's life for many years, and the scene of the great triumph that brought him fame. The *Agamemnon*, in which he now enjoyed the life as well as the responsibilities of being her Captain, was to live up to her famous name.

Nelson was happy aboard her in a way he had never been before, and would hardly be again – at least not in the same degree. She was the last ship to be his own and sole command, she sailed well, and he had confidence in both his officers and his crew. Aboard her he probably had, if not as much space, just as much comfort as in the simple Parsonage at Burnham. His cabin was about the size of a small low-ceilinged room, lit through square windows by day, with ever the sight of the sea, hushed and flat, or rising with the wind. At night the soft glow of lanterns would have been reflected from the captain's table when he entertained. Mostly, though, his life like that of all sea captains was an extremely lonely one: it was this which induced the immense stresses and strains (quite apart from those of command itself) that turned some captains into brutal tyrants and made of others drunken eccentrics. Nelson was lucky in that from a boy under his father's influence he had learned self-discipline, and had learned also, even in recent years, how to cope with loneliness, silence and monotony. Not that the life aboard a man-of-war could ever have been considered monotonous, for in daylight hours there were exercises to test the crews, and to ensure that manoeuvres were carried out as smartly as the Admiral in charge of the fleet required. And Lord Hood was known as a man who required a great deal. But, quite apart from all this, there was the ever-changing pattern of the ship herself; the relief of one watch for another, the call for 'All hands!' if the wind piped up and sail had to be shortened, daily gunnery drills, and never-ending ship maintenance. Meal times and evening breaks after supper, when the sailors would dance to flute and fiddle, rounded off the day. All this was accompanied by the rhythms of wind and sea, the patter of bare feet, the rush and roar of wind-filled canvas as the vessel tacked, the squeal of ropes through blocks and tackles, and the hushing sigh as she settled away on her new course. But the loneliness of command remained absolute.

John Masefield, who knew the sea as few poets have done, having served in windjammers round the Horn, wrote of this in his *Sea Life in Nelson's Time* (1905):

> A captain of a ship at sea is not only a commander, but a judge of the supreme court, and a kind of human parallel to Deity. . . . He has power over his subjects almost to the life. That he could not touch, without the consent of his equals, but he had the power to flog a man senseless, and authority to break some of his officers and send them forward. He had power to loose and to bind, and perhaps no single man has ever held such authority over the fortunes of his subordinates as that held by a sea captain over his company at sea during the Napoleonic wars. He lived alone, like a little god in heaven, shrouded from view by the cabin bulkheads, and guarded always by a red-coated sentry, armed with a drawn sword. If he came on deck the lieutenants at once shifted over to the lee side, out of respect to the great man. No man on board dared to address him, save on some question relating to the duty of the day. No sailor could speak to him with his hat upon his head. One uncovered to one's captain as to one's God.

All this was true enough, but Nelson – as there is plenty of evidence to show – was not one of those remote and uncaring 'gods' who only show themselves in order to hurl thunderbolts. He cared about his men, because he knew that a sick ship is an inefficient ship. He laid down stringent rules about the ventilation of the below-deck areas; about the supply of wine (when available) as being good for the health; and the issue of lime or lemon juice as a prevention against scurvy. As he cheerfully wrote to the Duke of Clarence that July, while the ships made their way northward towards the French coast: 'Our fleet continues healthy : we sail in three divisions, led by *Victory*, *Colossus*, and *Agamemnon*. . . .'

Hood's first objective was to contain, or bring to battle, the large French fleet which was lying in the French harbours of Marseilles and Toulon. The latter, being also the principal Mediterranean dockyard for the French fleet, was the immediate target for investment and it was reported that nearly thirty ships-of-the-line were ready for sea

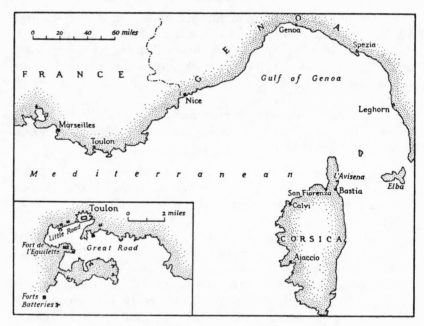

Toulon and the South of France in 1793

under the command of Rear-Admiral Trogoff. This was a slight exaggeration (they were nearer twenty) and, in any case, few of them were in a condition to come out and give battle. The condition of the French Navy at that time was chaotic; discipline had broken down; and many of the Royalist officers had been hauled away to the guillotine. Toulon itself was in a desperate state, starvation was rife, and the citizens were divided into bitter factions of revolutionaries and royalists.

The blockade continued through the long hot summer, the fleet beating up and down that tawny coast, with few diversions except a visit to Genoa – to remonstrate with the Genoese republic for supplying the French with grain. Day after day, with slatting sails when the wind failed and only the swell continued, or reefed down when the mistral blew from the north, hard and hot off the land, the ships drove back and forth. On 4 August, off Toulon, Nelson sent a letter to Fanny by a ship that was detaching from the fleet and returning to England:

Whether the French intend to come out, seems uncertain: they have a force equal to us. Our Jacks would be very happy to see

THE *AGAMEMNON*   93

them; and as our fleet is in the fullest health, I dare say we should
give a good account of them. I hardly think the war can last; for
what are we at war about? How I long to have a letter from you :
next to being with you, it is the greatest pleasure I can receive. . . .
Indeed I look back as to the happiest period of my life the being
united to such a good woman; and as I cannot here show my
affection to you, I do it doubly to Josiah, who deserves it, as well
on his own account, as on yours; for he is a real good boy. . . .
Lord Hood has sent me an offer of a 74, but I have declined it;
as the Admiralty chose to put me into a 64, there I stay. I cannot
give up my officers.

He was happy in the *Agamemnon*, which had lived up to her
reputation as a smart ship, 'for as we sail fast, we are always
employed'. Even the lure of a 74 could not induce him to leave her.

'Hunger will tame a lion' : Nelson had quoted the old saying in
another letter, and the effect of the blockade, coupled with the
internal struggles in the city, brought the desired result in late August
when the white flag was run up and the anti-revolutionary faction in
Toulon surrendered to the British. The fleet, the dockyards, 'the
strongest place in Europe' submitted without a struggle. Lord Hood's
immediate concern was to secure enough troops to hold Toulon
against the attack which must be inevitably mounted against it. The
Agamemnon's sailing qualities made her Hood's natural choice for the
ship which should proceed with despatches for Sir William Hamilton,
the British Envoy and Minister Plenipotentiary to the Court of the
Two Sicilies in Naples. Hood's request was for as many troops as could
be spared to be sent to the defence of Toulon. This was in accordance
with an agreement which had recently been negotiated by Sir William
and the French-born Englishman Sir John Acton, who was Prime
Minister to King Ferdinand IV and his Queen, Maria Carolina, sister
of Marie Antoinette. In this treaty between Britain and Naples, the
Neapolitan merchant fleet was to receive the full protection of the
British Navy in the Mediterranean, provided that there was no trading
with France; nor was any separate peace to be concluded by Naples
without British consent. It was one of the triumphs of Sir William
Hamilton's diplomatic career, and it was hardly surprising that the
arrival of the first British man-of-war after its conclusion should have
been heralded as something of an event. Nelson concluded a long
letter to Fanny 'Begun off the Island of Sardinia, September 7th,
finished at anchor off Naples, September 11th, 1793' : 'We are now
in sight of Mount Vesuvius which shows a fine light to us in Naples

Bay where we are lying to for the night and hope to anchor early tomorrow.'

Five years later, when he was to become deeply involved in the affairs of the Kingdom of the Two Sicilies, Nelson was to learn a great deal more about their ramifications, and about the central actors and actresses upon the stage – although he was still to remain conspicuously ignorant of half the operatic plots that were to surround him. As a post-captain, with little or no knowledge of the libretto, he observed in the few days that he was there only the charm of the performance. It is best, for the moment, to try to glimpse people through the eyes of the *Agamemnon*'s commander, who was quite inexperienced in the ways of the great world. Sir William at sixty-three, for instance, was gracious and distinguished, the very model of a diplomat, with a fine taste for collecting the antiquities of the ancient world. His wife Lady Hamilton had a beautiful face and a voluptuous figure. As for the King and the Queen – well, to Nelson, the eminence of their rank precluded any likelihood of judging their natures. The fact that King Ferdinand was a coarse buffoon, and that Queen Maria Carolina (despite her innumerable pregnancies) was the real power behind the throne will inevitably have escaped him. Sir John Acton, who had succeeded to his English title and estates in 1791 and had served in the navy of Tuscany, had at least an element of nautical experience in common with the visitor – but little else. Sir John was a politician to his fingertips, and a proficient one, and it was he who, in combination with Sir William, had devised the policy of substituting British influence at Naples for that of Spain. Both Sir William and Nelson took to one another, and Lady Hamilton was kindness itself to young Josiah, to whom she showed the sights of the city. Nelson, for his part, was treated with exceptional courtesy by Sir William Hamilton, who broke one of his long-standing rules about not having visitors to the city as house-guests, and gave Nelson a fine bedroom and all the hospitality of the Palazzo Sessa where he lived. King Ferdinand had the thirty-four-year-old captain of the *Agamemnon* sit at his right hand at a dinner given in his honour in the Royal Palace (the Queen was not present, being in the later stages of a pregnancy). As Nelson wrote to Fanny : 'We are called by him the Saviours of Italy, and of his dominions in particular.' Of Lady Hamilton he wrote : 'She is a young woman [she was about twenty-eight] of amiable manners, and who does honour to the station to which she is raised.' He must, of course, have been familiar with her common birth, but he could hardly have known the circumstances by which she had risen from being a blacksmith's daughter to being the wife of Sir William. Emma's later story, that her husband before first introducing her to Nelson had advised her that this 'little man and far from handsome' would become 'the greatest man that England ever produced', must be considered very suspect. Sir William honoured this as yet unknown captain partly perhaps because he liked his open manner, but principally because it was politic to do so at this historic moment. The arrival of the *Agamemnon*, proof of British naval power in the Mediterranean, set the seal upon the treaty just concluded between Naples and Britain. The practical ratification of this was the assembly of 6,000 troops to be transported to Toulon in accordance with Lord Hood's wishes.

Nelson was on the point of returning the King's courtesy by having him, the Hamiltons, and other notables aboard his ship for a formal visit and entertainment. But, before the King could arrive, and while all the others awaited the royal barge, the signal was received that a French warship escorting a convoy had been sighted off Sardinia. Although there were several Neapolitan men-of-war at anchor in the Bay, Nelson observed that they were showing no inclination to up-anchor and go in chase. 'I had nothing left for the honour of our country but to sail, which I did in two hours afterwards.' The distinguished guests were put ashore and the *Agamemnon*, as representative of the protecting arm of Britain, showed how quickly a disciplined and well-manned fighting vessel could discard the trivialities, as well as courtesies, of the shore – and get to sea. The fact that by the time Nelson caught up with his quarry she was safely at anchor in neutral Leghorn did not detract from the impression made by his swift action. It showed an efficiency that must have inspired confidence in the heart of Sir William. Nelson had been only four days in Naples. Five years were to pass before he and the Hamiltons met again.

CHAPTER TEN

Action

THE *Agamemnon* rejoined the fleet at Toulon on 5 October, arriving at almost the same time as 4,000 troops from Naples. Lord Hood was delighted with the promptness of the response to his request for aid, and undoubtedly attributed it in some degree to Nelson's efficiency as a courier and an advocate. As a reward for his services, and with the knowledge that the *Agamemnon* (though long overdue for a refit) was, despite some sickness among the ship's company, still the smartest sailer among those under his command, he despatched Nelson under sealed orders to join a squadron that was operating under Commodore Linzee off Sardinia. It was already clear to Hood that, despite the arrival of the Neapolitan troops, the investment of Toulon by the Revolutionary forces, which grew daily in intensity, was likely to succeed in the long run. He was anxious, in the event of this happening, to have a further base for the British fleet to fall back upon, and he calculated that he had found this in Corsica. Being independent from the mainland of France, it would be easier to hold once captured, and the people were more likely to be of a conservative, or at any rate anti-revolutionary, nature. Curiously enough, even while this plan was being concerted, a young artillery officer of Corsican birth, 'Citizen Bonaparte, a trained captain', had just been appointed to assist with the artillery in the siege of Toulon, the previous French commander having been wounded. 'Buona Parte' (for his name was sometimes still spelled in the Italian fashion) was described by his advocates, who finally secured him overall command of the artillery and, in effect, of the whole conduct of the siege, as 'the artillery officer competent to plan these operations'.

Nelson meanwhile had his first real brush with the French on his way southward to join Commodore Linzee. The *Agamemnon* was short-handed, having been forced to land a number of men at Toulon, and with a complement of only 345 could not man all her guns. The

96

account given by twelve-year-old William Hoste, a midshipman from Norfolk and yet another parson's son, conveys with a fresh eye this small engagement, so typical of many others that were to take place all over the world during the following years :

On the 22nd of October, when running down the island of Sardinia, about two o'clock in the morning, being off Monte Santo, twenty leagues to the northward of Cagliari, we saw five sail of ships standing to the N.W. : on observing us, they tacked and stood to the eastward. Captain Nelson, suspecting them to be a French convoy, immediately stood after them. About three o'clock we were very near up with the hindermost; and at four got within gunshot. We hailed her in French, but receiving no answer, fired a gun for her to bring-to, and shorten sail; when we observed her making signals with sky-rockets to her consorts, who were at some distance to windward. After we had repeatedly hailed her to no purpose, we fired one of our eighteen pounders at her, to oblige them to shorten sail.

At the same time, the lower gun-ports were opened and the French-man, a frigate, realised that she had come up against a ship-of-the-line and crammed on sail to make away. They came up with her again at dawn and a lively engagement began, the frigate using her greater speed and manoeuvrability to avoid the *Agamemnon*'s full broadside, while managing to pour plenty of shot into her larger opponent. William Hoste gave the Frenchman full credit :

She bravely engaged us in this manner for three hours, both ships sailing at the rate of six knots an hour. . . . The other frigates were coming after us with a fresh breeze; consequently we expected to have warm work, and were therefore anxious to dispatch this gentleman before they arrived : but, about eight o'clock, by an alteration of the wind, our antagonist got out of the reach of our guns. Our last broadside did infinite damage; nor was what we had received inconsiderable, as our rigging was shot away, and our main top-mast broken, which prevented us from going after the frigate.

The ships which the *Agamemnon* had come up against were four large frigates, a corvette and a brig. All in all, against the *Agamemnon*'s 64 guns and 345 men they composed a force of 170 guns and some 1600 men. Nelson's own comment is explicit : 'Had they been English a 64 never could have got from them.' Nevertheless the crack frigate *Melpomène*, against which he had been in action, had shown admirable spirit. Although she was so badly damaged that she must have sunk or surrendered if her companions had not come up to help, she had shown that, even in the disorganised state of revolutionary France, the French Navy was not one to be despised. The *Agamemnon* had only one man killed and a few wounded, but her rigging was so cut to pieces, quite apart from the loss of her main topmast, that she was in no condition to continue the fight – even if the French had so wished – without a breathing space. As it happened the other ships were too concerned in rescuing the *Melpomène*, which had 24 dead, many wounded, and was almost completely disabled, to continue the engagement any further. Nelson, however, was expecting that they would do so, and called his officers together to ask them their opinion as to whether the *Agamemnon* was 'fit to go into action with such a superior force against us, without some small refit and refreshment for our people?' His action in itself shows that trust in his subordinates which was so rare in its day, and which he was to continue to show to all who came under his command, even when he was an admiral. On receiving their opinion that the ship must certainly have a rest, his orders were : 'Veer the ship, and lay her head to the westward; let some of the best men be employed refitting the rigging, and the carpenters getting crows and capstan bars to prevent our wounded spars from coming down, and get the wine up for the people, with some bread; for it may be half an hour good before we are again in action.'

On arrival at Cagliari to join Commodore Linzee and to present him with Hood's sealed orders the crew of the *Agamemnon* were busy 'all night fishing our masts and yards and stopping shot holes, mending sails and splicing rigging'. Although they had just been in action there was no time for rest, for the orders revealed that the squadron was to sail immediately to Tunis, to expostulate with the Bey on his pro-French policy. (The five ships with which Nelson had been in action had, in fact, just left Tunis.) William Hoste ended his letter home with the account of this action with the words: 'Captain Nelson is acknowledged one of the first characters in the Service, and is universally beloved by his men and officers.' The letter would only be seen by his father. It was not designed for posterity, and there was no censorship in those days.

The Bey of Tunis like the Dey of Algiers occupied a position first held by those famous Turkish sailors-of-fortune, the Barbarossa brothers, who early in the sixteenth century had established all along the North African coast a series of kingdoms and principalities dedicated to harassing the trade of Europe. These rulers of the North

African coast lived by plunder and pillage, and by blackmail – extorting, from those powers who were willing to pay, vast sums of money to permit their ships to pass unmolested through the Mediterranean. At the moment the Bey was favouring the cause of France, as was proved by a large French convoy escorted by a frigate and a ship-of-the-line lying in the Bay of Tunis. Linzee's orders were to try and convince the Bey that he should not support a revolutionary regime and be on terms of friendship with people who had murdered their King and Queen. To this latter, the Bey smoothly replied that it was of course quite wrong for people to have done such a thing, but he believed that in the history of the country which his visitors represented it was reported that the English themselves had once beheaded their sovereign. Nelson, who in company with the other captains had accompanied Commodore Linzee at the interview, was thoroughly dissatisfied with the outcome. 'The English seldom get much by negotiation except the being laughed at, which we have been; and I don't like it. Had we taken, which in my opinion we ought to have done, the men-of-war and convoy, worth at least £300,000, how much better we could have negotiated : – given the Bey £50,000, he would have been glad to have put up with the insult offered to his dignity.' Linzee, however, had no instructions from Lord Hood to do anything other than negotiate. He did not have Nelson's impetuous spirit which, had it been given rein, would very likely have achieved success. It is fair to say, though, that it might have left a hostile Tunis to the south, while all British ships available were engaged in the north. Nelson, in any case, was glad to be gone : 'Thank God ! Lord Hood, whom Linzee sent to, for orders how to act after having negotiated, has ordered me from under his command. . . .' He was put in charge of a squadron of frigates off Corsica, ordered to protect British trade and that of her allies, and to prevent any vessels getting into the port of Genoa. The command was a high compliment from Hood, for there were five captains in the fleet senior to Nelson.

It was with relief that the *Agamemnon*'s captain put the sultry Bay of Tunis behind him. He knew already that action and not negotiation was his forte, and an independent command gave him the chance to use his initiative. He was disappointed to find that the French ships he sought – the same with which he had been in action off Sardinia – were tucked away in San Fiorenza and Bastia, while the badly damaged *Melpomène* was lying in Calvi. *Agamemnon* herself was in need of a refit, and, as he wrote to Captain Locker, 'we have only had our anchor down thirty-four times since we sailed from the Nore, and then only to get water and provisions'. The time at sea put in by men-

of-war at this period of history has never been equalled, even by the
Americans in the Pacific, or the British in the Atlantic, during the
Second World War. And these men had no diversions; poor food that
got poorer the longer they stayed at sea; and the only opportunity to
communicate with their homes was when a frigate went off with orders,
or a ship was detached from the fleet for Gibraltar or England. They
knew the face of the sea as no modern sailor can know it: not even
single-handed yachtsmen who, despite their self-enforced loneliness, can
still communicate by radio. On the other hand, the sailing ship had
her own life and, although for some it must have been miserable, for
the great majority it had its own dignity and simple pleasures. Under
these conditions of many months at sea, it was the captain who could
make or break a ship, for his influence was all-pervasive. As the old
navy saying has it: 'If the captain wakes up with a headache he takes
it out on the First Lieutenant. And so it goes on right down the ship,
until the youngest ordinary seaman kicks the ship's cat over the stern.'

Meanwhile at Toulon it had become clear that everything hinged
on the Fort of L'Eguilette which dominated the harbour. Bonaparte
on taking command of the artillery had said, pointing to it: 'Toulon
is there!' His judgement was soon to be proved right. While Nelson
was at sea, protecting merchantmen and searching in vain for the
French frigates, the French army investing Toulon, skilfully aided by
the relentless deployment of his artillery by Major Bonaparte, was on
the verge of making the harbour untenable. The *Agamemnon* had
put into Leghorn and was busily engaged in provisioning ship when
the news reached Nelson that Toulon had fallen. Shortly afterwards
the ships full of refugees, of wounded, and of exhausted soldiers began
to arrive in the port. Nelson outlined to various correspondents those
only too familiar, dismal and confusing scenes that accompany
evacuations: 'One family of a wife and five children are just arrived,
the husband shot himself . . . the recital of their miseries is too afflict-
ing to dwell upon. In this scene of horror Lord Hood was obliged to
order the French fleet of twenty sail-of-the-line, and as many other
ships of war, together with the arsenal and powder magazines, to be
set on fire: report says that one half the miserable place is in ashes.'
The forces of the Revolution that swept Toulon did not spare their
fellow countrymen, for no war is more horrible than a civil war.
Nelson was never to forget the stories that he heard in Leghorn and
later from brother officers who had been present at the fall of Toulon.
Whereas Napoleon in subsequent years was to regale listeners with his
feelings of triumph as city, harbour and ships went up in flames and
the red tide ran through the streets, Nelson was only to recall the

misery of it all, and to pin the blame where it lay – on revolutionary France. 'In short, all is horror. I cannot write all : my mind is deeply impressed with grief. Each teller makes the scene more horrible.'

Corsica, as Lord Hood had foreseen, now became even more important. The possibility of gaining the island from the French was reinforced by the fact that General Paoli, a Corsican patriot who was a friend of James Boswell, had ambitions to secede from France and unite the island with the British crown. Hood was very sensible of this, and far more perspicacious than fire-eating Captain Nelson (who had already quite wrongly supposed that the 'sea war is over in these seas'). But it was this able subordinate whom Hood now ordered to conduct a series of commando-like raids upon the island. This was something which, as history has proved over and over again, can be achieved by superiority of sea-power. In the war between the Elephant and the Whale, which was to follow over the next eleven years, the advantages enjoyed by each side are immediately obvious : the land-power having its great mass for central organisation and dominance, while the sea-power is, within limits, free to strike at its opponent from whatever quarter it chooses. The disadvantages to those who espoused a sea-power as ally had already been felt by the unfortunate citizens of Toulon (as they were to be felt by the French during the Second World War when they were abandoned to the Germans while the British withdrew their forces from Dunkirk). It was something which, only too naturally, gave the Continental nations pause for thought whenever it came to deciding on the respective merits of alliance with Britain or with France.

While Lord Hood moved the main body of his fleet to the Bay of Hyères, a few miles east of Toulon, Nelson was able to initiate the first of a number of raids upon Corsica intended to turn the island into the main British base in the Mediterranean. The weather off the northern coast of Corsica can be unpredictable or dangerous, even in the more settled times of the year, but in January Nelson and the *Agamemnon* encountered everything that the uneasy stretch of sea can throw at the sailor. His letters to Fanny, to whom he remained as always a good and regular correspondent, tell something of those days : 'I was unfortunately drove from my station with the whole squadron on the 28th by the hardest gale of wind almost ever remembered here. The *Agamemnon* did well but lost every sail in her. Lord Hood had joined me off Corsica the day before and would have landed the troops but the gale has dispersed them over the face of the waters. The *Victory* was very near lost. . . .' However, in the same letter, which is dated 30 January 1794, at Leghorn, he goes on to

report the first of those small successes which he was over-confident
would give the British control of Corsica in 'a week or two'.

A thing happened a few days past which gave me great satisfaction.
The 21st January the French had their store house of flour near a
water mill close to St Fiorenza. I seized a happy moment, landed
60 soldiers and seamen. In spite of opposition at landing the sailors
threw all the flour into the sea, burned the mill the only one they
have, and returned on board without the loss of a man. The French
sent 1,000 men at least against them and gunboats etc, but as the
French shot went over them they were just within reach of my
guns. It has pleased the Lord [Hood], if this dreadful gale has not
blown it out of his memory.

Nelson continued with more lightning raids on coastal shipping and
defences, designed to draw attention away from San Fiorenza where
Hood planned to land a force of 4,000 men. Twelve vessels loaded
with wine were burnt, another four being taken as prizes. At
L'Avisena, just north of Bastia, a fort was captured and its garrison
forced to withdraw. Elsewhere a small castle was seized, Nelson leading the landing party and striking the hated French colours with his
own hand. A courier boat was boarded and captured 'in high style',
and everywhere Nelson's 'Agamemnons' inflicted a series of pinpricks
which kept the defenders on their toes and convinced them that Bastia
must be the first British objective. This was as Hood wanted for,
although Bastia's harbour must ultimately prove essential to his plans,
he had his eye on San Fiorenza as the first base for the British and
their fleet. In mid-February 1794, San Fiorenza fell to a British
assault, the only real opposition being provided by the Tower of
Martella which yielded after two days' bombardment at close quarters.
(Anglicised into 'Martello', this tower was later to give its name to the
series of small round forts which were built along Britain's coasts as
a defence against Napoleon's projected invasion.)
    Nelson was now detached by Lord Hood to blockade Bastia. This
was an important service, for upon its success largely depended
whether the Army could take this strongly fortified town which Nelson
described as 'walled in with a Battery to the north and south of it, a
Citadel in the middle, defended by thirty pieces of cannon and eight
mortars, four stone redoubts on the nearest hills and three other posts
above them'. The blockade was so successful that not a boat got
through, and Nelson was confident that a determined assault would
soon have the city and port in their grasp. His opinion was reinforced

by an engagement on 23 February, during which *Agamemnon* and
two frigates bombarded the city for nearly two hours. Two days later
he noted in his journal : 'Lord Hood with five sail is to leeward. Two
Corsican boats came off to beg some ammunition, and to tell me that
our troops were on the hills.' So indeed they were, but, much to
Hood's irritation and Nelson's fury, General Dundas in command of
the army based on San Fiorenza was of the opinion that Bastia could
not be taken without strong reinforcements, which he sent for from
Gibraltar. Nelson, recalling no doubt his experiences all those years
ago with the military on the abortive San Juan expedition in
Nicaragua, deplored the refusal of soldiers to move without long
preparation and intensive planning. 'What would the immortal Wolfe
have done?' he cried. 'A thousand men would to a certainty take
Bastia. With 500 and the *Agamemnon* I would attempt it. . . .' It was
not to be, and when Dundas was succeeded by Brigadier-General
D'Aubant the opinion of the new commander remained unchanged.
Nelson, who had heard from sources ashore that his bombardment
had so shaken morale that St Michel, the French Commissioner, had
been obliged to hide himself from the townsfolk's fury, and had only
been able to restrain them from sending out a boat to treat for peace
by threatening to blow up the Citadel, was convinced that the army
was not only dilatory but in the wrong. By the middle of March, his
ship having been at sea for three months, he described in a letter to
Hood how not a man aboard slept dry (through lack of deck-caulking
and harbour maintenance) and that they were without fuel for the
galley, 'wine, beef, pork, flour, and almost without water. The ship
is so light she cannot hold her side to the wind.' He added that, if
they could be spared for a few days, he could get to Porto Ferraio and
Leghorn, water and provision within twenty-four hours, and be back
on station. He was absolutely determined to be in at the assault of
Bastia. He knew the mettle of his crew to be 'almost invincible. They
really mind shot no more than peas.'

The spring came slowly to Corsica, the weather remained variable
and often rough, with the ships compelled to leave their station and
stand offshore for safety. But still, day in and day out, they kept up
their relentless blockade – a foreshadowing of that blockade with
which England would in due course surround the whole continent
of Europe. Lord Hood, meanwhile, who disagreed with D'Aubant
just as much as he had with Dundas, was as confident as Nelson that
Bastia could be taken without the elaborate planning and reinforcements that the Army called for. In the end, he managed to procure a
force of a little over a thousand troops and marines, while Nelson sent

off to Naples for artillery and ammunition, which the Army had also refused to provide. On the night of 3 April, this small force under the command of Lieutenant-Colonel Villettes and Captain Horatio Nelson landed unopposed, three miles to the north of Bastia. The military at San Fiorenza, who had been openly contemptuous of Nelson's optimistic views about the feasibility of taking Bastia without waiting for reinforcements, had sarcastically nicknamed him 'The Brigadier'. Who was this thirty-five-year-old naval captain, they argued, to be disputing with professionals like themselves, let alone with their general? Nelson was soon to prove that he was as deserving of his military title as his naval one.

CHAPTER ELEVEN

Corsica Campaign

So FAST did the small force move that, by noon on the day after landing, they were encamped 2,500 yards from the citadel. Nelson's 'Agamemnons' had disembarked and brought up to their lines eight of the ship's 24-pounders, which were later augmented by a number of large mortars supplied by Sir William Hamilton from Naples. It took a further six days for the seamen to haul the guns up to the heights commanding the town. The means by which this was done astonished not only the Corsican patriots who had joined the British force, but even Sir Gilbert Elliot, future Viceroy of the island, who was an admiring witness of the versatility of Jack Tar : 'They fastened great straps round the rocks, and then fastened to the straps the largest and most powerful purchases, or pullies, and tackle, that are used aboard a man-of-war. The cannon were placed on a sledge at one end of the tackle, the men walked down hill with the other end of the tackle.'

In somewhat the same way that they sent topmasts and spars aloft, the seamen hoisted the guns that were to dominate Bastia. Eight days after the landing, the batteries opened fire. Lord Hood was lying off in the *Victory* and, from the heights above, Nelson and his sailors could see *Agamemnon* at anchor in the bay. The French Commissioner was still confident of the strength of his position and, when Hood sent off a flag of truce before engagement commenced, he made the reply : 'I have hot shot for your ships, and bayonets for your men.' Nelson, in a letter to Fanny dated 22 April, wrote : 'My ship lays on the north side the town with some frigates and Lord Hood on the south side. It is very hard service for my poor seamen, dragging guns up such heights as are scarcely credible. The town and citadel is most amazingly battered and many of their batteries ruined.' Although he did not mention it at the time, he himself had been wounded just over a week earlier, receiving 'a sharp cut in the back'.

Bastia held out longer than he had anticipated and it was natural that the issue should prove very worrying, for it was largely on his advice – against that of the Army – that the siege had been initiated. He was also well aware that, while the forces at San Fiorenza were still refusing to co-operate until they had received reinforcements, they would, as soon as Bastia was prepared to surrender, be only too eager to march in and take the glory for themselves. Two further batteries were installed, only 1,000 yards from the citadel, and day after day the cannonading continued, losses on both sides mounting. Five 'Agamemnons' were killed – 'they are not the men to keep out of the way'. On 1 May, he wrote to Fanny that he was confident Bastia would fall, adding 'all my joys of victory are two fold to me knowing how you must partake of them, only recollect a brave man dies but once, a coward all his life long. We cannot escape death, and should it happen to me in this place, recollect it is the will of Him in whose hands are the issues of life and death.' There can be no doubt that these words were not written just to reassure his wife, or to console her if he fell : they represent the essential core of his nature and his belief.

Extracts from the journal that Nelson kept at this time show quite clearly that the siege of Bastia was not so simple an affair as has sometimes been made out : 'Our batteries kept up an incessant fire. . . . On the 16th they got a thirteen-inch mortar which kept up a constant fire through the night . . . three boats attempted to get into the town with powder and provisions; two were taken but one got in . . . the Enemy fired more than usual both night and day. We had also often five shells in the air all at once, going to Bastia.' But, in the end, on 19 May, the garrison sent out a flag of truce and terms were arranged for the surrender of the town. As Nelson had expected, the army from San Fiorenza now arrived on the heights above : their presence, at long last, gave the defenders the excuse of honourably surrendering to a large force. It would have been somewhat ignominious to have capitulated to what was no more than a handful of sailors and soldiers. In effect, though, this was what had really happened. It reinforced Nelson's long-held opinion that 'one Englishman was equal to three Frenchmen; had this been an English town, I am sure it would not have been taken by them. They have allowed us to batter it without once making an effort to drive us away. I may truly say that this has been a Naval Expedition; our boats prevented anything from getting in by sea and our sailors hauling up great guns, and then fighting them on shore.' Fanny's son, Josiah, whom Nelson had kept out of the way most of the time aboard the *Agamemnon*, being determined – despite Josiah's eagerness to be in the field – that if she were to lose her husband she should not lose a son as well, now had the honour of being put at the head of the British Grenadiers who were taking over the citadel and strong-posts of Bastia. The British forces engaged had lost 19 dead and 37 wounded, the enemy over 200 dead and 540 wounded, 'most of whom are dead'. 4,500 men in a strongly fortified place had laid down their arms to a mixed force of 1,200 troops and seamen.

With San Fiorenza and Bastia in his hands, Lord Hood now only needed Calvi on the west side of the island to give him control of Corsica. He would then have a pistol pointed at the heart of southern France, and adequate bases for his ships from which to keep watch and ward over Toulon. Calvi, small though it was – and remains – was nevertheless a place strong by nature and heavily fortified. It presented more challenge to the attackers than Bastia had done, for the terrain behind the port and town was arid, rocky and barren. It was not until mid-June that the *Agamemnon* together with two smaller warships and a convoy of transports and storeships could be got into a position not far from Revellato Point, some three miles to the west of their objective. This time, however, there could be no doubt about the willingness of the Army to co-operate, and the subsequent attack on Calvi can truly be called a 'combined operation', Nelson being in charge of the naval forces and General the Hon. Charles Stuart of the military. Fortunately both men – despite subsequent disagreements – were matched in their eagerness and efficiency. The disembarkation, despite the difficulties of an iron-bound coast with uncharted rocks and great depths between them, went ahead swiftly. But the savage weather off western Corsica was to lead to many difficulties: on one occasion, when only part of the landing force was ashore, the ships were compelled to stand out to sea rather than be trapped on a lee shore. Those who know the difficulties of putting troops, guns, supplies and all the impedimenta of war ashore on a hostile coast from modern landing craft and transports, can have some small idea of what all this entailed when the ships themselves were dependent upon canvas and the boats upon men at the oars. A combined operation in the eighteenth century was an astounding test of men and of ingenuity.

Nelson's natural pride in the taking of Bastia received a severe blow. In Hood's despatch he was credited with no more than 'the command and direction of the seamen in landing the guns, mortars, and stores', while Captain Anthony Hunt was given credit for having 'commanded the batteries'. This was quite untrue, and Captain Serocold, a friend of Nelson, soon to be killed in the attack on Calvi, was so infuriated by the inaccuracy and injustice of the despatch as to have been prepared to publish a report on his own account to the effect that Hunt 'never was on a battery, or even rendered any service during the siege'. The fact was that Hunt, who had lost his ship through no fault of his own, was in need of the assistance that a favourable report from Hood could give him. Hood himself knew well enough the true circumstances of the case, and was prepared – as now at Calvi – to give Nelson the position of command which he had genuinely earned. Even so, it was galling, and the fact that General Stuart was to take nearly all the credit for himself on the successful conclusion of the attack on Calvi was to add further bitterness to Nelson's feelings. Yet, as before in the West Indies, where he had seen the credit for his dutifully carrying out the Navigation Act assigned to others who had, in fact, opposed him, so now he did little more than comment that 'We will fag ourselves to death before any blame shall lie at our doors.'

He was immensely happy in the achievements of his seamen: 'By computation we may be supposed to have dragged one 26-pounder with its ammunition and every requisite for making a battery upwards of 80 miles, 17 of which were up a very steep mountain.' When it is recollected that the siege of Calvi was undertaken in midsummer, the achievements of the attacking force are remarkable. The smiling face of Corsica, which the men had known on the east coast at Bastia in the spring, was now eclipsed by Mediterranean man's enemy – the summer. The wild flowers, the scent of the tangled maquis under the dews of dawn, those had been invigorating: they now yielded to the harsh realities of a land where malaria was rife and where the sun was no friend but an implacable enemy. The naval officers in their cocked hats and blue frock-coats, knee-breeches and stockings, the sailors in their miscellaneous but heavy sea-going clothes and tarpaulin hats, the military encumbered by uniforms that were suitable for northern Europe or for ceremonial parades, all suffered grievously from the heat. In one of his letters to the Duke of Clarence, whom he regularly kept posted as to his actions, Nelson described the conditions:

It is now what we call the dog-days, here it is termed the Lion-Sun; no person can endure it: we have upwards of one thousand sick out of two thousand, and others not much better than so many phantoms. We have lost many men from the season, very few from the enemy. I am here the reed among the oaks: all the prevailing disorders have attacked me, but I have not strength for them to fasten upon. I bow before the storm, while the sturdy oak is laid low.

It was not long after writing this that Nelson received the wound to his right eye which was to trouble him for the rest of his days.

The military, following their accustomed habit which Nelson had long ago deplored of advancing their trenches and batteries by pedantic zigzags, were now commanding the town, which meant of course that their advanced batteries were well within range of the enemy fire. Nelson had been knocked down, but uninjured, only the day before by a shot landing close by him, but this time he was not so lucky. On 10 July at 7 a.m., being up as usual for the day's early bombardment, he was standing in the parapet between two embrasures when a shot struck it and he was hit by sand, stones and splinters kicked up from the merlon. Blood poured from a deep cut made over his right eyebrow while the eye itself was damaged. (Much later, when the Royal College of Surgeons examined him for compensation, it was agreed that the wound was 'fully equal to the loss of the eye'.) The surgeons who now attended him held out hopes that he might get his sight back in some degree. His resilience and courage were extraordinary, for the very same evening with his head throbbing and a field-dressing over his eye he wrote to Lord Hood : 'I got a little hurt this morning: not much, as you may judge from my writing.' To Hood's subsequent inquiry as to whether he needed relieving at his post he replied that his eye was better and that he was quite capable of superintending the work. Knowing how much Fanny constantly worried about his safety, he did not tell her the news until over a month later when he was back aboard the *Agamemnon* off Leghorn :

You may hear, therefore as it is all past I may tell you that on the 10th of July last a shot having struck our battery the splinters and stones from it struck me most severely in the face and breast. Although the blow was so severe as to occasion a great flow of blood from my head, yet I most fortunately escaped by only having my right eye nearly deprived of its sight. It was cut down, but is as far recovered as to be able to distinguish light from darkness, but as to all the purpose of use it is gone. However, the blemish is nothing, not to be perceived unless told. The pupil is nearly the size of the blue part, I don't know the name.

The pathological result of the injury was never fully established, but modern eye specialists have conjectured that he received either a

haemorrhagic retinal lesion (a ruptured choroid or eyeball) or retinal
detachment; in either case followed by gradual optic atrophy. Hence-
forth the eye was as good as useless to him, although many who met
him afterwards were unable to distinguish any difference between his
good eye and his bad. He did not, as is sometimes supposed, wear an
eye-patch over the right eye because it was disfigured, but he had a
green shade made to protect his *left* eye from the glare of the Mediterranean sun and sea. In later years he always wore a green shade
covering both eyes under the brim of his cocked hat. This is shown in
an anonymous contemporary portrait, and can also be verified at
Westminster Abbey where there is a cocked hat made by James Lock
of St James's Street, London, with this shade attached. Later popular
engravings often show him with an eye-patch, indifferently over the
left or over the right eye. (Contrary to popular belief, his statue in
Trafalgar Square is accurate – showing him with no eye-patch.)

While the British ashore were suffering from fever and the climate
generally, the besieged were suffering the inevitable shortages of both
food and ammunition which must always befall those who have need
of sea-borne supplies, but are blockaded by an enemy having control
of the sea. On 28 July, the French Governor sent word that he would
surrender within twenty-five days if he had had no succour or
reinforcements. Four vessels did in fact manage to slip through Hood's
blockade but, although they had some grain aboard, they had no
ammunition, and the garrison's magazines were almost empty. Calvi
had never been designed to repel a long siege but only to hold out
for a limited time against a sea-borne attack. This was where Stuart
and Nelson, with their troops and batteries ringing round the city
from the rear, made its fall almost inevitable. On 10 August the town
surrendered. It was only just in time from the point of view of the
British, for General Stuart himself was sick, Nelson half blind, and the
men were dropping from malaria like flies. It is doubtful if the siege
could have been prosecuted for a further fortnight.

Although Nelson and Stuart had got on well enough during the
campaign, it was to Nelson's great chagrin that he learned later from
Stuart's despatch that the General had taken all the credit for himself.
'One hundred and ten days', he wrote, 'I have been actually engaged,
at sea and on shore, against the enemy; three actions against ships,
two against Bastia in my ship, four boat actions, and two villages
taken, and twelve sail of vessels burnt. I do not know that any one
has done more. I have had the comfort to be always applauded by my
Commander-in-Chief, but never to be rewarded. . . .' A further piece
of news that filled him with great sadness was to hear of the death

of Lieutenant James Moutray of the *Victory*, the only son of the lady whom he had admired so much all those years ago in Antigua. Mrs Moutray whom he had adored more than any other woman he had ever met . . . He had the ship's carpenter cut a stone to the young man's memory and had it placed in the church at San Fiorenza.

Nelson knew that Lord Hood, whose health had been failing, was almost certain to return home and he had every hope of accompanying him – 'I think if he can with propriety take me I shall be one of the ships.' He was soon to learn, however, that although the *Agamemnon* was well overdue for a major refit there was no chance of depleting the fleet any further at the moment : particularly since the French had already got at least thirteen ships-of-the-line ready for sea at Toulon. A visit to Genoa impressed him with the magnificence of that city, 'superior in many respects to Naples', and it was from here that he wrote to Fanny that Lord Hood was definitely leaving but, as for himself, 'I stand no chance of seeing you at present.' He hankered after Burnham, and then added a small fatherly postscript : 'Josiah is very well 5 feet high he says he is 5 feet 1 inch.'

Hood was succeeded by a man whom everyone liked but no one admired, the old and easy-going Admiral Hotham. He was no fit successor to the fierce and ever-zealous Hood, particularly at that moment in Mediterranean affairs. Meanwhile the endless blockade of Toulon carried on, the winter gales hurling off the land as the storm-battered ships furled their ragged canvas before them, or set all their patched sails once again when the weather grew temporarily fair. The sea and the wind, the monotony of the blockade, ate into the men as well as the ships. Well was it said of old-time sailors that every finger was a marlinespike and every hair a bunch of spun-yarn. They were, as Conrad was to write of a later generation, '. . . a good crowd. As good a crowd as ever fisted with wild cries the beating canvas of a heavy foresail; or tossing aloft, invisible in the night, gave back yell for yell to a westerly gale.' 'The gale moderates', Nelson wrote to William Suckling from Leghorn in October, 'and I am just going to get under weigh again.' He had lost fifty of his best men since leaving Calvi, had been into the Bay of Hyères, looked carefully into Toulon and seen how many ships were being assembled to sweep the British from the sea – 'Twenty-two sail of ships in the inner Harbour.' He had reported to Sir Gilbert Elliot, now Viceroy of Corsica, on the extent of the French preparations, and had made some suggestions as to the defence of Ajaccio (Napoleon's birthplace) in the event of an enemy attack. Yet, despite all that had happened to him in recent months, he could still say : 'I don't know that I ever had such good health as since I have been in Italy, not one day's illness.' By the end of November the *Agamemnon* was at last able to get into Leghorn for long enough to undergo a proper refit and to let the sailors ashore for the first time in many weeks, to enjoy those pleasures of the land – women and drink.

Nelson, except for a short period at Palermo when he was under the spell of Emma Hamilton, excessive adulation, and a luxurious court life, seems always to have been a very temperate man. He liked a glass or two of wine, as did most others, but he was never by nature a drinker. On the other hand, as his early history has shown, he always had an eye for a pretty girl, and it was hardly surprising that after the hardships and exigencies of the recent campaign he should fail to live a life of monastic seclusion while aboard *Agamemnon* secure in port. Most officers had their affairs ashore, many kept a mistress, and Nelson was no exception. James Harrison, whose biography has so often been condemned on the score of partiality or inaccuracy, nevertheless often comes out with anecdotes about Nelson which have all the ring of veracity – more particularly since much of his information came from Lady Hamilton. And no one was more likely to have known about Nelson's love-life than she. At a later date, after they had become lovers, on hearing that he was bound for Leghorn she was strictly to forbid him to go ashore there; thus clearly indicating she knew he had had a previous affair with some woman in that port. Harrison hints at his nature in as clear a way as the oblique references of the time would permit about a national hero :

> . . . though by no means ever an unprincipled seducer of the wives and daughters of his friends, he was always well known to maintain rather more partiality for the fair sex than is quite consistent with the highest degree of Christian purity. Such improper indulgences, with some slight addition to that other vicious habit of British seamen, the occasional use of a few thoughtlessly profane expletives, form the only dark specks ever yet discovered in the bright blaze of his moral character.

So Nelson, like most sailors, was given to swearing on occasions! He was also, parson's son or not, sometimes guilty of adultery – even before Lady Hamilton came into his life. Captain Thomas Fremantle, one of 'the band of brothers', who was with him in Leghorn commanding the frigate *Inconstant*, has a few brief references to this phase in Nelson's life.

December 1794. Wed. 3. Dined at Nelson's and his Dolly. Called on old Udney [the British Consul], went to the opera with him. He introduced me to a very handsome Greek woman.

August 1795. A convoy arrived from Genoa. Dined with Nelson. Dolly aboard who has a sort of abscess in her side, he makes himself ridiculous with that woman.

August. Sat. 28. Dined with Nelson and his Dolly.

September. Sun. 27. Dined with Nelson and Dolly. Very bad dinner indeed.

Leghorn at that time was well known as a very free and easy city for both officers and men, something which was to result in many of them landing up in the British hospital that had recently been opened in Ajaccio. It is worth remarking on this score that the condom was well enough known in the eighteenth century, and in 1783 a Mary Perkins of Half Moon Street in London advertised that she 'had lately had several large orders [for condoms] from France, Spain, Italy, and other foreign places'. Venereal disease was rife in the eighteenth century, and sailors and soldiers with the irregularity of their sex-lives were inevitably more prone to it than most. At one time in his life Nelson suffered from a 'fleshy excrescence' between his upper lip and jawbone 'which when he shaved, gave him uncommon pain'. The doctors at Haslar Hospital, Portsmouth, diagnosed a venereal infection and proposed to give him mercurial treatment, to which he agreed. A distinguished French dentist who was present disagreed with their diagnosis and removed the growth with a scalpel, after which it would seem that he had no further trouble. But the fact that Nelson accepted the Haslar diagnosis is significant in itself.

The *Agamemnon* had completed her refit by mid-January and was back at sea, once more guarding the northern approaches to Corsica. The weather was as bad as any he had ever known. 'We have had three gales of wind in thirteen days. Neither sails, ships or men can stand it.' But he was as happy with his ship as ever, writing to Fanny : 'We have had nothing but gales of wind and a heavy sea, so much so that one of the ships lost all her masts last night. In *Agamemnon* we mind nothing. She is the finest ship I ever sailed in and was she a 74 nothing should induce me to leave her whilst the war lasted.' The war, which he had at times optimistically believed would be over swiftly, was only just beginning. The new year, and those that were to follow it, was to bring him into a steadily increasing sphere of action where the thunder of the guns would far outweigh the hazards of winter off Corsica.

CHAPTER TWELVE

Riviera

In March 1795 Rear-Admiral Pierre Martin was ordered to take his fleet out of Toulon and clear the way for an invasion of Corsica and the re-establishment of French control in that island. Martin had only been made Lieutenant in 1792 and, such was the shortage of naval officers in revolutionary France, he had been promoted to Captain within a year, and then to Rear-Admiral. He had, as he knew well, no real experience of handling a fleet at sea; many of his ships were not fit for battle; while out of his ships' companies of 12,000 men something like 7,500 had never been to sea before. This was hardly the material with which to drive the British from the Mediterranean. Even if many of the latter's ships were in need of refitting, they were well-tried and proven from their long experience off Corsica and the coast of France. Their officers and men had been constantly at sea, were finely disciplined, and completely attuned to their environment.

On 8 March, hearing that the French had left Toulon on a course for Corsica, Hotham led out fourteen British ships-of-the-line together with one Neapolitan to intercept the seventeen French vessels. The wind was light and variable and, although British frigates were quite soon in touch with the enemy, the prospect of an immediate fleet action seemed remote. If the French had their problems with untrained and inexperienced officers and men, the British vessels were, in Nelson's view, about 'half-manned'. However, he wrote cheerfully to Fanny on 10 March: 'I shall commence a letter at this moment to assure you, although I flatter myself that no assurance is necessary, of my constant love and affection. We are just in sight of the French fleet and a signal out for a general chase.' Next day he added to the letter: 'Did not get sight of the French fleet this morning. I suppose they stood to the westward all night. The Admiral has just got information that the French . . . on the 8th off Cape Corse took the *Berwick* of 74 guns.' The *Berwick* had been dismasted and was struggling along under jury rig when the French came up with her. On 12 March Nelson concluded this letter on an exuberant note : 'The French are now within 4 miles of *Agamemnon* and *Princess Royal.* Our fleet 10 miles from us, we standing towards our fleet, the enemy attempting to cut us off.' For years Nelson had hoped and waited for a fleet action, and now it seemed as if he was about to see one. But the erratic winds and the uninspired conduct of Admiral Hotham, who failed to follow home a dispirited enemy, were to frustrate his hopes. From the very beginning the inadequacies of the French were manifest. The *Mercure* lost her main topmast in a squall and had to stand away for Golfe Juan, while the *Ça-ira* and the *Victoire* collided, the former losing her topmasts and falling off to leeward between the two fleets. Nelson in *Agamemnon*, who was out-distancing the rest of the fleet, saw his chance and took it. Although the *Ça-ira* was an 84-gun ship, 'absolutely large enough to take the *Agamemnon* in her hold', Nelson made straight for the crippled giant which was being supported by a frigate despatched to take her in tow.

The *Agamemnon* now took on the grim face of action, the marine drummer beating to quarters to the rousing tune of 'Hearts of Oak'. Everywhere men were busy at their tasks, the wooden bulkheads being unshipped between the officers' quarters and the captain's furniture and private gear being sent down below. Meanwhile extra hammocks were brought up to join those which ran all round the upper deck, some being lashed over the dead-eyes and lanyards of the standing rigging. Far aloft, the sails were being doused with water, while everywhere fire buckets were being ranged in their allotted places, and wet sand sprinkled on the deck to lessen fire-risk and give the seamen a surer footing. The guns' crews were all at their stations, flint-locks ready, slow-matches burning, the lashings cast off the guns, and the ports opened. Powder-monkeys scurried to and fro bringing up the cartridges for the first broadside, while high above them all nets were spread from main to mizzen masts to catch men falling from aloft as well as topmasts and other gear crashing on to the deck. The carpenter and his men were standing by below with their wooden plugs and tools to deal with underwater damage, while in the blood-red cockpit the surgeon, Mr Roxburgh, and the surgeon's mates waited with instruments, water, rum, tourniquets, and bandages for the first casualties. If time permitted, as it did now, the officers changed into clean linen, fresh breeches, and silk stockings, to obviate the risk of infection from dirty clothes being driven into a wound. The men, for their part, stripped to the waist; their black silk handkerchiefs which were normally worn loosely knotted round their necks were now bound

tightly around their heads over their ears. The concussion of the guns
in the confined space below decks could deafen a man for life. The
hatches leading from the gun-deck to the orlop-deck below were
guarded by marines or midshipmen with pistols, who would permit
no one to pass except the powder-boys and authorised messengers.
That formidable figure representative of discipline, the master-at-arms,
made his rounds : it would be his duty, once action commenced, to
keep a tally of losses, of guns out of action, and of the general fighting
capacity of the ship. It took a little over five minutes for a ship-of-the-
line to come down from cruising trim to a state of instant readiness.
When all was prepared the First Lieutenant made a complete tour of
the ship, to encourage the men, and to issue final orders to all officers
and senior ratings.

The French were now running as fast as they could for the security
of their shore with the British in pursuit. Captain Fremantle in the
frigate *Inconstant* was the first to come up with the crippled *Ça-ira*.
Two French ships-of-the-line, the *Jean Bart* and the *Sans Culotte*,
were dropping back to afford protection, while one of their own
frigates had passed her tow and was struggling to get the *Ça-ira*
underway. The *Inconstant*, coming under heavy fire, was forced to
retire leaving the field clear for *Agamemnon*. The wind being south-
west and squally, Nelson decided to lay his ship across the enemy's
stern. Although this meant that the *Agamemnon* was subjected to a
heavy and accurate fire from the enemy's stern guns, the way in which
he manoeuvred his ship meant that the larger Frenchman could never
bring her broadside to bear. The action, which began at about 10 a.m.
on the thirteenth, was in effect almost over by 1 p.m., by which time the
Ça-ira was 'a perfect wreck'. *Agamemnon*, veering back and forth
under her stern, poured broadside after broadside into her. As Nelson
wrote later to William Suckling : 'Could I have been supported, I
would have had the *Ça-ira* on the 13th.'

On the following morning it was seen that the *Ça-ira* had now
been taken in tow by the 74-gun *Censeur*, and a confused action
began in which two British 74s, the *Bedford* and the *Captain*, were
badly damaged. The *Ça-ira*, however, was completely dismasted and
the *Censeur* lost her mainmast. 'Our fleet', Nelson wrote to the Duke
of Clarence, 'closed with *Ça-ira* and *Censeur*, who defended themselves in the most gallant manner; the former lost 400, the later 350
men.' During the previous day's engagement the *Agamemnon* had
only 7 wounded as compared to 100 lost aboard her superior
opponent. The two crippled Frenchmen now struck their colours, at
which, to Nelson's profound disappointment, Admiral Hotham decided

that two prizes of such calibre were sufficient to call it a day, and broke off any further pursuit of the fleeing French. 'We must be contented. We have done very well,' he remarked. Nelson was convinced, as was his friend Goodall in command of the *Princess Royal*, that if the fleet had been energetically led they could have come up with the French and in a general action secured complete victory.

He later confided to Locker that he did not think Hotham was 'intended by nature for a Commander-in-Chief, which requires a man of more active turn of mind'. It must be said in Hotham's defence that he had achieved the main object of the engagement. The French fleet had been forced to retreat to Toulon, and Corsica was saved. There was one detached observer on the sidelines, however, who saw matters in exactly the same terms as Nelson. This was Sir William Hamilton, far away in the Palazzo Sessa in Naples, who commented that 'my old friend Hotham is not quite awake enough for such a command as that of the King's Fleet in the Mediterranean . . .'. Hotham's mild success in the capture of the two French ships-of-the-line was also somewhat nullified by the fact that the *Berwick* had already been captured prior to the engagement, and that the 74-gun *Illustrious* was now lost, being driven ashore by a gale between Spezia and Leghorn. Nelson, agitated beyond belief at the prospect that the French might cut off a convoy from England which was eagerly awaited at Leghorn, or that they might sally out again and descend on Corsica, could hardly contain himself.

I am absolutely at this moment in the horrors, fearing from our idling here, that the active Enemy may send out two or three Sail of the Line, and some frigates, to intercept our Convoy, which is momently expected. . . . In short, I wish to be an Admiral, and in command of the English Fleet. I should very soon either do much, or be ruined. My disposition cannot bear tame and slow measures. Sure I am, had I commanded our Fleet on the 14th, that either the whole French Fleet would have graced my triumph, or I should have been in a confounded scrape.

His general depression at the state of things in the Mediterranean was later to be further deepened by the news that Lord Hood, who had been expected back aboard *Victory* to resume his command, had fallen foul of the Board of Admiralty. Hood had argued in his fierce and imperious way that the reinforcements their Lordships intended to send out to the Mediterranean were inadequate to deal with the situation. Never a man to temper the wind of his wrath, Hood had not overstated his case, but he had stated it in a manner that was found offensive. He was ordered to strike his flag, and this magnificent old seaman ('the first officer in our Service', Nelson reckoned him) was to end his days as Governor of Greenwich Hospital – a post he discharged as honourably and efficiently as all else in his life.

Under Hotham, meanwhile, the fleet continued to be inadequately and somewhat inefficiently employed. On 6 July the *Agamemnon* and four frigates while halfway between Nice and Genoa fell in with the whole French fleet which Hotham, tucked away in San Fiorenza and clearly with very poor information at his command, ought certainly to have known was at sea. Nelson and the ships with him only managed to escape by running with a prevailing northerly back to the security of the British base. The French numbered seventeen ships-of-the-line. By the time that Hotham and his fleet could get to sea – for they had been bottled up in harbour by the same wind that had saved Nelson – the French topsails had retired over the horizon. With a shift of wind the British got to sea and, on 13 July, the *Agamemnon* and half a dozen others came up with the enemy rear, and in the engagement that followed the 74-gun *Alcide* was so badly damaged as to be forced to strike her colours. Unfortunately, before she could be taken in tow as a prize, a fire aboard reached her main magazine and she blew up and sank. A calm then fell leaving the French, who were well inshore, with just sufficient air from the *brise soleil* to make for the Gulf of Fréjus. (The *brise soleil*, a solar wind to be remarked in calm summer months when no real winds are blowing, tends to follow the sun's course throughout the day and towards sundown usually blows westerly on to the Riviera coast.) 'It was impossible for us to close with them,' Nelson wrote the Duke of Clarence, 'and the smoke from their Ships and our own made a perfect calm; whilst they, being to windward, drew in shore.' He added bitterly: 'Thus has ended our second meeting with these gentry. In the forenoon we had every prospect of taking every Ship in the Fleet; and at noon, it was almost certain we should have had the six near ships. The French Admiral, I am sure, is not a wise man, nor an Officer: he was undetermined whether to fight or run away: however, I must do him the justice to say, he took the wisest step at last.'

Despite the *Agamemnon*'s proven efficiency as a fighting ship, it was a frustrating time in his life, though somewhat compensated for by learning in July that he had been appointed a colonel of the Marines. This was an honorary command, a reward for his distinguished services ashore, carrying a remuneration but no duties, and Nelson wrote to Earl Spencer, who was now First Lord of the Admiralty, to express his thanks. At the same time he did not forget to remind his Lordship that he had as yet received no compensation for the loss of sight of his right eye at Calvi. He had the satisfaction, though, of being appointed by Hotham to an independent command of a small squadron of frigates, designed to assist the Austrian General de Vins at Vado Bay near Genoa. Baron de Vins had hopes of advancing on Nice, sweeping all opposition before him, and causing the whole of Provence to rise. His optimism, as Nelson soon discovered, was quite ill-founded, and the only success during these long-drawn-out operations was achieved by Nelson's blockading squadron which, to quote Napoleon, 'has suspended our commerce, stopped the arrival of provisions, and obliged us to supply Toulon from the interior of the Republic'. For Nelson this was a very worrying period in his life, for he was now in a position far more taxing and much more complicated than he had been in even in the West Indies. If he, or those under his command, were to make a mistake in the detention of neutral shipping he personally could be sued for damages by the vessel's owners. The Genoese authorities were even more furious with him than had been the planters and merchants of Nevis all those years ago, while his detention of vessels from Algiers caused such a furore that it looked as if those long-time pirates of the Mediterranean sea-lanes would declare war on all English shipping. Nelson wrote to Fanny, 'Political courage in an Officer abroad is as highly necessary as military courage', and to Sir Gilbert Elliot in Corsica, '. . . is England to give up the almost certainty of finishing this war with honour, to the fear of offence of such beings?' The same strict sense of moral obligation, which in the West Indies had seemed to many merely the presumptuous officiousness of a young captain 'on the make', served him in good stead in war. 'I am acting not only without the orders of my commander-in-chief, but in some measure contrary to them. However, I have not only the support of his Majesty's Ministers, both at Turin and Genoa, but a consciousness that I am doing right and proper for the service of our King and Country.'

Quite apart from the normal responsibilities of command, he was constantly oppressed by anxiety about his conduct of the blockade and, even worse, his good, left eye was troubling him. The glare of the sea and sky endured day after day in the white heat of August left him for a brief period almost totally blind. Later he was also to complain of a tautness in his chest 'as if a girth were buckled taut over my breast'. This was uncomfortably reminiscent of pains in his chest and lungs which he had had in *Boreas* in 1784, which, a surgeon has commented, were somewhat suggestive of tuberculosis. In addition to all this, he was to find out that General de Vins, whom he had at first believed to be reliable, was no more than a broken reed: a professional, true, but without any of the fire and aggression that could possibly cope with those very two qualities which the revolutionary French possessed in abundance.

Nelson had some small successes, however, to compensate for his general feeling of frustration about the land campaign. On 26 August, for instance, he and six of his squadron made a raid on the small port of Alassio, and captured a large gunboat, a corvette, two galleys and several other smaller vessels. Since Alassio was occupied by the French, and the ammunition and provisions aboard the ships were all destined for their army, the raid was a good illustration of the proper use of sea-power. It made Nelson 'feel better in every way'. But he could not feel the same about the overall conduct of the operations: 'We are doing nothing here,' he told Fanny. 'The Austrians cannot get over the mountains and I cannot get the Admiral to come here to give us his assistance in carrying a part of the army a small distance by water, but Hotham will not entangle himself with any co-operation.' Hearing that his old friend Collingwood was on his way out to join the station, he wrote to put him in the picture. 'You are so old a Mediterranean man, that I can tell you nothing new about the country. My command here is so far pleasant as it relieves me from the inactivity of our Fleet, which is great indeed, as you will soon see. . . . Our Admiral, entre nous, has no political courage whatever, and is alarmed at the mention of any strong measure. . . .'

By the end of 1795 Nelson's gloomy prognostications about the fate of the war ashore were confirmed. Massena, who was to become the greatest of Napoleon's marshals, had given proof of his abilities by routing the Austrians and their allies at Loano. 'General de Vins, from ill-health, as he says,' Nelson wrote bitterly, 'gave up the command in the middle of the battle, and from that moment not a soldier stayed at his post. . . . The Austrians ran eighteen miles without stopping.' Perhaps if Hotham had supported Nelson's offshore squadron, and had given the full assistance of the British fleet to the land operations, things might have turned out differently. But one doubts it: 'The French, half-naked, were determined to conquer or die.' They now had possession of the whole coastline from Savona to Voltri; the Austrians were cut off from their British allies at sea; and the path to the subsequent French invasion of Italy was laid open. No one emerged with any credit from the whole of this operation except Nelson – and, of course, the other captains of his inshore squadron. The Agamemnon, so worn out by her year off the Riviera coast that she had had to be frapped with cables (three or four huge hemp hawsers being passed round the hull amidships to keep her weakened frame together), returned to Leghorn. She was in need of a refit beyond the capacity of any dockyard available to the fleet outside England.

CHAPTER THIRTEEN

Commodore

NELSON was at Leghorn when he learned that he now came under the command of Admiral Sir John Jervis, who had been appointed to take over the Mediterranean station in succession to Admiral Hotham. No greater contrast between two commanders-in-chief could have been found. Hotham had been unsure in his judgement, and was always prone to take the middle way both in the discipline of the fleet and in the conduct of operations. Sir John Jervis, on the other hand, was a fire-eater, a martinet indeed, and a man whose record in the Seven Years War, the War of American Independence, and as Commander-in-Chief in the West Indies, had established him as one of the foremost officers in the Service. He arrived at San Fiorenza on 27 November, and it became evident within days of his arrival that everything was to change. This was 'to the great joy of some, and sorrow of others', but it was to prove in Nelson's case the formation of a friendship that was to last his lifetime. Indeed, Jervis's influence on Nelson was such that he, above all other admirals, must be regarded as the man who added the stamp of authority to a nature that had already shown itself zealous and brave. Jervis put the steel in his soul, and some of Nelson's subsequent actions – particularly when it came to disciplinary matters – can only be judged in the light of the fact that he was an ardent pupil of this iron-bound sixty-year-old admiral.

Since Jervis was to have so great an influence upon Nelson, and indeed upon all the captains who served under him, it is worth quoting the viewpoint of another, later admiral, Lord Charles Beresford, who was also known as a disciplinarian and a man who could always be relied upon to act with firmness and efficiency:

In character he [Jervis] was the typical, grim, cold, reserved Englishman of his day – a Duke of Wellington at sea. To the incapable he was terrible; the lazy captain and the mutinous sailor found in him the harshest of judges. Zeal and courage he favoured and distinguished. Of character he was a consummate judge; the captains whom he 'made and formed' in the Mediterranean were the 'band of brothers' rendered glorious by the victory of the Nile. His merciless severity was untempered by the milk of human kindness; he had no hesitation in ordering men to be flogged or hung; he never attempted to govern by love. But to repair defects in discipline, to keep a fleet in thorough order, to train it for battle, he was the very man we needed. . . . The energy of Jervis was as furious as that of Nelson himself, though he had attained the ripe age of sixty years [on taking over the Mediterranean station]. He had not, however, Nelson's genius for war, or Nelson's power of winning his officers' and men's affection. His tastes were cultivated, his conversation charming, his table well-appointed – and yet he was not liked. 'Where I should take a penknife,' said Nelson, 'he takes a hatchet.'

At that moment in the war, with the French triumphant, with the Austrians ineffectually trying to hold the gates of Italy, and with the British Mediterranean fleet run-down and weak in morale through having been inefficiently used, a hatchet was just what was needed.

Throughout the early months of 1796 Nelson continued the arduous and exhausting blockade of Toulon. But, like most such blockades, though the fruits of it were not evident to the seamen who in the gales and blizzards held the blinkered coast during those months when the Riviera reveals a very different face from that known to the sun-lover in summer, its effects were grimly felt by the French ashore. Even though it was almost impossible to stop all the small coasters that scurried close inshore from port to port, no major traffic could move while the French fleet lay bottled up in Toulon. Meanwhile Corsica still had to be guarded, British trade with the eastern Mediterranean protected, and such help as could be afforded to the Austrians provided. It was fortunate that Jervis took to Nelson at once, while the latter was quick to see in him those qualities which had been so sadly lacking in Hotham. As he wrote to Fanny: 'Our new Admiral will not land at Leghorn. The late one was so much here that Sir John is determined to act the contrary. Reports say the French will have their fleet at sea again. If they do I think they will now lose the whole of them, for we have a man of business at our head.' As nearly always he appended his best regards to his father, and added the note: 'Josiah is very well and is daily threatening to write you a letter.' No one could ever deny that to his wife, to his friends, to the Duke of Clarence, and to sundry others, he was the most admirable of correspondents; and all this in addition to the daily business of the ship and the many formal letters and despatches required by the Service. While saying this, it must equally be added that Fanny was the most regular, concerned and tender letter-writer that any naval officer could have dreamed of.

Bonaparte, not yet quite twenty-seven years of age, had now been appointed General of the Army of Italy. His military genius and political sense were already apparent to those who had been in close contact with him and although there was much against him – his Corsican accent, his unimpressive appearance, and the judgement of some like Suchet (a future Marshal of the Empire) that he was 'an intriguer' – he had that special fire which men like the *sans-culottes* would follow. He understood them well enough, these veterans 'who had grown hoary in battle. . . . I had to act with *éclat* to win the trust and affection of the common soldier : I did so.' His army consisted of 30,000 hungry and ragged men, in want of everything – and many of those wants caused by the British blockade. But on 27 March 1796 Napoleon found the words that would rally them : 'Soldiers! You are almost naked and you are starving. . . . I am about to lead you into the most fertile plains in the world. Before you are great cities and rich provinces; there we shall find honour, glory, and riches.'

Curiously enough, the two great antagonists (who were never to meet) both married ladies from the West Indies, both of whom were widows. But Nelson was more fortunate in his choice of Frances Nisbet than was Napoleon in Josephine de Beauharnais, who was to make his life miserable with her unfaithfulness, and for whom he cherished a passion that was as violent as his Corsican temperament. One other singular coincidence emerges : on almost the very day that Bonaparte issued his famous call to his troops, Nelson received the order from Jervis to fly a pendant as Commodore aboard the *Agamemnon*. Midshipman William Hoste acquainted his family: 'It gives me infinite pleasure to be able [to inform you] that our good Captain has had this additional mark of distinction conferred upon him, which, I daresay, you will agree with me, his merit richly deserves.' The broad pendant, denoting a commodore second class, which Nelson now hoisted, was not a rank in itself, but a post that enabled a senior captain to exercise an admiral's duties in advance of the time that he was actually promoted to flag-rank.

In June that year, the *Agamemnon*, far and away the ship most in need of a major refit of all in the fleet, was ordered home. Nelson hoped to have gone with her, he might indeed even now have stayed aboard, but the health of another captain was even worse than his own and, as he wrote to Sir John Jervis: 'I cannot bear the thought of leaving your command.' Just as, all those years ago at Sandy Hook, he had opted for Lord Hood's squadron, having come to the conclusion that with Hood he would find honour and action, he realised that he had found in Jervis another commander who would lead him where that 'radiant orb' beckoned. Although few of the original officers were left aboard *Agamemnon*, and the ship's company through sickness and wounds had also largely changed, although his wonderful 64 was 'old and worn out', he cannot have watched her go without great emotion. He had been aboard her over three years, and in her he had experienced everything that the fickle Mediterranean could do – from infuriating summer calms to long dead swells, to white squalls off the coast of Toulon and black gales off Corsica. With her departure in the direction of Gibraltar a chapter of his life ended. He was now a commodore, and would never again be sole and simple captain of a ship, but would have a captain under his command. He had learned in her how to handle a man-of-war in every kind of weather and had tried her, himself, and his fellow officers and sailors, against the navy of revolutionary France. The Homeric Agamemnon had been 'The King of Men', and in the ship that had been called after him Nelson himself had learned something of the grandeurs and the miseries, the glories and the concerns, of kingship.

His broad pendant was transferred to the 74-gun *Captain*. As captain of her he was to have a fine seaman, Ralph Miller, New York born, who had seen much action and who was to become one of Nelson's devoted followers. The year 1796, which saw Nelson well on the way to becoming an admiral, was not to prove a happy one for the British in the Mediterranean. Everywhere the French were on the advance, sweeping through Italy, capturing Leghorn in July, and fomenting revolution in Corsica. Leghorn and Genoa were now closed against the British, and Corsica, although an admirable source of timber, had always required supplies from the mainland to feed the fleet. As it appeared that the island would soon become untenable, Nelson was despatched to capture nearby Elba whose main harbour of Porto Ferraio, as well as a good anchorage at Porto Azzurro, could easily accommodate the fleet, while its proximity to the mainland would make the matter of supplies easier. He was rewarded for the success of this venture in August by being confirmed substantive commodore, which gave him an increase in pay. The small island of Capraia, forty miles east of Corsica, was subsequently taken to provide a further lookout point from which the blockade of Leghorn could be maintained, and also as a riposte to the action of the Genoese Government in seizing British property. On all sides it could now be seen that the triumphs of Bonaparte ashore – 'they are masters on shore, and the English at sea' – were having the inevitable effect of swaying weak and vacillating kingdoms and principalities to join the French camp. In the battle between the Elephant and the Whale it is always the triumphs of the Elephant that are visible to the landsman. The city-dweller or the peasant sees the passage of conquering armies – tangible proof of power and success – but what he does not see are what Admiral Mahan described as 'those far-distant, storm-beaten ships, upon which the Grand Army never looked, but which stood for ever between it and the dominion of the World'.

By the autumn, with Spain as well as Holland now allied with France against Britain, nothing in Europe stood against the French advance. It was clear that Corsica must be abandoned, and this most successful evacuation was carried out in October despite gale-force winds. Nelson could happily announce that 'Every man and vessel [is] safely moored in Porto Ferrajo, for its size the most complete harbour in the world.' Eighteen years later, long after Nelson was dead, the forty-five-year-old ex-Emperor Napoleon was to be landed here in an English frigate, sighing at the sight of what territory was left to him : 'My island is very small.' Nelson, the seaman, could admire an excellent harbour, but Napoleon (the man responsible for more death and destruction in the western world than any individual until Adolf Hitler) could only regret the scant acres of an island that, however delightful, could not satisfy the vanity of his ambition. Nelson, however, was not without his small vanities, as he readily confessed to Fanny in a letter that August : 'A person sent me a letter, and directed as follows, "Horatio Nelson, Genoa". On being asked how he could direct in such a manner, his answer, in a large part, was "Sir, there is but one Horatio Nelson in the world." ' He went on to more practical matters : 'Lord Spencer has expressed his sincere desire to Sir John Jervis, to give me my Flag. You ask me when shall I come home? I believe, when either an honourable peace is made, or a Spanish war, which may draw our Fleet out of the Mediterranean. God knows I shall come to you not a sixpence richer than when I set out.'

San Fiorenza, Bastia, Calvi, all the places where he had spent so much time and arduous endeavour with his 'Agamemnons' in making secure bases for his country, were already abandoned. Many a commander in subsequent centuries has had to see hard-fought-for gains

turned over to the enemy, but Nelson was to suffer even more disillusionment. In December, the decision was taken in London to
withdraw the fleet altogether from the Mediterranean. 'As for
Corsica,' he wrote, 'I have seen the first and last of it. I was the cause
of giving many lucrative employments for the army which they were
incapable of getting for themselves and I took them off the island
when they were equally helpless.' As for the decision to leave the
Mediterranean entirely to the French, it made him frantic with
distress: 'They at home do not know what the Fleet is capable of
performing – anything and everything. Of all the Fleets I ever saw,
I never beheld one, in point of officers and men, equal to Sir John
Jervis's, who is a Commander-in-Chief to lead them to glory.' But the
final evacuation, Elba, was to be his next mission.

Only Gibraltar, 'this dark corner of the world', was now left to the
British. It was early in December that Nelson wrote to Fanny:

> I . . . am going on an arduous and most important mission, which,
> with God's blessing, I have little doubt of accomplishing. . . . It is
> not a fighting mission, therefore be not uneasy. I feel honoured in
> being trusted in the manner I am. . . . If I have money enough
> in Marsh and Creed's hands, I wish you would buy the cottage in
> Norfolk, and be assured that I believe it to be impossible that I shall
> not follow the plough with much greater satisfaction than viewing
> all the magnificent scenes in Italy.

There can be no doubt, for the theme recurs so often in his letters,
that, like many a sailor, he always retained the dream of a quiet rustic
life. But the idea of Nelson 'following the plough' is laughable. One
of his great predecessors, 'Old Dreadnought', Admiral Edward
Boscawen, expressed himself better in a letter to his wife written
during the Seven Years War: 'To be sure I lose the fruits of the earth,
but then I am gathering the flowers of the sea.' Nelson knew well
enough, despite all its hardships and monotony, that he would never
have exchanged the wake of a ship for the chocolate-dark curl behind
a Norfolk plough. Even the seagulls dipping over that rich earth would
have reminded him of those other, salty acres.

The mission on which he was sent, transferring his broad pendant
from the *Captain* to the frigate *Minerve*, was no less than to cross the
enemy-dominated Mediterranean all the way to Elba, and take off
as much as he could of the garrison marooned there. To assist him
he had the frigate *Blanche*, and it was with these two small ships that
he set out from Gibraltar on 15 December. It proved to be a passage

which could certainly never have been described as 'not a fighting mission'. Hardly were they further east than Cartagena than they fell in with two Spanish frigates, the *Santa Sabina* and the *Ceres*. After all his years as commander of a 'capital ship', Nelson was to show that he had not forgotten his early training, and that he could still, in modern terms, fight a 'destroyer action'. The *Minerve* and the *Blanche* took on their opposite numbers in a simple and traditional ship-to-ship engagement. Nelson, again according to old-fashioned custom, hailed 'the Don' and asked his surrender; to which came back the reply: 'This is a Spanish frigate, and you may begin as soon as you please.' A spirited duel followed, in which the Spaniard lost her fore, main, and mizzen masts – some tribute to the gunners of the *Minerve*. It was not until all was gone that her captain could be prevailed upon to strike his colours. Nelson's comment was: 'I have no idea of a closer or sharper battle : the force to a gun the same, and nearly the same number of men; we having two hundred and fifty. I asked him several times to surrender during the action, but his answer was – "No Sir : not whilst I have the means of fighting left." When only he himself of all the other Officers was left alive, he hailed, and said he could fight no more, and begged I would stop firing.' The strange intimacy of warfare in those days is what strikes the modern sailor : the courtesies, and the captains' hailing each other in between the thunder of the guns. Nelson spoke no more Spanish than French, so the ability of his opponent to exchange shout for shout in English should have surprised him. When the defeated captain came aboard, however, to surrender his sword the explanation was strangely simple. He was none other than Don Jacobo Stuart, great-grandson of James II by his mistress Arabella Churchill. Nelson was moved enough at having defeated the descendant of a king of England, as well as by his opponent's gallant fighting style, as to restore to Don Jacobo his sword. Meanwhile, the *Blanche* had equally defeated her opponent, and both ships had prize crews aboard the Spaniards and had taken them in tow. Next morning, however, a Spanish frigate hove up and Nelson was compelled to cast off his tow, while the arrival soon after of two Spanish line-of-battle ships removed any possibility of the *Minerve* and the *Blanche* getting away with their prizes. Both Spanish ships were cast adrift, and the two British frigates – their presence in the Mediterranean now only too well known to the enemy – were lucky to get away scot-free. Among those who had to be left behind with the boarding-parties aboard the now recaptured frigates were Lieutenants Culverhouse and Hardy. Nelson was able in due course to arrange an exchange of prisoners. Don Jacobo Stuart, 'reputed the best officer in Spain', was to prove not only a gentleman, but also a valuable asset when it came to arranging the exchange.

Nelson suffered a hard winter in every sense of the term. The weather was cold all over Europe with heavy falls of snow; the King of Naples had made peace with the French; and there were many complications involving Sir Gilbert Elliot as Viceroy and the military commander, General de Burgh, as to the validity of the orders for the withdrawal from Elba. There were seventeen ships on station at Porto Ferraio and Sir John Jervis's orders were, to Nelson at any rate, quite clear. They and all troops and stores were to be withdrawn, some destined for Gibraltar, and the rest for Lisbon. But it was not until the end of January that Nelson could successfully effect the major part of the evacuation, by which time everyone concerned had received further written and concise orders that 'cleared their yard-arms'. Among other items of minor consideration, Nelson's friend, Captain Fremantle of the *Inconstant*, had married a Miss Betsy Wynne in Naples. Both the new bride and her sister kept journals, and it is from these that we learn much about the happenings of those days. Lady Emma Hamilton also had played a large part in making the match during a visit by Fremantle to Naples. The seventeen-year-old bride, upon her return to Elba aboard the *Inconstant* with her husband, was to record of their first dinner party that 'Old Nelson [was] very civil, but does not say much.' He was thirty-seven. Disease, wounds, and long years at sea must indeed have made him seem 'old' to a young woman. His taciturnity was due not to moroseness – he had a lively nature – but to the loneliness of command.

CHAPTER FOURTEEN

A Famous Indiscipline

It WAS not until the end of January 1797 that Nelson was free to leave Elba. He had long been fretful to be gone, for all the months that, in his view, had been largely wasted in prolonging the weak British sphere of influence in the central Mediterranean had been months when he was quite certain that under Jervis they could have forced an action on the French and Spaniards and resoundingly defeated them. But, as Pitt and his ministers had seen fit to withdraw the fleet from the inland sea, then the sooner they were gone the better. He fretted with anxiety, too, that Jervis, during his absence, would take the fleet out of the Tagus – where the bulk of the ships were secured – and manage to provoke a major action with the French and Spaniards in the Atlantic. Having missed his chance of participating in a real fleet action through the sluggishness of Hotham off Toulon, he was desperate not to miss another. As it turned out, he was only just in time to be present at the engagement that came to be known as the Battle of Cape St Vincent.

The *Minerve* reached Gibraltar on 9 February, where they learned that the bulk of the Spanish fleet from Cartagena had passed through the Strait four days before. Pausing only to water and collect Lieutenants Hardy and Culverhouse, together with the other members of the prize crew who had been returned from the *Santa Sabina*, Nelson weighed anchor and set off westward for the Atlantic. It looked very much as if what he had feared was about to take place – a fleet action in which he would have no share. Two Spanish ships-of-the-line, which had been at anchor in Algeciras Bay keeping an eye upon Gibraltar, immediately gave chase, seeing an easy prey in the lightly armed frigate. The incident which followed has become immortalised because, among the guests whom Nelson had aboard the *Minerve* was Colonel John Drinkwater, who had served throughout the great siege of Gibraltar and had become famous as its historian (his *Siege of Gibraltar* being a best-seller of its time). Drinkwater, gazing astern at the pursuing Spanish ships, asked Nelson if he thought that there was any likelihood of an engagement, to which the latter replied that it was very possible but, looking aloft at his commodore's broad pendant, 'Before the Dons get hold of that bit of bunting, I will have a struggle with them, and sooner than give up the Frigate I'll run her ashore.'

Shortly after this, with true British *sang-froid*, the visitors and several of the officers of the *Minerve* sat down to dine at the Commodore's table. Colonel Drinkwater was in the process of congratulating Lieutenant Thomas Masterman Hardy, First Lieutenant of the *Minerve*, on his being no longer a prisoner of the Spaniards, and was expecting no doubt to hear some detailed story of the circumstances of his captivity when one of the most alarming cries that can ever be heard at sea rang out – 'Man overboard!' The sailor, then as now, had his code and, no matter what the circumstances, if a man had fallen into the sea every effort must be made to rescue him. The sea was always the enemy – far more than those other enemies in men-of-war who moved upon its surface. Very few sailors could swim, for almost no one at that time considered swimming to be a useful or even a healthful exercise. It is doubtful, for instance, if Nelson could swim. Men who fell overboard, or who were blown off ships in action, could usually do little more than 'dog-paddle' until they reached a boat or piece of floating wreckage. But there were always these basic codes that governed life at sea, one of which is cynically expressed in an old navy saying: 'Messmate before shipmate, shipmate before soldier, soldier before dog.'

The dinner party immediately broke up and Colonel Drinkwater commented:

The officers of the ship ran on deck; I, with others, ran to the stern-windows to see if anything could be observed of the unfortunate man; we had scarcely reached them before we noticed the lowering of the jolly-boat [a small ship's boat always kept at the ready], in which was my late neighbour, Hardy, with a party of sailors; and before many seconds had elapsed, the current of the Straits [which runs strongly to the eastward] had carried the jolly-boat far astern of the Frigate, towards the Spanish ships. Of course, the first object was to recover the fallen man, but he was never seen again. Hardy soon made a signal to that effect, and the man was given up as lost. The attention of every person was now turned to the safety of Hardy and his boat's crew; their situation was extremely perilous, and their danger was every instant increasing, from the fast sailing of the headmost ship of the chase, which by this time had approached nearly within gun-shot of the *Minerve*. The jolly-boat's crew pulled 'might and main' to regain the Frigate, but apparently made little progress against the current of the Straits. At this crisis, Nelson, casting an anxious look at the hazardous situation of Hardy and his companions, exclaimed 'By God! I'll not lose Hardy: back the mizen topsail.' No sooner said than done, the *Minerve*'s progress was retarded, *having the current carry her down towards Hardy* [sic] and his party, who seeing this spirited manoeuvre . . . naturally redoubled their actions to rejoin the Frigate. To the landsmen on board the *Minerve* an action now appeared to be inevitable; and so, it would appear, thought the Enemy, who surprised and confounded by this daring manoeuvre of the Commodore (being ignorant of the accident that led to it), must have construed it into a direct challenge.

The captain of the leading ship, the *Terrible*, almost immediately shortened sail, and his consort followed suit. The only conclusion that can be drawn from their doing so is that the two Spanish ships-of-the-line, seeing the *Minerve* drop back, must have assumed that the frigate was in touch with the main body of the British fleet, and that they were being drawn into a trap. Nelson's humane foolhardiness has never escaped note – especially since Thomas Hardy went on to become his captain aboard *Victory* and to share in his last triumph. What has often been misconstrued, however, is his action (as described by Drinkwater) of backing the mizzen topsail and 'having the current carry her down towards Hardy'. Of course, both the ship and the jolly-boat were being impelled eastward, backwards, towards the enemy – for a current has the same effect upon a ship as upon a ship's boat. What Nelson did by 'backing' the topsail was, in landsman's terms, rather similar to putting on a brake. The *Minerve* was still subject to the same current as Hardy's open boat, but Nelson had carefully reduced his forward rate of progress so that the oared boat could come up with him. Nelson had no intention whatsoever of coming into action with two heavily armed ships – especially when he wanted to catch up with his own fleet and join Sir John Jervis. Studding-sails, those light-weather sails, which have been compared with 'wings upon the yardarms', were now run out and the frigate drew away from her pursuers. With Hardy and his crew safely back aboard, the *Minerve* altered course slightly to the south and lost her pursuers.

The adventures of the night were far from over. The easterly wind that had been blowing brought up its usual companions in the Strait of Gibraltar – humidity, mist, and then fog. The warm air flowing out of the Mediterranean felt the colder touch of the Atlantic, and the frigate moved slowly and stealthily through a thick night – a night in which they gradually became aware of the presence of other ships. Sighs of sails and the creaking of rigging, the discharge of minute guns, the soft wallow and wash as they passed quite close by a large vessel, showed them that they were in the middle of a great fleet. Nobody could be quite certain whether it was the Spanish battle fleet they were passing through, or a large convoy bound for the West Indies. Fortunately for all aboard the little *Minerve*, so thick and dark was the night that no one aboard the other ships could know that it was a British frigate which was gliding through their midst. The *Minerve* was, in fact, passing through the Spanish fleet, which was guarding a valuable convoy of mercury ultimately destined for the Spanish colonies overseas (where it was used in the amalgamation of silver ore). Blown out into the Atlantic by the same Levanter that had lofted Nelson through the Strait, they were waiting for a favourable wind to take them into Cadiz. The major part of this fleet was ultimately intended to join up with the French at Brest and then, combined with the Dutch from the Texel, to form a massive armada that would pave the way for the invasion of England. Despite the failure of a recent attempt on Ireland and another on Wales, it was still felt that, given sufficient naval superiority in the Narrow Seas, the French could land and crush the only power in Europe that still resisted them. The battle that was to follow blew their design to pieces.

On the morning of 13 February, having passed unscathed through the enemy, Nelson came up with Sir John Jervis and the British fleet some twenty-five miles to the west of Cape St Vincent. The south-western extremity of Portugal, Cape St Vincent is an imposing mass of rock, steep-to on all sides. Of it the Admiralty Pilot says: 'The western side of the cape is so precipitous and full of caves, that the noise produced by the sea breaking on it may be heard at some distance.' It is a formidable natural phenomenon, the place where Europe contemplates the long expanses of the Atlantic. It was from nearby Sagres that the great Portuguese prince, Henry the Navigator, in the early fifteenth century had first begun the systematic exploration of Africa and the islands of the Ocean Sea. A place of destiny.

Nelson transferred his broad pendant to the *Captain*, while two of his guests in the *Minerve*, Sir Gilbert Elliot and Colonel John Drink-water, were put aboard the frigate *Lively* which was destined to carry back the news of the impending action to England. For there could be little doubt now that the first great trial of strength at sea between Britain and her enemies was soon to take place. The Spanish fleet should, in fact, have been in Cadiz harbour watering and provisioning prior to its northerly excursion to the Channel, but having been blown out into the Atlantic by the Levanter, it was now running back under a wind which had just switched to slightly south of west. The British fleet to the north of them numbered fifteen sail-of-the-line, of which the *Britannia* and the *Victory* mounted 100 guns, the *Barfleur* and *Prince George* 98, and the *Blenheim* and *Namur* 90. These were all three-deckers. There were in addition eight 74s; the *Captain*, *Colossus*, *Culloden*, *Egmont*, *Excellent*, *Goliath*, *Irresistible* and *Orion*. There was also a 64, the *Diadem*, four frigates and a sloop – making a grand total of twenty ships, but only fifteen sail-of-the-line.

The fleet through which Nelson had passed on the previous night and which, as he informed Jervis on his arrival, seemed to have gone about and headed in an easterly direction was considerably larger than that of the British. Jervis should, in fact, have had under his command a further seven ships-of-the-line, but Admiral Man – at a time when Jervis was still in the Mediterranean – had taken his squadron home from Gibraltar, against orders and supposing that the Mediterranean was lost and that England would welcome seven ships rather than none at all. For this desertion, except that it was not in the face of the enemy, he might well have been shot – rather than, as happened, merely ordered to haul down his flag. Jervis would almost certainly have been happy to see Man undergo quarter-deck execution – as had happened for much less reason to Admiral Byng in the year before Nelson's birth.

Jervis was to confront a Spanish fleet of twenty-seven sail-of-the-line, accompanied by ten frigates, under the command of Admiral Don José de Córdoba. The Admiral's flagship, the *Santissima Trinidad*, was the largest warship in the world, being a four-decker mounting 136 guns. Córdoba also had with him six three-deckers of 112 guns and one of 80 guns, the rest being 74s. All were excellent ships, but they were ill-manned and, as Nelson had previously observed, 'The Dons can make fine ships, they cannot however make men.' This was a natural enough observation for a partisan of the time, but, as history has often shown, the Spaniards are a very brave race. No, the trouble with the Spanish Navy at that time was that it was officered by noblemen who, in general, considered the trade of the sea a common one; and it was manned by soldiers and a leavening of fishermen among a mass of conscripted peasants who knew an ox and a plough better than a rope and a gun. In this respect the Spaniards had learned little or nothing about the essence of nautical matters since the failure of the Armada in 1588.

It was not until the morning of 14 February, St Valentine's Day, that the two fleets were engaged. The wind was now almost due west, almost dead astern for the Spaniards running back towards the port of Cadiz, and comfortably on the starboard beam for the British. The Spanish fleet was in haphazard array. Those long months at sea which had become native to the British – coupled with the iron discipline of Jervis – had given them a superiority which could not be matched by larger ships and greater fire-power. There was mist again over the water and the first sight of the Spanish fleet was something that the greatest of all British artists, William Turner (who was half a sailor at heart) would have loved to see : 'Thumpers, looming like Beachy Head in a fog'. The First Captain of the *Victory*, walking the quarter-deck in the company of Sir John Jervis, began to count the enemy ships as they emerged out of what the log-book of Nelson's ship describes as 'moderate and foggy' weather. Their topsails shimmered first over the opaque mist, then their lower courses – fore, main, and mizzen – and then the hulking shadows of their hulls.

'There are eight sail-of-the-line, Sir John.'

'Very well, sir.'

'There are twenty sail-of-the-line, Sir John.'

'Very well, sir.'

'There are twenty-five sail-of-the-line, Sir John.'

'Very well, sir.'

'There are twenty-seven sail-of-the-line, Sir John; near double our own !'

'Enough, sir,' came the answer. 'No more of that ! If there are fifty sail, I will go through them. England badly needs a victory at the moment.'

Captain Ben Hallowell, a Canadian-born officer who had been Nelson's constant companion in the batteries at Calvi, and whose ship had been wrecked through no fault of his own a few months before, was serving as a supernumerary aboard the *Victory*. He was present on the quarter-deck during this exchange and so far forgot himself as to thump his formidable Commander-in-Chief on the back, with a hearty : 'That's right, Sir John, that's right ! And, by God, we'll give them a damned good licking.'

Jervis's remark that England needed a victory was true enough. The country's situation was somewhat similar to that which was to occur

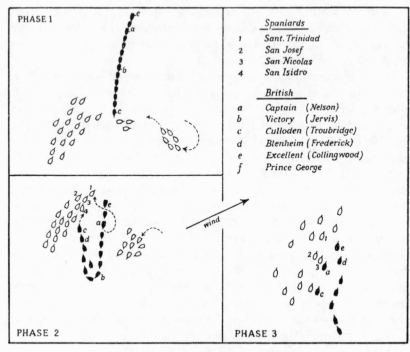

The Battle of Cape St Vincent

in the summer of 1940, with all the continent of Europe lined against her. But in 1797 the position for England was, if anything, somewhat worse. Not only was the enemy everywhere triumphant, but in Ireland revolutionary agitators were creating even more ferment than usual in that unhappy country. Britain's commercial interests were threatened on all hands, and, to make matters worse, dilatoriness in the payment of the men, coupled with inefficiency and brutality, had produced a state where the Channel fleet was on the verge of mutiny.

The Spaniards, who had lost their formation when driven into the Atlantic, were now trying under the welcome westerly wind to get themselves back into some semblance of order. But, at the moment that they sighted the British – something which 'took them completely by surprise' – they were straggling along in two main groups. There was a gap of about seven miles between the leading ships, six in all, and the main body of twenty-one ships bringing up the rear. But even these were ranged in a slovenly fashion, some abreast of one another, and others standing along on their own. 'We flew to them as a hawk to his prey,' as Collingwood put it. Shortly after eight in the morning Jervis made the signal: 'Form line of battle as convenient.' This meant that the British, who had been proceeding in two columns, now drew together into one single column with a precision that was second nature after their many months at sea. In close order, Nelson's *Captain* being third from the rear, the British sails came down on a south-westerly course towards the enemy, a deadly spear with Troubridge's *Culloden* at the tip.

Jervis, as he wrote, 'confident in the skill, valour, and discipline of the officers and men I had the happiness to command, and judging that the honour of His Majesty's arms, and the circumstances of war in these seas required a considerable degree of enterprise', had decided to take advantage of the enemy's divided fleet and pass his own clean between the two sections. The *Culloden* in the van, the *Blenheim*, *Prince George*, *Irresistible*, *Colossus* and *Orion* were ordered to cram on all sail and make straight for the gap. Seeing the danger, the Spanish division in the lead altered back from their easterly course, in order to try to rejoin the main body. Nine Spanish ships all told were to the eastward of him as Troubridge in the *Culloden* burst through the line and opened fire at 11.30 a.m. So close did he come to the leading Spanish vessel that it looked for a moment as if a collision was inevitable. 'Let the weakest fend off,' was Troubridge's dry comment just before he opened fire. The *Culloden* poured into her opponent two double-shotted broadsides, 'as if by a second's watch, and in the presence of a port-admiral's inspection'. When the fire and smoke and thunder was over, it was seen that the Spanish three-decker had fallen away in such a state of disrepair and confusion that she had not even fired her guns. The British were through – the Spanish backbone was broken.

The *Culloden*'s consorts came into action as they too drove into the gap between the two sections of the Spanish fleet. The main body of the enemy now altered to the north, so that they and the British were passing each other on reciprocal courses. To prevent their escape Jervis made the signal for his ships to tack in succession. This meant that they came about one after another, still forming the same line-of-battle sequence as when they had gone in. It was at this moment that the Spanish van, which had been cut off to leeward, came beating back in an attempt on their part to cut the British line at the point where they were turning. They received such heavy fire from the British, who maintained so close a station that it was not like the broadsides of individual ships but one solid wall of shot, that they were driven off and fell away. Only one vessel managed to pass through and rejoin the main body of their fleet. The British, however, were still turning as they altered course in succession – so that they presented, could they have been observed from the air, a V extended over the water. One side of this was returning to engage the main body of the Spaniards while the other side was still inoperative as it sailed down to the bottom of the V. Admiral Córdoba had already given up any thoughts of victory. He saw that he had but one chance of extricating his fleet, and that was by pressing on under full sail so that he and the ships with him could slide across the top of the V, rejoin the van and make safely away eastward for the welcome arms of Cadiz harbour.

It was at this point that Nelson, seeing exactly what the Spanish Admiral had in mind, committed his famous indiscipline. His action required immense courage, for it ran completely counter to those *Fighting Instructions* which governed the conduct of the British fleet in battle. To depart from the *Fighting Instructions*, which specifically laid it down that no ship might leave the line-of-battle without orders from the Commander-in-Chief, was usually seen as an act of cowardice, and invariably entailed a court-martial. Nelson's action, however, was the very reverse of cowardice for, seeing how the leading Spanish ship, the immense *Santissima Trinidad*, at the head of her column was on the point of slipping across the top of the British V, he wore his ship round through 180 degrees to port. (Wearing ship, turning a vessel round so that her stern comes into the wind, was a far quicker operation than tacking.) He passed astern of the *Diadem*, Captain Towry, who was immediately behind him, hauled across the bows of the *Excellent*, his old friend Collingwood, and made straight for the giant *Santissima Trinidad*. He had seen with that quick eye which made him a genius of naval warfare that, if the Spanish van – and the largest ship in the world – could be held in check, it would give the rest of the British sail-of-the-line time to execute their turn and come up with the enemy. '. . . Passing between the *Diadem* and the *Excellent*,' as he later wrote, 'at ten minutes past 1 o'clock, I was in close action with the Van, and, of course, leewardmost of the Spanish Fleet. . . . I was immediately joined and most nobly supported by the *Culloden*, Captain Troubridge. The Spanish Fleet, from not wishing, I suppose, to have a decisive Battle, hauled to the wind on the larboard tack . . .'

Captain Frederick in the *Blenheim* and Collingwood in the *Excellent* were soon up with him, and Collingwood's crew proved themselves such master-gunners that the Royal Navy was later to call its gunnery school at Portsmouth H.M.S. Excellent. Collingwood was a stern disciplinarian and a great believer in gunnery training, and his ship now proved herself; discharging into the Spaniards whom she engaged three broadsides to every one that the enemy managed to fire in return. As Nelson put it :

The *Salvador del Mundo* and *San Isidro* dropped astern, and were fired into in a masterly style by the *Excellent*, Captain Collingwood, who compelled them to hoist English colours, when, disdaining the parade of taking possession of beaten enemies, he most gallantly pushed up to save his old friend and messmate, who was to appearance in a critical situation : the *Blenheim* having fallen to leeward, and the *Culloden* crippled and astern, the *Captain* at this time being actually fired upon by three First-rates and the *San Nicolas* and a Seventy-four, and about pistol-shot of the *San Nicolas*.

Collingwood now drew up to help his old friend, and, with every sail set, passed within ten feet of the *San Nicolas*, 'giving her a most awful and tremendous fire'.

Collingwood's magnificent action gave Nelson's devastated *Captain* something of a respite. All four ships, *Captain*, *Culloden*, *Blenheim* and *Excellent*, which had been in the forefront of this dramatic action, suffered heavy damage. The *Captain*, which had initiated the move, almost inevitably suffered worst of all. Her sails were in tatters, her rigging was torn to pieces, her fore-topmast gone, and the wheel itself had been shot away, so that she had to be steered by emergency tackles. The *Captain* fell away in the direction of the *San Josef* which had fallen foul of the First-Rate *San Nicolas* and become inextricably entangled with her. The confusion, the thunder of guns, the dense smoke, the chaos as rigging, yards, topmasts, and men with them, came falling from aloft, presented an inferno that even Dante could hardly have envisaged. Fleet actions in the days since sail gave place to machinery have also their attendant horrors, but not in quite such a devastatingly personal way as when ships actually ran alongside ships, firing at point-blank range. While the wood splinters howled and screamed, and the sharp-shooters opened fire from aloft, the soldiers, marines, and sailors waited to board. Now, as the *Captain* came alongside the *San Nicolas*, her out-jutting port cathead (the heavy oak frame that carried the anchor) fell foul of the Spaniard's gallery on the quarter, while the spritsail yard of Nelson's ship hooked itself into the enemy's main rigging.

Familiar though they are, Nelson's own words can never be bettered :

I directed Captain Miller to put the helm hard-a-starboard, and calling for the Borders, ordered them to Board.

The soldiers of the 69th regiment, with an alacrity which will ever do them credit, were among the foremost on this service. The first man who jumped into the enemy's mizen chains was Captain Berry, late my first lieutenant (Captain Miller was in the very act of going also, but I directed him to remain). A soldier having broke the upper quarter-gallery window, jumped in followed by myself and others as fast as possible. I found the cabin doors fastened, and some Spanish officers fired their pistols; but having broken open the doors, the soldiers fired, and the Spanish Brigadier [Commodore, with a distinguishing pendant] fell as retreating to the quarter-deck. Having pushed on the quarter-deck, I found Captain Berry in possession of the poop, and the Spanish Ensign hauling down. The *San Josef* at this moment fired muskets and pistols from the Admiral's stern-gallery on us. Our seamen by this time were in full possession of every part: about seven of my men were killed, and some few wounded, and about twenty Spaniards.

Having placed sentinels at the different ladders, and ordered Captain Miller to push more men into the *San Nicolas*, I directed my brave fellows to board the First-Rate, which was done in a moment.

So, from the captured *San Nicolas*, Nelson's men now swarmed over her decks and began to board the huge *San Josef* which lay alongside her with her spars and rigging foul of her compatriot.

When I got into her main-chains, a Spanish Officer came upon the quarter-deck rail, without arms, and said the Ship had surrendered. From this welcome information, it was not long before I was on the quarter-deck, when the Spanish Captain, with a bended knee, presented me his Sword, and told me the Admiral was dying with his wounds below. I gave him my hand, and desired him to call to his Officers and Ship's Company that the Ship had surrendered, which he did; and on the quarter-deck of a Spanish First-rate, extravagant as the story may seem, did I receive the Swords of the vanquished Spaniards, which as I received I gave to William Fearney, one of my bargemen, who placed them, with the greatest sang-froid, under his arm.

He went on to add that a number of those involved in the capture of the two Spanish ships, among them Captain Berry and the unemotional William Fearney, were old 'Agamemnons'. The circumstances in which Nelson's *Captain* took these two ships, using the one to board the other – later described as 'Nelson's patent bridge for boarding first-rates' – were remarkable enough. What must not be forgotten is that the condition of these two ships, which had been so heavily hammered and rendered unnavigable, was not all due to the fire of the *Captain*. Far from it : a considerable amount of the credit for the success of this part of the action must go to the other British ships also engaged with them, and in particular to Collingwood's *Excellent*. Nevertheless, the spectacle of the three vessels locked together, with the British ensign triumphant over an island of ships, was something that those who saw it could never forget. Sir Gilbert Elliot, who was aboard the frigate *Lively*, later wrote to Nelson that : 'Nothing in the world was ever more noble than the transaction of the *Captain* from beginning to end, and the glorious group of your ship and her two prizes . . . was never surpassed and I dare say never will.' The crew of *Victory*, surging past after the fleeing enemy, lined her rails and gave three cheers as the men looked with wonder at the astonishing sight.

The battle, which had been hard fought for over two hours, ended with four Spanish ships taken as prizes. The mighty *Santissima Trinidad* had been so badly damaged that Córdoba had to transfer his flag to another vessel. Unfortunately for British hopes, this vast man-of-war, which everyone had hoped to see among the prizes, managed to slip away under tow as darkness fell. What prevented the Battle of Cape St Vincent from being the overwhelming victory that it might well have been was that the junction of the two sections of the enemy fleet was finally effected when 'the day was too far advanced', as Nelson put it, for further action. In any case, Jervis, in view of the damage to his own ships, could hardly have prosecuted the action once the two halves of the Spanish fleet had come together, some of their ships being quite fresh, not having been in action. What Sir John could not have known, of course, was that complete disorder and indeed nigh-chaos prevailed in Córdoba's fleet. The unfortunate Admiral and his officers were destined in due course to share much the same fate as had Medina Sidonia and those who had failed with the Spanish Armada. He, his surviving Rear-Admiral, and several of his captains were court-martialled and dismissed the Service, while it was said that in Cadiz 'the officers cannot come ashore for fear of the populace'.

Nelson had shifted his flag from the *Captain* to the *Irresistible*, which was undamaged, in the hope of coming up with the *Santissima*

Trinidad. After the signal to discontinue action was received, he must, despite his astounding success, have felt somewhat uneasy about his first meeting with Sir John Jervis. The latter, after all, was known as the strictest disciplinarian in the Service, and Nelson had committed a court-martial offence by hauling out of line during a battle. But Jervis was great enough a seaman to have instantly recognised what Nelson's action had achieved. Indeed, immediately upon seeing the *Captain* wearing out of line, he had signalled Collingwood in the *Excellent* to support Nelson. Jervis received his Commodore aboard the quarterdeck of the *Victory* in a most untypical manner – with open arms. Nelson's appearance was remarkable : part of his hat shot away, his face darkened by gunpowder and his clothes in tatters. Jervis, as Nelson recalled, '. . . having embraced me, said he could not sufficiently thank me, and used every expression to make me happy'. The Commander-in-Chief himself had narrowly escaped death, a marine standing by him having been killed by a shot, while Nelson had also been wounded by a flying splinter of wood or metal. He was later to write, underestimating his injury, to Sir Gilbert Elliot that 'it is only a contusion and of no consequence, unless an inflammation takes place in my bowel, which is the part injured'. In fact he was in great pain for a number of days and the husband who regularly kept Fanny posted as to every event could manage no more than a line : 'I am well, Josiah is well.' As late as 1804, seven years after the action, a lump sometimes appeared on the site : 'brought on occasionally by coughing'. Modern diagnosis is that he was probably badly ruptured.

But on that night, while the shattered Spanish fleet regrouped and mourned their losses – in the *Santissima Trinidad* and the *San José* alone over 400 men – and the British also buried their dead and fished their yards and spars, it was quite clear where the victory lay. It was the greatest naval engagement since the Battle of the Saints in the West Indies in 1782, when Rodney had decisively defeated the French. There could be no doubt in anyone's mind that a large part of the credit for the victory must be accorded to Commodore Horatio Nelson.

CHAPTER FIFTEEN

Rear-Admiral

CAPTAIN CALDER of the *Victory* is credited with having said to Jervis, when Nelson had hauled out of line and had only the *Culloden* to help him: 'Sir, the *Captain* and *Culloden* are separated from the fleet and unsupported, shall we recall them?' only to receive the reply, 'I will not have them recalled. I put my faith in those ships.' Calder's anxiety, as First Captain, was natural enough, but what later may seem to stem from envy of Nelson's success is provided in an anecdote related by Benjamin Tucker, secretary to Jervis: 'In the evening, while talking over the events of the day Captain Calder hinted that the spontaneous manoeuvre which carried Nelson and Collingwood into the brunt of the battle was an unauthorised departure by the Commodore from the prescribed mode of attack. "It certainly was so," said Jervis, "and if ever you commit such a breach of your orders, I will forgive you also." '

It has sometimes been suggested that it was through Captain Calder's influence that Sir John Jervis's original draft relating to the action was toned down in such a way that only he, Calder, received personal praise in the Commander-in-Chief's official despatch. It is extremely unlikely, however, that a man like Jervis could have been influenced in his depatch by anyone, let alone his Captain, whom he had in fact told off during the day for ordering a premature broadside. Jervis's despatch can only be seen in the light of events: everyone had fought their ships well and, as it turned out, everyone was duly rewarded. Jervis, in a private letter to Earl Spencer, wrote: 'Commodore Nelson, who was in the rear on the starboard tack, took the lead on the larboard, and contributed very much to the fortune of the day.' He also went on to single out for special commendation Vice-Admiral Waldegrave and Captains Berry, Hallowell, Collingwood and Troubridge.

From aboard the *Irresistible* in Lisbon, on 28 February, Nelson wrote to Fanny: 'We got up here with our prizes this afternoon: the more I think of our late Action, the more I am astonished; it absolutely appears a dream. . . . I believe this Spanish War will give us a Cottage and a piece of ground, which is all I want.' Then, on 3 March: 'I shall come one day or other laughing back, when we will retire from the busy scenes of life : I do not mean to be a hermit. The Dons will give us a little money. . . .' Only on 23 February Fanny had written to him from Bath, where she was staying with his father, that 'Yesterday's Gazette authorises our good father and myself to congratulate you on being a flag officer, may it please God your fame and successes increase and continue under this promotion.' Nelson did not receive the news until 1 April. He had in fact been promoted to flag rank on 2 February, so that at the time the Battle of Cape St Vincent was fought he was, unbeknown to himself or any others present, already a Rear-Admiral of the Blue. His promotion was accorded him in the normal course of events, nine other post-captains all of eighteen years' seniority being promoted at the same time.

On 11 March Fanny wrote him again, having been reassured by Locker that reports that he had been slightly wounded were untrue. She had by now received Nelson's note that he and Josiah were well, and she had been more than flattered by the attentions of Lady Saumarez (wife of Sir James Saumarez who commanded the *Orion* in the battle) who had heard from her husband that, Fanny quoted : 'He speaks generously and manly about you, and concluded by saying, "Commodore Nelson's conduct was above praise". You were universally the subject of conversation.' But that deep concern for his safety, that concern so natural yet so misplaced since she must by now have understood his nature, breaks through : 'I shall not be myself till I hear from you again. What can I attempt to say to you about Boarding? You have been most wonderfully protected : you have done desperate actions enough. Now may I – indeed I do – beg that you never Board again. *Leave it for Captains.*' On reading this no doubt he must have smiled, affectionately – and wryly. Unlike the wives of so many sea-officers, who came from the same stock and who had grown up surrounded by tales of their ancestors, and of battle and high courage and inevitable loss, Fanny was from so very different a background. Why, a man was just as likely to be cut down on his own quarter-deck by a cannon ball, chain-shot, or a sharpshooter's bullet as he was in the action of boarding. . . . It was something he had no intention of explaining to her.

England had needed a victory, and now the honours came pouring in thick and fast. Nelson, who had been very concerned, as he had said earlier in conversation with Colonel Drinkwater shortly after the battle, that he might be made a baronet (a hereditary title which he did not have the means to sustain) was delighted to have the Order of the Bath conferred upon him. This would not involve him in the kind of financial outlay that a baronetcy would have entailed, but it was a very high mark of distinction. Sir John Jervis became Earl St Vincent, and received a pension of £3,000 a year, Rear-Admiral Parker and Vice-Admiral Thompson were made baronets, and the Admirals, Commodore Nelson, and all Captains of ships-of-the-line received gold medals. Captain Calder, who had carried Jervis's despatch home, was knighted. Nelson, ever mindful of his origins, sent the sword which had belonged to the dead Spanish Rear-Admiral Don Xavier Winthuysen, and which he had received aboard the *San Josef*, to the City of Norwich, writing: 'I know no place where it would give me or my family more pleasure to have it kept, than in the Capital City of the County in which I had the Honour to be born.' The local hero received the freedom of Norwich, while the freedoms of London and Bath were also conferred upon him. At the age of thirty-eight he was now Rear-Admiral Sir Horatio Nelson, K.B. – so far had the 'radiant orb' led him over the years. There would also be prize money. The sailors, too, those without whose blood and strength and iron endurance no victory could ever be won, would also get prize money – but theirs would be minimal compared with that of the officers. Certainly, even their share would finally enable them to enjoy the pleasures of the shore for, as an old song puts it in the words of the sailors' women:

> Don't you see the ships a-coming?
> Don't you see them in full sail?
> Don't you see the ships a-coming
> With their prizes at their tail?
> Oh! my little rolling sailor,
> Oh! my little rolling he;
> I do love a jolly sailor,
> Blithe and merry might he be.

But one cannot help wondering if over the years, as the Orders and the medals and other distinctions came – and rightfully came – his way, Nelson recalled those words which had so impressed him as a young seaman in the West Indies: *'Aft the most honour forward the better man.'* Perhaps he did, or he would never have included that saying in his brief autobiography.

The *Captain* still being unserviceable, Nelson remained aboard the *Irresistible*, being despatched early in March with two other sail-of-the-line in quest of the Viceroy of Mexico, who was reputed to be on his way home to Spain with three sail-of-the-line escorting a large convoy of treasure ships. The idea of overcoming their escort and capturing a wealth of gold, silver, and emeralds from the rich mines of Spanish America inspired Nelson, just as it had inspired Drake in earlier days. But, despite an intensive search, cruising between Cape St Vincent and the African coast, the treasure train eluded him. He could not be sure whether it had managed to get into Cadiz un-observed – though he doubted this – or had temporarily taken refuge in the Canary Islands; most probably at Santa Cruz in Tenerife. He cannot have helped recalling how Blake in 1657 had fallen upon Santa Cruz, subdued the castle and forts protecting the anchorage, and sailed out again having destroyed sixteen Spanish ships including four that contained the silver upon which so much of Spain's finance depended. The thought haunted him that such an exploit could be repeated.

On his return from this abortive search he was once more ordered back into the Mediterranean. Not all the troops had been taken off from Elba on his previous expedition, nearly three thousand of them being still on the island, in an exposed situation where the arrival of even a small squadron from Toulon could have compelled their surrender. Nelson had at the back of his mind the conviction that they could be better employed elsewhere, but St Vincent required a little convincing that it was worth risking a squadron in the French-dominated inland sea for so few men. Nelson managed to prevail, sailing aboard the *Captain* once again (he described her : 'she is little better than a wreck') and having in company the *Colossus* and the 50-gun *Leander*, as well as a number of smaller ships. Their passage across the Mediterranean was uneventful, although this was more by luck than judgement, for only a north-west gale hurling out of the Gulf of Lions prevented their interception by a strong French force of four ships-of-the-line. Nelson sailed back with the convoy, and the remaining troops and stores, from the last British outpost in the Mediterranean. It was the kind of convoy that occurs often enough in times of war and which is hardly mentioned in the official histories – or only if it is unsuccessful. If Nelson's small force had run into the French ships-of-the-line they might have given a good account of themselves, but they would certainly have been captured or sunk. As it was, he reached Gibraltar safely in May and the complete British evacuation of the Mediterranean had been effected.

It was while he was at Gibraltar that a small incident occurred which, while seemingly insignificant in itself, shows that he had learned over the years some of the essentials of diplomacy. Despite the fact that on 11 April he had been compelled to write to the American and Danish Consuls at Cadiz that, in view of the war with Spain, no neutral vessels could be permitted to enter or leave Cadiz, he now came to the rescue of some American merchant ships which were at anchor in the harbour of Malaga. Nelson, who had been so adamant about the application of the Navigation Law against the Americans in the West Indies and who had also certainly regarded these former colonials with dislike, was now appealed to by the American Consul at Malaga to come to his aid. Although the United States and France were at peace, the Consul had been informed that some French privateers which were lying in the port had been instructed by their government to seize the American vessels as soon as they put to sea. Nelson immediately sent a frigate to lie off Malaga, to protect the Americans when they came out, and with orders to escort them to their required destination – whether ports on the Barbary Coast or out of the Strait of Gibraltar. To the Consul he wrote: 'I am sure of fulfilling the wishes of my Sovereign, and I hope of strengthening the harmony which at present so happily subsists between the two nations.'

On 15 May 1797, Fanny wrote to her husband from Bath, mentioning among much else:

> You will see by the papers the unhappy situation this country has been from the seamen, wishing for an increase of pay and their dislike for some particular officers. Sir Bickerton [Admiral Sir Richard Bickerton whom Nelson had known in the West Indies] . . . although the sailors have suffered him to return to his ship, still threaten his life. After they had once driven him on shore and allowed him to return he addressed them on the impropriety of their conduct, the great lenity of his Majesty etc. (it would have been well had he stopped there) but he said he knew he had a set of rascals to deal with, that expression had made them even more inveterate than ever.

Nelson had long known all about the troubles in the Channel fleet, and he was later (1803) to make a number of recommendations to St Vincent, who was then First Lord, about manning, inducements to join the Navy rather than impressment, and improvements in pay and prize money. But at the moment, with England's back against the wall, he could have no more tolerance towards indiscipline, let alone the suggestion of mutiny, than St Vincent himself. In July that year, for instance, there was a trial by court-martial of four mutineers aboard the *St George*, in which it was disclosed that they had confederates aboard four other ships (one of them being Nelson's former *Captain*). They were found guilty and sentenced to be hanged from the yardarm on the following morning, which chanced to be a Sunday. St Vincent's second-in-command, Vice-Admiral Thompson, 'presumed to censure the execution on the Sabbath' : as St Vincent reported, 'I have insisted on his being removed from the fleet immediately.'

Nelson thoroughly approved his commander-in-chief's implacable resolve that the infection which had attacked the Channel fleet, and which was brought out in ships coming from home, should be eliminated at source. He commented : 'Had it been Christmas Day, instead of Sunday, I would have executed them.' But, before this happened, and shortly after his rejoining the fleet off Cadiz, his flag was transferred to the *Theseus* which had been sent out from the Channel fleet because she had been one of the ships in which there had been mutinous conduct. St Vincent had carefully selected Nelson and his captain Ralph Miller because he knew that, though both were disciplinarians, they were humanitarians also, and that Nelson possessed that especial quality which men will invariably follow. It was not a happy appointment for Nelson or for Miller, but Nelson knew well enough how seamen's rations were underweight and sold by contractors at fraudulent prices, and he had fought before for their inalienable rights to be properly paid for the services that they had rendered. His sympathies were with the sailors – provided always that they knew their limits within the reins of decent and fair authority.

The *Theseus*, he discovered within hours of being aboard her, had left England without proper provisioning – almost destitute indeed of everything from victuals to all the necessaries for the maintenance of a ship. She had never seen any service. He was lucky at this point that, quite apart from an admirable captain in Miller, he had a number of old 'Agamemnons' with him who were able to infuse into the broken-spirited crew a sense of what it could be like to live under a good commanding officer in a 'happy ship'. Nelson was very quick in acquainting St Vincent with the fact that he would soon be calling on the commissariat for the supply of practically everything from clean-casked food to rope, and even nails.

On 24 May Nelson had transferred to the *Theseus* and by 15 June he was able to write in a letter to Fanny :

The *Theseus* was one of the ships concerned in the business at home for which scare her late Captain Aylmer left her fancying her crew intended to carry her into Cadiz and had always a party of marines under arms. I have found a more orderly set of men. A few nights ago a paper was dropped on the quarter-deck. I send you a copy.

Success attend Admiral Nelson
God bless Captain Miller we thank
them for the officers they have placed over us.
We are happy and comfortable and will shed every drop
of blood in our veins to support them, and the
name of *Theseus* shall be immortalised as high as
Captain's SHIP'S COMPANY.

Like so many essentially humane men Nelson was intensely practical: never a sentimentalist. While liberals of his own day (like ours) might bewail in words and print the plight of the sailor or the working man, Nelson *did* something. On 30 June, for instance, on blockading station aboard *Theseus* off Cadiz, he wrote in another letter to Fanny: 'With your approbation I intend my next winter's gift at Burnham to be fifty good large blankets with the letter N wove in the centre that they may not be sold. I believe they may be made for about 15 shillings of the very best quality and they will last some person or other for seven years at least, and it will not take off from anything the parish might give.'

Meanwhile the continuous blockade of Cadiz occupied his time. Nelson constantly expected that the Spanish fleet would come out, and that this would coincide with a Levanter which would boost the remainder of their ships from the Mediterranean into the Atlantic, thus making a fleet of forty sail-of-the-line; against which St Vincent could oppose no more than twenty. He had no fear of the outcome: 'We in the advance are, night and day, prepared for battle: our friends in England need not fear the event.' On 3 July, on instructions from his Commander-in-Chief, who hoped to make Cadiz so unpleasant that the enemy would come out rather than cower within the harbour walls, Nelson conducted a bombardment of the town. Although he was the most junior flag-officer, he was entrusted with half of the sail-of-the-line for the operation. This was a sign of St Vincent's trust which far outweighs all the arguments that have been raised as to his having slighted Nelson in his report on the recent battle, or having in any way undervalued his brilliant junior.

Nelson, disregarding, as usual, Fanny's urgent demands that he should not expose himself in positions which were not normally those required of an admiral, was present in a small-boat action. This was something that not even a captain would normally have engaged in, for such missions were those assigned to a lieutenant or, at the most, a commander. Nelson, of course, was never one to disguise his valour and, if the sentence from his autobiography reads like rodomontade, one must at the same time accept it as truth :

> It was during this period that perhaps my personal courage was more conspicuous than at any other part of my life. In an attack of the Spanish gun-boats I was boarded in my barge with its common crew of ten men, coxswain, Captain Fremantle and myself, by the commander of the gun-boats; the Spanish barge rowed twenty-six oars, besides officers, thirty men in the whole. This was a service hand to hand with swords, in which my coxswain, John Sykes, now no more, twice saved my life.

An anonymous correspondent who was present during this boat-to-boat affray wrote that :

> Don Miguel Tyrason, singled out the Admiral's barge; in which was John Sykes, as gallant a sailor as ever took slops from a purser, or shared his grog with his mess-mates. . . . Nelson parried a blow which would have saved him from being at the Nile. . . . It was a desperate struggle, and once we were nearly carried. John Sykes was close to Nelson on his left hand, and he seemed more concerned for the admiral's life than for his own : he hardly ever struck a blow but to save his gallant officer.

Sykes, who had stood next to Nelson on the quarter-deck of the *San Josef*, was another East Anglian (from the Fen district of Lincolnshire). He not only saved Nelson's life twice but, as the account goes,

> saw a blow descending which would have severed the head of Nelson. In that second of thought which a cool man possesses, Sykes saw that he could not ward the blow with his cutlass. . . . He interposed his own hand! We all saw it – we were witnesses to the gallant deed, and we gave in revenge one cheer and one tremendous rally. Eighteen of the Spaniards were killed, and we boarded and carried her : there being not one man left on board who was not either dead or wounded.

As a result of this action St Vincent made Sykes a warrant gunner. He was dead within a year, killed by the explosion of a cannon. Sykes goes largely unrecorded in the history of his country. But for him, England's greatest naval genius would never have survived to fight the Battles of the Nile, Copenhagen, or Trafalgar.

CHAPTER SIXTEEN

Failure

WRITING to Fanny on 14 July 1797, Nelson had some good news about prize money, adding laconically: 'I fancy you will not find it amount to much, £7 or 800. . . .' He then went on to say: 'You must not expect to hear very soon from me as I am going on a little cruise.' This, in fact, was the attack on Tenerife which had been in his mind ever since he had failed to intercept the Spanish squadron that had been reported on its way with the treasure fleet. Nelson may possibly have been familiar with Clarendon's verdict on the great Robert Blake that 'He was the first man that declined the old track. . . . He was the first man that brought ships to contemn castles on the shore, which had ever been thought very formidable, but were discovered by him to make a noise only, and to fright those who could rarely be hurt by them.' Nelson had had experience in Corsica against castles and fortifications, and had come away with a rather poor opinion of them. He had seen that a comparative handful of determined sailors and marines could make short work of such shore defences. He was just modest enough to say that 'I do not reckon myself equal to Blake', but he still felt that what Blake had done before him at Santa Cruz he could do again.

He was not confident, however, that such an operation could easily be conducted by ships alone. Nelson knew his Atlantic, and he knew how the north-east trade winds blow home upon the Canary Islands. Ships could sail into the harbour of Santa Cruz but they certainly could not rely upon a wind to blow them out. One of the reasons that Nelson had been so eager to see the withdrawal of the remaining troops of the Elba garrison was that he hoped they could be used in the operation which he proposed to St Vincent should be made against Santa Cruz. General de Burgh, however, whose men had been unemployed ever since they had been evacuated, was unwilling to allow them to take part in an enterprise where, most probably, he saw little purpose or profit for the Army, and only a great deal for the Navy – if there should chance to be a treasure ship lying in the harbour. This was natural enough, and only historians prejudiced in favour of the Navy can see it as otherwise. The object, after all, was not to capture Tenerife or any of the Canary Islands. From a military point of view the whole expedition might only be regarded as something that might possibly give the sailors and their officers some prize money. On a wider aspect, however, it should have been seen that the deprivation of the gold and silver, upon which the unstable Spanish economy relied, would greatly contribute to the weakening of France's ally and England's enemy. Neither General de Burgh nor General Charles O'Hara, who was in command of the garrison at Gibraltar, was prepared to see things in this light. Their viewpoint must not be disregarded. After all, it was only fourteen years since the Great Siege of 'The Rock' had ended; the memory of it was fresh in everyone's mind, and Nelson's admirer, Colonel Drinkwater, had helped to ensure that it was not forgotten. If Gibraltar was yet again to be besieged, it was the duty of the Army to see that it could resist efficiently. Furthermore, if Gibraltar were to fall, there would be little or no chance of a British fleet ever again being able to make its way into the Mediterranean. As was to appear in the following year, this was far more salient than any cutting out of treasure-ships.

Although the idea for the attack on Santa Cruz had originally been discussed between St Vincent and Nelson as early as April, it was not until July that it was finally carried out. Indeed, in view of the Army's disinclination to be involved, nothing might have come of it at all if the frigates *Lively* and *Minerve*, with Lieutenant Hardy in charge of the boats, had not carried out a neat action at the end of May. They descended on the harbour of Santa Cruz, cut out the French frigate *Mutine*, and made off safely. All this had been achieved in daylight. It seemed to indicate that a larger force, coming in at night with all the advantage of surprise, might achieve considerable success. Even so, nothing would have come of the plan if the bait had not arrived. But when it was heard that a large treasure-ship, *El Principe d'Asturias*, had reached Santa Cruz from Manila and was lying there not daring to risk the homeward passage back to Spain, the scene seemed set.

Nelson, although he had always seen the Santa Cruz expedition as a combined operation, now conceded that he thought the Navy could do it on their own, provided that he could have an additional 200 marines for the shore party. Neither he nor St Vincent can have failed to see how attractive it would be to have a solely naval success, and both had learned from the experience of Corsica that this was feasible. It would also be pleasant to wipe the eye of the military. St Vincent, for his part, did Nelson very handsomely, giving him a squadron of three fine 74s, Nelson flying his flag in the *Theseus*, with Miller as his Captain: Troubridge was in the *Culloden*, and Samuel Hood (a cousin of Lord Hood) in the *Zealous*. In addition, there were the *Leander* of 50 guns, three frigates and a cutter. What may seem strange to those familiar with modern warfare was that Captain Fremantle of the frigate *Seahorse* was allowed to take along with him his newly married wife – a strange form of honeymoon! But ordinary sailors' women were not infrequently carried on the lower deck of men-of-war – this depending upon the captain's feelings on the matter – and Mrs Fremantle, who had asked to go, was a great favourite with St Vincent.

The latter's orders to Nelson were clear and concise. He was to proceed to the island of Tenerife and capture the port of Santa Cruz. He was then to seize *El Principe d'Asturias* with all her cargo, while any enemy warships should be sunk, burned and destroyed. St Vincent concluded: 'God bless you and prosper you. I am sure you will deserve success. To mortals it is not given the power of commanding it.' Nelson's reply was: 'Ten hours shall either make me a conqueror or defeat me.' The expedition sailed in fair weather and Nelson, who had earlier written to Fanny that 'I have had flattery enough to make me vain, and success enough to make me confident', must have felt that with so fine a squadron, and captains selected by himself, he was on the eve of the greatest moment of his career. The capture of the treasure-ship would not only be a harsh blow to Spain, but would also enrich every officer and man concerned, and delight the king whom he served with such determined devotion.

Their passage southward to the Canaries was uneventful, and on 20 July at sundown, after five days at sea, they sighted the giant peak of Mount Teide rising 12,000 feet from the sea, and feathered with its usual stratum of sea-cloud. Like the other islands in the group, Tenerife was of volcanic origin, a vast upsurge standing out from the bed of the ocean, rich from its volcanic earth in the vine, the date-palm, and the sugar cane. But if the earth made it a kindly land to its Spanish inhabitants, the harbour for which Nelson and his squadron were bound was of a very different nature. Lying on the east coast of the island, Santa Cruz is on a plain, bounded by volcanic rocks. In those days it was open and unsheltered, except for a small mole. The rocks which ran down into the sea were worn smooth by the incessant pounding of the surf. The only anchorage that could be called at all safe was close inshore – under the protective guns of the forts. The island at that point is steep-to, and the land drops away rapidly into great depths.

The plan, which Nelson had carefully studied over with his captains and other officers involved, was for the three 74s to lie off out of sight, while the frigates closed the island after dark. Seamen and marines were to be landed by boats with their oars muffled by canvas, and were to make for the area to the north-east of the town near a valley known as the Lion's Mouth. Troubridge, designated 'General' in command of the land forces, was to lead them to the attack before daybreak, starting on the forts to the east, and making use of scaling ladders and other equipment that had been especially constructed for the operation. Nelson's ships-of-the-line would come in at dawn, and bring their broadsides to bear. It was hoped that with the fall of the two forts which protected Santa Cruz from the east the Governor of the city would be prepared to treat for peace. The ship's boats carrying the assault troops were to be roped together in six divisions, each in a long line so that there would be no danger of their losing one another in the darkness. Little or nothing had been left to chance, from the weapons that the men would carry to their escalading gear, and to the movements of the frigates and, subsequently, of the 74s. A bomb-vessel, the *Cacafuego* (Spanish for 'Shit-fire'), which had been added to the squadron, was to open fire on the town itself, 'the moment the Boats are discovered by a firing being made on them . . .'.

Unfortunately the only thing that could not have been accounted for, in a detailed and carefully thought-out plan, was that the wind and the sea might fail to prove co-operative. Contrary to normal conditions and expectations, the wind instead of remaining onshore blew off the land, dead in the teeth of the advancing boats, while strong currents hindered their approach and that of the frigates which were escorting them. By daybreak, when Nelson with his 74s advanced to make their ominous threat against a town whose eastern forts should have already been taken, it was seen that the boats had not yet been able to get their troops ashore. There, clearly visible to even the sleepiest Spanish sentry, was the whole British squadron with lines of small boats, laden with men, clearly intended to attack their city.

It was a moment when almost any commander would have hesitated. The element of surprise, upon which the whole operation hinged, was totally lost. Some have been critical of Troubridge for not pressing on with the landing and the attack even at this moment. Lord Charles Beresford, for instance, wrote : 'But even now the British landing-party might have carried the heights which dominated the town had not Troubridge feared the responsibility of the attack.

He did not, like Nelson at St Vincent, seize his golden opportunity, but delayed to consult the rear-admiral, and when the consultation was over the opportunity had slipped from his grasp. The Spaniards crowded men upon the heights; the attack was hopeless; and the seamen were re-embarked.' The salient words here are *'might have carried the heights'*, but almost equally well – or almost certainly – might not. Men struggling ashore from open boats and under full view of an alarmed and expectant enemy are in a very poor condition to make an assault that has any likelihood of success. With the benefit of hindsight it is easy to say that Troubridge did right to return and consult with Nelson, and that a less ambitious or less self-assured commander would at this moment have called off the whole operation.

Nelson's own account goes on : 'Thus foiled in my original plan I considered it for the honour of our King and country not to give over the attempt to possess ourselves of the town, that our enemies might be convinced that there is nothing that Englishmen are not equal to. . . .' Nelson's experience of the Spaniards at sea had given him no good reason to respect them, but he had never encountered them ashore – except briefly in Nicaragua. He was unaware what magnificent fighting soldiers the Spaniards could be, and how – in those days – their colonial outposts were often manned by their best troops. Any immediate fresh attempt was, in any case, foiled by the weather, and the squadron withdrew. For two days the British were forced to stand off the land, two days in which the Spaniards, now thoroughly alerted, had plenty of time to make their preparations against any renewed attempt at invasion. It was not until the evening of 24 July that Nelson was able to get his ships back into position, coming to anchor at 5.30 p.m. about two miles to the north of the town. His intention now was for the landing to be made on the mole itself, from which point the men would make straight for the town square of Santa Cruz. This time he himself would be in one of the boats and lead the attack.

Nelson was far from unaware of the dangers involved in this second attempt (he himself had made his will) and he was very disturbed when Josiah, now a lieutenant, begged to be allowed to accompany him. 'Should we both fall, Josiah,' he said, 'what would become of your poor mother? The care of the *Theseus* falls to you; stay, therefore, and take charge of her.' Josiah was adamant. 'Sir, the ship must take care of herself. I will go with you tonight, if I never go again.' Unwillingly Nelson acceded. The Spaniards, meanwhile, seeing the British ships anchored as if their intention was, as before, to attack the forts to the east of the town, had despatched troops in that direction. They were not so ignorant of the science of war, however, as not to realise that this might be no more than a feint on the part of the British, and leave the central defences of Santa Cruz undermanned.

While waiting for complete darkness, which could not be expected in that latitude in July until close on midnight, Nelson and his captains dined aboard the *Seahorse* with Mrs Betsy Fremantle as their hostess. Whatever the private anxieties of these officers and her husband may have been, they were certainly in no way communicated to Betsy. She was to record in her diary : 'As the taking of this place seemed an easy and almost sure thing, I went to bed after they had gone apprehending no danger to Fremantle.' As soon as it grew dark enough for their movements not to be detected from the shore the seamen and marines, numbering about 700 in all, began to board the boats that rose and fell alongside the ships in the long Atlantic swell. The cutter *Fox* embarked a further 180, while a Spanish merchantman which had been captured that dawn took another 80. The orders were clear enough : they would attack in six divisions, with Nelson leading the centre, land at the mole, and make straight for the town square.

The heavy sea that was now running helped to conceal the boats' approach, and it was not until they were within half-gunshot of the mole that they were sighted labouring out of the darkness. All hell now broke loose, the bells of the town ringing, the Spaniards everywhere running to arms, and the cannon that commanded the approaches opening up with canister and grapeshot. In the wind, darkness, white-capped waves, and rain that had begun to fall, some of the boats missed the mole altogether. Among them were those containing Troubridge and Waller, who found themselves on that menacing shore in a roar of pounding surf. As their boats were overwhelmed, torn to pieces on the volcanic rocks or, in a few cases, managed to turn about and get seaward, rockets began to illuminate the night sky. In every respect the British – which means above all Nelson – had underestimated their enemies.

Troubridge, who has been censured by some for his previous reluctance to take action without consulting his Admiral, was among the small band who actually managed to get ashore and, although most of the special gear such as scaling ladders was lost in the stormy landing, he gathered together the remnants of his men. They, and they alone, crossed the wind-and-rain-swept terrain. He and Waller with about three hundred men managed to fight their way into the piazza, where, in Nelson's words, 'they took possession of a convent from whence they marched against the citadel, but they found it far beyond all their power to take'. The Admiral himself, together with Captains Thompson, Fremantle, and Bowen, had found his way correctly to the mole which was, of course, the area that the Spanish garrison had long ago decided was the most important outpost of Santa Cruz. Not only had they had their guns trained upon the mole, but they had also stationed musketeers in every house or situation that commanded the approach. The cutter *Fox*, inevitably more conspicuous than the ship's boats, was singled out for cannon fire. Struck between wind and water, she went down taking with her her captain and nearly all the ship's complement.

The one redeeming feature, from the British point of view, about the utter débâcle of that night was the competence of their seamen. It was little short of astounding that they managed to get so many boats to the right place and, despite the bursting surf, to land as many men as they did. In fact, the leading division in which Nelson was present managed, in the face of all the fire, to land sufficient men to overwhelm the immediate defenders of the mole and spike the cannons that were sited on it. Further than that they could not go, for the Spanish defences beyond were far too strong and well-organised. Nelson's report sums up the situation : '. . . such a heavy fire of musketry and grape shot was kept up from the citadel and houses at the head of the mole that we were nearly all killed and wounded'.

Among those wounded was Nelson himself who, in the act of drawing the sword which had been a present to him from Captain Maurice Suckling, was hit in the right arm. There are two accounts of how it happened, one stating that he was stepping out of the boat on to the mole, and the other that he had already landed and was leading the charge towards the guns. In any event, it is clear that he was wounded within seconds of his boat coming alongside and that, although conscious enough (under the immediate anaesthesia of pain) to transfer his sword to his left hand, he was from that moment on no longer in command of the action. It was well that Fanny's son was with him on that night. Josiah was largely instrumental in saving his step-father's life. Helped by one of the crew he got Nelson laid down safely in the boat, took a scarf from around his neck and applied a simple tourniquet. Nelson's arm was so shattered that there was nothing for it but to withdraw him from the battlefield. The 'Brigadier' had fought his last campaign ashore.

CHAPTER SEVENTEEN

Aftermath

A SEAMAN named Lovel tore up his shirt and made a simple sling for the Admiral's arm. In the darkness, the general confusion, the thunder of guns, and with most of the boat's crew advanced along the mole with the other attackers, it was difficult to find hands enough to get the boat manned and under way. When Josiah Nisbet had finally found a scratch crew, the night was torn apart by the sinking of the cutter *Fox*, the thunder of the cannonade being sufficient to arouse Nelson from his semi-coma to order the boat's crew to put to the assistance of any survivors. He knew already that he must lose the arm. He knew already that the whole attack had been a failure. The main assault up the mole had been stopped and, even though the Spaniards had suffered casualties and some of the guns been spiked, the British had not been able to advance any further. What he did not know was that Troubridge and his party, who had landed in the wrong place, were to make their way into the square and – if they had had the assistance expected from the main landing force – might possibly have taken Santa Cruz.

From now on, and until the end of his days, he would live with pain. The loss of his eye had been something that he had accepted as stoically as he accepted most things. But the loss of the arm was always to remind him of failure. He had said earlier that he would return from the expedition either crowned with cypress or with laurel but, in effect, he returned with neither. Over-confidence had betrayed him. Midshipman Hoste, that faithful correspondent to his parents, who had been with Nelson since the days in the *Agamemnon*, recorded:

At two in the morning Admiral Nelson returned on board, being dreadfully wounded in the right arm. I leave you to judge my situation, when I beheld our boat approach with him, who I may say has been a second father to me, his right arm dangling by his side, while with the other he helped himself to jump up the ship's side, and with a spirit that astonished every one, told the surgeon to get his instruments ready, for he knew he must lose his arm, and that the sooner it was off the better.

Fanny Nelson's memorandum on the events of that night based on her son's recollections was that :

When the boat reached the side of the ship Nisbet called out 'Tell the surgeon the Admiral is wounded and he must prepare for amputation', upon which they offered to let down the chair. Sir H. Nelson said 'No, I have yet my legs and one arm,' and he walked up the side of the ship, Lieut. N. keeping so close that in case he had slipped he could have caught him.

On getting on the quarter deck the officers as usual saluted him by taking off their hats, which compliment Nelson returned with his left hand as if nothing had happened.

There were two surgeons aboard the *Theseus*, Thomas Eshelby and Louis Remonier, the latter a French Royalist refugee. Eshelby was the ship's official surgeon and Remonier was his assistant. Eshelby's journal records that Nelson had a 'Compound fracture of the right arm by a musket ball passing through or a little above the elbow, an artery divided : the arm was immediately amputated and opium afterwards given.' There was no general anaesthetic in those days, the wounded sometimes being given a tot of rum or a leather pad to bite on during the operation itself. John Masefield in his account of *Sea Life in Nelson's Time* has perhaps the clearest distillation from varying sources of exactly what it was like in a ship's cockpit when the wounded were brought in : 'It was the strict, inviolable rule, that a wounded man should take his turn. The first brought down was the first dressed. No favour was shown to any man, were he officer or swabber. The rule was equitable, but not without its disadvantages. Many men were so torn with shot or splinter that they bled to death upon the sail [laid over the operating platforms] long before the surgeon worked his way round to them.'

In Nelson's case, of course, the ship was not in action and at that moment he was almost the only wounded man aboard the *Theseus*. (He is reported to have said, when asked if he wanted the arm preserved, 'Throw it into the hammock with the brave fellow that was killed beside me.') The other wounded would come later to their various ships, among them Betsy Fremantle's husband who also, like

Nelson, was hit in the right arm, although in his case amputation was not necessary. Silk ligatures were used to tie up the arteries of Nelson's arm and were left long; the second ligature probably included the median nerve as well as the artery. This was to cause Nelson a great deal of pain, and was not to come away until the December of that year. The surgeon also recorded of him that during the night he 'rested pretty well and quite easy. Tea, soup and sago. Lemonade and Tamarind drink.' While undergoing the amputation in the cockpit of the *Theseus* Nelson noticed the cold – and the coldness of the knife itself. Later he was to issue orders that portable stoves should be installed in the cockpits of ships, and also that there should be a kid of hot water so that the surgeons could warm their saws and knives before operating. This was done not with the idea of sterilising the instruments – something unknown at that time – but so that some of the shock of the cold metal should be obviated. Thomas Eshelby was subsequently paid £36 for amputating Nelson's arm and for further attendance upon him, while his assistant, Louis Remonier, received £25 4s 0d. The arm was to require a great deal of further attention by doctors in Bath and London when he went there to recuperate.

Meanwhile, despite the success of Troubridge and his small company getting into the main square of Santa Cruz, the expedition was in ruins. As Troubridge's own account has it: 'As the boats were all stove, and I saw no possibility of getting more men on shore, the ammunition wet, and no provisions, I sent Captain Hood with a flag of truce to the Governor, to declare, "I was prepared to burn the town, which I should immediately put in force, if he approached one inch further." ' One can only admire his spirit, but Troubridge knew as well as the Governor did that, with his few hundred men opposed against about 8,000 Spanish troops and well-placed gun sites, his position was hopeless. The Governor, however, was willing to accord the honours of war to this brave but misguided enemy. His terms were handsome in the extreme. The British might embark with all their arms aboard their boats and, if they had not enough of their own, he himself would lend them some, provided that neither they nor the ships lying off committed any further action against the town. Don Juan Gutierrez had seen his plans for the defence of Santa Cruz so perfectly put into practice that he could well afford the luxury of old-time courtesy. Gentlemanly to the last he directed that, after an exchange of prisoners, any of the British wounded who were unable to be transported back to their ships might be accommodated in the town hospitals, while the ships might send boats ashore to purchase any provisions they wanted. He himself provided a liberal amount of wine and bread 'to refresh the people'. Before he left the island Nelson, in some attempt to repay his generosity, asked the Governor if he would kindly accept a cask of English beer and a cheese. The memory of that fateful night is still preserved in the church of Nuestra Señora de la Concepción in Santa Cruz where a number of British ensigns captured from the boats serve as legitimate spoils of war – and a reminder of Nelson's defeat.

The squadron remained offshore for three days after the abortive attack on Tenerife – three days in which to tend their wounded, bury their dead, and trade for fresh provisions with the indulgent enemy. They had lost seven officers, among them Captain Bowen of the frigate *Terpsichore*, 139 seamen and marines killed, and a further five officers and one hundred other ranks wounded : roughly a quarter of the original landing force. Nelson, suffering acute pain from his amputation and possibly suspecting that he might not survive it, was anxious to see that Fanny's son Josiah was not forgotten. His famous letter to St Vincent written with the left hand three days after the disaster is quite explicit :

I am become a burthen to my friends, and useless to my country; but by my letter wrote the 24th, you will perceive my anxiety for the promotion of my son-in-law, Josiah Nisbet. When I leave your command, I become dead to the world; I go hence, and am no more seen. If from poor Bowen's loss, you think it proper to oblige me, I rest confident you will do it; the Boy is under obligations to me, but he repaid me by bringing me from the Mole of Santa Cruz. I hope you will be able to give me a frigate, to convey the remains of my carcase to England. God bless you, my dear Sir, and believe me, your most obliged and faithful, Horatio Nelson.

You will excuse my scrawl, considering it is my first attempt.

Since it was only three days after he had had his right arm amputated 'very high, near the shoulder', it is remarkable enough. Both style and script may ramble a little but the Admiral, even at this nadir of his fortunes, remained as solid as a piece of salt-seasoned oak. His request that Josiah receive promotion was noted by St Vincent, who made him a commander. 'Pretty quick promotion,' commented Hoste, who knew Josiah well, and had observed from close quarters that Fanny's son was singularly lacking in those qualities which Nelson would have liked to find in him. Hoste himself, however, was to profit from the disaster of that night for the death of his great friend Lieutenant John Weatherhead also brought him promotion, although, as he wrote in a letter home, 'Admiral Nelson gave me a commission to act as Lieutenant in his vacancy; happy would it have made me, had it been in any other.'

The Fortunate Islands, as the ancients had termed the Canary group on account of their indulgent climate and rich volcanic soil, had been singularly unfortunate for the British. The failure of the expedition can be laid only at Nelson's door. Not having achieved his surprise attack, he had then made the tactical error of attempting a frontal assault on a well-defended position, with under a thousand men – landing from open boats direct in the teeth of shore batteries. 'My pride suffered,' Nelson was to write. The parson's son should have known the Proverb, 'Pride goeth before destruction, and an haughty spirit before a fall.' Meanwhile, as the squadron struggled north, the wind which had refused to drive them to their destination now blew as it should have done before, north-east and dead in their teeth. Nelson's servant Tom Allen looked after his sick master with the attention and care of a loving woman. He even arranged a cord leading from Nelson's bunk which he attached to his own collar when he himself was turned in, so that the Admiral had only to twitch it with his left hand and Allen would spring awake and see what the sick man needed. Meanwhile aboard the *Seahorse* the eighteen-year-old Betsy Fremantle was tending her husband who had a bad flesh wound in his right arm. It required constant dressing and for some weeks it remained a case of touch-and-go whether he also would not have to endure an amputation.

On 16 August the squadron came in sight of St Vincent and the blockading fleet off Cadiz. Nelson immediately sent a boat across : 'I rejoice at being once more in sight of your Flag, and with your permission will come on board the *Ville de Paris* [a French prize to which St Vincent had earlier shifted his flag] and pay you my respects. . . . A left-handed Admiral will never again be considered as useful, therefore the sooner I get to a very humble cottage the better, and make room for a better man to serve the State. . . .' St Vincent was full of sympathy for his brilliant junior who had failed so signally on this occasion : 'Mortals cannot command success,' he reiterated. 'You and your Companions have certainly deserved it, by the greatest degree of heroism and perseverance that ever was exhibited. I grieve for the loss of your arm, and for the fates of poor Bowen and Gibson, with the other brave men who fell so gallantly. I hope you and Captain Fremantle are doing well; the *Seahorse* shall waft you to England the moment her wants are supplied. . . . Give my love to Mrs Fremantle. I will salute her and bow to your stump tomorrow morning, if you will give me leave.'

Hardly had the *Theseus* dropped anchor than Tom Allen was instructed to get his master into his coat : he was going straight across by boat to St Vincent that very afternoon. So much for the letters to his Commander-in-Chief, to Fanny, and to William Suckling about 'humble cottages' and 'a hut to put my mutilated carcase in' ! The fact was that Nelson was as eager as ever to show that he was still hale and active, and would in due course be available for further duty. St Vincent, who may possibly have expected a man physically ruined and morally at low ebb, was impressed. He reported in a letter to the First Lord that Nelson 'dined with me, and I have very good ground for hope he will be restored to the service of his King and Country'.

Four days later, the *Seahorse* being ready for sea, Horatio Nelson joined her, bringing with him his Burnham Thorpe manservant, Tom Allen, his surgeon, Mr Eshelby, and a number of other sick and wounded homeward bound. Betsy Fremantle recorded that he 'is quite stout', an expression hardly applicable to Nelson, 'but I find it looks shocking to be without one arm. He is in great spirits.' She too had her own concerns, not only about the state of her husband's arm (which did not seem to be healing properly), but because she had just realised she was pregnant. This was something Eshelby confirmed, and morning sickness hardly went well with the quick leap of a frigate through the Biscay seas. Nelson, despite the constant pain in his stump, was cheerful enough as long as the wind proved fair, but when it turned foul he proved fractious and irritable – 'a very bad patient'. Meanwhile the sick and wounded below decks did not add any cheer to the atmosphere or suggest a happy return to 'England, Home and Beauty'. Nelson confessed himself 'very indifferent'. The man whom Eshelby and Tom Allen tended was now to all outward appearance the Nelson of legend, the face familiar from so many portraits. His once sandy hair was now white, the sightless eye (though indistinguishable from his good one) necessitated his turning his head if addressed from the right-hand side, and the right sleeve of his jacket was empty. It was only his vitality that impressed, and his enthusiasm and deep knowledge when it came to professional matters. Other than that, despite Betsy's description, he was never 'stout' – or had not been since those faraway East India days – while his 5 foot $5\frac{1}{2}$ inch frame was only kept from insignificance by the fact that his back was still as straight as when his father had made the children sit erect so that their backbones did not touch the chairs. The habit of command was evident in the face, in the set of the jaw, while the distinct, arching eyebrows retained their brown colouring. The mouth, which lifted slightly at the corners, was well-moulded with a full, somewhat sensual,

lower lip that belied the austerity of the rest of the Admiral's appearance. There was, though, and all who came in contact with him –
having searched vainly for other remarkable features – remarked upon
it, a kind of electric quality. The 'radiant orb' which he had seen all
those years ago, while it still beckoned him, cast a light around him.
Despite the pain from his arm – with which she was soon to become
sadly familiar – he wrote cheerfully to Fanny :

> As to my health, it never was better; and now I hope soon to
> return to you; and my Country, I trust, will not allow me any
> longer to linger in want of that pecuniary assistance which I have
> been fighting the whole war to preserve to her. But I shall not be
> surprised to be neglected and forgot, as probably I shall no longer
> be considered as useful. However, I shall feel rich if I continue to
> enjoy your affection. The cottage is now more necessary than
> ever . . . I am fortunate in having a good surgeon on board; in
> short, I am much more recovered than I could have expected. I beg
> neither you nor my father will think much of this mishap : my
> mind has long been made up to such an event. God bless you, and
> believe me Your most affectionate husband HORATIO NELSON.

On Friday, 1 September, the *Seahorse* dropped anchor at Spithead.
It was raining, the wind was squally, and the weather was unsuitable
for Betsy Fremantle to go ashore in an open boat with her husband.
But Nelson was all fever and impatience to leave the ship, strike his
admiral's flag, and get to Bath to see Fanny and his father. Tom
Allen had his master's cases and gear all ready, for he was to accompany Nelson on his visit while his surgeon was left behind to deal with
his other duties. On a grey day, so typical of the Channel and of
Portsmouth, Rear-Admiral Horatio Nelson, K.B., set foot on shore
in England for the first time in over four years.

He was to receive a hero's welcome. Just as England had needed a
victory at the time of the Battle of Cape St Vincent, now the populace
badly needed a figure around whom they could weave their webs of
fantasy and of hope. The disaster of Tenerife was not made light of
in the papers, the total loss of the cutter *Fox* figuring prominently in
the columns, but – curiously enough perhaps – the author of the
disaster was excluded from blame. Nelson, with his one eye and one
arm, was taken into the public heart. The process of mythologising
had begun. The same thing had happened to Drake after the defeat
of the Armada, but that at least had been a victory. Nelson, it was
true, had the astonishing success of Cape St Vincent behind him, and

his 'patent bridge' had been widely celebrated, but he returned now as the author of a dismal failure. He was not seen as such, but as the gallant commander who had done all he could to make a success of what was intrinsically faulty planning on the part of the Earl of St Vincent, or even Dundas, the Secretary for War, or (for the politically minded) of William Pitt. No blame was allowed to attach to the man who had actually been responsible. His wounds absolved him from all criticism. As a Bath paper put it : 'The Rear-Admiral, who was received at Portsmouth on the 1st with a universal greeting, reached Bath on Sunday evening in good health and spirits to the great joy of his Lady and Venerable Father. . . .'

He was *not* in good health, as Fanny was soon to find out when she had to learn from her doctor, Mr Nicholls, how to clean and dress the stump of an arm that was swollen and inflamed, and from which one ligature refused to part. Fanny who had consistently advised caution on his part, and whose letters had always been full of intense concern about his health and safety, was now faced with an unpleasant task resulting from his constant determination to be in at the heart of the action – wherever it was. Only opium could secure him a night's sleep. But Fanny now had in this wounded and weakened man the child that they had never managed to have together, and her maternal instincts were satisfied in looking after him, cutting up his food, and helping him to dress and undress. Throughout the years that they had been parted, their letters had been full of tenderness and affection : it can never be doubted that this was no pretence on either side. They were to all intents and purposes a model married couple, whose friendship had perhaps deepened because they only had each other. Now Fanny was to add to her other duties and responsibilities that of writing many of Nelson's letters for him. There can, however, have been little sexual exchange between them. Nelson was far too run-down and in much too great pain from his arm, while Fanny, whose nature we can only guess at but from what little we know was probably somewhat unresponsive, found the operation of dressing his wound so repulsive as to make her husband physically unattractive. At a time which Nelson was to describe in the words 'I found my domestic happiness perfect', the seeds of a future estrangement were inadvertently being laid.

On the recommendation of their Bath physician the Nelsons moved to London to find more expert opinion on the condition of the arm, which was still very painful and inflamed. Horatio's brother Maurice found them rooms in Bond Street where a succession of doctors and surgeons examined the stump and the persistent ligature, the final conclusion being that it was best to leave all to time and nature to heal. In view of the limited surgical knowledge of the day Nelson was fortunate that a further operation was not attempted. It was while they were in London that news was received of Duncan's victory over the Dutch at Camperdown, a victory which resulted in the annihilation of their fleet; something which caused Nelson to exclaim that he would have given his other arm to have been present. He had long ago seen that the inconclusive type of action which had characterised so much of the war to date, and indeed naval warfare in the past, was not what was required in this struggle of life and death between Britain and revolutionary France. Annihilation was to be his watchword.

On 13 October when the news reached the capital, all London, in the fashion of the time, was illuminated, flambeaux being lit outside the grand houses and state buildings, while people had their curtains drawn back and candelabra placed on tables in their windows to show their pride and pleasure in a victory which had done much to remove the threat of invasion from England's shores. The Nelsons had retired early and the windows of 141 Bond Street were all darkened, in marked contrast to those of their neighbours. Nelson lay in a fitful feverish sleep induced by opium when a group of roisterers, who were breaking the windows of houses which were not celebrating the victory, hammered on the door to demand an explanation. On being informed that the hero of St Vincent, the badly-wounded leader of the Tenerife expedition, was staying there and must not be disturbed, they withdrew with the words, 'You will hear no more from us tonight.'

During these weeks in London Nelson had pursued his usual active life, calling constantly at the Admiralty, visiting Lord Hood at Greenwich Hospital as well as his old 'sea-daddy' William Locker who also lived in the Hospital. It was Locker who prevailed on a never very reluctant Nelson (when it came to sitting for portrait painters) for another picture, to succeed the one which he had by Rigaud. This resulted in the commissioning of the little-known Lemuel Abbott who was inspired to produce one of the best, and certainly the best-known, of all representations of Nelson. Meanwhile engravers, working from the Rigaud portrait and changing Nelson's rank from Captain to Admiral and taking away his right arm, were busy producing for the general public the popular image that was to stir the imagination during the years that were to follow. Some weeks before Camperdown Nelson had been presented at a levée to the monarch whom he served with such diligence and devotion all his life, during which George III had invested him with the Order of the Bath. Upon the King's remarking, 'You have lost your right arm!' Nelson had replied with grace: 'But not my right hand, as I have the honour of presenting Captain Berry.'

Quite apart from the pleasure he derived from having been invested by his monarch in person, Nelson had also received the Freedom of the City of London, and had been granted a pension of £1,000 a year. This necessitated his submitting a formal statement or 'memorial' to George III, outlining the services which he had rendered during the present war. It is of the greatest interest, for it details a war record which would have been impressive even if it had not been followed by his three great victories. He had been present at four fleet and three frigate actions, six engagements against batteries, ten boat actions cutting out harbours, and in the capture of three towns. He had served ashore with the Army for four months and had been in command of the batteries during the sieges of Bastia and Calvi. He had been engaged against the enemy over one hundred and twenty times, and had been present in engagements during which 7 sail-of-the-line had been captured, 6 frigates, 4 corvettes, and 11 privateers, and about 50 merchantmen had been taken or destroyed. During the course of this service he had lost his right eye, his right arm, and been 'severely wounded and bruised in his body'. The pension which he was now awarded meant that at long last he and Fanny could think about getting themselves a home of their own for the first time. It was not quite the humble 'cottage' about which he had so often written, but 'a gentleman's house', Round Wood Farm near Ipswich in Suffolk. Here at last, it would seem, was the haven in East Anglia where he and his wife would spend their declining years. He was never to live there. Round Wood would indeed provide a home for Fanny, his father and family, but by the time he next returned to England the whole pattern of his life would have changed.

CHAPTER EIGHTEEN

The Vanguard

On the morning of 4 December 1797, something long hoped for occurred. Nelson awoke after a night's deep sleep that had been untroubled by any fevers or fancies to find that the pain in his arm had almost entirely disappeared. The surgeon was summoned and the bandages were undone, the cause of Nelson's relief being immediately evident. During the night, the central ligature which had given all the trouble and led to the inflammation and poisoning, had come away, leaving a stump that would now heal easily. It was close on four and a half months since he had been hit in the arm at Santa Cruz. Only four days later he was to write to Captain Berry, who was at Norwich and engaged to marry a Norfolk girl : 'If you mean to marry, I would recommend your doing it speedily, or the to be Mrs Berry will have very little of your company; for I am well, and you may be expected to be called for every hour.'

He had been promised the 80-gun *Foudroyant* which was due to be launched in January but, her completion being delayed, he had settled quickly for the 74-gun *Vanguard*. She was lying at Chatham and, as he reported to his former captain, Ralph Miller, was to be 'well manned and soon'. Despite his anxiety to be back aboard ship again and once more involved in the war, he did not forget his other duties. The clergyman at St George's, Hanover Square, London, received a request for a Thanksgiving : 'An Officer desires to return thanks to Almighty God for his perfect recovery from a severe Wound, and also for the many mercies bestowed upon him.'

The *Vanguard* was ten years old and had been built at Deptford on the Thames in the dockyard that had originally been established by King Henry VIII. The first distinguished ship to bear her name had seen service against the Spanish Armada. In his *Vanguard* Nelson was soon to write another chapter in British naval history. Since she was delayed in her completion and in her working up for foreign

168

service, he had time for a further visit to Bath. Round Wood was not yet ready for occupation so to Bath, which suited both Fanny and his ageing father, he went with all the confidence of a man recovered in health and sure of his future. As early as September 1797, when Nelson was very far from recovered of his amputation, St Vincent had written to Lord Spencer at the Admiralty: 'I beg that Admiral Nelson may be sent to me.' Lord Minto (formerly Sir Gilbert Elliot, the Scots Viceroy of Corsica, with whom Nelson had got on so well) was also to press upon Spencer that, if the Mediterranean was to be considered once again as a field for British activities, the man to be in command of them was undoubtedly Horatio Nelson. 'He is as well acquainted with the Mediterranean', he remarked, 'as your lordship is with this room we are sitting in.' Both men knew that something was brewing in France and, since England was the only enemy left, whatever it was must be a campaign against their country's interests. The fact that a great number of troops and ships were being accumulated in the French ports of the Mediterranean suggested they must be designed for that theatre. Further than that nothing for sure was known, and there remained a number of alternative destinations – the Kingdom of Naples and Sicily, Greece and its islands, with Constantinople as the main target, Egypt or the Levant, with a view to threatening India, or even Gibraltar, whose fall would close the Mediterranean finally and forever to the British and permit the French full access to that fortress-harbour which was the key to the inland sea.

In March 1798, having heard from his Captain, Berry, that the *Vanguard* was ready at Portsmouth, Nelson and Fanny went up to London. He attended a levée on 14 March, and took leave of his sovereign, while he was also invited to the Spencers' before taking up his new command. Lord Spencer and his wife had had good opportunity for meeting, and assessing, their one-eyed, one-armed Admiral during his convalescent days in London and had formed their own conclusions – Lady Spencer's at first being not at all favourable. 'The first time I saw him', she was to recall, 'was in the drawing-room of the Admiralty, and a most uncouth creature I thought him. He was just returned from Tenerife, after having lost his arm. He looked so sickly, it was painful to see him, and his general appearance was that of an idiot; so much so, that when he spoke, and his wonderful mind broke forth, it was a sort of surprise that riveted my whole attention.' Her husband had long known from his record that he was far from 'an idiot'. Lady Spencer, however, having been so agreeably relieved to find that this frail, suffering (and painful to regard) small man possessed intellectual brilliance, even forgave him for upsetting her seating arrangements at dinner. He asked for his wife to be allowed to sit next to him, saying that he saw so little of her that he would not willingly lose a moment of her company. In reality, of course, this had been largely due to the fact that he had not yet acquired the dexterity to cut up his own food, which Fanny did for him. Lady Spencer, having observed his difficulties, had a table instrument made for him (now to be seen at Lloyd's of London), which was a combined knife and fork in gold, with a steel cutting edge. Nelson constantly used it.

On 29 March he hoisted his blue flag at the mizzen of the *Vanguard* at Spithead. After a certain amount of confusion about his personal stores and belongings, Tom Allen no doubt silently blaming her Ladyship for neglect and Nelson exchanging messages with his wife ashore about absence of silk stockings and so forth, the Admiral could grow used to his surroundings. The wind blew foul, dead from the west, and Nelson wrote to Fanny that 'as I am now fixed on board, it is my intention not to move out of the ship, to which I begin to be reconciled'. The letters went back and forth, but it was not until 7 April that he was able to get a last note ashore to say: 'The wind is fair and we are getting under sail.' He went on, 'I pray God to bless you and soon to send us peace when believe me nothing in this world can exceed the pleasure I shall have in returning to you.' The loving affection expressed in both their letters over all the years can hardly be equalled in the known correspondence of any married couple. Meanwhile, on 30 March, Lord Spencer had written to St Vincent that he was very happy to be sending him Sir Horatio Nelson, 'because I have reason to believe that his being under your command will be agreeable to your wishes'. On 1 May, the day after he had joined St Vincent's flag on the familiar blockading station off Cadiz, the latter was to write back to the First Lord that '. . . the arrival of Admiral Nelson has given me new life : you could not have gratified me more than in sending him, his presence in the Mediterranean is so very essential'. All was now set for one of the most dramatic moments of the war – the re-entry of the British fleet into the Mediterranean.

At this moment in Nelson's life no assessment can better that of Admiral Mahan :

As the sails of the *Vanguard* dip below the horizon of England, a brief interlude begins, and when the curtain rises again, the scene is shifted, – surroundings have changed. We see again the same man, but standing at the opening of a new career, whose greatness exceeds by far even the high anticipations that had been formed for him. Before leaving England he is a man of distinction only;

prominent, possibly, among the many distinguished men of his own profession, but the steady upward course has as yet been gradual, the shining of the light . . . is still characterised by sustained growth in intensity rather than by rapid increase. No present sign so far foretells the sudden ascent to fame, the burst of meridian splendor with which the sun of his renown was soon to rise upon men's eyes, and in which it ran its course to the cloudless finish of his day.

At the time when the *Vanguard* joined St Vincent's fleet off Cadiz there was only one friend left to Britain in the whole of Europe, and that was Portugal; a somewhat timorous neutral who might be expected to fall into the enemy camp if France's successes continued. Without the use of the Tagus for her fleet Britain would have had nowhere except Gibraltar, and 'The Rock' itself was heavily menaced by Spain. Elsewhere the revolutionary tide rolled unchecked over the continent. Austria had fallen in 1797, her defeat being largely attributed to the withdrawal of the British fleet from the Mediterranean. Lord Malmesbury's peace mission, on which St Vincent among many others had placed great hopes, had broken down at Lille after the death of Catherine the Great of Russia, for the French felt that they had little to fear from her successor, the half-mad Paul I. Napoleon, who had been appointed by the Directory to command the army of the invasion of England, had come to the conclusion by February 1798 that this was impossible because 'we shall not for many years acquire the control of the seas'. Instigated by Napoleon, the Directory had looked eastwards. He had suggested that the fleet under Vice-Admiral Brueys should descend upon Malta, that linch-pin of Mediterranean strategy, and seize the island from the Knights. The Order of St John had long been in a state of decline and, under their German Grand Master von Hompesch, was now completely apathetic, many of the French knights even being in correspondence with revolutionary France. With Malta as a base, with Sardinia and Corsica safe behind them, with the British absent from the inland sea, the way to Egypt and the East lay open to the army of France. India would be at their mercy, the Ottoman Empire would either remain their ally or would easily fall, and with the whole of the Mediterranean secure and the riches of the East to support him Napoleon could return 'and give the enemy its death-blow'. Such was the grand strategy at which the British could only vaguely guess, but one thing they did know for sure was that the preparation of a vast armament was going ahead in southern France, and that the fleet at Toulon and Genoa was being readied for some large-scale expedition.

It was to ascertain what was going on at Toulon as well as to keep an eye on the eastern Mediterranean generally that St Vincent despatched Nelson from the fleet, in the latter's own words 'with a small squadron; not on any fighting expedition . . .'. He added for Fanny's benefit, 'England will not be invaded this summer. Bonaparte is gone back to Italy, where 80 thousand are embarking for some expedition.' He reached Gibraltar with two other 74s in company, the *Orion* under Sir James Saumarez, and the *Alexander* under Captain Ball, together with four frigates and a sloop. The hospitality of the military in that strange limestone garrison was more than willingly extended to Sir Horatio, especially since he came with the news that once more the fighting ships of England were going to pass through the Strait and invade a Mediterranean that had seemed on the point of becoming no more than a French lake. On 8 May, having waited until dark so that no Spanish eyes should remark their eastward route, the squadron set course for the Gulf of Lions with the intention of running along the French coast to Toulon. In his final orders to the squadron Nelson had stressed the importance of the ships maintaining close contact and not getting separated at any cost. The weather, which continued good for several days, was to play him foul on 20 May – the very day after Napoleon had sailed from Toulon with over 30,000 troops in 300 transports, together with an escort of thirteen line-of-battle ships and seven frigates. A great game of hide-and-seek was soon to begin in the eastern Mediterranean.

The disaster which struck the *Vanguard* and its effect upon Nelson is best told in his own words to Fanny :

Figure to yourself a vain man, on Sunday evening at sunset, walking in his cabin with a Squadron about him, who looked up to their Chief to lead them to glory . . . Figure to yourself this proud, conceited man, when the sun rose on Monday morning, his Ship dismasted, his fleet dispersed, and himself in such distress, that the meanest Frigate out of France would have been a very unwelcome guest. But it has pleased Almighty God to bring us to a safe Port, where, although we are refused the rights of humanity, yet the *Vanguard* will in two days get to sea again, as an English Man-of-war.

What had happened was that, shortly after sunset, the wind which had blown from the north-west the previous day, driving the British off their station on the French coast, suddenly roared up again in one of those gales 'which no canvas will withstand'. The Mediterranean, as many sailors have found, is a fickle sea, the wind in summer usually being too light for all but the smallest and fastest of sailing boats or else, with little warning, storming up to gale force and bringing with it as suddenly as it comes a short, dangerous, and breaking sea. (Being excessively saline and almost uncorrected by tides or tidal currents, the sea's surface stirs up far more quickly than that of an ocean.) Berry had quickly got the *Vanguard* snugged down to a main storm-staysail, but the sea which built up, coupled with the violence of the wind, caused the ship to roll her masts out. 'On Monday at half past one A.M.,' in Nelson's words, 'the main top-mast went over the side, as did the mizen-top-mast soon afterwards . . . about half past three o'clock the foremast went in three pieces, and the bowsprit was found to be sprung in three places.' In the darkness and the roar of the storm the squadron had lost contact with one another and no signals could be exchanged. Dawn found the *Vanguard* a wallowing semi-hulk some 75 miles south of the islands of Hyères, with the *Alexander*, *Orion*, and the frigate *Emerald* still in company, the others lying to under bare poles. Throughout the day, during which the gale continued to blow as hard as ever, the *Vanguard* and the three still present out of the squadron laboured south-easterly in the direction of Sardinia. Over the next night the *Emerald* parted company; no doubt, being so much smaller, she was forced to heave to and her rate of drift was not so great as that of the 74s. It was not until Tuesday afternoon that the wind fell sufficiently for Ball in the *Alexander* to pass a tow to his disabled chief.

Nelson was now to be heavily beholden to a man whom, all those years before in France, he had dismissed as a coxcomb for wearing epaulettes in the French style. He was to find in Ball one of his greatest friends, and one of the closest of the 'Band of Brothers'. Ball, who was to become the first governor of Malta after it was ultimately recaptured from the French, was a handsome man who was as intellectually distinguished as he was brave in action. Years later, when Samuel Taylor Coleridge was to go to Malta and become secretary to Sir Alexander Ball (as he had then become), the poet was to write of the seaman that his stay with Ball was 'in many respects the most memorable and instructive period of my life'. This was the man whose seamanship now saved Nelson's crippled vessel, towing her to within the safety of St Pietro Bay in southern Sardinia. Here the *Vanguard* was able to drop anchor in the lee of the rugged little island, secure from the westerly swell which had earlier very nearly had her on the rocks. Nelson, indeed, had at one moment signalled Ball to cast off the tow, shift for himself, and leave the *Vanguard* to her fate. Ball, with a Nelsonian disregard of orders, had managed to claw offshore – a magnificent example of seamanship, seeing that he was towing a heavy, part-filled hulk (the lower deck of the flag-ship had been cleared) under totally adverse conditions. He was to oblige his Admiral even further once the crippled man-of-war was securely anchored by helping his junior Berry with advice on the repair of the damage, and by lending his warrant carpenter, an old hand who had been thirty years in the Service, to assist in the rigging of jury masts. So well was the operation effected that only four days later *Vanguard* was once more on station with *Alexander* and *Orion*, having 'a main top-mast for a fore-mast, and a top-gallant-mast for a top-mast, consequently everything else reduced in proportion'. The fact remains that, out of the three 74s to see out the gale, it was only the *Vanguard* that suffered damage – something which points to bad maintenance and, no matter whose fault this was, the responsibility must inevitably be laid upon the shoulders of her Captain.

Another event of major significance which resulted from the dis-masting of the *Vanguard* and the scattering of the squadron was that Napoleon's armada had slipped out of Toulon at the time that the British had been driven far to the south off their station. The fleet and the army destined for Egypt had passed through the Gulf of Genoa and had then headed southward between Corsica and Italy. All that Nelson knew at this juncture, after interrogating a French merchant-man out of Marseilles, was that the French expedition had sailed for an unknown destination. He still could only guess at it, and it might be anywhere from Spain (to attack Portugal), to Naples and Sicily (to overthrow the Kingdom of the Two Sicilies), or east to Egypt or even Constantinople. His frigates, in any case, had regrettably dis-appeared. He had news of them on 4 June, when the brig *Mutine* hove in sight. That stalwart friend whom he had saved in the Strait of Gibraltar, Captain Thomas Hardy, was in command. He was soon aboard to tell Nelson that the frigates had all repaired to Gibraltar, their captains being convinced that the *Vanguard* was so severely damaged that she would require the dockyard attention which only Gibraltar could provide. Frigates, the eyes of the fleet! The lack of them was to hamper him so severely over the coming weeks that Nelson no doubt resorted to that sailor-like language which pious biographers have deplored. Hardy, however, had very good news as well as bad. On 2 May an urgent message had reached St Vincent off Cadiz from the Admiralty ordering him to reinforce the Mediterranean. St Vincent, given the option of either coming in with his whole fleet or appointing an admiral in charge of a strong squadron for this purpose, had chosen Nelson. The Commander-in-Chief still felt that the Spaniards might come out and he was unwilling to abandon the blockade of Cadiz. He had chosen Nelson over the heads of two senior admirals (something which was to lead to a considerable amount of friction) and was sending him the flower of the fleet or, as he described them, 'some choice fellows of the in-shore squadron'.

On their way to join Nelson was Troubridge in the *Culloden*, that old friend whom St Vincent himself regarded as even superior to Nelson ('the very best Sea-officer in His Majesty's Service'), along with Gould in the *Audacious*, Darby in the *Bellerophon*, Peyton in the *Defence*, Foley in the *Goliath*, Westcott in the *Majestic*, Louis in the *Minotaur*, Ben Hallowell in the *Swiftsure*, Miller in the *Theseus*, and Samuel Hood in the *Zealous*. All were 74s, commanded by some of the finest officers in the Navy, and St Vincent by despatching them under Nelson's command had deprived himself of a large number of his best ships. They were also joined by the 50-gun *Leander* under Captain Thompson.

Nelson was now to be in command not of a squadron but of a fleet. His orders were explicit. He was to proceed 'in quest of the Armament preparing by the enemy at Toulon and Genoa. . . . On falling in with the said Armament, or any part thereof, you are to use your utmost endeavours to take, sink, burn, or destroy it.' St Vincent informed him that, in a private letter received from Lord Spencer, he had been told that Nelson was 'perfectly justifiable in pursuing the French Squadron to any port in the Mediterranean, Adriatic, Morea, Archipelago, or even into the Black Sea'. He added his own note of encouragement that 'thoroughly sensible of your Zeal, Enterprise, and Capacity at the head of a Squadron of ships so well appointed, manned, and commanded, I have the utmost confidence in the success of your operations'.

After sending off Hardy in the *Mutine* to look into Talamone Bay on the west coast of Tuscany south of Elba – one of the few anchorages where a large fleet could assemble – Nelson set off round the northern-most point of Corsica, Cap Corse. He wrote to Sir William Hamilton with whom he had kept up a friendly correspondence over the years asking him, in view of the good relations between Britain and the Court of Naples, for his help in ensuring water and supplies while his ships were in the Kingdom of the Two Sicilies. Sir William could do little, for King Ferdinand was naturally enough eager to preserve an apparent neutrality, much though his Queen, Sir John Acton and the British Minister Plenipotentiary might long for the defeat of the French. He, like all other Continental observers, could hardly have failed to remark what had happened at Toulon when the royalist citizens had turned to the British nor, indeed, the fate of Austria. It was clear enough that the Whale could always move seaward and abandon its friends, while the march of the Elephant was inexorably committed. *Sub rosa*, though, as later events were to show, the inclinations of Ferdinand and his advisers towards helping the British were to be implemented – though always with an outward show of unwillingness.

On 15 June, in the form of a diary letter to St Vincent, Nelson wrote that he was off the Ponza Islands some sixty miles to the north-west of Naples. The *Mutine* had rejoined with the news that Talamone Bay was empty, while a Tunisian cruiser when interrogated said that she had spoken to a Greek merchantman which reported that she had passed through the French fleet off the north-west coast of Sicily heading eastward. This was all second-hand information, though better than none, but the absence of his frigates was sorely felt. Meanwhile Nelson sent Troubridge, who 'possesses my full confidence, and has been my honoured acquaintance of twenty-five years standing', into Naples aboard Hardy's *Mutine*. The rest of the ships lay off Naples outside neutral waters while Troubridge saw Sir John Acton and Sir William Hamilton. While awaiting his return Nelson received a letter from Lady Hamilton assuring him of the best wishes of herself and the Queen of Naples in his pursuit of the French. She enclosed a letter from the Queen which she enjoined him – in high romantic vein – to kiss before returning. She ended the note in an affectionate and curiously familiar tone, seeing that she had not seen Nelson for close on five years, 'Ever yours Emma'.

Troubridge returned with one portion of his mission incomplete : he had been unable to prevail upon the Government in Naples to secure the loan of any frigates. This was hardly surprising since any such act would have severely compromised Neapolitan neutrality. Acton, however, had provided him with a credential in the King's name which enjoined all the governors of ports in Ferdinand's realms to give Nelson every necessary assistance.

On 9 June, while the British were still at sea bound for Naples, Napoleon in *L'Orient* had joined the advance guard of his fleet which had been anchored off Malta for three days. As a French observer among the Knights of St John commented : 'Malta had never seen such an enormous fleet in its waters. For miles around the sea was covered with ships of every size. Their masts looked like a huge forest.' The island surrendered with hardly even a token resistance, the armistice being signed on 11 June. Napoleon took up residence in

Valetta, the island's magnificent fortified capital, and drafted new regulations for the islanders in accordance with the ideas of revolutionary France, while the churches and the palaces were systematically plundered of their age-old treasures of silver, gold and precious stones. The conqueror, who commanded both the army and the fleet, could look round him with satisfaction. Over three centuries before the Grande Turke, Sultan Suleiman the Magnificent, had hoped 'as universal lord, from that not unpleasant rock, to look down upon his shipping at anchor in its excellent harbour'. The Knights of St John in those days had been the foremost warriors of Christendom, and the Turkish invasion had been defeated after a siege of several months. The ambition of Suleiman was achieved by Napoleon in a matter of days.

CHAPTER NINETEEN

The Hunters and the Hunted

THE quartering wind sat fairly in their sails – steady out of the north-west. They had left Naples on 18 June, and were headed southerly over the Tyrrhenian Sea for the Strait of Messina. Nelson still had no clear idea as to Napoleon's objective, and could do little more than surmise, as Sir William Hamilton had already done, that the French were bound for Malta. And Malta was the stepping-stone to Sicily.

By night off their bows to starboard 'the lighthouse of the Mediterranean', the volcanic island of Stromboli, signalled to them that they were nearing the Lipari Islands. '. . . From the deck of a vessel, a glow of red light is seen to make its appearance from time to time above the summit of the mountain; it may be observed to increase gradually in intensity, and then as gradually to die away. After a short interval the same appearances are repeated, and this goes on until the increasing light of dawn causes the phenomenon to be no longer visible.'

To port of them by day they could see the pale shores of Calabria sliding past, the inland mountains shining in the blue distance. An inhospitable shore, no ports, no anchorages even, only a few scattered villages where the fishermen hauled their boats up the beach for safety during the winter or, in the calms of high summer, let them idle at their mooring-stones. The thirteen 74s, the 50-gun *Leander*, and Hardy's brig *Mutine* swept smoothly over that historic sea, trimming their sails slightly as they altered course when the Liparis were abeam.

Nelson was in a fever of impatience. As he wrote to Sir William: 'Were I commanding a fleet attending an army which is to invade Sicily, I should say to the general, "If you can take Malta, it secures the safety of your fleet, transports, stores &c., and insures your safe retreat should that be necessary; for if even a superior fleet of the enemy should arrive before one week passes, they will be blown

178

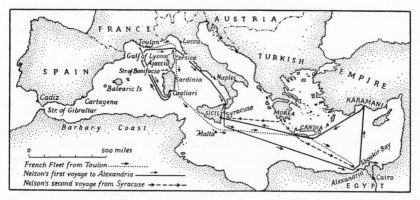

The Mediterranean Lands in 1798

leeward, and you may pass with safety . . . I repeat it, *Malta is the direct road to Sicily.*" '

The letter like others reveals Nelson's accurate appreciation of strategy. He could see, as so indeed could Bonaparte, that the island of Malta, 'the navel of the Sea', commanded the east–west trade routes as well as those north and south between Europe and North Africa. Nelson well knew, though he had not yet seen, the capabilities of the magnificent harbour of Valetta, from which the Knights of St John had operated so successfully for centuries. Nelson's words also justify his claim to be 'an old Mediterranean man'. He was well aware that in the central area of the sea the prevailing winds are north-westerly throughout the summer. The southerly wind, the unpleasantly humid sirocco, which dominates the months of spring, yields as the cooler air surges down from the north, to take the place of the hot air rising off the desert land of North Africa. A square-rigged ship, caught to the east of Malta, would have some difficulty in beating back again and, since about fifty degrees off the wind was as close as she could lay, would be 'blown to leeward'. Had Nelson in fact come across the French fleet while it was in Malta he might have had some difficulty in conducting a conclusive action. The protecting fleet and the great convoy of merchantmen were, as we know, either watering in Grand Harbour or anchored close offshore, near the city of Valetta. The British would have had to attack from the lee side and the French would have had that all-important advantage of the weather gauge.

They were now approaching the Messina Strait and, on 20 June, the finest squadron of 74s the Mediterranean had ever seen altered course to make its run down the coast of Sicily. On their port hand, where the toe of Italy jutted out into the two-mile-wide strait, gleamed the small fishing village of Scylla, its name commemorating the Homeric monster which had snatched six sailors from the open boat of Odysseus. The rocky shore held no terror for the dark oaken sides of the pursuing ships. To starboard, however, the whirlpool of Charybdis still presented a minor hazard. In 1783, fifteen years before Nelson's ships passed this way, the famous whirlpool had become greatly diminished owing to changes in the seabed following upon a great earthquake at Messina. Yet, even as late as 1824, one of Nelson's successors, Admiral Smyth, could write : 'To the undecked boats of the Rhegians, Locrians, Zancleans, and Greeks, it must have been formidable; for even in the present day small craft are sometimes endangered, and I have seen several men-of-war, and even a seventy-four-gun ship, whirled round on its surface. . . .' But now, with their fair following wind, the British vessels passed easily through the strait.

Sicily appeared peaceful. No vessels came out to meet them with news of any French invasion. The island slept under the June sun, the peak of Etna smoking lazily south of Taormina above the long fertile plain of Catania. It was from this area, as well as from other citrus-producing parts of Sicily like the Conca d'Oro behind King Ferdinand's other capital, Palermo, that the British Navy bought the lemons which provided the necessary anti-scorbutic in their diet to keep the scurvy at bay.

They passed the fishing village of Riposto, mellow beneath the seaward flanks of the great volcano, the vast empty harbour of Augusta (whose possibilities as a naval base were not appreciated until the days of Mussolini) and were down off the ancient city of Syracuse. This had once been the queen of the Mediterranean, the richest city-port in the ancient world, when Sicily had beckoned the colonising Greeks as the wealth of the New World now beckoned modern Europeans. It shimmered dusty under the sun, part of Ferdinand's bedraggled kingdom. The officers turned their telescopes on the old castle that guarded its entrance. Nothing. Only the eyes of a few sun-dazzled sentries watched their passage. Here, where the Athenian empire had finally collapsed in the fatal Syracusan expedition, no little interest was felt about this new battle for the control of the Mediterranean. It was comforting for the watchers to see that these ships flew the British ensign. It was no secret that relations between the Court of Naples and that of St James's were good – even if it was necessary to obscure the fact for fear of the French. Had it been the tricolour that flickered above the ships, it would have been a very different matter. The passage of this imposing British squadron indicated that something was definitely stirring in the central Mediterranean. Nothing had been seen of their flag since their fleet had withdrawn from the inland sea two years before. Weeks would pass before the Syracusans knew for certain what all this unexpected activity foreshadowed.

The long hump of Murro di Porco faded astern as the ships drove on to the south. Two days after leaving the Messina Strait they had their first news. Off Cape Passero, the low south-eastern point of Sicily, where only an old thirteenth-century fort watched over the end of Ferdinand's dominions, Hardy's *Mutine* which was scouting ahead sighted a foreign sail – an Italian brig. At last, after so much uncertainty, they had the news they had been waiting for; the French armada had anchored off Malta and their troops had captured the island. The brig, under a Genoese master, had left Malta the previous day – it was only seventy miles from Valetta to Passero. His report was that the French had left Malta six days before and were bound for some unknown destination.

At almost the exact time of speaking to the brig the sails of two French frigates were sighted on the far horizon. This certainly confirmed the veracity of the Genoese master, for where there were frigates there, almost inevitably, somewhere hull down and out of sight was the fleet. Once again Nelson cursed the absence of his own frigates. If he only had them now they could have been sent in chase. It was unthinkable to divert any of the ships-of-the-line to try to intercept. The enemy frigates would have two knots or more over them in the fresh wind that was blowing, and in any case would certainly only lead the British on some wild goose chase away from the prey.

Valuable, then, though the news was, there remained the lack of certainty as to the French objective. Also, although no one could know it at the time, a salient item of information was either misheard or mistranslated. The French had not left six days before, but only three. It is possible that the brig's captain said that they had *begun* to leave six days before, a quite different matter. Since the advance guard had originally appeared off Malta three days ahead of the slower main body composed of the merchant ship convoy and its escorts, they would have left in much the same manner. Napoleon, having left 4,000 men behind to garrison Valetta, did not himself leave aboard *L'Orient* until 19 June. He had a head start of the British of no more than three days – little enough when his fighting ships were tied to the slower rate of advance of the convoy.

The incident of the intercepted brig and the sighting of the frigates has often been treated as if it had no more significance than that Nelson learned the enemy had taken Malta, and had a six-day start on him for some conjectural destination. It was far more important than that. The frigates seen by the British did not fail to sight the approaching fleet. After all, that was exactly what frigates were designed for, to be the lookouts and eyes of a battle fleet. The fact that they did see and report back to Napoleon is confirmed by a letter from Louis Bonaparte, who was in the expedition, to his brother Joseph. Napoleon and Admiral Brueys now learned that, contrary to prior reports and expectations, the British had returned to the Mediterranean. Proof of this is the subsequent course taken by the French armada : a temporary diversion from their real objective which had the intended effect of throwing the hunters off the scent.

One minor puzzle remains. At a later date, after his return to Sicily, Nelson was to write to Sir William Hamilton in Naples : 'It has been said that to leeward of the two frigates off Cape Passaro was a line-of-battle ship, with the riches of Malta on board, but it was the destruction of the enemy, not riches for myself, that I was seeking. These would have fallen to me if I had had the frigates, but except the ship-of-the-line, I regard not all the riches in the world.' The ship to which Nelson here refers (although he was not to know it at the time) was clearly Brueys' flagship *L'Orient* with Napoleon on board, which had *left* Malta three days before the two frigates were sighted. It is clear that, while watering in Syracuse before the second stage of the chase, Nelson and others heard many details as to the activities of the French during their initial occupation of the island. Among them was the despoliation of churches and palaces, and in particular the looting of the great cathedral of St John in Valetta. This wealth had indeed been embarked aboard *L'Orient*, but even if she was the last in the line to leave Malta she would hardly have still been in sight on the twenty-second, when the *Mutine* spoke to the Italian brig. Here, later information has been imposed upon previous observation : observation in which there is no mention of any French being in sight except the frigates.

Nelson had long suspected that, if Sicily were not Napoleon's objective, then it must most likely be Egypt, which in its turn meant Alexandria, the only port on that inhospitable shore capable of harbouring a large fleet. He was not alone in his thinking, for Henry Dundas, the Secretary for War, in a letter to Lord Spencer at the Admiralty written early in June had suggested he had a feeling that Egypt – with India as the ultimate objective – was at the heart of Napoleon's plans. Rumour had also been rife on the Continent that the French expedition was embarking notable savants, historians and antiquarians with a view to uncovering the treasures of the East as well as setting up schools and administrative centres which would spread the language and culture of France over what would soon be her new possessions. Captain Sidney Smith, at that time a French prisoner of war, had managed to get a letter out of France as early as January that year, with a warning to the effect that the aims and ambitions of the Directory extended to Egypt and beyond. After Sidney Smith's release Lord St Vincent had personally heard his tale, and undoubtedly passed it on to Nelson.

So, despite the excellent security maintained by the French – which still at this moment off Cape Passero had Nelson and his senior officers unsure as to what move to make – there had been straws in the wind of gossip as well as enlightened speculation about Bonaparte's real intentions. Indeed, two days before reaching Naples, Nelson had written to Lord Spencer that he had learned from a Tunisian vessel off the Italian coast that the French had been seen off Trapani in western Sicily, headed towards the east. 'If they pass Sicily I shall believe they are going on their scheme of possessing Alexandria – a plan concocted with Tippoo Sahib, by no means so difficult as might at first be imagined.' Well, they had indeed bypassed Sicily, taken Malta en route, and were now certainly eastward bound. Yet even so, and convinced as he was of their destination, Nelson wanted to sound out the opinions of his captains. If they trusted him, he equally trusted them. It was this mutual value set upon each other, this shared confidence, as well as steady exchange of views between the 'Band of Brothers' that set the British fleet quite apart from the French – quite apart indeed from possibly any other fleet that had previously existed.

Berry, Nelson's own Captain aboard *Vanguard*, held the same opinion as his Admiral. But then he might have been influenced by so forceful a personality. Saumarez, not entirely a Nelson partisan (more experienced in fleet actions, he had referred to Nelson, whose ambitious nature was alien to him, as 'our desperate Commodore') was summoned aboard the flagship together with Ball, Darby and Troubridge for a discussion. Saumarez later gave his opinion in writing that : 'Under all the circumstances I think it most conducive to the good of His Majesty's service to make the best of our way for Alexandria, as the only means of saving our possessions in India should the French Armament be destined for that country.' Although both Corfu and Constantinople were mentioned as possibilities, the general concurrence was that Alexandria was more likely. Troubridge also confirmed in a letter that, in his opinion, 'their getting of Alexandria or any port in Egypt will put our possessions in India in a very perilous situation'. The order was given and the fleet 'crowding sail' dropped the flanks of the Sicilian foothills behind them and altered course to the south-east. The chase was on. But the hounds which pursued were deprived of their eyes. They had only their sense of smell (their deductive intelligence) to rely on as to the direction taken by the hunted.

Napoleon himself had every reason to feel content – even though he was upon this infernal element the sea, where things could not be directed as they could ashore by his critical and strategic evaluations, let alone determined by his will. Here, whatever revolutionary France might say as to 'God is dead', fate or the imponderable powers of nature still held sway. Napoleon would almost certainly have agreed with the words of 'Amr, that great general and passionate follower of Mahomet, who had himself conquered Alexandria and subdued Egypt in the seventh century. Contemplating the sea and ships upon it, he had remarked : 'If a ship lies still, it rends the heart; if it moves, it terrifies the imagination. Upon it a man's power ever diminishes and calamity increases. Those within it are like worms in a log, and if it rolls over they are drowned.'

Nevertheless, for the moment Napoleon was relaxed. Malta had been, as he had always known it would be, a fruit so over-ripe that it had fallen into his hand with scarcely a touch. 'Certainly,' as he wrote, 'it possessed vast physical powers of resistance, but no moral strength whatsoever.' He had secured this essential base, and General Vaubois with his troops would be able to hold Valetta and prevent any British ships entering the great harbour. Before joining L'Orient at Toulon Napoleon had asked Brueys to make sure that a comfortable berth was ready for him, since he expected to be sick throughout most of the voyage. On the contrary, the weather had been fair; the Mediterranean climate suited his Corsican blood better than the raw north; and even the favourable wind from astern seemed to augur well for his ambitions. The news that an English fleet was in the central Mediterranean was not so pleasant, but there were thousands of miles of water and a simple stratagem might well lose them. It might also cause any merchantmen which sighted the armada to assume that their destination lay further to the north – toward Greece, the Aegean, and possibly Constantinople. Brueys was ordered to steer as if making for Crete – a course a little south of due east.

On the night of 22 June, not long after Nelson's ships had put Sicily behind them and were heading direct for Alexandria, a heavy summer mist – not uncommon in the Ionian Sea at that time of year – hung over the water. Nelson's ships, unencumbered with any convoy, were so close on the enemy's heels that the dull thud of the British

Nelson, aged eight
Miniature

The Parsonage at Burnham Thorpe
Oil by Pocock

Lady Nelson (Frances)
Miniature by Orme

Lord Nelson
Miniature

Sir John Jervis
Oil by Beechey

Lord Nelson
Oil by Abbott

The Battle of the Nile

Victory in the Bay of Naples
Drawing by Pocock

Emma Hamilton
Pastel by Schmidt

Sir Hyde Parke
Oil by Romne

The Battle of Copenhage
Poco

Lord Nelson
Oil by Beechey

Horatia Nelson
Miniature by W. Ross

The Orders on Nelson's Uniform:
top Order of the Bath
left Order of St Ferdinand and Merit
right Turkish Order of the Crescent
bottom Order of St Joachim

Nelson in his cabin on board
Victory
Print by Lucy-Sharpe

signal guns could be distinctly heard aboard the French. (As early as 1558 a British naval instruction had laid down that in fog, or if a ship was seen to be standing into danger, contact should be made by 'ringing bells, blowing horns, beating drums and firing guns'.)

'The devil's children', as Nelson wrote, 'have the devil's own luck.' But it was not entirely luck. Napoleon's alteration to the north of his original course meant that throughout the night the two fleets gradually diverged. Some hours after dawn, when the sun had burned the mist away, they were no longer within touch of one another. But once again, if the British had had frigates scouting to port and starboard of their van, they would almost certainly have found the French.

It was not to be. Napoleon could enjoy his dreams and his books, among them a copy of the Koran and an account of the voyages of Captain Cook, as well as envisage a future infinitely more grandiose than anything even Alexander the Great had contemplated. The Directory, certainly, had agreed with his stated plans. These, as has been seen, included the foundation of a French colony in Egypt, a threat in concert with Tippoo Sahib to British Indian interests, and a triumphal return to Paris prior to the great invasion of the arrogant island. 'Turkey', as he had said, 'will welcome the expulsion of the Mameluke. . . .' The Mamelukes, an élite corps which had originated as a bodyguard of Turkish slaves first formed in the days of Saladin's successors, had long been the effective rulers of the country. They, like the Knights of St John in Malta, were a medieval anachronism. Napoleon did not think that with his superb soldiers of revolutionary France he had much to fear on their score. His dreams went much further than the establishment of a French Empire of the East. As he was to write in his journals many years later – when exile which made everything impossible seemed on the contrary to make everything possible – he had greater ambitions. Although Turkey was at the moment an ally of France, and had long entertained good relations with the French (ever since the 'infamous alliance' of the sixteenth century when the Ottomans were the enemies of the rest of Christian Europe), Napoleon saw her as a threat to his plans. Leaving Egypt, the Near East, and India secure and friendly behind him, he would sweep up north through Turkey, calling on the thousands of Christians in the Ottoman Empire to rise against their masters. A revived Roman Empire which looked to France as its head would include not only all the Mediterranean territories that had once belonged to Rome, but also the eastern empire of Alexander the Great, and beyond that all the wealth of India and the Orient. 'Only in the East can one do great things,' he said. On 15 August Napoleon would be twenty-nine years old.

Nelson would be forty in the September of that year. He was a badly damaged man – not only the physical damage to his arm and his eye. Far more than that, he was strained to the utmost of his ability, and he did not enjoy the confidence of a nation that sat so easily on Napoleon's shoulders. His captains and ships' companies admired and trusted him, but he was well aware that in this new command he had acquired considerable unpopularity with some of his senior officers. It was true that Lord Spencer had suggested him for the post, and that St Vincent had complete confidence in him. He had seen that in Nelson he had the commander with the dash and enterprise which might bring Napoleon's plans to ruin. But even St Vincent himself had come up against the opposition of Nelson's seniors. Vice-Admirals Sir William Parker and Sir John Orde had voiced their complaints at being passed over for this special independent command by a junior. The latter had even gone to the length of writing direct to the First Sea Lord complaining about the appointment of 'a junior officer, and just arrived from England' over and above his head. He had subsequently had a furious argument with St Vincent, and been ordered home. Quite apart from all this (and the row between St Vincent and Orde was of epoch-making proportions) Nelson was well aware that already people would be saying that he had failed in the main part of his mission. Malta was lost to the French and he had let the enemy get to the east of him. Tongues would be wagging back in London.

Admiral Goodall, a supporter and friend of Nelson ever since the action under Hotham against the French in March 1796, was to write that he was being asked: 'What is your favourite hero about? The French fleet has passed under his nose. . . .' Nelson had additional worries for, whatever he might say to the contrary, he needed both money and renown. The latter he had deservedly gained at the Battle of St Vincent, but it had been somewhat diminished by his failure at Tenerife, and money, in any real form, was something which had always eluded him. To come up with the French armada, to destroy their battle fleet, and to capture a vast quantity of prizes – these were comparatively simple dreams compared with Napoleon's, which drove him so anxiously across the Mediterranean. But over and above all this was his intense patriotism and his loathing of everything that revolutionary France represented.

> The fair breeze blew, the white foam flew,
> The furrow followed free. . . .

The fleet made a sparkling run, but the empty horizon taunted them. Saumarez, his misgivings yielding to admiration, confessed that the responsibility would have been more than he could endure : 'Some days must now elapse before we can be relieved of our cruel suspense, and if at the end of our journey we find that we are upon a wrong scent, our embarrassment will be great indeed. Fortunately, I only act here *en second*; but did the chief responsibility rest with me, I fear it would be more than my too irritable nerves would bear.' No one saw them pass. They were in those sun-varnished waters of the mid-eastern sea where, before the opening of the Suez Canal, little shipping ever moved. The main routes lay to the north of them, and the sleepy North African trade well to the south. In six days they covered the 700 miles that separate Cape Passero from Alexandria.

Even assuming that the fleet was consistently able to steer the direct course – approximately east-south-east, or 120° true – this gave them an average speed of five knots. Since it is more than likely that at this time of the year the wind varied between west and north-west and it is improbable that the ships maintained the direct 'chart' course all the time, they may well have covered nearer 800 miles in their pursuit, giving them a speed of over five and a half knots. Under ideal conditions of wind and weather, and with a ship straight from the dockyard and perfectly clean underwater, seven knots was considered good for a ship-of-the-line. It is clear then that the British fleet was consistently maintaining not far from maximum speed in its rate of advance. The French, even with their great convoy of merchantmen, also made good progress as they headed up to come under the lee of Crete. Brueys well knew that as he neared the mouth of the Aegean – to which Crete acts as something like a cork in a bottle – he would find that towards the end of June the *Meltemi* had set in to blow. These northerly winds which persist throughout the summer over the Aegean, as well as the sea south of Crete, would give him a fine boost on his second leg down towards Alexandria. It is the *Meltemi* which, funnelling over the ancient harbour and through the narrow streets of that city, make life supportable during the summer heats that turn most of Egypt into a trance-laden siesta-land.

The city towards which both fleets were headed was a far call from the Alexandria which had been one of the glories of the ancient world, second only to Rome in its wealth and power. The Alexandria where Antony and Cleopatra had ruled in Ptolemaic splendour, and which young Octavian had entered in triumph, had long been no more than a dream on the far limits of man's memory. The centuries of Arab rule, followed by the even more desiccating centuries of Turkish indifference, had reduced the proud former capital to little more than an obscure trading port. A recent English visitor had been Mrs Eliza Fay who had landed here in 1779 and had found nothing to commend it; being a Christian she was not allowed to disembark in the Western Harbour, nor to ride anything nobler than a donkey. 'I certainly deem myself very fortunate in quitting this place so soon,' she wrote to her sister. Over a century before another English traveller, John Sandys, had lamented over the decay that surrounded him : 'Such was this Queen of Cities and Metropolis of Africa : who now hath nothing left but her ruins. . . .'

There were, however, still a number of foreign communities in the city for, although the wealth of the East now largely flowed round the Cape of Good Hope, Alexandria still held the reins of a great deal of Near Eastern trade. Among the foreign residents was a Mr George Baldwin, who, in addition to his own business activities, held the office of British Consul. It was to call on him that Hardy was despatched by Nelson, the brig *Mutine* steering ahead and leaving the fleet on 26 June.

Hardy found the old port to the west of the city empty except for one old Turkish man-of-war and four frigates. The eastern harbour, known as 'the Franks' Port', contained a number of merchantmen of various nationalities. That was all : no French armada, no advance guard even. Nelson had been wrong. Wherever Napoleon had been bound, it was clearly not for Alexandria. Hardy landed and made his way to the British Consul's house. Once again fate was on the side of the French. Mr Baldwin was away, had been away according to his deputy for several weeks, and it was not known exactly when he might return. The Vice-Consul was not English, had no real powers, and could not or would not attempt to secure the necessary permission for the British squadron to enter harbour. Egypt was neutral in the war or, as a vassal state of the Sultan, was pro-French. (The ostensible object of the French, as set out by Napoleon on his arrival, was the suppression of the Mamelukes and the restoration of the Sultan's authority.) There was nothing left for Hardy to do but make his way back through the squalid streets, the tumble of 'mud houses, window-less except for a few holes in the walls', conscious of a great feeling of despair.

On 28 June, the British squadron was within sight of Alexandria. Nelson, still cursing his lack of frigates, was overwhelmed by the sight of the barren harbour. He could hardly believe that his own supposition, reinforced by those of his senior captains, had been proved wrong. The French must have gone east, and where else could they have gone to but here? It was at this point that the false or misunderstood report of the Genoese captain off Cape Passero proved so damaging. If the French had indeed been six days ahead of their pursuers they must by now either have been overhauled and engaged at sea, or be in Alexandria. The fact that they had only a three-day start, and that they had made a detour to the north, could not be known or hardly have been foreseen.

If the British Consul had been available things would have proved very different, as Nelson made clear in answer to a letter which he received from Mr Baldwin three years later. What effect would it have had, asked Baldwin, if he had been in the city when Nelson's ships arrived? 'I should have been off Alexandria', was the reply, 'when the French fleet arrived, and most assuredly the Army could not have landed in the complete order it did, had an action taken place on the first of July which . . . it would have done had the Turks received me as a friend instead of an enemy, for the answer I received was that neither English nor French should enter the port of Alexandria. And I believe that if you had been there to explain between me and the Turkish Government that I should have remained a few days to get some water and refreshments.' L'Orient, with Napoleon aboard, could well have suffered the same fate as she was to do a few weeks later. There would have been no Battle of the Pyramids. Mr Baldwin's absence from Alexandria – so small a thing at the time – had a profound effect on European history.

Nelson's 'active and anxious mind', according to Berry, 'would not permit him to rest a moment in the same place'. It was hardly surprising that the Admiral was 'anxious'. He was tuned to such a pitch that any inactivity seemed intolerable. The fleet was ordered to sail on to the east. It was just possible that the French had made for that old home of their crusading ancestors, L'Outremer as it had been called – the Holy Land and Syria. The threat to India might come from further away than he or anyone else had supposed. A great word of approbation in the Navy was 'zealous', and it was this quality above all which Nelson had consistently shown. It was this which now, by driving him to a further, immediate course of action, lost him the opportunity of bringing the French to battle at sea. The motto of Augustus Caesar, Festina Lente – 'Hasten Slowly' – was not Nelson's. Taking the wind on their port beam, the ships turned east along the coast and were soon passing the spacious Bay of Aboukir. It was named after an obscure Coptic Saint, Father Cyrus, and was void of shipping.

Three days later, on 1 July, while the British drew the empty coverts of the Levant, Napoleon landed in Alexandria.

CHAPTER TWENTY

The Patience of Job

NELSON had written to George Baldwin, the Consul, on 26 June, that he had 'reason to believe, from not seeing a Vessel, that they have heard of my coming up the Mediterranean, and are got safe into Corfu'. This was an alternative to Alexandria which he had already discussed with his captains, and it must have seemed to him now, as the fleet fruitlessly searched the East, that this was what had happened. Nevertheless, he could not presume upon it, for his earlier judgement as to their objective seemed to have been quite wrong. His confidence was shaken, but not his resolve to cover every possible square mile of the wind-freckled sea. Stretching out the fleet, using his 74s in the way he would have used those missing frigates, he headed north for the coast of Turkey, which they sighted on 4 July. Nothing. West-about, then, to comb the sea south of Crete, where they would find that at the best the wind was on their beam, and at the worst that it was heading them.

In the meantime, landing almost unopposed at Alexandria, Napoleon seemed to have his youthful dream of the East and of the great conquest well within his grasp. His tame poet, Parseval-Grandmaison (a more imposing name than his poems merited) stood at hand to record the conquests of this new Alexander. Napoleon felt the utmost confidence. His star was in the ascendant; it seemed that no judgement of his could be wrong. As he later told his friend, the politician and economist, Roederer: 'It was by making myself a Catholic that I ended the war in the Vendée; by making myself a Moslem that I established myself in Egypt. . . . If I were ruling a people of Jews, I should rebuild the Temple of Solomon.'

At the same time – and he could not disguise it – there was something arid and disillusioning about the taste of the East. 'I am particularly disgusted with Rousseau since seeing the Orient,' he said, 'the uncivilised man is a dog.' So much for all the French dreams of the 'noble savage'! Napoleon was still young, and was learning the hard way. Personally distressing was the fact that it was while he was in Egypt that he heard that Josephine was betraying him. He, who had written his name upon history, who had at the same time written ardent love letters to her during his campaign in Italy, celebrating conquest after conquest, was a cuckold. Did he recall, one wonders, his early definition of love as 'une sottise faite à deux'? But, as he wrote to his brother Joseph : 'Grandeur wearies me. Sentiment has dried up, glory is dulled. At twenty-nine I have drained all the cup.' The much older Nelson, sailing wearily back across the Mediterranean after his elusive enemy, could never have echoed those sentiments at any time in his life.

If Napoleon and Nelson had their problems, so did the French Admiral. Brueys had successfully achieved his main objective. He had brought the Army of the East safely down through the Tyrrhenian Sea and past Sicily, had landed the forces necessary to capture Malta (and had seen this most useful stepping-stone secured behind him), and had now disembarked Napoleon and his men at the required harbour. Some naval historians, intent only on the career of Nelson, have tended to ignore the skill of his naval opponent. But, if Brueys had been incompetent, could he have done what he did? Could he by a ruse (generally attributed to Napoleon, but possibly inspired by his Admiral) have thrown Nelson so efficiently off the scent during the long run down from Malta to Egypt? There is no such thing as a great boxer unless he has proved himself against great opponents. The same thing might equally be said of admirals and generals. There would be comparatively little to Nelson's credit if he had just defeated an inefficient admiral with an inefficient fleet. Neither Brueys nor the other officers and men under his command merit such a description.

After seeing the transports into Alexandria and disembarkation begun, Brueys had three options open to him. The first was to enter Alexandria itself. This he rejected; it is generally said on the grounds that there was insufficient water for the deeper draught of his men-of-war. But a surveying officer reported that, with a small amount of blasting, adequate entrance could be made for the fleet. Almost undoubtedly Brueys dismissed the idea for the reason that, if he were caught inside Alexandria harbour by a blockading fleet, his ships would be inextricably trapped. His second option was to retire to Corfu. But the island was a long distance away, his stores might not hold out, and – far more important – he would then leave the merchantmen and transports unprotected if the British fleet, which he now knew was in the Mediterranean, should arrive upon the scene.

The shore defences of Alexandria, he calculated, would not hold out against a determined seaborne assault. He had already seen at Valetta, in Malta, how even the strongest of bastions and walls would yield to a determined force.

Brueys' third option, for which he has often been criticised, was to sail eastward down the coast and anchor in the Bay of Aboukir. Letters which he wrote to Napoleon at the time show him to have been indecisive, but at the same time they seem to confirm his final judgement. Until the French Army had established its supremacy in Egypt, Napoleon needed his fleet near to hand. He himself raised no objection to Brueys' decision. It was not until after his triumph over the Mamelukes and his victorious entry into Cairo that Napoleon felt sufficiently secure to send a message to Brueys ordering him to withdraw to Corfu. The courier was killed en route (not only many Egyptians but also the desert Arabs detested this invasion of their land by 'the Franks' – a name they would always associate with the bloody wars of the Crusades), and the message never arrived. Brueys remained at anchor in Aboukir Bay.

The coastline of Crete disclosed nothing to the British as they beat to windward, finding that the north-westerly wind which had so happily driven them down to Egypt was no longer a friend. It was hot in July, the pitch tacky in the deck-seams, the sun and the salt wind hard on the canvas, and both officers and men seeking, below-decks, for the best place where a draught drew in, or a slant of air, caught by the sails aloft, spiralled down into their quarters. It says a great deal for Nelson, it says a great deal for his captains, and indeed for all the ships' companies that they were not dispirited and that morale remained high. Much credit for this must go to the victualling arrangements. But, perhaps above all, it was their good fortune to be at sea, in the environment that they had made their own, which preserved their spirits and their health. As Nelson was to write later to Sir William Hamilton, after they had returned to Sicily : 'At this moment we have not one sick man in the Fleet.'

The same could not be said for the French anchored in Aboukir Bay. They were, in any case, short by some seventeen hundred men of their proper complement of about ten thousand, and they had already found that the desert shores of Egypt provided little in the way of provisions. All this was quite apart from an actively hostile population. The principal reason for the French shortage of complement was that, on their outward voyage, the ships had been crowded with soldiers, many of whom could have helped fight the guns in action. But these were now removed to further Napoleon's military ambitions and, as E. H. Jenkins remarks in *A History of the French Navy*, 'the seamen were often of poor quality, ill-disciplined, and in a naval sense largely untrained'. That they were later to fight so gallantly is all to their credit, and was due to a passion fired by their revolutionary zeal. At the same time, it was their misfortune that, especially when it came to gunners, the demands of the Army were set by Republican France well above those of her Navy.

The British, meanwhile, held on with all sail to the westward, endeavouring to keep between latitudes 36° and 37° North, thus covering the approaches to the Grecian archipelago, and cutting an observant swathe through the centre of the sea, as they crossed the Ionian headed for the Malta–Sicily channel. Vessels spoken to convinced them that the French had certainly not gone to Corfu, nor – as had at times been anticipated – headed north for Constantinople. They had vanished into the clear midsummer air as if by magic. There was nothing for it but to cross the empty spaces of the Ionian once again and see whether Sicily was still safe. Water and stores were already beginning to be needed urgently, and only the ancient harbour of Syracuse could provide them.

On 20 July the dazzling dried coast of Sicily confronted them, the same walls and fortress that they had passed nearly four weeks ago. Ship after ship entered a still harbour, where only a coaster or two and a scatter of fishing boats idled on the water. The great urgency was to water ship and revictual. There were obvious difficulties. The weak Kingdom of Naples did not dare to offend the French although, as has been seen, the King, and especially his Queen and his Prime Minister Sir John Acton, were pro-British and passionately anti-French. But, on the surface at least, the Governor of Syracuse could do nothing but make an official complaint about the usage of his harbour by a belligerent power. Nelson, whose nerves were strung to breaking point, remonstrated angrily in letters to Sir William Hamilton, and his Commander-in-Chief, at the treatment of the British fleet. But all this was little more than a charade, and in fact all their wants were supplied during the three days that the ships lay there at anchor.

Superficially it was a scene of confusion, to the landsman's eye at least; yet it was in fact a perfect exercise in supplying ship in an unfamiliar foreign anchorage. The long-boats plied backwards and forwards between the vessels and the shoreline of the island of Ortygia, on which stood the ancient city. The Fountain of Arethusa provided them with water, just as it had done the Greeks who had first settled there over two thousand years before. From dawn to dusk barricoes were rising and falling alongside the ships, for each vessel required about 250 tons of water, and every bit of it had to be brought aboard by manual labour. Live pigs, the carcases of bullocks, fowls in hampers, and great baskets of fresh fruit and vegetables soared upwards suspended on tackles. 'As no fleet has had more fag than this', Nelson wrote to Sir William, 'nothing but the best food and the greatest attention can keep them healthy.'

He had already written to St Vincent, in a letter which Ball had advised him not to send – on the grounds that he was defending his conduct of the chase before it was yet over, and before any criticism had been made. But his nerves were on fire, and he knew that officers senior to him were ready at any moment to point to the folly of sending a junior on so important a mission. In later years he was to tell Troubridge how the return to Syracuse had almost broken his heart, and to counsel him : 'Do not fret at anything. . . . I wish I never had.' Now, at his desk in the sun-laced cabin of the *Vanguard*, with the rhythm of the ship's operations assuaging his anxieties a little, he wrote on 20 July, in a quieter manner, to his wife. Poor Fanny must not be unduly disturbed. At the same time he never concealed from her whatever lay at the core of his real feelings :

. . . I have not been able to find the French Fleet, to my great mortification . . . we have been off to Malta, to Alexandria in Egypt, Syria into Asia, and are returned here without success. However, no person will say that it has been for want of activity. I yet live in hopes of meeting these scoundrels; but it would have been my delight to have tried Buonaparte on a wind, for he commands the Fleet, as well as the Army. . . . Glory is my object, and that alone. God Almighty bless you.

To Sir William and his wife he expressed himself in terms which reflected his invariably high-romantic nature : 'Thanks to your exertions, we have victualled and watered; and surely, watering at the Fountain of Arethusa, we must have victory. We shall sail with the first breeze, and be assured I will return either crowned with laurel, or covered with cypress.'

The first breeze came, the sultry harbour stirred under the north-westerly : the only wind that makes life supportable in Sicily, Malta, or the central Mediterranean during July and August. The wind came off the land, the fleet was unmoored, and, as he wrote to Sir William : '[We] shall go out of this delightful harbour, where our present wants have been most amply supplied, and where every attention has been paid to us.' This last sentence in itself completely belied his previous complaints – complaints made in letters which he undoubtedly expected either to be anticipated by the French, or shown to them if necessary as proof that the British had not been made welcome in the Kingdom of the Two Sicilies.

Napoleon, far absent in the hot sands of Egypt, had in the meantime achieved his triumph. On 8 July, while Nelson was searching for him off the southern coast of Crete, Napoleon had moved his army out of Alexandria on the march to Cairo. It was indeed 'le commencement d'une grande chose', something that was confirmed by his defeat of the Mamelukes at Chebreiss and the Pyramids. On 24 July, the day before Nelson sailed from Syracuse, Napoleon entered Cairo. The East lay at his feet.

He now set about reorganising the affairs of Egypt. A proclamation printed in Arabic was issued everywhere that he, Napoleon, reverenced Mahomet and the Koran far more than the defeated Mamelukes ever had. In accordance with the doctrines of the Revolution, it was proclaimed that all men were equal, with the necessary rider 'except in so far as they were distinguished by their intellectual and moral excellences'. The overthrow of the papal authority in Rome was put forward as a proof of the fact that the French were sincere Moslems. Such casuistry would have been quite beyond the Protestant Nelson (who might possibly have approved of the overthrow of papal authority, but never that of Christianity). But, as always with Napoleon, there was constructive sense in many of his words. In the future, for instance, all posts in the country were to be open to all men of whatever class. The hereditary autocracy of the Mamelukes was thus overthrown at a blow. Somehow or other Napoleon – and the Eastern mind is adept at tortuous thinking – was accepted as the Sultan's emissary, while at the same time being regarded as a new Sultan of Egypt himself.

Dropping the shores of Sicily behind them, the British were once more headed eastward. Before leaving Syracuse Nelson had already informed his commanders: 'I now acquaint you that I shall steer direct for the Island of Cyprus, and hope in Syria to find the French fleet. . . .' He knew from his sources of information in Naples that the French had certainly not got to the west of him, but he could still hardly believe his original judgement that their destination was Alexandria could be correct. It must have been that he had missed them in the Levant. Their paths had somehow crossed while he was searching the shores of Turkey, and the French Army was now headed inland through Persia to join forces with Tippoo Sahib and reduce

British India, while their fleet lay at anchor in one of the ancient ports that had once housed the ships of the Crusaders.

Crowding on all sail, with studding-sail yards hauled out and their gull-wings spread, mizzen, main and even maintop staysails set, the ships took the favourable north-westerly on their port quarter and sped on their way. During their beat back from Alexandria, Nelson had his captains aboard whenever possible, to discuss every eventuality if and when they came up with the French – whether at sea or at anchor. Gunnery practice and the exercise of the marines in small arms had not been neglected.

Still hoping to catch the enemy at sea, he disposed the squadron in order of battle in case such good fortune came their way. They ran down the wind in three divisions, two of them designed to take care of the French fleet, while the third was to engage and capture the transports. If their first passage of six days had been excellent, this second was even better. The gods of chance, to whom Napoleon paid such respect, might favour him ashore, but at sea – even though he had been led astray for many weeks – the ancient gods were to smile upon Nelson. He himself would have rightly disparaged any such expression. The God he worshipped was the one whom he had known since childhood in the Burnham parsonage. He had been tried like Job, but he cou'd answer 'Yes' to God's question : 'Hast thou entered into the springs of the sea, or hast thou walked in the search of the depth?'

Despite Nelson's original intention of making direct for Cyprus, he had decided to take one more look into Alexandria. The reason was simple. On the way, as they had passed the great Gulf of Kalamata, north of Cape Matapan, Troubridge had gone into the anchorage of Koroni and had found a French wine-brig there. This was a double delight, for not only did the good pressed grapes of the Morea help to serve the fleet, but she held the key to the door at which Nelson had so long and so obstinately been hammering. A month ago the French fleet had passed on a course to the south-east of Crete. Alexandria!

CHAPTER TWENTY-ONE

Brought to Bay

ON THE morning of 1 August 1798, the *Alexander* and *Swiftsure*, which had been sent on ahead the previous night, made their landfall off Alexandria. They signalled back that the French flag was flying over the city and that the harbour was full of merchantmen. Of the French fleet itself there was not a sign. The officers in the *Vanguard*, who had breakfasted that day with Nelson, commented that their Admiral had constantly asked for the time throughout the night. It was difficult even for them to understand how dangerously stretched were his nerves. At times it seemed to him that the mission upon which he had been sent had been beyond his powers, and that he had failed his 'Dear Lord', St Vincent.

The *Vanguard*'s log reads : 'On the 1st of August at 1 PM moderate breezes and clear : the wind north. We saw Alexandria bearing S.E. seven or eight leagues. . . . At half past two hauled our wind, unbent the best bower, took it out of the stern port and bent it again.' The dilapidated Pharos – that wonder of the ancient world which the Arabs had been unable to maintain – came into sight, and beyond it Pompey's lonely tower. The reason for taking the principal anchor to the stern was that Nelson envisaged he might have to commence an action against the battlements of Alexandria and French men-of-war within, which would entail anchoring by the stern so as to position the ships accurately. On learning that there were no men-of-war within either of Alexandria's harbours fear must have clutched at his heart, but the presence of the French transports was in itself reassuring. He knew that the warships were not in Corfu, and from his previous investigation he knew also that if their fleet was in Egypt there was only one other place where it could anchor – Aboukir Bay. He immediately turned the fleet to the east.

It seemed to almost everyone that their hopeless quest was to begin yet again, and Captain Saumarez was later to recollect how

197

despondent he felt. At four in the afternoon everything changed dramatically. The masthead lookout of Captain Hood's *Zealous* had sighted the French fleet off the starboard bow, at anchor in that large sandy bay called after the Coptic saint. The enemy had been sighted at almost the same moment by the *Goliath*. The main meal of the day had begun half an hour beforehand, and the cloth was just being removed from the table in front of Captain Saumarez, when Midshipman Elliot came running to acquaint him with the news : 'Sir, a signal is just now made that the enemy is in Aboukir Bay and moored in a line of battle.' As Clarke and M'Arthur recorded :

> Nothing could equal the joy that prevailed throughout the British squadron at the sight of the French flag, unless it were the calm determination and awful silence by which that joy was succeeded. Sir Horatio, for many preceding days, had hardly eaten or slept; but now, with a coolness peculiar to our naval character, he ordered his dinner to be served, during which the dreadful preparation for battle was made throughout the *Vanguard*. On his officers' rising from the table and repairing to their separate stations, he exclaimed, *Before this time tomorrow, I shall have gained a Peerage, or Westminster Abbey.*

His officers knew his high style (it was part of the rhetoric of their day), but they had to address themselves to their tasks with no such assurance.

The preparations that had been made for engaging the enemy, if they were found at anchor in Alexandria, were to hold equally good for Aboukir Bay. All ships were ready to anchor by the stern, all the preparations for a fleet action had been made, and every man from gunner to marine was at his post with the sure knowledge of his exact duties. As Falconer puts it in his *Dictionary* : 'When the admiral, or commander in chief, of a naval armament has discovered an enemy's fleet, his principal concern is usually to approach it, and endeavour to come to action as soon as possible. Every inferior consideration must be sacrificed to this important object. . . .' Nelson after so arduous a chase had no doubt at all about his duty. With the French, however, it was a very different matter. They had been under the assumption that their enemy had lost them and was far away to the west, and this had led to an over-confidence which was to prove disastrous. It had not been anticipated that the British would retrace their steps all the way across the eastern Mediterranean. Brueys had also taken unfortunate comfort in the fact that two British admirals, Hood and

Barrington, had previously succeeded in fighting a successful action from just the kind of position in which he had anchored his fleet. Theoretically it should have been almost impregnable, for the shores of the bay provided a protection from the windward, or northerly, side and he had mounted guns on Aboukir Island which the enemy must round in order to come to grips with his fleet. This battery was, however, to prove ineffective, being ill-sited, under-gunned, and not having the necessary range to hit their opponents when they came sailing in.

One French flag-officer who survived the Battle of the Nile, Rear-Admiral Blanquet-Duchayla, left the clearest account of how the action appeared from the French point of view. The British were sighted about two o'clock in the afternoon, and the French Commander-in-Chief immediately called a council of war. Many of the men were away on shore, digging wells and foraging for provisions. Because of the attacks of the Bedouins upon the shore-parties, each ship had also had to send twenty-five additional men to protect their companions which meant that not only they but the ships' boats were away. All must be recalled. In fact, many of them never did get back in time to be at their posts when battle commenced. The French frigates, which should have been permanently on the lookout against just this eventuality – the surprise arrival of their enemies – were at anchor. Brueys was betrayed by over-confidence. It was a known fact that men-of-war stood little chance against powerful, well-sited shore batteries and he should, in theory at any rate, have converted his ships into an impregnable defence-line. He had thirteen ships-of-the-line, nine of them of 74 guns, three of 80 guns, and in the very centre he had anchored his own flagship *L'Orient* with her 120 guns. This should have been more than enough to cope with Nelson's thirteen 74s and his 50-gun *Leander*. The ships were anchored in a line stretching from north-west to south-east and certainly, by every rule of naval warfare, should have been more than capable of giving a good account of themselves. In view of the late hour, with darkness about to fall, they could hardly believe that the enemy would attack at once and risk a night action in uncharted waters. They had underestimated Nelson, who had constantly said, 'I will bring the French Fleet to action the moment I can lay hand on them.'

Only Blanquet-Duchayla had suggested at the council that they should up-anchor and stand out to sea. Brueys, however, who was also constrained by having to wait for the shore-parties to return, felt reasonably confident that the British would not engage that day. The normal procedure would have been for the advancing squadron to

reconnoitre the position, make their calculations, and then lie off overnight, inviting the French to come out the following day. If, on the
other hand, they intended to attack them at anchor, they would not
press home their attack in an unknown bay until daylight. Brueys, as
Blanquet-Duchayla tells us, did briefly consider taking the fleet out
to sea, and even had his top-sail yards set up. He changed his mind
because he saw that, with his shortage of crew and so many men not
yet returned from shore, he was in no position to fight a ship-to-ship
action at sea. There was nothing for him but to stay at anchor, man
all the starboard guns, and rest confident that if the British did enter
the bay he could pick them off one by one as they came to anchor. A
further reason for his staying at anchor was that the prevailing
northerly wind would have meant his tacking out of an awkward
position while the British would have had the weather gauge.

Although the wind favoured the British approach, they were at the
great disadvantage of having no proper charts of the anchorage. This
in itself was hardly surprising since it was an area where little or no
trade existed, so it had never engaged the attention of British
hydrographers. Brueys had naturally concluded that this might be the
case, something which may have accounted for the somewhat lax
disposition of his fleet. Nelson had only a sketch of the area which
he had been given by Hallowell of the *Swiftsure*, who had taken it
from a captured French merchantman. As it turned out, neither this
nor another chart owned by Hood proved of any use. The only up-to-
date information about the area belonged to Foley of the *Goliath* and
this was given in a recently published French atlas. It was perhaps to
some extent owing to this that it was Foley who initiated the action
and got inshore of the French van – the manoeuvre which was to give
the British their supreme advantage.

As the British bore down ominously, their sails illuminated by the
westering sun, Brueys despatched the brig *Alerte* with orders to 'stand
towards the enemy until nearly within gunshot, and then to manoeuvre
and endeavour to draw them toward the outer shoal lying off that
Island'. The bait was to be ignored. Blanquet-Duchayla guessed that
this was because Nelson had experienced pilots aboard. But, as we
know, there were no local or other pilots with a knowledge of Aboukir
Bay in any of the British ships. Their amazing achievement was due
to the fact that their captains and officers were seamen of such
experience that they could make their way into an unknown foreign
anchorage against a larger fleet, and still bring up their ships where
they wanted them.

At three that afternoon Nelson had hoisted 'Prepare for battle' and

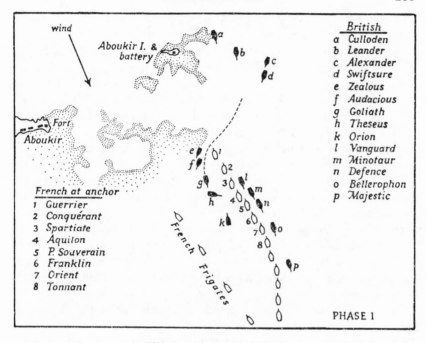

The Battle of the Nile 1

at four 'Be ready to anchor by the stern'. At half-past five on that ever-memorable 1 August, the simple signal was made to form line of battle 'as most convenient'. No more needed to be said. It is this which distinguishes Nelson and his captains from their enemy. Just one signal to commence a battle that ranks in the history of the world. . . . The discussions at sea, the conferences in Syracuse, these had left them with a shared knowledge and such an understanding of their mutual problems under whatever conditions action might take place, that the eleven 74s acted as if they were one great marine animal, directed by a single intelligence.

The reason why there were no more than eleven 74s present at this all-important moment was that the *Alexander* and *Swiftsure* had been detached on reconnaissance (a duty the missing frigates should have fulfilled), and the *Culloden* was lying some distance astern with her captured French wine-brig in tow. The latter was ordered to cast off her prize, while all three were signalled to rejoin with the utmost expedition. In the event, Troubridge in the *Culloden*, coming in astern of Captain Thompson's 50-gun *Leander* as darkness fell, was to ground on the Aboukir shoals and remain there throughout the battle.

The other two, arriving late upon the scene, were to act like a reserve – coming fresh into battle at a crucial moment.

As the British drew into the mouth of the bay, the leadsmen in the chains heaving and hauling the dripping lines, Hood of the *Zealous* called across to his Admiral that he had eleven fathoms on the lead. 'If you will allow me the honour of leading you into battle, I will keep the lead going.' Nelson gave him leave and wished him success, at which Hood in courtesy to his Commander-in-Chief removed his hat – only to have it snatched out of his hand by the breeze. 'There it goes for luck,' he said jocularly. 'Put the helm up and make sail.' As Nelson's *Vanguard* dropped back slightly to allow him to muster the rest of the line, the *Goliath* on the lee bow of the *Zealous* moved up to race her for the lead. Foley, who was one of the most experienced captains in the Navy, had served under the great Rodney some twenty years earlier and had been Flag-Captain in the *Britannia* at St Vincent. Since he had the only practical chart of the bay, it was perhaps fortunate that it was Foley who won the privilege of leading the British fleet into action.

Brueys, in accordance with correct naval thinking of the time, had placed his strongest ships at the centre of his line, for it was here that the main blow might be expected to fall. *L'Orient* was seventh in the order, with the 80-gun *Le Franklin* and *Tonnant* on either side of her, sixth and eighth respectively. Where he had made a grave mistake, however, was in placing his weakest five 74s in the van, while concentrating his other strong ships to the rear. With the prevailing wind from the north this meant that the latter could not without great difficulty make their way up to reinforce their centre and their van. And it was upon this part of the fleet that Nelson fell like a fury. He had announced his intention to attack the enemy's van and centre, and this is exactly what he did.

The 74 *Le Guerrier* was anchored at the head of the French line and Foley, spurring ahead past Hood's *Zealous*, saw, as Nelson had said, that 'where there is room for a French 74 at single anchor to swing, there is room for a British 74 to anchor'. His lookouts gazed anxiously ahead to descry on the darkening water the Frenchman's anchor-buoy. This would mark the very place where *Le Guerrier*'s bower anchor lay. It would give Foley an immediate indication that, where the Frenchman had dropped it, there was room for his own ship to pass. There it was! And there was some 200 yards between it and the bows of *Le Guerrier*. Foley bore up to clear it, the White Ensign flying high above what would soon be the darkness of night and the smoke of battle. Although Nelson was a Rear-Admiral of the

Blue, and the Blue Ensign was the proper colours of the ships under his command, all of them went into action flying the White, since it was more easily distinguishable from the French tricolour of blue, white and red. The ancient banner of England, the Red Cross of Saint George that had been borne on a thousand battlefields, now went into battle against the new enemy, Revolutionary France.

Hood of the *Zealous* remarked, as the *Goliath* drew ahead of him : 'Well, never mind, Foley is a fine, gallant, worthy fellow.' He was now a close spectator of the opening round as the *Goliath* crossed the bows of *Le Guerrier* to take up an inshore berth on the Frenchman's port side. As he passed by close under *Le Guerrier*'s bows Foley raked her with a broadside at point-blank range. He had accurately assumed that, from the way the French had drawn up their line, they had presumed they would only be attacked on the starboard side and therefore that the larboard would be less ready for action. He was to be proved right. But now, as he made to place himself alongside *Le Guerrier* his sheet anchor failed to run out as quickly as it should have done, so he swept on to drop a stern anchor along the second in the French line, *Le Conquérant*. It was Hood who brought up the *Zealous* just astern of him against *Le Guerrier*. The first shots were fired at 6.28 p.m. at which time the French hoisted their battle ensigns. Following upon Foley's lead, the next three ships in the British line, the *Orion*, *Theseus*, and *Audacious*, also steered inboard to place themselves on the port side of the French. The ineffective batteries on Aboukir Island played no part in the action. As the sun set and the sky above the desert began to glow with that astonishing green and orange which precedes the sudden onset of night over Egypt, the van of the French fleet was already heavily engaged. It was to be remarked, so confident had they been of the security of their landward side, that many of their larboard upper-deck gun-ports were cluttered up with lumber and rubbish.

Within ten minutes of the action's opening, the fire from *Zealous* had so overwhelmed *Le Guerrier* that all her masts had gone by the board. *Le Conquérant*, closely assailed by the *Goliath* and raked by the *Audacious*, was subjected also to the fire of the *Orion* and the *Theseus* as they swept past to find their main targets further down the line. Although the dismasted *Le Guerrier* was to fight on gallantly until nine o'clock, when she surrendered to the *Zealous*, the carnage aboard the luckless *Le Conquérant* was such that her captain struck his colours after no more than twelve minutes.

This first phase of the battle is best exemplified by Hood's account of his action against *Le Guerrier* :

I commenced such a well-directed fire into her bow within pistol shot a little after six that her foremast went by the board in about seven minutes, just as the sun was closing the horizon; on which the whole squadron gave three cheers; it happening before the next ship astern of me had fired a shot and only the *Goliath* and *Zealous* engaged. And in ten minutes more her main and mizzen masts went; at this time also went the main mast of the second ship, engaged closely by the *Goliath* and *Audacious*, but I could not get *Le Guerrier*'s commander to strike for three hours, though I hailed him twenty times, and seeing he was totally cut up and only firing a stern gun now and then at the *Goliath* and *Audacious*.

By this time darkness had fallen. 'At last being tired of firing and killing people in that way, I sent my boat on board her, and the lieutenant was allowed . . . to hoist a light and haul it down to show his submission.' The British, prepared for the eventuality of a night action, had all hoisted four lamps in a horizontal line at their mizzen-peaks so that they could distinguish one another from the enemy.

Meanwhile Nelson's *Vanguard*, the sixth in the line, had come into action, being the first of the British ships to anchor on the outside of the French, dead abreast *Le Spartiate*, the third in the enemy line, and within pistol shot of her. As she engaged her, *Vanguard* also came under fire from *L'Aquilon*, fourth in the line. She was not to be relieved of this double fire until Louis brought the *Minotaur* to port of his Admiral and put her abreast of *L'Aquilon*. The next two ships to run in were less fortunate than their predecessors: the *Bellerophon* – missing her companions in the darkness and the dense smoke of battle – ran too far down the line and anchored abeam of Brueys' flagship, the mighty *L'Orient*. A 74 on her own could be no match for a ship of 120 guns and in the end the *Bellerophon* was completely dismasted and forced to wear out of line to the lee side of Aboukir Bay. (The *Alexander* and the *Swiftsure*, running down to throw their weight against *L'Orient*, all but fired into the *Bellerophon* since she no longer bore her distinguishing lanterns.) Westcott's *Majestic* having fallen foul of *Le Tonnant*, spiking her jib-boom through the Frenchman's main shroud, received a point-blank and devastating fire, Westcott being killed by a musket ball. Her First Lieutenant, having finally managed to get his ship free, dropped further down the line and came to anchor on the port bow of *L'Heureux*.

The long-sustained horror of naval action in the days of sail has already been described, but a night action like this was something that had not been known before. It was bad enough in the roar and thunder of the guns during daylight, but then at least the men could have some understanding of what was happening and how the battle progressed, and daylight itself lends man a certain confidence. But now, in the dim light of the lanterns, their flames wavering to the concussion of the guns, and often obscured by the smoke of battle, the scene aboard each and every ship was like an image of hell. The French van was steadily being crushed to pieces. Masts and yards – and men with them – came falling down to add to the confusion between ships that were lying almost alongside one another.

It was about eight o'clock when Nelson, standing with Berry on the quarter-deck, was struck across the forehead by a piece of langridge shot (langridge, or langrel, consisted of scraps of chain and pieces of old iron tied by rope into cylindrical form and principally designed to cut up sails and rigging). Nelson's forehead was cut to the bone right above his old wound, and a flap of flesh falling down covered his good eye, rendering him blind. Half-stunned and conscious of the darkness engulfing him, he felt sure that it was the darkness of death. Berry caught him as he fell to the deck. His last words (as he imagined them to be) were : 'I am killed. Remember me to my wife.' The Admiral was immediately taken below to the smells and screams of the red-painted cockpit. He insisted that the Principal Surgeon should not be told that he was wounded. He was convinced in fact that he was dying and asked for the Chaplain, renewed his message to Fanny, and sent for Captain Louis of the *Minotaur*. Louis had been ably assisting him and drawing some of the fire of *L'Aquilon* and *Le Spartiate*, both of which, until the *Minotaur*'s timely arrival, had been combining their fire on *Vanguard*. 'Your support', Nelson told Louis, 'has prevented me from being obliged to haul out of line.' Losses aboard the flagship were in fact very severe, only being exceeded by those of the *Majestic* and the *Bellerophon*.

Surgeon Michael Jefferson examined Nelson's head and found 'the cranium bared for more than an inch, the wound three inches long'. While Nelson was waiting for attention, Berry had come bustling down with the happy news that *Le Spartiate*, dismasted, had just ceased firing. This was at 8.30 p.m. and not long afterwards Galwey, the First Lieutenant, who had been sent to board her, returned with the French Commander's sword. The surgeon meanwhile had brought the edges of the wound together, applied strips of adhesive, and given Nelson a sedative. Then there was further good news – *L'Aquilon*, their other immediate opponent, had struck her colours as had *Le Souverain Peuple*. '. . . It appeared that Victory had already declared itself in our favour.' Nelson, after being attended to, had withdrawn

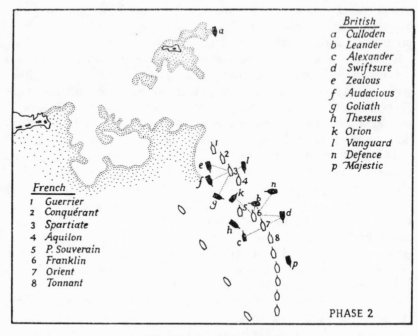

The Battle of the Nile 2

himself to the darkness of the bread-room to be clear of the steady
stream of wounded. Quite apart from the throbbing pain of his wound
he was badly concussed. (He was to suffer from the effects of that
langridge shot for many weeks to come.)

Removed from all the action, cursing his luck and trying by every
means in his power to get his badly damaged ship off the shoal,
Troubridge in the *Culloden* was a furiously impotent spectator. The
night was lit only by the flashes of the guns, the whole area obscured
by dense smoke, the air shaken by the cannonades, and he could not
know what fortune or what disaster might be befalling his friends.
One of them, for instance, Captain Darby of the *Bellerophon*, upon
whom the whole weight of *L'Orient's* firepower had fallen like the
wrath of Zeus, had managed to hold out against the giant for a whole
hour. This astonishing achievement singles out Darby and his ship for
special distinction – almost as much as Foley for his initial thrust
inboard of the anchored fleet. By nine o'clock it was clear that the
first part of the battle was over. The whole of the French van was,
as Captain Miller put it, 'completely subdued'. It was now to be the
turn of the centre and especially of *L'Orient*. She was heavily engaged

by Captain Ball's *Alexander*, Captain Hallowell's *Swiftsure*, and finally by Captain Thompson's 50-gun *Leander*. The moon had just risen, cool and impersonal, over the fiery and sulphurous arena. Nelson, having dismissed his secretary, who had been overcome by emotion on seeing the Admiral apparently blind with a bandaged head ('He has not activity for me,' Nelson was later to write on assigning him to another ship), had decided it was time to compose a despatch. He pushed up the bandage – he could see after all through his 'bright eye' – and began : 'My Lord, Almighty God has blessed His Majesty's Arms in the late Battle.'

Berry came down again, this time to report that the stern of the French Admiral's flagship appeared to be on fire. Nelson, disregarding the surgeon's orders that he must remain quiet and inactive, insisted on being helped on deck. Mistily the scene unfolded before him. Yes, there could be no doubt that fire had started aft aboard *L'Orient*! It has been said that the French had been experimenting with shot containing combustibles, but they had also been painting ship, and paint and oil in jars lay along *L'Orient*'s after-deck. Sinister yellow tongues of fire were already beginning to dart towards her mizzen-chains. Aboard the *Swiftsure*, anchored close off the flagship's weather side, Captain Hallowell ordered every available gun to be trained upon this bright aiming-mark. The fire was spreading fast, and soon it lit up the whole night battle-scene, disclosing *Le Conquérant*, *Le Guerrier* and another French 74 already struck. Men could now see for the first time what damage had been inflicted upon their own ships and what upon those of the enemy. Already the fire, fanned by the northerly wind, was spreading fast, threatening not only *L'Orient* but the ships engaging her. It was an impressive but terrifying sight, for in those wooden ships – each one of which was a floating magazine – fire was the most terrible of enemies.

L'Orient had been fought with consummate gallantry throughout the night's action. Brueys had lost both legs early in the battle, but had had tourniquets applied so that he could still conduct operations from an armchair on his quarter-deck. He was seated there, giving directions for putting out the fire, when a shot from the *Swiftsure* nearly cut him in two. When his men tried to take him below he refused saying : 'A French Admiral must die on his quarter-deck.' He was dead before Nelson had staggered up top to survey the scene from *Vanguard*. The latter now ordered Berry to do what he could to pick up the survivors, for it was quite clear that *L'Orient* was doomed. There was only one boat left aboard the flagship in seaworthy condition, but she was immediately despatched under Galwey to come to the aid of the French sailors who were already beginning to throw themselves into the water to escape from the inevitable holocaust. Other boats from the British ships were to be sent to pick up survivors. Even in the middle of a fight to the death, the seaman's code was recognised – a man in the water is a man to be rescued.

The British men-of-war in the vicinity of *L'Orient* veered to get clear of her, only Hallowell in the *Swiftsure* holding his place. He reckoned that he was so close that the flying debris from the inevitable explosion would pass clean over his ship. John Theophilus Lee, who was serving aboard the *Swiftsure*, left a record of the events which is all the more interesting coming as it does from a midshipman of under eleven, who had already seen service at the Battle of Cape St Vincent. He wrote how '. . . the ports were ordered to be lowered, the magazines and hatchways closed, and every man to go under cover, provided with wet swabs and buckets of water in order to extinguish any burning fragments which might come on board during the explosion'. Among the many wounded aboard *L'Orient* was the son of Commodore Casabianca who had lost a leg. His father, according to one account, could not be induced to leave the ship while his son was still among the wounded below and went down with him. Another version has it that both Casabianca and his ten-year-old son were in fact sighted, clinging to some wreckage, after *L'Orient* sank, but were never recovered. It was soon after ten o'clock that the fire finally reached *L'Orient*'s magazines and she went up with an explosion so shattering that it was heard over ten miles away and noted by Monsieur Poussielgue in Alexandria. The sky lightened as if the door of some enormous blast-furnace had suddenly opened – and then as suddenly closed again. In the darkness that followed, timbers, masts and spars, lumps of burning debris and the pulverised bodies of men rained down on the ships around. So cataclysmic was the concussion, so deep the silence that followed after the last pieces of wreckage had thundered down, that all firing ceased throughout the two fleets as if everyone present had been stunned.

The destruction of the French flagship seems in retrospect symbolic of the fate of Napoleon's dreams. It had also a very real and practical effect upon his plans, for *L'Orient* contained a large part of the financial resources upon which he had relied. In her hold lay quantities of bullion and precious stones extracted from the Roman State and the Swiss Republic, as well as a fortune in artistic and material terms from the loot of Malta. The remains must lie there to this day, but buried so deep beneath the silt of the shifting Nile mouth that they are almost certainly irrecoverable.

After the brief lull that followed the destruction of *L'Orient*, firing broke out once more. *Le Tonnant*, *Le Mercure*, and *L'Heureux* had all slipped their cables before the flagship exploded, the last two grounding in the bight of the bay, whither they were pursued and forced to strike. *Le Spartiate* had struck her colours at eleven, and *Le Franklin* at midnight. Both had scarcely a gun left that would fire, and both had been fought with the greatest courage. Admiral Blanquet-Duchayla in the dismasted *Le Franklin* had fought to the last, although wounded in the head, urging his men: 'Fire, fire, steadily. The last shot may give us victory.' Captain Dupetit-Thouars in *Le Tonnant*, who was almost dismembered, gave orders that he should be placed in a bran tub so that he might encourage his men to the last.

Nelson had been finally persuaded to go below; he was in no fit state to stay on deck. Had he not been seriously concussed it is possible that the follow-up of the battle would have resulted in the destruction of every single French ship. Even so, it is somewhat doubtful whether the men could have fought any longer. They had been in action for six hours and more, and were dropping at their posts. Foley's signal midshipman, Elliott, recalled that he fell asleep 'in the act of hauling up a shroud hawser', while Miller of the *Theseus* wrote in a letter to his wife that: 'My people were so extremely jaded, that as soon as they had hove our sheet anchor up, they dropped under the capstan-bars and were asleep, in a moment, in every sort of posture.'

As dawn came brilliant and crystalline over the desert and the bay, the extent of the victory could be seen. *L'Orient* had disappeared, three French 74s had been captured and later burnt, and six ships-of-the-line had been captured (two of them of 80 guns). Only Rear-Admiral Villeneuve in *Le Guillaume Tell* (80 guns) and *Le Généreux*, which had been anchored at the end of the line, managed to cut their cables and escape. Villeneuve was to meet Nelson at Trafalgar. 'The Ships of the Enemy, all but their two rear ships, are nearly dismasted,' as Nelson wrote to St Vincent, 'and those two, with two frigates, I am sorry to say, made their escape; nor was it, I assure you, in my power to prevent them. Captain Hood most handsomely endeavoured to do it, but I had no Ship in a condition to support *Zealous*, and I was obliged to call her in.'

Whatever anyone might say, it was the most complete victory ever recorded in naval history.

CHAPTER TWENTY-TWO

Laurels for the Victor

DURING the strange, punch-drunk days that followed, the victors had time to collect themselves. The effort of knocking out their opponent had left them almost equally exhausted, spread-eagled on the translucent battlefield under the hot midsummer sun. The day following the battle, Nelson had signalled his captains: 'Almighty God having blessed His Majesty's Arms with Victory, the Admiral intends returning Public Thanksgiving for the same at two o'clock this day, and he recommends every Ship doing the same as soon as convenient.' The French prisoners, most of whom had adopted the prevalent atheism of the Revolution, were surprised to see the ships' companies grouped together for divine service, against a background of shattered masts and torn rigging. They were also filled with a reluctant admiration. Nelson congratulated his officers and men, desiring that 'they will accept his most sincere and cordial thanks for their very gallant behaviour in this glorious battle'.

While they fished their spars, rigged jury masts, and attended to their own damages – as well as re-rigging such of the enemy as were capable of being sailed or towed away as prizes – the British had time to remember, in the quiet aftermath, some of the events which they, as individuals, had remarked upon in the storm of that night. Midshipman Elliott recalled how great a value to morale was the British habit of cheering as they went into action. This was something the French did not understand: 'No other nation can cheer. It encourages us and disheartens the enemy.' John Nicol, a cooper by trade and an 'old man' of forty at the time, remembered how, from his station in the powder magazine, hearing only the thud of shot, the roar of the cannonades and the howl of battle, he and the gunner were at a loss as to what was happening: 'Any information we got was from the boys and women who carried the powder.' This is the first mention of women being aboard during the action although, as has been said, it

210

was not uncommon for them to be carried in men-of-war, whether they were legitimate or common-law wives. 'I was much indebted', he goes on, 'to the gunner's wife who gave her husband and me a drink every now and then, which lessened our fatigue much. There were some of the women wounded and one woman belonging to Leith died of her wounds. One woman bore a son in the heat of the action; she belonged to Edinburgh.' This was clearly one child at least who deserved the old sobriquet of 'son of a gun'.

All of them in this curious corner of the world, far away from Europe where the main issues were to be decided, had contributed in striking a blow, the immensity of whose effect the victors could hardly visualise. In his first action in command of a fleet Nelson had all but annihilated his opponent. More than that, he had in one stroke regained command of the Mediterranean for the British: all that was now needed was for the opportunity to be seized. Sicily and the Kingdom of Naples were secured, Austria was emboldened to chance her arm once more, while Turkey and Russia were both in due course, despite their long mutual enmity, to declare against the French. India was saved, and all Bonaparte's dreams of the great conquest of the East were blown sky-high as *L'Orient*. As Monsieur Poussielgue, Controller-General of Napoleon's finances, wrote at the time, assessing the effects of the battle:

The fatal engagement ruined all our hopes; it prevented us from receiving the remainder of the forces which were destined for us; it left the field free for the English to persuade the Porte to declare war against us; it rekindled that which was barely extinguished in the heart of the Austrian Emperor; it opened the Mediterranean to the Russians, and placed them on our frontiers; it occasioned the loss of Italy and the invaluable possessions in the Adriatic which we owed to the successful campaign of Bonaparte; and finally it at once rendered abortive all our projects, since it was no longer possible for us to dream of giving the English any uneasiness in India. Added to this was the effect on the people of Egypt, whom we wished to consider as friends and allies. They became our enemies, and, entirely surrounded as we were by the Turks, we found ourselves engaged in a most difficult defensive war, without a glimpse of the slightest advantage to be obtained by it.

As Napoleon was to remark many years later when, a prisoner aboard the *Bellerophon*, he sailed for St Helena, 'In all my plans I have always been thwarted by the British Fleet.'

Meanwhile no one in England knew of this action which had changed the whole balance of power. The 50-gun *Leander*, with Captain Thompson in command and Nelson's Captain Berry bearing the despatches, fell in off Crete with the escaped *Le Généreux* and, after an action in which both Berry and Thompson were wounded, was captured. Fortunately a duplicate set of despatches had been prepared and sent aboard the brig *Mutine* to go to the Admiralty by way of Naples. It was not until two months after the action that the despatches reached England with Captain Capel of the *Mutine*. Speculation in the meantime had been rife, and many of the rumours which had been circulating were detrimental to Nelson. He had missed Napoleon, he had returned to Syracuse, there had been a great battle : who had won? Lord Spencer was moved to comment that he hoped Sir Horatio would have 'a pretty good story to tell at least'. In the event, when he did finally hear the news, the First Lord fell to the floor in the Admiralty in a dead faint. Emotions had already run riot in Naples where the 'vapours' had immediately attacked Lady Hamilton on Capel's arrival there. She, too, fainted and, as Nelson was to write some weeks later, 'she . . . is not yet properly recovered from severe bruises'. A tidal wave of emotion swept not only England, but also all Europe. So, the French were not in fact all-powerful, but as subject as all others to defeat. In England, of course, the emotion generated was immense, provoking even the cool and patrician Lady Spencer (who had been so scathing about Nelson's appearance on their first meeting) to write a letter almost as extravagant as those which he was later to receive from Emma Hamilton :

Joy, joy, joy, to you, brave, gallant immortalised Nelson! May that great God, whose cause you so valiantly support, protect and bless you to the end of your brilliant career! Such a race surely never was run. . . . All, all I *can* say must fall short of my wishes, of my sentiments about you. This moment the guns are firing, illuminations are preparing, your gallant name is echoed from street to street, and every Briton feels his obligations to you weighing him down.

She concluded, 'I am half Mad, and I fear I have written a strange letter, but you'll excuse it. Almighty God protect you. Adieu.' There could be no doubt now that the 'radiant orb' had led him to the Valhalla of fame, folklore, and legend. He would be known throughout his homeland – as indeed Drake had been before him – by ballad and broadsheet, on tobacco boxes and tankards, and on a hundred and one simple pieces of pottery that served as ornaments in country homes.

It was as if all Europe heaved a sigh of relief, and with it came foreign orders, messages of congratulation, and rich presents – a miniature from the Tsar of Russia, a gold-hilted scimitar and a diamond-set turban ornament from the Sultan of Turkey, a sword from the City of London (he had sent the City the sword of Blanquet-Duchayla), and gifts from places as remote from one another as Palermo and the island of Zante. Parliament voted him a pension of £2,000. The East India Company also made Nelson a grant of £10,000, while Alexander Davison, who was the sole prize agent, had medals struck to commemorate the action : in gold for Nelson and his captains, and in silver and bronze for the other ranks. In November Nelson was to receive a peerage, being created Baron of the Nile and of Burnham Thorpe : a reward which all his friends thought was less than his due. After all, Jervis after the much lesser action of St Vincent had been made an earl, and Duncan a viscount after the Battle of Camperdown. The award aroused criticism in the House of Commons for being insufficient, but it was pointed out that it was the highest honour that had ever been conferred upon an officer of Nelson's rank, and that he was not a commander-in-chief, but merely a junior admiral in charge of a detached squadron. What certainly pleased him was that the first lieutenants of all the ships engaged received immediate promotion. His captains had also formed an 'Egyptian Club' to commemorate the event and had commissioned a sword to be made for him, which was later to become one of his cherished possessions. Ben Hallowell, who had known him so long and had a deep affection for him, showed that he also possessed a dry sense of humour. He set *Swiftsure*'s carpenter to work on making a coffin from part of the mainmast that had been salvaged from the wreck of *L'Orient*. This *memento mori* was afterwards to adorn Nelson's cabin, and to stand behind the Windsor chair in which he commonly sat. One day in Palermo, some time later, finding some officers new to the *Vanguard* gazing with interest at this noble if morbid piece of craftsmanship, Nelson remarked : 'You may look at it, gentlemen, as long as you please; but depend upon it, none of you shall have it.'

'My head is ready to split, and I am always so sick,' he wrote to St Vincent; 'in short, if there be no fracture, my head is severely shaken.' References to his wound occur in other letters, among them one to the Hon. William Wyndham, the British Minister in Florence : 'My health, from my wound, is become so very indifferent, that I am thinking of going down the Mediterranean, so soon as I arrive at

Naples. . . .' It might have been best if he had done so. In one of the last letters written to Fanny at Round Wood in Suffolk before he sailed from Aboukir Bay, he said: 'I am thank God as much better as could be expected. . . .' As always in the past, he did everything he could to disguise from his sensitive and caring wife the extent of the damage to his health. He sent his love to his father and all his friends and again, as ever, signed himself 'your most affectionate husband'. Jefferson, his surgeon, noted in his journal that 'I applied every night a compress [to Nelson's forehead], wet with a discutient embrocation, which was of great service.' The wound was healed after a month but it is likely that the effects of concussion remained with him for a great deal longer. For the rest of his life he would wear his hair trained down over his forehead to conceal the scar.

On 14 August Sir James Saumarez sailed from Aboukir Bay for Gibraltar with seven of the squadron, taking with him six of the prizes. The previous day some of the missing frigates had at last rejoined, and Nelson detailed off three of them to stay on station with three ships-of-the-line and maintain a blockade off Alexandria. He himself in *Vanguard*, together with Troubridge in the *Culloden* and Ball in the *Alexander*, sailed for Naples on the nineteenth. They were the three most heavily damaged ships and it seemed imperative to take them to the nearest efficient dockyard in the Mediterranean, Castellammare in the Bay of Naples. Ball had received a great part of *L'Orient*'s fire and his ship was badly cut up, while the *Vanguard* was under jury rig, and Troubridge had had to fother the damaged bottom of the *Culloden* with oakum and canvas to keep her afloat. Nelson, who at this moment still hoped that he might go home to recover his health, as always placed his trust in Troubridge. He knew him for a far better diplomat than himself, and he felt sure that he could more than adequately take over the command. It was clear that, though the victory had given the British the command of the inland sea, the changed complexion of things would now occasion a general increase of activity: 'These are not times for idleness', as Nelson wrote, and later, to Hood off Alexandria, that he relied upon him to maintain a close blockade, thus ensuring the ultimate destruction of the French Army. As for himself – for he was feeling slightly better – 'I shall not go home until this is effected, and the islands of Malta, Corfu, &c., retaken.'

Meanwhile, with light and contrary winds, the three ships slowly retraced their track across the eastern Mediterranean. The news of the Battle of the Nile had reached Napoleon long before it reached his enemies in Europe. He fully realised its implications: 'I wanted to create a new religion,' he said years later. 'I saw myself on the high road to Asia, seated on an elephant, a turban on my head, a new Koran, which I should have composed to suit my interests, in my hand. I saw myself assailing Britain's power in India. But fortune decided otherwise.' Fortune had many more tricks up her sleeve. Nelson, who disliked the idea of spending much time away from the eastern area – for he envisaged the main interests of his command as stretching from Sicily to Malta and then to Egypt and the Levant – wrote to St Vincent, 'I detest this voyage to Naples. Nothing but absolute necessity could force me to the measure. Syracuse in future, whilst my operations lie on the eastern side of Sicily, is my port. . . .' To Sir William Hamilton he wrote that he hoped not to be 'more than four or five days at Naples'.

Nelson had rightly concluded that the next operation in securing the Mediterranean for the British fleet was to expel the French from Malta. With this in mind, he instructed a Portuguese squadron of four ships-of-the-line, which had been ordered to place itself under his command, to blockade the island. Once more the *Vanguard* passed through the Strait of Messina, but this time headed north with her mission accomplished. Further delayed by the loss of her jury-rigged foremast and her main topmast in a sudden squall – during which several men were lost and others injured – it was not until Saturday 22 September that Nelson's battered flagship came into the bright Bay of Naples. Under tow by a frigate, the other two ships-of-the-line having preceded him by six days, the *Vanguard* made an impressive spectacle as she passed the steep sides of Capri. On that calm autumn day, she and her Admiral sailed into the land which, since the days of the Greeks, had been known as the haunt of the Sirens.

CHAPTER TWENTY-THREE

Siren Land

FROM the moment that the *Vanguard* hove in sight all was *opéra bouffe*. The blue waters of the famous bay were untroubled by even a ripple as hundreds of pleasure boats put out to welcome the victor of the Nile, the saviour of not only their own kingdom but also all Europe, as his crippled flagship wallowed along behind her tow. Across the water came the sound of music, and 'Rule Britannia' sounded somewhat incongruously against the background of idly smoking Vesuvius and the golden glimmer of the houses and palaces of Naples. King Ferdinand, who fancied himself as something of a sailor, had himself rowed out in the state barge to meet and congratulate the hero. 'Sir William and Lady Hamilton came out to sea attended by numerous boats,' Nelson wrote to Fanny. He continued, 'Alongside my honoured friends came, the scene in the boat appeared terribly affecting. Up flew her ladyship and exclaiming : "Oh God is it possible," fell into my arms more dead than alive.' (Not for nothing was Lady Hamilton famous for her 'attitudes'.) 'Tears however soon set matters to rights, when alongside came the King. The scene was in its way affecting. He took me by the hand, calling me his deliverer and preserver, with every other expression of kindness. In short all Naples calls me "Nostro Liberatore" for the scene with the lower classes was truly affecting.' The note which was sounded on this first meeting was never to diminish. From now on all was to become more and more truly Neapolitan. As Emma Hamilton herself wrote : 'My dress from head to foot is *alla Nelson*. Even my shawl is in Blue with gold anchors all over. My ear-rings are Nelson's anchors; in short we are all be-Nelsoned. . . .'

The characters who were now to circle around the diminutive figure of the Admiral were all in their way equally strange, fantastic even, when set against the sombre hull of the *Vanguard* and the other men-of-war : the sun-tanned, tar-stained sailors, the lowering guns that had destroyed the French fleet, and the shot-riddled oak sides, scarred masts and torn rigging of the victors. Ferdinand IV, who might be cast as the buffoon in this opera, was known to his subjects as 'Old Nosey' for his physiognomy, and also affectionately by the working people, and contemptuously by the other classes, as 'Il Re Lazzarone' for his fondness for the beggars and riff-raff of his city. In an age when monarchs kept strictly aloof from their subjects he enjoyed the simple pleasures of the people, fishing, gaming, drinking wine and, above all, the pleasures of hunting. It has been said of him that 'Few sovereigns have left behind so odious a memory', but at the time that Nelson met him he presented no more than an affable and coarse bonhomie. His Queen, who was unable to come with him, being ill as well as in mourning for the death of her youngest child, was an altogether more formidable figure. Of her Bonaparte remarked that she was the only man in Naples. Sir William Hamilton's first wife (who was a great deal more perspicacious than his second) had recorded of Maria Carolina that :

She is quick, clever, insinuating when she pleases, hates and loves violently . . . there is no dependence on what she says as she is seldom of the same opinion two days. Her strongest and most durable passions are ambition and vanity, the latter of which gives her a strong disposition towards Coquetry, but the former, which I think is her principal Object, makes her use every Art to please the King in order to get the Reins of Government into her hands in as great a measure as is possible.

The Prime Minister of this southern kingdom was an expatriate Englishman, Sir John Acton, who had been born in France and had served in the French Navy as well as those of Tuscany and of Naples. An excellent administrator, and an honest man in a land where such a virtue was rare, he had made himself invaluable to Ferdinand and his Queen. He had inherited his English title seven years before and, although he spoke the language fairly fluently, had never visited his native country. His policy as Prime Minister was largely devised in concert with Sir William Hamilton, its principal aim being to sub-stitute the influence of Britain and Austria for that of Spain in the Bourbon Kingdom of Naples. He shared the Queen's dislike, if not quite her impassioned hatred, of all things French – a language which he spoke as easily as he did Italian. As an administrator in a corrupt kingdom he was exceptional, but in matters of higher policy he was not astute or perspicacious enough to have risen to the rank of statesman – the role in which he fancied himself.

Sir William Hamilton was the son of a Scottish duke. He had
served in the Army but, after marrying a Welsh heiress, had turned
to the diplomatic world and had become British envoy to the Bourbon
Court in Naples in 1764. On his first wife's dying in 1782 he had
inherited her estate near Swansea, the money from which he had
largely devoted to his pursuit of works of classical art, the production
of beautiful and lavishly illustrated books on antiquity and on
volcanoes – the latter being his second passion. He had made twenty-
two ascents of Vesuvius and was one of the first and foremost
volcanists in history. By the time that Nelson knew him he had become
so perfectly assimilated to this kingdom in the sun that a British
visitor had remarked of him, 'As to Sir William Hamilton, he was a
perfect Neapolitan both in mind and manners.' This was to be
less than fair to a man who might better have been described as
the epitome of an eighteenth-century English aristocrat. Civilised,
courteous, urbane, he took a Horatian view of life. His relationship
with his second wife has often aroused controversy, but it is best
perhaps summed up by his biographer Brian Fothergill :

After seven years of marriage and twelve years living under the
same roof as Emma Sir William had no complaints to lay at her
door; he was still devoted to her. The exact nature of their relationship must remain a matter for speculation, but it is probable that
he was not a very ardent or demanding husband. The fact that he
had no children by either of his marriages . . . might well suggest
that he was either impotent or sterile. Emma, as we know, had a
child long before he met her and was later to present Nelson with
a daughter and possibly another child who was still-born. Hamilton's amorous adventures during his first wife's lifetime have a note
of comic opera about them and consisted in no more than mild
philandering; there is no evidence that he ever had any illegitimate
children. His lifelong love of beauty, the 'attitudes' that featured
so early in his life with Emma, his whole manner of treating her like
a wonderful *objet d'art* which so often amused his friends, the
swimming boys who performed for his entertainment at Posillipo
(as Tischbeing witnessed) are all indications that in matters of sex
Sir William was possibly one of those men for whom a feast for the
eyes is banquet enough.

Goethe in his *Travels in Italy* summed up his impressions of the
ambassador with the words : 'Hamilton is a person of universal taste,
and after having wandered through the whole realm of creation has

found rest at last in a most beautiful companion, a masterpiece of that great artist – Nature.'

His companion, now his wife, and thirteen years older than when Goethe had met her, was Emma, née Amy Lyon, born the daughter of a Cheshire blacksmith. Taken early to London by a shrewd mother, she had swiftly graduated to a so-called Temple of Health in the Adelphi, which would appear to have been a cross between a quack apothecary's shop and a fashionable house of assignation. Her beauty had infatuated Romney who had drawn and painted her innumerable times, catching in her youthful skin, lips and eyes a perfection of natural health and glowing vitality. Taken up by a young baronet, Sir Harry Fetherstonehaugh of (appropriately named) Up Park on the South Downs, she proceeded to live a life which she was herself later to describe as 'wild and thoughtless'. After less than a year she found herself pregnant and the gates of this wanton Eden were closed behind her. It was at this point that one of Sir Harry's friends, the cool and cultivated Charles Greville, stepped in to become her protector. He not only adopted her child, a daughter named Emma, but kept her as his mistress for four years in his small house in Edgware Row. She had now changed her name to Emily Hart. Greville found that he had a devoted mistress who truly loved him for the kindness he had shown her, together with an efficient housekeeper in her mother. He taught her how to spell (though this was never to be her forte), had her instructed in music, and indeed made out of his wild country rose a flower that sat elegantly in the buttonhole of a young man about town. It was he who introduced her to Romney. Greville was Sir William Hamilton's nephew and, like his uncle, though well born he had no fortune, so it was incumbent upon him to find an heiress to maintain his style of life. (Unlike his uncle he was never to find one.) But in the search for an heiress it was necessary to disencumber himself of his mistress. Hamilton, already a widower, had visited England and had been much taken with the beauty of his nephew's young protégée, but his interest was decidedly no more than an admiring platonism. Greville thought that this situation could easily be improved upon and arranged, after Hamilton's return to Naples, for Emma and her mother (Mrs Cadogan as the latter now called herself) to visit the envoy in his romantic city. Sir William was a reluctant lover, and it was some time before Emma became his mistress. Indeed Emma, who genuinely loved Greville, was most unwilling to exchange him for his elderly uncle, however kind and gentle the latter might be. Indeed, it is quite clear from the numerous tragic letters that she wrote Greville from Naples, that he was perhaps the only man she ever loved with simple passion unmixed with artistry. (Her love for Nelson, as will be seen, was of another calibre.) 'You are everything', she wrote, 'that is dear to me on hearth, and I hope happier times will soon restore you to me, for endead I would rather be with you starving then from you in the greatest splender in the world.'

She did not starve, however – *she* made the rich marriage that Greville never did – and she returned to Naples, after Sir William had paid another visit to England, as Lady Hamilton, wife of the envoy extraordinary and minister plenipotentiary to the Kingdom of the Two Sicilies. Before passing on to consider what Emma looked like when Nelson came to know her on this visit in *Vanguard* it is worth considering the judgement of genius, of Goethe who saw Emma as a young woman :

. . . an English girl of about twenty years of age. She is very handsome with a beautiful figure. The old knight has made a Greek costume for her which becomes her extremely. Dressed in this, letting her hair fall loose, and making use of a couple of shawls, she exhibits every possible variety of pose, expression, and aspect, so that in the end the spectator almost imagines himself in a dream. Here one sees in perfection, in ravishing variety, in move-ment, all that the greatest artists have loved to express.

At the time that they all now met Emma was thirty-three; Sir William nearly sixty-nine; and Nelson would be forty within a few days.

Nelson's original intention was to settle himself into a hotel, for he knew that there would be much coming and going of naval officers and couriers : he had after all to consider the whole disposition of the ships throughout the central and eastern Mediterranean as well as prosecute the blockade of Malta. Napoleon was still triumphant in Egypt, even if deprived of his fleet, and the host of French transports were still at anchor in Alexandria harbour. Sir William, however, was determined to have the Admiral as his guest and the hero must of necessity be lodged in the Palazzo Sessa. This was Sir William's town house, a palace of considerable grandeur that had been further enriched by his magnificent collection of antiques and old masters. Here an upper-floor room had been set aside for Nelson, from which a curving window gave out upon the whole prospect of the Bay of Naples. It was a far call from the cramped quarters and low head-room of his cabin aboard the *Vanguard*, from that simple wooden home from which, as he remarked, he had not been absent for some six months. Nelson was still ill from his head-wound, and his frail appearance, his one arm, his sightless eye, and the evidence of considerable fatigue dating from all those weeks of relentless chase, culminating in the thunder of the Nile, made him an obvious subject for rest and careful nursing. Emma took this upon herself. She was, it must be pointed out, no longer quite Goethe's vision of loveliness, although her face had retained the glowing charm that Romney had loved to paint. She was, as one observer described her, 'full in person, not fat, but *embonpoint*'. She was also, though 'ill-bred, often very affected', a woman who had learned throughout her curiously chequered career to discern the nature of men and know how to please them. It did not take her very long to discover that Nelson's greatest weakness was his vanity. Indeed, as he himself wrote to Fanny, 'The preparations of Lady Hamilton for celebrating my birthday tomorrow are enough to fill me with vanity. Every ribbon, every button has "Nelson" etc., the whole service are "H.N. Glorious 1st August". Songs, sonnets are numerous beyond what I ever could deserve. I send you the additional verse to "God save the King" as I know you will sing it with pleasure.' The verse read :

> Join we great Nelson's name
> First on the roll of fame
> Him let us sing
> Spread we his praise around
> Honour of British ground
> Who made Nile's shores resound
> God save the King.

Even the cool and imperturbable Troubridge might have had his head slightly turned by all the adulation that now fell upon Nelson.

The Admiral's fortieth birthday – marred only by the fact that Josiah Nisbet got outrageously drunk – was a fantasy of lights, decorations, triumphal arches, and all the fanfaronade that came so easily to the Neapolitan temperament. Nelson was celebrated in much the same way as the Caesars had once been hailed in this bright bay of the Sirens. It is significant, however, that he had not yet quite succumbed to those blandishing voices, that his letters to his wife are still the letters of a loving husband, and that he could write to St Vincent on the day after his birthday : 'I trust, my Lord, in a week we shall be at sea. I am very unwell, and the miserable conduct of this Court is not likely to cool my irritable temper. It is a country of fiddlers and poets, whores and scoundrels.' One suspects that the

Admiral may have had a hangover, but his judgement was still sound. His immediate preoccupation was to capitalise upon the victory of Aboukir Bay and to take advantage of the rising tide of hope throughout Europe. It seemed essential to strike on land, while Napoleon was still immersed in the affairs of the East, and unable to return so long as the Royal Navy held the seas between Egypt and France. All seemed set for a military expansion, moving northwards to free Rome, with the intention of ultimately driving the French out of Italy. On the surface of it, the overall plan was reasonable enough, but what Nelson neglected to appreciate was that the material with which to effect it was sadly wanting. The Neapolitan troops, with whom he hoped to effect this thrust, were – as he should well have known from his previous experience in western Italy and France – ill-trained, and incompetently officered. However, the tide was at the full : the Queen was fired by the desire to see the hated French expelled from Italy, Ferdinand even was carried along by Nelson's enthusiasm, and Sir William Hamilton cast aside his better judgement to join the war party. Negotiations were already afoot for a coalition against France in which Britain, Austria and Russia were to act in concert. Early in October General Mack arrived from Vienna. He was unfortunately a very typical example of an Austrian general of the period – and Nelson had had good reason to mistrust their capabilities from previous experience. But he felt himself borne forward on the shining wave of success, and the atmosphere by which he was surrounded was hardly conducive to clear thinking, even by one who was less susceptible to flattery than Nelson or, indeed, of a less amorous disposition. One letter to St Vincent is revealing enough for, after commenting sensibly on the general procrastination and inefficiency in Naples (with the exception of the Queen), he goes on : 'We all dine this day with the King on board a ship, he is very attentive. I have been with the Queen, she is truly a daughter of Maria Theresa. I am writing opposite Lady Hamilton, therefore you will not be surprised at the glorious jumble of this letter. Were your Lordship in my place, I much doubt if you could write so well; our hearts and our hands must be all in a flutter : Naples is a dangerous place, and we must keep clear of it.' The words spring clear enough from the page – Nelson was already half in love with the Ambassadress. If he had heeded his own sound advice, history would have been very different.

On 14 October, he sailed for Malta where a Portuguese squadron had joined Captain Ball to assist in the blockade of the island. It was a long slow passage from Naples, ten days at sea, but on arrival Nelson was able to see for himself that the islanders were actively conducting

a siege of their capital, Valetta, where General Vaubois and his troops
were besieged with little food, and almost no hope of receiving any
assistance from the sea. It seemed at that time as if Valetta must soon
fall, and this last French base be eliminated from the middle sea. In
fact, Vaubois and his men were to hold out for many months. Before
making his way back to Naples Nelson had the satisfaction of seeing
the French in the little northern island of Gozo, invested by Ball, come
to terms and capitulate. Five ships-of-the-line were left behind to help
in prosecuting the blockade of Malta itself and Nelson felt that he
could now turn his attention to the march on Rome – something
which, if General Mack and the Neapolitans had been anything but
dilatory, should have been almost ready.

Not even the atmosphere of war, as Nelson quickly found out, could
bring any sense of urgency or real understanding of the task ahead of
them to either King Ferdinand, General Mack, or their officers and
troops. Although some thirty thousand men had been assembled at
San Germano for manoeuvres and for a personal inspection by Nelson,
it could not escape the latter's critical eye that all was not well. He
drily observed, 'I have formed my opinion. I heartily hope I may
be mistaken.' Coletta, the historian of Naples during this period,
describes the scene :

The King had taken up his quarters in this camp, prepared to
march with the army; the queen, attired in a riding-habit, constantly drove along the lines in a chariot and four, accompanied by
the Ambassadors from friendly sovereigns, and other foreigners of
distinction, the barons of the kingdom, and Lady Hamilton, who,
under pretence of escorting her Majesty, displayed her own beauty
in all its magnificence to the camp, and paraded her conquest over
the victor of Aboukir who, seated beside her in the same chariot,
appeared fascinated and submissive to her charms.

There were as yet no grounds for real gossip. All was pretence, at
least on Emma's part, who was merely striking one of her 'attitudes'
as the constant companion of Victory, embodied in Nelson. Nor had
Sir William any reason to suspect that a wife who had been faithful
to him for so many years, and who had never in any way been touched
by the constant scandal of a scandalous city, could possibly be acting
in any other way than as the proud friend of a great and noble man.
Sir William regarded Nelson as the son he had never had : the
embodiment of old English values and virtues.

It was not until late November that any action was initiated against the French in Italy, and had more careful thought been applied to the situation the Neapolitan army would have stayed where it was. The Austrians had refused to commit themselves to what they regarded as a rash adventure, while the Marquis de Gallo, Ferdinand's Foreign Minister (who had always been opposed to any military action), began to weaken the King's resolution – which in any case had only been lent any form of strength by the presence of Nelson. Sir William Hamilton was also in something of a quandary, for he had explicit instructions from London to avoid any action being taken against the French unless he could be sure of 'the fullest assurance of support' from the Austrian government. It was Nelson and his insistence on the necessity of attack that won the day, and forced the irresolute Ferdinand and the (as it proved) incompetent General Mack to make a move. In a sense, it was a Tenerife all over again. Nelson's belief that any activity was better than none – that action would always solve everything – was once more to prove fatal.

The army set out from San Germano on 22 November, at the same time as Nelson and his squadron sailed for Leghorn. The plan was for the ships to land troops and make a surprise attack in the rear of the French while Ferdinand and Mack attacked Rome from the south. The first part succeeded admirably, Leghorn surrendering unconditionally. For a brief moment success also attended the Neapolitan Army, the French withdrawing from Rome to reorganise themselves outside the city. They were indeed, if only momentarily, taken by surprise, since for one thing their country was not at war with Naples. On 29 November Ferdinand entered Rome in triumph – a little over a week later he was in full flight. The French under General Championnet had turned to the attack and, although they were only half the number of Mack's army, soon proved that they were much more than a match for it, that they were without doubt the finest soldiers in Europe. The retreat of the Neapolitans – 'la plus belle armée d'Europe' as Mack had earlier called them – became a shameful rout, officers throwing aside their arms and seizing horses and carriages to escape, while the body of the army abandoned all discipline and ran south for Naples as fast as it could go. Nelson commented bitterly: 'The Neapolitan officers have not lost much honour, for God knows they had but little to lose, but they lost all they had.' Foremost in the retreat, disguised as a civilian, was King Ferdinand.

CHAPTER TWENTY-FOUR

Palermo

A DOCUMENT headed *Most Secret* tells the tale of the next few days. Dated 'Naples, *December 20, 1798*', it reads:

> Three barges, and the small cutter of the *Alcmene*, armed with cutlasses only, to be at the Victoria at *half past seven* o'clock precisely. Only one barge to be seen at the wharf, the others to lay on their oars at the outside of the rocks – the small barge of the *Vanguard* to be at the wharf. The above boats to be on board the *Alcmene* before seven o'clock, under the direction of Captain Hope. *Grapnells to be in the boats.*
>
> All the other boats of the *Vanguard* and *Alcmene* to be armed with cutlasses, and the launches and carronades to assemble on board the *Vanguard*, under the direction of Captain Hardy, and to put off from her at half-past eight o'clock *precisely, to row half way towards the Mola Figlio. These boats to have 4 or 6 soldiers in them. In case assistance is wanted by me, false fires will be burnt.*
>
> NELSON
>
> *The Alcmene to be ready to slip in the night, if necessary.*

The Neapolitan attack on Rome had given the French the opportunity, and a valid reason, for a move on Naples. The city had a strong Republican faction, particularly among the educated middle-classes, and King Ferdinand's regime was doomed from the moment that he and his army fled back to the illusory safety of his kingdom. In reality there was no safety, and only the *lazzaroni*, the sturdy riff-raff of the Neapolitan slums and waterfront, held their King in any regard. Sir William Hamilton had already seen to his effects and had arranged for the safety of the British residents in Naples. Meanwhile the Queen had sent countless boxes, trunks and jewel cases to Emma Hamilton at the Palazzo Sessa, whence they were surreptitiously forwarded to the waiting British. One letter from the Queen reads, 'I

225

venture to send you this evening all our Spanish money, both the King's and my own, they are sixty thousand gold ducats.' She wrote further on 19 December, 'I abuse your goodness and our brave Admiral's. Let the great boxes be thrown in the hold and the little ones be near at hand. It is so, because I have unfortunately an immense family. I am in the despair of desolation and my tears flow incessantly. The blow, its suddenness has bewildered me, and I do not think I shall recover from it.' In the midst of all this secrecy and of the preparations for the flight of the royal family, Emma Hamilton was in her element. She relished the high drama of it all but, quite apart from that, she was a competent organiser. For so long the Queen's closest confidante (a role in which she saw herself as dominant, unknowing how much the Queen manipulated her), Emma now found a real *raison d'être* in acting as the link between her 'adorable unfortunate Queen' and her heroic Admiral.

Extracts from the *Vanguard*'s journal show the pattern of those last feverish days as the royal family together with their court prepared to flee from the city that they rightly saw as doomed – not by the eruption of Vesuvius but of revolutionary sentiments among many of their own people, and by the uncontested advance of the French Army.

December 18th. Sailmakers making cots for the Royal Family: Painters painting the wardroom and offices under the poop; getting ready for sea, and getting off the valuable effects of Her Sicilian Majesty in the night time.

Thursday, 19th. Smuggling on board the Queen's diamonds &c. [Sir William Hamilton estimated that the treasure and money carried aboard the *Vanguard* and other ships amounted to two and a half million sterling.]

Friday, 21st. At 10 AM, their Sicilian Majesties and the Royal Family embarked on board, as did the British Ambassador and family, the Imperial Ambassador and suite, several of the Neapolitan nobles and their servants, and most of the English gentlemen and merchants that were in Naples.

Nelson had been present at the corner of the Arsenal at half-past eight that night and had gone to the palace by a long tunnel which communicated with the Victoria landing stage. He had supervised the departure of the royal family (cloaked and hooded) into the waiting barge which rose and fell in a long swell that presaged the advent of bad weather. The evacuation of the royal family and of all their dependants was carried out with the minimum of fuss. Only one man was deeply troubled and aggrieved by the fact that the King and Queen were seeking safety aboard Nelson's flagship *Vanguard*. This was Commodore Caracciolo, Bailli of the Order of Malta, who was in command of the Neapolitan Navy. He had pleaded for the privilege of taking his monarch to his other capital, Palermo, but had had his application refused – on the good ground that there was trouble in his fleet, and some of the ships' companies had even gone ashore and refused to man their ships. The only security was to be found with Nelson and the British.

Among those who did not leave Naples was Baron Mack. He had nothing to report to the departing King but total failure. His army had largely melted away, and his only instructions now were to fall back on Sicily if he was unable to hold Naples. Even Nelson, who held no brief for him, was forced to comment: 'My heart bled for him, he is worn to a shadow.' As for King Ferdinand, not even the loss of his beautiful capital and of the major part of his kingdom could bring him to his senses or afford him any realisation of the gravity of the situation. When Sir William Hamilton stood by him, as the *Vanguard* made sail and drew out of the bay, he listened with close attention for any words from the King which might indicate his future plans. Ferdinand drew a deep breath of air, inhaling the salty tang of the winter wind, and said comfortably: 'We shall have plenty of woodcocks, *Cavaliere*, this wind will bring them in – it is just the season, we shall have rare sport. You must get your *cannone* ready!'

But the wind which was just beginning to blow brought them far more than just rare sport. Nelson was to record how, 'On the 23rd, at 7 PM the *Vanguard*, *Sannite*, and *Archimedes*, with about twenty sail of Vessels left the Bay of Naples; the next day it blew harder than I ever experienced since I have been at sea.' Christmas Eve was certainly a day to remember, with a storm of such violence that all communication was lost between the wallowing ships. The *Vanguard* split her three topsails and was even in some danger of foundering, while the confusion and sickness among the already dejected evacuees was such that many would have wished themselves back in Naples – even if the French had already arrived. Sir William Hamilton, having helped his fellow passengers as far as he could, adopted a philosophic attitude and retired to a cabin, where Emma found him seated with a brace of loaded pistols in his hands. He was determined, he said, not to go down with 'the guggle, guggle, guggle of salt water in his throat' but to shoot himself the moment he felt the ship sinking. It was Emma who was the heroine of the voyage, the only civilian, it would seem, to retain her head and to try to put some spirit into her demoralised companions. If there was one virtue that Nelson held above all others it was courage, and he saw it in Emma. It probably was to count almost as much with him as her beauty, for he now admired a high spirit and an indomitable quality that he had probably never seen in a woman before. In his letter to St Vincent describing the evacuation in detail, and the stormy passage southward to Sicily, he wrote of his concern about the safety of the royal family and how :

On the 25th, at 9 AM Prince Albert, their Majesties' youngest child, having eat a hearty breakfast, was taken ill, and at 7 PM died in the arms of Lady Hamilton; and here it is my duty to tell your Lordship the obligations which the whole Royal Family as well as myself are under on this trying occasion to her Ladyship. They necessarily came on board without a bed, nor could the least preparations be made for their reception. Lady Hamilton provided her own beds, linen, &c., and became *their slave*, for except one man, no person belonging to Royalty assisted the Royal Family, nor did her Ladyship enter a bed the whole time they were on board.

Beauty allied with courage and endurance, glimpsed against the background of storm and of sick and frightened human beings, made an unforgettable impression.

Two events marred the peace of mind both of Sir William Hamilton and Nelson not very long after their arrival in Palermo. Sir William had sent the pick of his collection of classical vases to England in a transport which, while sheltering in Scilly Roads, dragged her anchor and sank. Only a few cases were recovered some months later, and it remained until the twentieth century for diving expertise to develop sufficiently for any fragments of the rest to be salvaged. Nelson's unease, and indeed downright anger, stemmed from the fact that the Admiralty, seeking for some way in which to employ his undoubted talents, had despatched Captain Sir Sidney Smith to the Levant with the joint task of exercising naval command in that area as well as diplomatic powers in conjunction with his younger brother Spencer, who was British Minister in Constantinople. Sir Sidney held the order of the Sword of Sweden (Nelson referred to him bitterly as 'the Swedish knight'), and was a colourful and histrionic character cast in somewhat the same mould as Nelson himself. Nelson saw in this new Admiralty appointment an intolerable situation, where a captain was being sent to take over a salient part of his own command – and in the very area where he had just won so resounding a victory. '*I do feel, for I am a man,*' he wrote to St Vincent, 'that it is impossible for me to serve in these seas under a junior officer : – could I have thought it ! – and from Earl Spencer ! Never, never was I so astonished as your letter made me. As soon as I can get hold of Troubridge, I shall send him to Egypt, to endeavour to destroy the Ships in Alexandria. If it can be done, Troubridge will do it.' His temper erupts again later in the same letter when he begs permission to be allowed to retire and return to England aboard the *Vanguard* along with 'my friends, Sir William and Lady Hamilton'.

In the event, St Vincent managed to cushion the arrival of Sir Sidney in the Levant against Nelson's anger and maintain the same dispositions, with the latter in overall command. Smith went on fully to justify the Admiralty's confidence in him, becoming the hero of the hour in his conduct of the defence of Acre. In command of Turkish troops reinforced by British sailors, he ensured so stout a resistance that Napoleon was forced to abandon the siege of the city. Already worsted by Nelson at Aboukir Bay, Napoleon was to find an indomitable opponent in 'the Swedish knight', who became the first Englishman to defeat the great Frenchman on land. The stubborn and successful defence of Acre, coupled with the immense losses (largely from malaria) of the Army of the East, checked Napoleon's eastern ambitions and proved a turning point in his career. He was later to say of Sir Sidney Smith : 'That man made me miss my destiny.'

The Hamiltons had settled into a draughty and uncomfortable house in Palermo, the Villa Bastioni, where Sir William promptly caught cold and took to his bed for several weeks. He had much to disturb him, for his political career was deeply damaged by his espousal of the Neapolitan adventure of attacking Rome. Nelson, who had been so largely responsible for the whole affair, seems to have felt that no blame could be apportioned to him. Like Sir William he blamed General Mack, the cowardice and inefficiency of the Neapolitan Army, and above all the failure of the Austrians to invade Italy from the north. Living in the minister's house, seeing more of courtiers than of sailors, his vanity constantly stirred by such companions – and above all by Emma – Nelson began only too rapidly to take on something of the hue of that strange southern kingdom, more remote even from his English background than the absurdities of Naples. A grave disappointment to him was the conduct of Josiah Nisbet, an officer whom those who knew him well had long realised would never be 'an ornament to the service'. Despite all that Nelson had done to promote his interest over the years, the fact was that Fanny's son had been a constant source of embarrassment. In January 1799 he was finally

impelled to tell her so : 'I wish I could say much to your and my
satisfaction about Josiah, but I am sorry to say and with real grief
that he has nothing good about him, and must sooner or later be
broke, but I am sure neither you or I can help it. I have done with
the subject, it is an ungrateful one.' Although he was writing to Fanny
in the same month about his desire to return home in March, and
about buying 'a neat house in London near Hyde Park', the links
binding him with home were gradually snapping. There can be no
doubt that by now he acknowledged to himself that he had fallen in
love with Emma Hamilton. It would only be a matter of time before
that love would be consummated.

Nelson's patent subservience to Emma, his dog-like devotion, could
hardly escape comment and could hardly fail to distress his fellow
captains, especially those who knew him well and knew how susceptible
he was to women and flattery. Emma herself was seen with a sharp
eye by a British visitor to Palermo that winter, Pryse Lockhart Gordon,
who was travelling with Lord Montgomery and, as was natural, called
on the British Minister upon his arrival in Palermo. After describing
his presentation 'to Sir W. Hamilton and Lord Nelson, who lived
with him', he goes on :

> Our introduction to the fascinating Emma Lady Hamilton was an
> affair of more ceremony, and got up with considerable stage effect.
> When we had sat a few minutes, and had given all our details of
> Naples, which we thought were received with great *sang froid*, the
> Cavaliere retired, but shortly returned by a *porte-battante*, and on
> his arm or rather on his shoulder was leaning the interesting
> Melpomene, her raven tresses floating round her expansive form
> and full bosom. . . . The ceremony of introduction being over, she
> rehearsed in a subdued tone a *mélange* of Lancashire and Italian,
> detailing the catalogue of her miseries, her hopes and her fears, with
> lamentation about her dear queen, the loss of her own charming
> Palazzo and its precious contents, which had fallen into the hands
> of the vile republicans. But here we offered some consolation, by
> assuring her Ladyship that every article of the ambassador's
> property had been safely embarked in an English transport, and
> would be despatched in a few days. All this we afterwards learned
> she knew, as the vessel had actually arrived.

But, where a cool and aristocratic eye could see only affectation and
vulgarity, the simple eye of a sailor could see only a full-blown beauty
that captivated him.

While the cold Palermitan winter drew on and arrangements were

made for the Hamiltons to move into a larger and more comfortable
house, the Palazzo Palagonia near the harbour-mole, the affairs of
Naples had passed from bad to worse. Only the *lazzaroni* had continued to defy the French and by the close of January all resistance
was at an end. The city capitulated to General Championnet and
although the Parthenopean Republic, which was now established in
Ferdinand's former capital, could hardly be said to be based on
popular support it rested firmly enough, so it seemed, upon the
indisputable strength of French arms. Cardinal Fabrizio Ruffo, a
type of worldly prelate familiar enough in the southern world, who
owned large estates in Calabria, now left Sicily to attempt to organise
the peasantry from his own lands and lead a general uprising. He was
to prove himself a skilled and able revolutionary leader who, within
a short space of time, managed to provoke a widespread movement of
revolt against the French. Troubridge similarly was successful in the
mission on which he was despatched by Nelson – to get control of the
islands commanding the Bay of Naples. By early April that year both
Procida and Ischia were in his hands, but he was soon to find that
the ambivalent, indeed mercurial, nature of southern patriotism was
altogether too complicated for his conservative nature to understand.
Nelson proposed to send him some soldiers as well as a judge, so that
the hard-pressed Troubridge did not have to concern himself over-
much with Neapolitan political affairs. These were deep waters where,
as would soon be proved in Nelson's case, straightforwardness and
simplicity, coupled with a belief in immediate action, were no sub-
stitutes for shrewdness, guile, and an understanding of the complexity
of Latin natures.

Nelson meanwhile had made the Palazzo Palagonia his home and
here the *Tria juncta in Uno* – Sir William's graceful usage of the
motto of the Order to which both he and Nelson belonged, and which
was no more than a delicate euphemism for a *ménage à trois* – quietly
established itself. Sir William had long ago accustomed himself to the
idea that he must one of these days yield to a younger man (naturally
hoping that the arrangement could be conducted with suitable
discretion). The fact that Nelson had clearly fallen under Emma's
spell, and that she was prepared to reciprocate his affection, was
disturbing but not intolerable. He had found in Nelson not only a
missing son but a classical hero, a figure almost from Homer, whom
he loved for his achievements and for the shining light of his personality. Sir William, although naturally accredited as such by British
visitors, by the Court, and by the Palermitan populace, was never the
classic *cornuto* – that word of disparagement which still obtains in

Palermo as the ultimate insult for a blind cuckold. He was also a great deal more than the *mari complaisant*, a term which suggests a husband who does not mind his wife's taking a lover provided that she does not mind his having a mistress. He loved Emma for the kindness she had shown him over all the years, for the still singular beauty of her face, and he loved Nelson as the greatest and most admirable friend he had ever made. His conclusion was to be the simple Horatian one of autumnal acceptance. He was never to show about the whole matter the raging fury which he displayed to Greville when he heard of the loss of his great collection of classical vases.

CHAPTER TWENTY-FIVE

Mediterranean '99

In March 1799 Austria declared war on France – the very event which Nelson, Hamilton and Acton had hoped for the previous year. An Austrian and Russian army under General Suvarov marched into northern Italy, while a combined Russian and Turkish squadron captured the island of Corfu from the French. The result of this was that Cardinal Ruffo and his rapidly growing army of irregulars were able to continue their sweep from the south. The unfortunate citizens of Naples seemed inevitably doomed to be caught by the terror unleashed by the Jacobins in their city and the terror that would be unleashed when Ruffo and their compatriots finally reached it. During the same period, away in the western Mediterranean, General Sir Charles Stuart had captured Minorca, with its all-important naval base of Port Mahon, with such ease that the General was able to send two complete British regiments to reinforce the defence of Sicily. Troubridge meanwhile, from his vantage points of Procida and Ischia, continued to maintain a tight blockade of Naples. The failure of 1798 looked as if it was to be succeeded by resounding success throughout the Mediterranean. At such a moment, when the action for which he had earlier called seemed on all sides to be achieving a momentum that could drive the French out of the Mediterranean basin, the man whose victory at the Nile had inspired it all remained, as Lord Spencer was later to describe him, 'inactive at a foreign court'.

The reason for this is sadly apparent. Lady Minto, wife of the ambassador to Vienna, had all the news from Palermo imparted to her by two British travellers who had been in that city since the first arrival of the royal family after their flight from Naples. She wrote to her sister :

Nelson and the Hamiltons all lived together in a house of which he bore the expense, which was enormous, and every sort of gaming

233

went on half the night. Nelson used to sit with large parcels of gold before him, and generally go to sleep, Lady Hamilton taking from the heap without counting, and playing with his money to the amount of £500 a night. Her rage is play, and Sir William says when he is dead she will be a beggar. However, she has about £30,000 worth of diamonds from the royal family in presents. She sits at the Council, and rules everything and everybody.

The latter was very far from true, for the Queen, while making use of Emma Hamilton (and increasingly so as she observed Nelson's dependence upon her), was not the kind of woman to let any other take the reins of power into her hands. But the general tenor of Nelson's life during this period is well enough borne out by other accounts, including Lord Minto's comment : 'His zeal for the public service seems entirely lost in his love and vanity, and they all sit and flatter each other all day long. . . .'

The saddest comment of all, however, was to come from Troubridge, who wrote to his old friend as tactfully as possible : 'Pardon me, my Lord, it is my sincere esteem for you that makes me mention it. I know you can have no pleasure sitting up all night at cards; why then, sacrifice your health, comfort, purse, ease, everything, to the customs of a country, where your stay cannot be long?' He knew well enough the reason; he knew also that Nelson had never been a gambler, and that he appeared to be so now only because the woman with whom he was in love had a passion for high play. Troubridge goes on to say : 'I trust the war will soon be over, and deliver us from a nest of everything that is infamous, and that we may enjoy the smiles of our countrywomen. Your Lordship is a stranger to half that happens, or the talk it occasions; if you knew what your friends feel for you, I am sure you would cut all the nocturnal parties. The gambling of the people at Palermo is publicly talked of everywhere. I beseech your Lordship leave off.' Nelson was unable to, and, as far as we know, never even answered this letter.

At the time when Sir William had married Emma, the cynical Casanova, who knew Naples as well as so many other cities during the strange odyssey of his life, made the comment : 'He was a clever man, but ended by marrying a young woman who was clever enough to bewitch him. Such a fate often overtakes a man of intelligence when he grows old. It is always a mistake to marry, but when a man's physical and mental forces are declining, it is a calamity.' His words were now sadly confirmed. The date when Nelson and Emma first became lovers cannot be certainly ascribed but such evidence as there is suggests that it was most probably on 12 February of this year 1799. A letter written by Nelson to Emma, after the birth of their daughter in 1801, contains the lines : 'Ah my dear friend, I did remember well the 12th February, and also the two months afterwards. I shall never forget them, and never be sorry for the consequences.' Now, there were only two 12 Februarys to which Nelson could possibly be referring – those of 1799 and 1800. But on 12 February 1800 Nelson sailed from Palermo to Malta with Lord Keith, who had succeeded St Vincent as Commander-in-Chief, on the cruise during which he captured *Le Généreux*. Knowing Nelson's meticulous habit (long learned from his lifetime as a sailor) of recording dates with punctiliousness, there can be little doubt that it is to the 12 February of 1799 that he refers. In that year also he did not leave Palermo aboard *Vanguard* until 19 May, which would account for the 'two months afterwards'. Palermo, after its bone-chilling winters with the snows on the high mountains behind the Conca d'Oro, blossoms out in spring to become one of the most gracious cities in the southern world. There seems little doubt that it was in the Palazzo Palagonia in the early months of that year that the Admiral and the Ambassadress consummated a love that had begun on her part as something of a charade mixed with adulation, and on his part as a sop to his vanity and the very human desire of an impressionable man for female affection and comfort. A confirmatory note to this conclusion is added by the fact that it was in May 1799 that Nelson added a codicil to his will in favour of Emma (many others were to follow) to the effect that he was leaving her a diamond-set gold box 'as a token of regard and respect for her every eminent virtue (for she possesses them all to such a degree that it would be doing her injustice was any particular one to be mentioned)'. The nub here is what construction one puts upon the word 'virtue'. . . .

As far as Nelson was professionally concerned the crucial event of that year was to be the replacement of St Vincent as Commander-in-Chief by Lord Keith. The relationship between St Vincent and Nelson was so close, with such implicit trust on either side, that the latter feared – and rightly – that he would never possess such freedom of command under a newcomer as he had had under his old friend. 'Do not quit us,' Nelson wrote. 'If I have any weight in your friendship let me entreat you to rouse the sleeping lion, *GIVE NOT UP A PARTICLE OF YOUR AUTHORITY*, be again our St Vincent.' But the latter was ageing and unwell, and in June that year Lord Keith superseded him. It is tempting, but somewhat unprofitable, to speculate as to whether Nelson would have behaved differently if St Vincent had remained as his commander. His friendship for the latter, coupled with his deep admiration and respect, might have held him back from some of the folly that was to follow upon his entanglement with Emma Hamilton. In the event, Lord Keith took over in June at almost the same time that Nelson shifted his flag from the *Vanguard* to a new 80-gun ship-of-the-line the *Foudroyant*, which had just joined his forces at Palermo. In a general promotion in February Nelson had now become a Rear-Admiral of the Red.

While events on the mainland seemed to indicate that the moment would soon come for the return of the Bourbons to Naples, the news came through that a French squadron had entered the Mediterranean. Its destination was unknown – Malta, Alexandria and Sicily were all potentials – and Nelson decided that his best course was to cruise to the west of Sicily whence he could keep an eye on all the main sea-routes. The French, in fact, had made for Toulon and had managed to give the slip to Lord Keith who had himself come in hot pursuit on their heels. The news from Naples was confusing, but one thing was quite clear – Commodore Caracciolo, still smarting from the King's treatment of him in preferring British ships to his own, had turned coat and had sided with the republicans. Meanwhile Cardinal Ruffo and his irregulars were rapidly closing in on the city, the French had all but evacuated everywhere except the old castle of St Elmo, and the moment seemed ripe for the final overthrow of the Parthenopean Republic.

On the afternoon of 24 June Nelson and his squadron of seventeen ships entered once more the Bay of Naples intent on eradicating the last of the the French influence in the city and, in effect, making it safe for King Ferdinand and Queen Maria Carolina to return. (Neither would leave Palermo until they were convinced that Naples had been thoroughly 'cleansed' of the republicans.) Sir William Hamilton and Emma accompanied Nelson to act as representatives of the King and to assist as interpreters. Nelson now found himself in the uneasy situation of promoting the Bourbon cause, forcing unconditional surrender upon the King's subjects, and ensuring that the last of the French left the city within two hours of his terms being delivered to them. Moving in the murky waters of diplomacy and international politics he adopted the forthright air of the captain of a ship who is confronted by mutineers. 'That as to the Rebels and Traitors, no power on earth has a right to stand between their gracious King and them : they must instantly throw themselves on the clemency of their Sovereign, for no other terms will be allowed them; nor will the French be allowed even to name them in any capitulation.'

Nelson's first act was to annul a truce which had been agreed by Captain Edward Foote of the frigate *Seahorse* and Cardinal Ruffo on the one hand, and the French and rebel Neapolitans on the other. Ruffo very naturally complained that he had done his best by arranging the terms of truce in order to spare the city from destruction by the departing French, and that he could not possibly break his word and erase his signature. Many, or indeed most of his countrymen, he believed, who had espoused the Parthenopean Republic, had done so because they had no other option, and they should now be forgiven by their monarch. Ruffo was a politician, Nelson was not, and it was hardly surprising that the two men fell out from the very start. As Sir William was later to write to his nephew Greville, 'Nothing but my phlegm could have prevented an open rupture on the first meeting between Cardinal Ruffo and Lord Nelson. Lord Nelson is so accustomed to dealing fair & open, that he has no patience when he meets with the contrary, which one must always expect when one has to deal with Italians &, perhaps, His Eminency is the very quintessence of Italian finesse.' It was largely through Sir William's tact and his explanation of the real position ashore that an agreement was reached whereby the Jacobins were permitted to withdraw from the two castles, Ovo and Nuovo, where they were established, and to embark in a number of merchantmen which were lying in the harbour. These, however, were not permitted to sail, nor were they accorded the honours of war as had been agreed in the terms of the capitulation.

On 29 June, four days after Nelson had arrived at Naples, letters arrived from Palermo which made it quite clear that nothing other than unconditional surrender was acceptable to the King. Ferdinand had no use for clemency and he was prepared to be uncompromising enough so long as his wishes were being carried out for him by Nelson and his British men-of-war. Queen Maria Carolina's advice, given to Nelson via Emma, was to treat Naples 'as if it were a rebellious Irish town', and to act with 'the greatest firmness, vigour and severity'. Ruffo immediately felt himself compromised by these new orders, which nullified his efforts to settle things peacefully, and he refused to assist in the projected siege of Fort St Elmo. At the same time he issued an order that nobody in Naples was to be arrested without his authority. Nelson, who had been given carte blanche by the King, even contemplated having the Cardinal arrested. Fortunately he decided that the situation had reached a point where only the return of the King and the Queen and their Prime Minister, Acton, could unravel a knotted situation which by now had assumed Gordian proportions.

(He himself was naturally tempted to use Alexander's technique and cut it with the sword.)

On 10 July, the King hove up from the south in a frigate and the burden of coping with the whole Neapolitan situation was lifted from Nelson's shoulders. Before that was to happen, however, there occurred the incident which has long stained Nelson's reputation for his handling of events in Naples. On 29 June, Captain Hardy, who was on the deck of the *Foudroyant*, heard a great disturbance as a small boat drew alongside the ship. The word then reached him that 'the traitor Caracciolo was taken'. The Commodore, who had certainly taken an active part in the affairs of the Parthenopean Republic, was condemned almost from the very start by the violent passions that had been aroused in Naples among the anti-Jacobins and by the very nature of his fellow citizens. The fact remains that he should not have been condemned in the heat of the moment – something which must be put down to Nelson's desire to set an instant example to all French sympathisers.

There can be no doubt as to Caracciolo's guilt, nor of his own awareness of the fate that must be in store for him if he were caught (he had been discovered hiding down a well in peasant's clothing). Nelson immediately had a court-martial convened, consisting of five senior officers from the Neapolitan squadron under the presidency of Count Thurn, an Austrian commodore in the Neapolitan service. The result was a foregone conclusion. Caracciolo had commanded the republican fleet, he had attacked British and Neapolitan ships (firing on his own colours), and had clearly been a traitor to his king. He was condemned to death by four votes to two and, when the verdict was reported to Nelson, the latter ordered that he should be hanged from the yardarm of a Sicilian frigate that very evening. Thurn's suggestion that Caracciolo should be allowed twenty-four hours in which to make his peace with his Maker, and Caracciolo's own request that he should be executed as befitting a nobleman, were both disregarded. Nelson, as he had long ago made plain to St Vincent (when he had agreed with the latter's summary treatment of mutineers), believed that such matters were best dealt with swiftly.

Midshipman Parsons in his *Reminiscences* shows an evident sympathy towards the Italian admiral and records that his defence largely consisted in pointing out that it was King Ferdinand who had betrayed his people by running away to Palermo, taking all the royal treasure with him, and leaving General Mack's army unpaid. Parsons goes on to recall a macabre incident that occurred a few days after Caracciolo's execution :

. . . I was roused from my slumbers with an account of the king being on deck. . . . I hurried up, and found his majesty gazing with intense anxiety on some distant object. At once he turned pale, and letting his spyglass fall on deck, uttered an exclamation of horror. My eyes instinctively turned in the same direction, and under our larboard quarter, with his face full upon us, much swollen and discoloured by the water, and his orbs of sight started from their sockets by strangulation, floated the ill-fated prince . . . on Lord Nelson (who was suffering from ill health) being awakened from his uneasy slumbers, he ordered a boat to be sent from the ship to tow the corpse on shore.

As was only to be expected, the city of Naples was now subjected to a White Terror, in which the persecution of revolutionaries and Jacobins was conveniently used for their own private purposes by those who had their own grudges and family vendettas to be avenged. The King, who should by all right have stayed in his city, was only too eager to return once more to Palermo to enjoy his hunting and shooting and to abdicate – as usual – from all responsibility. Nelson's part in this whole affair was unfortunate, for there can be little doubt that he was used by Ferdinand to lend the weight of his authority and the power of the British fleet to condone a state of affairs that was to provoke Mr Fox in the House of Commons to refer to the 'horrors' that had taken place in Naples.

Nelson's position was an invidious one and, although he can in no sense be 'whitewashed', it is difficult to see what else he could have done under the circumstances. He could not control King Ferdinand's actions. He could not be responsible for, nor indeed could he understand, the passions of southern politics. His job as a British admiral was to see the Bourbons restored – that and nothing else. The internal politics of the kingdom were not his concern. There can be little doubt that he felt an infinite weariness towards Neapolitan affairs and the tortuous processes of Italian thought. Midshipman Parsons, recording the execution of Caracciolo, probably best sums up Nelson's whole attitude towards all the affairs of this hysterical kingdom: 'The seamen of our fleet, who clustered on the rigging like bees, consoled themselves that it was only an Italian prince, and an admiral of Naples, that was hanging – a person of very light estimation compared with the lowest man in a British ship.'

On 13 July, shortly after the King had reluctantly returned to Naples from Palermo once again, and when the last pro-French stronghold in the city, Fort St Elmo, had capitulated to the investing forces, Nelson received orders from Lord Keith to 'send such ships as you can possibly spare . . . [to] Minorca to await my orders.' Nelson, whose flagship was at the time acting as the seat of government of Ferdinand, and many of whose sailors had been landed to assist in the capture of the two cities north of Naples, Capua and Gaeta, refused. His action was a blatant disobedience of orders and Keith as his Commander-in-Chief had every right to tell his junior to send him every ship that he could spare. The fact that Nelson did not believe that Minorca was in danger had nothing to do with the matter. That he was proved right, and that Minorca was not attacked, did not exculpate him, any more than the fact that Capua and Gaeta soon fell to Neapolitan arms reinforced by British sailors. One sees Nelson at this moment putting the interests of the Kingdom of Naples and the Bourbon king before his own country's, and disobeying the explicit command of his senior officer.

A further order from Lord Keith, received only six days later, was to the effect that all or at least the greater part of Nelson's force should withdraw from Sicily and repair to Minorca to protect the island during Keith's absence on a search for the combined Franco-Spanish fleet. Nelson refused, giving as his excuse that until the French were driven out of Capua he thought it right 'not to obey your order'. He added : 'I am perfectly well aware of the consequences of disobeying the orders of my Commander-in-Chief.' Such behaviour, justified though it was by events, was hardly rational – nor, one may doubt, would Nelson have tolerated it from any subordinate of his. On the receipt of a further order from Keith, Nelson reluctantly sent Duckworth with three sail-of-the-line and a corvette, himself and the bulk of his forces still remaining in the vicinity of Naples. Even allowing for the fact that, in those days of poor communications, a great deal more latitude was allowed to the man on the spot than is conceivable today, Nelson's whole attitude throughout this exchange is one that merits the deepest censure. He may have had a poor opinion of Keith, but his behaviour by any standard was intolerable.

Keith was now engaged in the pursuit of a French fleet into the Atlantic, which left Nelson as acting Commander-in-Chief of the Mediterranean for the rest of the year, part of which time was spent aboard the *Foudroyant* at Naples and part back at the Palazzo Palagonia in Palermo. There was no reason or excuse for him to be based ashore when he was at Palermo, for the business of the fleet could just as easily have been conducted from his flagship as it could from a palace ashore. The fact is that in the corrupt and indolent atmosphere of the court, surrounded by adulation and besotted with Emma Hamilton, the victor of the Nile was rapidly succumbing – if he had not succumbed entirely – to a decline of morale that is only too often fatal to northerners who take up their residence in the indolent, lax and febrile south. His health was far from good, his eyesight was declining, and his involvement with Emma can hardly have failed to cause some tremor of conscience in the parson's son. His letters to Fanny this year are comparatively few and it would not be long before rumour of his activities (only too well known among his friends and equals in the Service) would invade the drawing-rooms and clubs of England. One letter alone from Naples, dated 4 August 1799, gives an idea of the adulation to which he was subject and the extent to which he revelled in it :

The first of August [the anniversary of the Battle of the Nile] was celebrated here with as much respect as our situation would admit. The King dined with me and when his Majesty drank my health a royal salute of 21 guns was fired from all H.S.M.'s ships of war and from all the castles. In the evening there was a general illumination. Amongst others a large vessel was fitted out like a Roman galley. On the oars were fixed lamps and in the centre was erected a rostral column with my name, at the stern elevated were two angels supporting my picture. In short the beauty of the thing was beyond my powers of description. More than 2000 variegated lamps were fixed round the vessel, an orchestra was fitted up and filled with the very best musicians and singers. The piece of music was in a great measure my praises, describing their distress, but Nelson comes, the invincible Nelson and we are safe and happy again. Thus you must not make you think me vain so far very far from it and I relate it more from gratitude than vanity.

What Fanny and his old father, sitting at Round Wood in the quiet of England, thought about it all is difficult to imagine. They could hardly visualise this world of wine and fireworks and Roman extravaganza. It must have been equally difficult for them to associate it with the man whom they had known in the past – the struggling sea-captain, often wounded in his country's service, but always obsessed with the desire to get to sea and find himself in the forefront of action against the French.

That August, in return for his services to the King and Queen, Nelson was offered the dukedom of Bronte, an estate lying in the foothills of Mount Etna, which was said to be worth £3,000 a year.

Although he made some mild show of reluctance at accepting the royal gift, Nelson yielded to the protestations of the King and Queen that it was little enough in return for his having restored them to their kingdom. He liked the name Bronte, meaning 'Thunder', and was soon to begin signing himself 'Bronte Nelson of the Nile', a signature which he later changed – after he had received his own monarch's permission to use his foreign title – to 'Nelson and Bronte'. Despite his preoccupations in Palermo it cannot be said that during Keith's absence Nelson did nothing at all towards looking after his widespread command. He was increasingly absorbed in the affairs of Malta where the Maltese, deprived of regular corn shipments from Sicily, were starving while the French were still holding out behind the magnificent fortifications of Valetta. Troubridge and Ball were increasingly distressed by the situation of the Maltese peasantry, who had proved the most redoubtable allies but who must inevitably collapse if their needs were not met. In the end an arrangement was made whereby corn shipments were brought down from eastern Sicily *sub rosa* (for it was contrary to the orders of the Government), and the island settled down to another long winter of siege. Nelson had also been to Minorca where he endeavoured, unsuccessfully, to prevail upon the military commander to spare him 2,000 men to assist him in the investment of Valetta.

Meanwhile, Napoleon, worsted by Sir Sidney at Acre, had escaped from the East which had now become not the pathway to his ambitions, but a trap from which he must escape at all costs. In France itself there seemed considerable likelihood of the monarchy being restored unless by some miracle a military leader could preserve the Republic. Emmanuel Sièyes, one of the five Directors, had remarked: 'I seek a sword.' And now, having by a series of seeming miracles evaded the British ships on watch throughout the Mediterranean, Napoleon slipped across the sea aboard the frigate *Muiron*. It might hardly be thought that to have abandoned an army, lost a fleet, and been worsted at Acre were the credentials to commend him to his fellow countrymen, but Napoleon still possessed an infinite glamour. Furthermore, so desperate was the situation in France, and so weak the leadership, that the return of this genie from the East was all that was needed to revive the vigour of his countrymen. On 9 October, Napoleon landed at Fréjus in southern France. Despite the proven superiority of the British Navy, he had twice escaped Nelson on the waters of the Mediterranean. Within a month of his arrival in France, he had not only given his country a new constitution but himself held the reins of power as First Consul. The British were now to be confronted not only with a fresh and intense activity of their enemies but with something that was to prove even more distasteful to them than the Revolution – a military dictatorship.

CHAPTER TWENTY-SIX

Malta

THE New Year brought a new century, one in which Napoleon's hold upon the Continent (despite Nelson's expressed belief that the war would soon be over) was immeasurably to strengthen. The year also started for Nelson with an unwelcome summons to Leghorn where Lord Keith, having returned to his command, was more than anxious to see his disobedient junior. Keith's behaviour throughout this period was a model of restraint. He was Nelson's senior by three years as a flag-officer, and twelve years in age; he was a man of irreproachable, even if unglamorous, record; and he was well aware of the predicament that Nelson had got himself into through his infatuation with the wife of the British ambassador. It was not the kind of situation that quiet Scottish admirals relish having to handle. Nelson for his part, accustomed to his diet of praise and his role as sole commander, did not take kindly to becoming second fiddle on the Mediterranean scene. The spoiled boy met the stern but just schoolmaster.

Keith's first action was to go down with Nelson to Sicily to take a look at things for himself, and then to proceed to Malta to see what further efforts could be made to bring the protracted siege to an end. One of the first things which must have pleased Keith – even if it had exactly the reverse effect on the other actors in the drama – was the news that Sir William Hamilton was being relieved of his post. He had been thirty-six years with the Kingdom of the Two Sicilies, and he had himself suggested the year before that he would like to return to England to look after his estates. It should have come as a shock to no one that a younger man, the Honourable Arthur Paget, had been appointed to relieve him. Nevertheless all was confusion in the court, the Queen 'half dead with grief', Emma lamenting in inconsolable attitudes, and even Sir William somewhat bemused at the prospect of leaving a world where he had become an 'Inglese Italianato', even if not the corollary 'diavolo incarnato'.

There was much to concern both Keith and Nelson in the affairs of Malta. The Russian Admiral Ushakóv had been ordered by the Tsar to abandon the blockade of the island and to withdraw his fleet from the Mediterranean. At the same time the Tsar, who was growing disillusioned with his allies and was contemplating making terms with the French, had instructed Marshal Suvárov to leave Italy and retire to Prague. It looked as if the siege of Valetta, which had promised to end in the near future, might be far from over. Keith was eager to see the state of things for himself and at the same time to remove Nelson from the idleness of Palermo, and concentrate his attention on the beleaguered island. Ironically enough, Keith's determination to take Nelson with him down to Malta was to add a further feather in the latter's cap during the last months of his career in the Mediterranean.

On 13 February, Nelson wrote to Emma Hamilton from the *Foudroyant*: 'We are now off Messina with a fresh breeze and fair. [He had picked up the northerly wind that often funnels between the straits.] . . . To say how I miss your house and company would be saying little; but in truth you and Sir William have so spoiled me that I am not happy anywhere else but with you, nor have I an idea that I ever can be.' He was soon to achieve the only true happiness that suited his nature : a successful action at sea that almost closed the book on the Battle of the Nile. *Le Généreux*, which had managed to escape from the net at Aboukir Bay, had been sent under Rear-Admiral Pérée in company with three smaller warships to escort three transports carrying 3,000 troops, as well as stores and munitions, to relieve General Vaubois in Valetta. Keith, who was aboard the *Queen Charlotte* off Malta, on receiving the news from a frigate that the convoy was off the west of Sicily heading for Malta with a favourable wind, despatched Nelson in the *Foudroyant* together with the *Northumberland* and the *Audacious* to beat to windward and endeavour to intercept the French squadron. There was a heavy sea and a thick fog, through which the British tacked back and forth covering the northern approaches to Malta and seeking the enemy.

It was at dawn on 18 February that they heard through a pearly grey mist the distant boom of cannon. The *Alexander*, which had been on patrol off the south-east of the island, had come across the reinforcing French squadron. It had come under the lee of Malta intending to cut up the coast on the short run into Valetta. They had anticipated a close watch being kept on the Malta–Sicily channel, and had hoped that by coming round from the south they would escape detection. Nelson and the ships with him, being to the north of the French, now had the weather gauge and turned promptly towards the sound of firing. 'Pray God,' he wrote in his journal, 'we may come alongside them.' The *Alexander* meanwhile had engaged the largest transport and had forced her to heave to, on seeing which the escorts had withdrawn in an attempt to escape – for it was clear that other British vessels would soon be on the scene. They were hotly pursued by the frigate *Success* under Captain Peard who, in Nelson's words, 'with great judgement and gallantry, lay across his hawse, and raked him with several broadsides'. The brief action which followed has been preserved in the amber of the account of Midshipman Parsons, who was himself aboard the *Foudroyant*. Although often quoted, it can hardly be omitted, for it is one of the only pictures that have survived the years to give a vivid picture of Nelson in action. ' "Deck there!" ' it begins,

' "the stranger is evidently a man-of-war – she is a line-of-battle ship, my Lord, and going large on the starboard tack."

' "Ah! an enemy, Mr Stains. I pray God it may be *Le Généreux*. The signal for a general chase, Sir Ed'ard . . . make the *Foudroyant* fly!" [Captain Sir Edward Berry had replaced Hardy in command of Nelson's flagship.]

'Thus spake the heroic Nelson; and every exertion that emulation could inspire was used to crowd the squadron with canvas, the *Northumberland* taking the lead with the flagship close on her quarter.

' "This will not do, Sir Ed'ard; it is certainly *Le Généreux* and to my flagship she can alone surrender. Sir Ed'ard, we must and shall beat the *Northumberland*."

' "I will do my utmost, my lord; get the engine to work on the sails [to pump water over the canvas to tauten it and make it draw better] – hang butts of water to the stays – pipe the hammocks down, and each man place shot in them – slack the stays, knock up the wedges, and give the masts play – start off the water, Mr James, and pump the ship."

'The *Foudroyant* is drawing a-head, and at last takes the lead in the chase.

' "The admiral is working his fin (the stump of his right arm), do not cross his hawse, I advise you."

'The advice was good, for at that moment Nelson opened furiously on the quarter-master at the conn. [Conning the ship.]

' "I'll knock you off your perch, you rascal, if you are so inattentive. Sir Ed'ard, send your best quarter-master to the weather wheel."

' "A strange sail ahead of the chase," called the look-out man. . . .

' "A sloop of war, or frigate, my lord," shouted the young signal-midshipman.

' "Demand her number."

' "The *Success*, my lord."

' "Captain Peard; signal to cut off the flying enemy – great odds, though – thirty-two small guns to eighty large ones."

' "The *Success* has hove-to athwart-hawse of the *Généreux*, and is firing her larboard broadside. The Frenchman has hoisted his tri-colour, with a rear-admiral's flag."

' "Bravo, *Success*, at her again!"

' "She has wore round, my Lord, and firing her starboard broad-side. It has winged her, my lord – her flying kites are flying away altogether. The enemy is close on the *Success*, who must receive her tremendous broadside."

'The *Généreux* opens her fire on her little enemy, and every person stands aghast, afraid of the consequences. The smoke clears away, and there is the *Success*, crippled, it is true, but bull-dog like, bearing up after enemy.

' "The signal for the *Success* to discontinue the action, and come under my stern," said Lord Nelson. "She has done well, for her size. Try a shot from the lower deck at her, Sir Ed'ard."

' "It goes over her."

' "Beat to quarters, and fire coolly and deliberately at her masts and yards."

'The *Généreux* at this moment opened her fire on us; and, as a shot passed through the mizzen stay-sail, Lord Nelson, patting one of the youngsters on the head, asked him jocularly how he relished the music; and observing something like alarm depicted on his countenance, consoled him with the information that Charles XII ran away from the first shot he heard, though afterwards he was called "The Great", and deservedly, from his bravery. "I, there-fore," said Nelson, "hope much from you in future."

'Here the *Northumberland* opened her fire, and down came the tricolour ensign, amidst the thunder of our united cannon.'

Berry now boarded the prize and received Rear-Admiral Pérée's sword, but the Admiral himself was dying from having had both legs taken off in one of the broadsides. Berry had last been aboard *Le*

Généreux when he had been wounded and taken prisoner after her capture of the *Leander* bearing the despatches about the Battle of the Nile.

Nelson was lucky – that quality which Napoleon required of his marshals. Had it not been for the initiative of Lord Keith it is extremely doubtful whether he would have left Palermo. As Ball wrote to Emma Hamilton, reporting the capture of *Le Généreux* and the dispersal of the rest of the convoy: 'We may truly call him a *heaven*-born Admiral, upon whom fortune smiles wherever he goes. We have been carrying on the blockade of Malta sixteen months, during which time the enemy never attempted to throw in succours until this month. His Lordship arrived here the day they were within a few leagues of the island, captured the principal ships, so that not one has reached the port.' Nelson for his part commented that twelve out of thirteen line-of-battle ships that had been at the Nile had now been accounted for, leaving only the *Guillaume Tell* which remained safe within Grand Harbour, protected by the guns of Valetta.

Keith magnanimously commended Nelson for his conduct in the affair – despite the fact that Nelson was under the impression that he had once again disobeyed orders by leaving Keith without making his intentions clear by signal. The Commander-in-Chief now sailed north to prosecute the blockade of Genoa, leaving Nelson in charge of the blockade in Malta. Before leaving he pointed out that Syracuse or Messina would be far better bases for the conduct of operations than Palermo, his remark tallying with Nelson's earlier expressed opinion that he would make Syracuse his home port. But that had been before Emma Hamilton had come upon the scene, and before his infatuation as a man had overcome his judgement as a seaman. There can be no doubt that he was at this time in his life extremely ill; run down physically, and no doubt in a fever of mental torment about the situation in which he and Emma found themselves. Despite Troubridge's plans for him to stay behind in command of the blockade he sailed back to Palermo. Once there, he transferred his flag to a transport lying off the Palazzo Palagonia and sent Berry back to Malta in command of the *Foudroyant*. By doing so he missed what would indeed have been the crowning glory to his Mediterranean career. Berry reached the Malta station just in time to fall in with the *Guillaume Tell* trying to escape, and captured the last of the ships that had survived from the Nile. Nelson immediately wrote to Berry with that enthusiasm and responsive recognition of others' achievements which always endeared him to those who served under him. 'Your conduct and character in the late glorious occasion stamps your

fame beyond the reach of envy. . . .' It seemed that, with this elimin-
ation of all Brueys' battle fleet, his last link with the Mediterranean
was severed. He had already applied to Lord Spencer for permission
to return to England. 'My task is done, my health is lost, and the
orders of the great Earl St Vincent are completely fulfilled.' Palermo
had begun to disgust him. He saw it all now, as he had first seen
Naples : 'a country of fiddlers and poets, whores and scoundrels'. His
feelings were reinforced by the marriage, by special dispensation, of
Sir John Acton, aged sixty-four, to his niece, who was three months
under fourteen. The comparison between this cynical, indulgent world
and that of his sea-officers must have been in his mind when he wrote
to Lord Keith in praise of the recent action : 'I thank God I was not
present; for it would finish me, could I have taken a sprig of these
brave men's laurels. They are, and I glory in them, my darling
children. . . .'

On 23 April, the *Foudroyant* sailed from Palermo bound for
Syracuse and Malta. Sir William had by now presented his letters of
recall and it was thus possible for him to take a short holiday at sea
with his friend. Apart from Emma there were four others in the sight-
seeing party, one of whom, Cornelia Knight, the daughter of an
admiral, has left a vivid account not only of this cruise but also of other
aspects of Nelson's life during these Mediterranean years. After calling
at Syracuse and inspecting the ruins, the great theatre, and all the
other evidences of that classical world which Sir William valued more
highly than the one in which he lived, the *Foudroyant* crossed the
Malta–Sicily channel and joined the blockading squadron off Valetta.
The flagship came under fire from the guns of Valetta and, unlike the
occasion of the action against *Le Généreux*, Nelson was not at all in
a congenial mood at the whistle of shot as the French ranged on
the *Foudroyant* – for it bore the precious burden of Emma. 'Lord
Nelson was in a towering passion, and Lady Hamilton's refusal to
quit the quarter-deck did not tend to tranquilize him.' Emma, who
generally professed not to like the sea, enjoyed it on this occasion : the
reason was not hard to find. Whatever dates may be put to the
beginning of their love affair, there can be no doubt that they were
now lovers, for a year later from the Baltic Nelson was to recall the
'days of ease and nights of pleasure' that unfolded during the three
weeks that they spent in Maltese waters. The *Foudroyant* lay for most
of the time in the large southern harbour of Marsa Xlokk where a
house is still pointed out as that in which Nelson and his party stayed
when ashore. Commodore Troubridge and General Graham, who
entertained them several times, were eager for Nelson to stay on longer

to witness the fall of the island, which then seemed imminent. During this period Ball, who was ultimately to become Malta's first governor, received the decoration of Commandeur Grande Croix from the Tsar (who had become Grand Master of the Order of St John after the knights had fled the island) while Emma, in recognition of her supposed services to the islanders in procuring grain supplies for them, was made a Dame Petite Croix. Everyone was happy, and Sir William could revel in an island which had been involved in the history of the Mediterranean ever since the Phoenicians had first established a trading post in the very harbour where the *Foudroyant* now idled at anchor. Nelson, however, was not destined to see the capitulation of the French, for Valetta under General Vaubois held out until the autumn – and by that time he was far away. It is very probable that Emma conceived during this Maltese holiday, for it was exactly nine months later that her daughter Horatia was born. On the return voyage to Palermo she was unwell, of a fever it was said, and Nelson had the ship run off before the wind at night so that she could rest more easily, as well as ordering silence to be observed so that her sleep should not be disturbed. Midshipman Parsons cynically referred to the *Foudroyant* as 'this Noah's Ark'.

Nelson had hoped to return to England together with the Hamiltons aboard the *Foudroyant*, but he was to find at Palermo that the usual state of confusion was even more compounded by Queen Carolina's decision to travel to Vienna with her family. King Ferdinand had no intention of returning to Naples and he was eager to be rid of his Queen for a few months. The burden thus fell on Nelson of transporting the Hamiltons, the Queen, her younger son, three unmarried daughters (the future Queens of France, Sardinia and Spain), as well as a retinue of fifty or more. His own decision to return home was further reinforced by a letter from Lord Spencer, in which the latter hardly bothered to conceal his disapproval of all that had been happening in this southern court :

It is by no means my wish or intention to call you away from service, but having observed that you have been under the necessity of quitting your station off Malta, on account of the state of your health, which I am persuaded you could not have thought of doing without such necessity, it appeared to me much more advisable for you to come home at once, than to be obliged to remain inactive at Palermo. . . . I am joined in my opinion by all your friends here, that you will be more likely to recover your health and strength in England than in an inactive situation at a Foreign Court, however pleasing the respect and gratitude shown to you for your services may be. . . .'

Keith meanwhile had written giving express orders for the *Foudroyant* and the *Alexander* to return to the station off Malta. But before the message reached Palermo, Nelson, together with the Hamiltons and the royal party, had already sailed north for Leghorn. For the *tria juncta in uno* the Sicilian and Neapolitan episode was finally and forever over.

On 14 June, Nelson and his party arrived in Leghorn aboard the *Foudroyant*. On that very day, although the Austrian-born Queen could not yet know it, Napoleon had resoundingly defeated her countrymen at Marengo. Once more the whole of Italy lay at his feet and, in the armistice that followed, all of the Italian provinces west of the Mincio river, including Genoa, passed under French control. In one stroke he had shattered the optimistic combination against France that had stemmed from the Battle of the Nile. He had shown that, whatever the British might do afloat, the French were supreme on land – and it was on land that the decisive victories were to be won. He could now look south towards Naples and Sicily, for, as he remarked : 'There is one power still in Italy to be reduced before I can give it peace.'

Under these circumstances it was hardly surprising that Lord Keith felt that he could not spare the *Foudroyant* 'to take the Queen to Palermo, and princes and princesses to all parts of the globe'. He was rightly concerned that the French fleet might now decide to enter the Mediterranean and capture Sicily. With Malta still in French hands, the British would then find that they had no hold anywhere in that sea other than Minorca. To the Queen's pleas that she be allowed to rejoin her husband aboard the *Foudroyant* he turned a deaf ear and made his decision quite explicit by ordering the ship to Minorca for repairs, whither the *Alexander* was also told to report. In view of the circumstances, it was considerate of him to offer Nelson the *Seahorse* frigate (in which he had returned to England after Tenerife) to transport himself and Sir William and party to England by sea. Alternatively, if the frigate was not large enough, Keith offered them a troopship out of Malta. Further than this he could not go and, since his private opinion was that 'Lady Hamilton had had command of the Fleet long enough', his behaviour was magnanimous. Lady Hamilton, however, was still to show that, if she had lost command of the fleet, she still commanded Admiral Nelson. She now announced that she detested the thought of travelling by sea and, in the words of Miss Cornelia Knight, 'wishes to visit the different Courts of Germany'. There was only one encouraging note at this nadir of Nelson's personal reputation, a letter delivered to him shortly before he left the *Foudroyant*. It read :

My Lord, it is with extreme grief that we find you are about to leave us. We have been along with you (though not in the same ship) in every Engagement your Lordship has been in, both by Sea and Land; and most humbly beg of your Lordship to permit us to go to England as your Boat's crew, in any Ship or Vessel, or in any way that may seem most pleasing to your Lordship. My Lord, pardon the rude style of Seamen, who are but little acquainted with writing, and believe us to be, my Lord, your most humble and obedient servants – Barge's crew of the *Foudroyant*.

Their plea was to go unanswered, for Lord Nelson was not returning to England in any ship or vessel. Obedient to Emma's wishes, he was going to travel overland across a continent that was increasingly troubled by the rising tide of Bonapartism, and where the route to Vienna was at one stage to take his party within only a few miles of French outposts. If his life or his career had ended at this moment, he would have been remembered only as an admiral who, after one astonishing victory, had compromised his whole reputation by an adulterous affair with the wife of his best friend.

CHAPTER TWENTY-SEVEN

Homecoming

NELSON'S departure from Leghorn was hastened by news from ashore that pro-French elements constituted a threat to the Queen, while loyalists, on the other hand, were eager to detain Nelson so that he might lead them in person against the French – who were no more than thirty miles away at Lucca. The royal party, shortly followed by Nelson and the Hamiltons, left precipitately, travelling in a convoy of fourteen coaches and three large baggage-vans. Sir Edward Berry saw his chief go with deep regret, and not without misgivings that he might well be captured on his way through Europe. The atmosphere of *opéra bouffe* which had prevailed ever since Nelson's first arrival in Naples was to be maintained to the very end. Only Emma's mother, the indomitable Mrs Cadogan, seems to have preserved any element of practicality. Sir William was so ill that he thought he was going to die, while Nelson was at a loss when coping with shore travel. Emma – despite the fact that Nelson was still thinking of making use of the *Seahorse* for his return home – adamantly refused to travel other than on land. The Queen, encumbered by her children and retinue, had no thought but to get to Vienna as fast as possible and exert her influence upon her daughter and son-in-law not to conclude a peace with the French. General John Moore who was present in Leghorn caught the atmosphere in his diary : 'Sir William and Lady Hamilton were there attending the Queen of Naples. Lord Nelson was there attending upon Lady Hamilton. He is covered with stars, ribbons and medals, more like the Prince of an Opera than the Conqueror of the Nile. It is really melancholy to see a brave and good man, who has deserved well of his country, cutting so pitiful a figure.'

From Florence this strange cavalcade proceeded to Ancona where an Austrian frigate, the *Bellona*, awaited the Queen to transport her to Trieste. Nelson, observing that most of the guns had been removed to make way for silk hangings and beds for the royal party, and hearing that the crew had recently mutinied, advised against it. A Russian squadron, consisting of three frigates and a brig, provided a more suitable alternative and, although Nelson could not help but compare the ships unfavourably with the British, they transported the travellers safely to Trieste. (The *Bellona*, which the French had long had their eye on, was captured in the Gulf of Venice.) At Trieste, safe now from any French threat, the party, with the notable exceptions of Nelson and Emma, nearly all collapsed with ill health, and it was not until a fortnight later that they could proceed on their way to Vienna. The British Ambassador in the Austrian capital, Lord Minto, viewed their arrival with considerable unease. He knew all about the Nelson–Emma imbroglio, and he found the Queen's presence more than embarrassing, for she had appropriated a sum of British money, designed for the defence of Naples, to her personal use. While both he and Lady Minto feared the worst from this visit ('He does not seem at all conscious of the sort of discredit he has fallen into') they were to find that Nelson himself, except for his dog-like devotion to Emma and his propensity for orders and decorations, was the same as ever. They found in fact that, so great was Nelson's popularity with the Austrian people, he served as an immense advertisement for their country at a time when Britain was not regarded with all that much favour in the court or country. 'You can have no idea of the anxiety and curiosity to see him,' Lady Minto wrote.

The door of his house is always crowded with people, and even the street, whenever his carriage is at the door; and when he went to the play he was applauded, a thing which rarely happens here. On the road it was the same. The common people brought their children to *touch* him. One he took up in his arms, and when he gave it back to the mother she cried for joy, and said it would be lucky through life. I don't think him altered in the least. He has the same shock head, and the same honest simple manners; but he is devoted to *Emma*; he thinks her quite an *angel*, and talks of her as such to her face and behind her back, and she leads him about like a keeper with a bear. She must sit by him at dinner to cut his meat, and he carries her pocket-handkerchief – he is a gig from ribands, orders and stars, but he is just the same with us as ever he was.

Her husband, Lord Minto, writing to Lord Keith on 30 August, maintained a somewhat more objective view of his visitors:

Lord Nelson arrived here with Sir W. and Lady Hamilton a few days after the Queen of Naples having been detained at Trieste some time by Sir William's illness. Sir W. has had a relapse here; and altho' he has recovered a little yet he is so feeble and so much reduced that I cannot see how it is possible for him to reach England alive. Lord Nelson has been received here by all ranks with the admiration which his great actions deserve, and notwithstanding the disadvantage under which he presents himself at present to the public eye. They talk of proceeding in a few days towards England; and I who am a lover of naval merit and indeed a sincere friend of the man, hope we shall again hear of him on his proper element. . . .

Sir William did indeed nearly die in Vienna, and the party had to stay there for a month before he was well enough to travel further. Nelson's expenses mounted with so much shore living, and an estimate of money drawn by him during the journey shows him as having spent well over £1000 during this period. He sat to the painter Heinrich Füger and later, in Dresden, the pastel artist Johann Schmidt, who also produced a portrait of Emma looking very young and demure and wearing the Order of the Knights of Malta. This portrait, which Nelson called his 'Guardian Angel', was afterwards always to hang in his cabin. The impression made by the strange trio as they proceeded on what more or less amounted to a triumphal tour through Europe was vastly successful with the general public, but far less so with their hosts and the upper echelons of society. All, however, conceded Nelson's immense merit – even if his slight and damaged frame gave little indication of the real quality of the man. Emma Hamilton, almost inevitably, came in for a good deal of adverse criticism from the ladies who met her. To have enslaved the Victor of the Nile was something that few could forgive in any case, but to be so obvious, so ostentatious, and so downright vulgar about it was intolerable. It was not only her own sex who saw her in unsympathetic terms. So, too, did many of the men who really cared about Nelson, and who could look ahead (which he seemed unable to do) to the situation that must inevitably confront him on his arrival in England. Lord Fitzharris, who had remarked, like Lady Minto, that Nelson appeared basically unchanged, and 'open and honest', could not bring himself to feel so kindly about Emma. 'Lady Hamilton', he wrote, 'is without exception the most coarse, ill-mannered, disagreeable woman I ever met.'

Before leaving Vienna for Prague and Dresden, Nelson and the Hamiltons had taken their farewell of Queen Maria Carolina. The latter saw them go not without real emotion, for she well knew that she would never find again a friend so devoted to her cause as Emma had been, nor a man like Nelson the weight of whose renown could be (and had been) used to further the fortunes of the Kingdom of Naples. She did not forget how large a part Sir William had played in her life over the past years, and sent 'a thousand compliments to the Chevalier' as well as 'to the hero', but to Emma, whom she hoped to see yet again in Naples, she sent 'everything'. Not all those of high rank, however, were prepared to tolerate this strange *ménage à trois*; for what might be acceptable in the lax court of Ferdinand and Maria Carolina was not so in the more strait-laced kingdoms of the north. The Electress of Saxony refused to receive Lady Hamilton, something which should have suggested to Emma, to Sir William, and even to the hypnotised hero that they might find on their return that their situation was considered downright immoral at the Court of St James's. King George III, while often despairing about the loose conduct of his sons, was himself an old-fashioned family man, who had no tolerance whatsoever in his immediate court for the sins of the flesh.

The whole atmosphere of this extraordinary European tour, which provoked the comments of so many, is best conveyed in the journal of a Mrs St George, who was a friend of Hugh Elliot, Lord Minto's brother and the British Minister in Dresden :

It is plain that Lord Nelson thinks of nothing but Lady Hamilton, who is totally occupied by the same object. Sir William is old and infirm, all admiration of his wife, and never spoke but to applaud her. Miss Cornelia Knight seems the decided flatterer of the two, and never opens her mouth but to show forth their praise; and Mrs Cadogan, Lady Hamilton's mother is – what one might expect. After dinner we had several songs in honour of Lord Nelson, written by Miss Knight and sung by Lady Hamilton. She puffs the incense full in his face; but he receives it with pleasure and snuffs it up very cordially.

It was not until 31 October that the party finally embarked outside Hamburg for a passage across the North Sea – Nelson's native environment, but one which he had forgotten amid the languors of the Mediterranean. He was back once more in the world of high tides, cold winds, and the mud-discoloured waters where he had first learned his trade. His long procession through Europe, which he was to describe in a letter to the Admiralty as 'my necessary journey by land from the Mediterranean', can only be seen as a pandering to Emma

Hamilton's wishes – and a desire on his part to put off facing the inevitable consequences of his involvement with her. The day of reckoning could not be pleasant (least of all for Fanny Nelson) and it is hardly surprising that he snuffed up the praise while it lasted, and on occasion took a glass or so of champagne more than his faithful servant Tom Allen reckoned was good for him. It is not insignificant that Nelson had written to the Admiralty asking for a frigate to take the party home – and that none was forthcoming. They travelled aboard the mailpacket *King George*, to land at Yarmouth after a stormy passage on 6 November 1800. It was two years and eight months since he had last seen England.

'I am a Norfolk man, and glory in being so.' These words addressed to the cheering throng at Yarmouth proclaim the real Nelson. But a most unreal one, a hero beyond even the dreams of eighteenth-century romance, was to be fêted about England during the weeks that followed his arrival. Nothing that had happened on the Continent could exceed the almost delirious reception that was now accorded to the Victor of the Nile. Then as now, people needed their heroes, needed – above all in a time of war to the death – the evocation of almost superhuman qualities. The wounded warrior, who had apparently transcended the fears and natural weaknesses of ordinary man, and who had set the seal on this by giving England a victory at sea that was without parallel in the country's history, could hardly be expected to pass unacclaimed. No sooner had Nelson set foot ashore than crowds surrounded him and drew his carriage to the inn where he and the Hamiltons were to spend the night. It was significant that Fanny Nelson had been previously advised not to make the journey from Round Wood to Yarmouth, but to meet him in due course in London. It was Emma Hamilton who stood on the balcony of the inn next to Nelson and responded to the plaudits of the crowd.

The following day, after a triumphal procession from Yarmouth to Ipswich, where the crowd once again took the horses from between the shafts and dragged their travelling coach round the town, the party proceeded to Round Wood. It was Nelson's first and last visit to the house where he never lived, to that country retreat which in the past he had so often promised to find for himself and Fanny, where they would retire in peace and quiet for the rest of their days. Symbolically enough the house was closed, for Fanny and Nelson's father were waiting to receive him in London. The East Anglian dream was finally and forever over.

His reception in London the following day was reported in the *Morning Post* :

His Lordship arrived yesterday afternoon at three o'clock at Nerot's Hotel King-street, St. James's, in the German travelling coach of Sir William Hamilton. In the coach came with his Lordship Sir William and Lady Hamilton and a black female attendant. The noble Admiral, who was dressed in full uniform, with three stars on his breast and two gold medals, was welcomed by repeated huzzas from the crowd which the illustrious tar returned with a low bow. Lord Nelson looked extremely well, but in person is very thin: so is Sir William Hamilton: but Lady Hamilton looks charmingly, and is a very fine woman. . . .

The regular reader of the *Morning Post* would have been familiar enough with the whole situation, for the paper had several times earlier that year featured accounts of Nelson. As early as 1 April, it had published the ironic comment: 'Of all the seeds lately sent home by Lord Nelson, that of "Love lays bleeding" was sown and gathered at Naples', while it commented less than obliquely during his visit to Vienna: 'The German State Painter, we are assured, is drawing Lady Hamilton and Lord Nelson at *full length together*. An Irish correspondent hopes the artist will have delicacy enough to put Sir William *between* them.'

The first meeting between Nelson and Fanny did no more than set the seal on what had clearly become a faded pile of long-dead correspondence, of early love letters and of hundreds of domestic letters between man and wife where mutual affection had once glowed, now tied up in a neat bundle for relegation to the bottom drawer of a desk. All was over now and, though Fanny for some time was very naturally unwilling to concede defeat at the hands of this large and loud lady, the antipathy which before had only existed in the imagination, based on gossip and on the scurrilous comments in newspapers, now flowered in actuality. Both women felt the same instinctive dislike of one another. Emma's was based very largely on a knowledge that she could never compete with this quiet, well-spoken, well-bred lady, who had not committed a single act that could be construed as in the slightest degree detrimental towards her husband or his career. Emma by nature was probably quite incapable of feeling any conscious guilt towards the forty-two-year-old impeccable wife, but she loathed her just the same, and felt 'an antipathy not to be described'. She had in any case triumphed in the most female way of all over her rival, for she was carrying her lover's child. She was deeply conscious of how much that meant to Nelson, whereas this delicate figure that confronted her – even though she was legitimately

Lady Nelson and accepted throughout the land as the wife of the great Admiral – was no more than a barren woman.

It was very soon clear enough that Nelson considered his marriage to Fanny at an end, and it was also soon made clear to him that his liaison with Emma was viewed with the gravest disfavour at Court. On the morning after attending the Lord Mayor's Banquet, where he had been presented with the sword that had been voted him by the City of London, Nelson made his way to St James's Palace to attend a levée, as was natural after his return on striking his flag in the Mediterranean. Sir William Hamilton was also present, for the reason that he too had returned after his long service at the Court of Naples. His wife had not been invited. The royal family had never countenanced his marriage to a woman of Emma's reputation and there could be no possibility under present circumstances that they would now change their minds as to receiving her at court. The saddened husband and the embittered lover made their way into the royal presence while the pregnant Emma languished out of sight in the London house that had been loaned to the Hamiltons by the millionaire William Beckford. The King, who had been talking to a number of courtiers, viewed Nelson with a cold eye and inquired abruptly as to the state of his health. Then, without waiting for an answer, he turned to engage a nearby military officer in a conversation that lasted half an hour. The dismissal was as clear as it was heavy-handed. Later the same evening Nelson and Fanny attended a dinner party at Admiralty House where his sullen humour and almost undisguised dislike of his wife was such that Lady Spencer was later moved to comment that she had never seen such a change in a man. On the last occasion when he and Fanny had dined with her he had shown his complete dependence upon her and the deepest affection.

What had been an open secret amongst those in the know was already public property. If the Victor of the Nile sat just as firmly in the popular heart, it was not for lack of cartoons and lampoons which showed the one-armed hero and the vast Emma and the emaciated Sir William as figures of fun caught in a comic eternal triangle. The ingenuous Miss Cornelia Knight, who had been with them for so long and had never been able to detect any impropriety in the relationship between Nelson and Emma, was at last disabused of her illusions by none other than Nelson's close friend Sir Thomas Troubridge. He advised her to keep other company while she was in London.

Little indeed did Miss Knight know that the very verses which she had added to the National Anthem in honour of Nelson had already suffered a strange sea-change at the hands of some anonymous parodist. The new verses now read :

> Also huge Emma's name
> First on the role of fame,
> And let us sing.
> Loud as her voice, let's sound
> Her faded charms around
> Which in the sheets were found,
> God save the King.

> Nelson, thy flag haul down,
> Hang up thy laurel crown,
> While her we sing.
> No more in triumph swell,
> Since that with her you dwell,
> But don't her William tell –
> Nor George, your King.

During this gloomy and dispiriting period the Hamiltons and Nelson lived together in a house in Dover Street which his friend and prize agent Davison had rented for him. Nelson made no attempt at any secrecy about his feelings for Emma Hamilton and his cruel indifference – that harsh reverse of the mask of love – must have been more than intolerable to a very sensitive woman. Nelson for his part was fully occupied, sitting to painters and sculptors, taking his seat in the House of Peers, and attending the theatre – where only the classic loose draperies of the time could conceal the fact that Emma Hamilton was heavily pregnant. On one occasion when Nelson and his old father and Fanny, together with Sir William and Emma, were in the stage box at Drury Lane attending a performance by the great Kemble, Fanny, overcome one suspects more by her own griefs than by those presented on the stage, suddenly cried out and fainted. The agony of their situation was such that it could inevitably only end one way, in a permanent separation.

There is more than one account of the final scene which led to their parting. The most familiar, and one which has the ring of truth since it shows so clearly the state that Fanny's nerves had reached, is that recounted by William Haslewood, a solicitor who was being employed by Davison in a legal tangle over prize money that had arisen between Nelson and St Vincent. According to Haslewood, he was breakfasting with the Nelsons, and

a cheerful conversation was passing on indifferent subjects, when
Lord Nelson spoke of something which had been done or said by
'dear Lady Hamilton'. Lady Nelson rose from her chair and
exclaimed with much vehemence, 'I am sick of hearing of dear
Lady Hamilton, and am resolved that you should give up either
her or me.' Lord Nelson, with perfect calmness, said : 'Take care,
Fanny, what you say. I love you sincerely; but I cannot forget my
obligations to Lady Hamilton, or speak of her otherwise than with
affection and admiration.' Without saying one soothing word or
gesture, but muttering something about her mind being made up,
Lady Nelson left the room, and shortly after drove from the house.
They never lived together afterwards. I believe that Lord Nelson
took a formal leave of her ladyship before joining the Fleet under
Sir Hyde Parker. . . .

One wonders why Fanny Nelson should, for a moment, have been
expected to utter a 'soothing word', or make any gesture at all –
except perhaps to throw something at her husband. But she remained
then, and to the end, a gentle and affectionate woman who was
unsuited to the storms of emotion. She was no match for her
tempestuous rival.

CHAPTER TWENTY-EIGHT

The Baltic Scene

On 17 January 1801 Nelson hoisted his flag aboard the *San Josef*, the great man-of-war which he had captured four years previously at Cape St Vincent. Despite his earlier expressed intention to retire on the grounds of health he had, immediately upon his arrival in London, expressed his wish to the Admiralty for a further appointment. On 1 January he had been promoted Vice-Admiral of the Blue. St Vincent, who was in command of the Channel fleet, now made it clear that he wanted no one but Nelson as his second-in-command.

The *San Josef* lay at Plymouth, Hardy was her captain, and Nelson had every reason to feel the greatest satisfaction at being aboard a ship which he declared would be the finest in the world. Once more in his native element he could assume the role for which nature had cast him, even though he could never forget the complexities of the shore and of his private life. Fanny had gone to Brighton to be with his old father, Round Wood was to be sold, but he had made ample provision for his wife for the rest of her life. He could never make amends, but he could at least freely admit that there was no blame attached to her: 'I call God to witness there is nothing in you or your conduct I wish otherwise.' But his main private concern, overlying all other things, was the fact that Emma was due to give birth in the near future. If the child survived, the problems involved would be considerable for, even if Sir William had been capable of overlooking the fact that his wife was pregnant, he could not overlook the existence of a child. While he sat in Hardy's cabin, for his own was not yet completed, listening to the bustle of the ship as efforts were made to complete her in advance of time, he had much to preoccupy him – not least the fact that his one good eye was giving him trouble and that he needed new shades made to protect both from the glare of sun on sea.

The world beyond these private preoccupations was bleak and menacing. Tsar Paul I of Russia, affronted by the fact that the

British had no intention of allowing him to annex Malta – which had now fallen – had become hostile. Although nominally at war with the French, the Tsar viewed the British blockade of the Continent as intolerable. He was not alone in this, for all the Continental countries had good reason to object to the search, control, and even seizure of their ships by the British. The latter, who could only strike at Napoleon's France by such measures, were in the unenviable position of making enemies of the very nations whom they wished to arouse to join them against the common foe. The Danes had particular cause for complaint, and an action in the Channel in which a Danish frigate together with her convoy of six merchantmen had been fired on and captured had produced an international storm that had very nearly led to war. Tsar Paul now proposed a treaty of Armed Neutrality, similar to that of 1780, whereby the Continental powers, whose trade was adversely affected by the British blockade, would deny Britain access to the Baltic, while at the same time the neutrals would band together against Britain to protect the freedom of their trade. It was not quite a declaration of war, but what it did in effect was to nullify British seapower. Without access to the Baltic, whose timber and other naval sources of supply were essential to the maintenance of her fleet, Britain was rendered impotent. The treaty was signed in December 1800 by Russia, Prussia, Denmark and Sweden, Russia at the same time seizing 300 British merchantmen which were in her ports. Napoleon was naturally delighted, for he saw his great adversary reduced once again to having no ally at all upon the Continent except Portugal. He declared that he regarded the French Republic as already at peace with the Tsar, even though the formalities of a peace treaty had not yet been concluded. The Tsar, who also had his eye on India, was quickly in touch with the First Consul, with the suggestion that influence should be brought to bear on Portugal to bring her within the Armed Neutrality, while approaches should also be made to the United States urging them to join. England faced the spectre of the deprivation of her sources of naval supplies and of a Continent united against her navy and her trade – the only weapons she had in her armoury against the might of the land power. The Danes proved more provocative than most of the other signatories of the treaty and, on 29 March 1801, placed an embargo on all British merchantmen within Danish ports. At the same time they entered Hamburg and declared the Elbe closed to British shipping. There was nothing left for Britain to do but to send a powerful fleet into the Baltic, in the hope that its presence would be enough to bring most of the signatories of the treaty to their senses – and, if it did not, to take appropriate action to destroy their navies. In the whole course of the war to date, England never faced a graver crisis than that which now stemmed from this new treaty of Armed Neutrality.

It was under these circumstances that Nelson now took the *San Josef* up the Channel to drop anchor in Torbay, where he at once went to report to St Vincent. Shortly after arrival he was ordered to transfer his flag to the 98-gun *St George*. She was of lighter draught than the *San Josef* and therefore considered more suitable for the shallow waters of the Baltic whither he would soon be bound. It was on this same day, 1 February, that he received the letter from London which he had been awaiting with eagerness. Its contents struck him like a blow in the heart. All his life he had longed for children, and it had been with saddened resignation that he had long ago accepted the fact that Fanny was incapable of bearing any. Now he had the longed-for news – Emma had given birth to a daughter! This child, which was to be christened Horatia (though Nelson would have preferred Emma), was the result of that warm and indolent cruise in the *Foudroyant* to Malta. She had most probably been conceived while the flagship lay at anchor in the warm waters of Marsa Xlokk Bay in the south of that sunny island. She was the product of their Mediterranean love and Nelson, only just returned from his first interview with St Vincent, was deliriously happy. The only trouble was that all must be concealed. The circumstances of the birth itself had been most adroitly handled by Mrs Cadogan and, after the child's delivery on 29 January, it had been smuggled out of the house concealed in a muff, and delivered to a wet-nurse in Marylebone.

Even if Sir William knew of the event (which he probably did) the arrangements made for the delivery and subsequent care of Horatia were so discreet that the world at large never had an inkling that Emma had borne a child. Indeed, so well concealed were all the circumstances of its birth that, even many years afterwards, there was considerable dispute as to whether she had had a child and, if she had, whose it was. There can be absolutely no doubt that Nelson was the father. Letters which passed in abundance between Nelson and Emma subsequent to the birth establish quite conclusively his proud parenthood. Of necessity, for the mails were not secure, this correspondence had to be concealed under a fiction that Nelson was concerned about a young father aboard his vessel who was named Thompson or Thomson (indifferently spelled by both) whose lady love had had a baby, but whose marriage to the mother was rendered impossible by an 'uncle'. Once this uncle was either dead or otherwise out of the way it was understood that the ill-starred lovers would get married.

Nelson's passion for Emma was more than reinforced by the birth of his daughter : 'My own dear wife, for such you are in my eyes and in the face of heaven . . . I love, I never did love anyone else. I never had a dear pledge of love till you gave me one, and you, thank God, never gave one to anyone else.' In this of course he was grossly mistaken (and Emma naturally would have been the last to undeceive him) for in the north of England a young woman of about nineteen named Emma Carew was still occasionally visited by Mrs Cadogan. Apart from Emma and her mother, only Charles Greville knew for certain of this daughter, Charles Greville of course having taken Emma under his protection when she had just borne the child. What Nelson's feelings would have been had he known of her existence cannot be imagined. All that is quite clear is that at this time of his life, separated from Emma, he cherished an almost mad jealousy on her score. The news that the unprincipled Prince Regent might be going to visit the Hamiltons was enough to throw him into a paroxysm of fear and rage. 'Does Sir William want you to be a whore to the rascal?' he wrote. The meeting in fact never took place, but Nelson must have been subconsciously aware that a woman with an early reputation like Emma's, and who had subsequently blatantly deceived her husband, might not be above seeking even higher favours than his own. If Emma's feelings towards Nelson may possibly have been tempered by material considerations and by the desire to have as lover the foremost figure of the time, there can be no doubt that his were totally inspired by that blind god from whom the ancients prayed to be preserved. 'What must be my sensations at the idea of sleeping with you! it sets me on fire, even the thoughts, much more would the reality. I am sure my love & desires are all to you, and if any woman naked were to come to me, even as I am this moment from thinking of you, I hope it might rot off if I would touch her even with my hand.'

Nelson was now made second-in-command under Sir Hyde Parker of the fleet that was destined for the Baltic. Parker was over sixty, an admiral of the old school, with little recent experience of warfare – a not undistinguished figure whom their Lordships may well have thought would be able to cope with the diplomatic niceties if, as they hoped, all could be settled in the Baltic without bloodshed. If, on the other hand, there was any necessity for naval action, then they felt that they could rely on the impetuous brilliance of his second-in-command to carry matters to a triumphant conclusion. The choice of Parker has often been criticised, but the idea of tempering the *élan* of the one with the moderation of the other was not without its boardroom reasoning. Nelson, for his part, had little reason to feel that Parker was active enough for this command. He had been acquainted with him in the Mediterranean under Hotham, in the action off Genoa and Hyères, and had observed how indifferently he had handled his division on that occasion. As he wrote privately to St Vincent: 'Our friend is a little nervous about dark nights and fields of ice, but we must brace up; these are not times for nervous systems.'

An elderly admiral, who had recently married a girl of eighteen (known to the irreverent as 'batter pudding'), was unlikely to have welcomed the arrival under his command of this famous firebrand. Nelson now paid a fleeting visit to London in order to see Emma and little Horatia. At the same time he arranged for the William Nelsons to stay near Emma during his absence to keep her company (and possibly to act as heavy clerical chaperonage if the detested Prince Regent should appear upon the scene). After three days' absence he returned to the St George at Spithead, where 600 troops under Lieutenant-Colonel the Hon. William Stewart were embarked. Stewart's presence was a fortunate circumstance for subsequent biographers, since he was the type of man who took Nelson's fancy and he left many vivid impressions of Nelson at this period of his life in a journal that he kept of the Baltic campaign. The latter had meanwhile sent the final letter to his wife, which forever sealed the closure of a long correspondence that had endured since his courtship of her in the West Indies. Its cruelty is readily apparent, but its venom was perhaps partly due to the fact that it had been reported back to Nelson that Josiah Nisbet, on seeing the one-armed admiral having difficulty in mounting the ship's side in bad weather, had loudly expressed the hope that his stepfather would break his neck. (Josiah had naturally always championed his mother, and deeply resented Nelson's infatuation with Emma Hamilton.) 'Josiah is to have another ship,' he wrote to Fanny from the St George on 4 March:

and to go abroad, if the Thalia cannot soon be got ready. I have done all for him, and he may again, as he has often done before, wish me to break my neck, and be abetted in it by his friends, who are likewise my enemies; but I have done my duty as an honest, generous man, and I neither want or wish for any body to care what becomes of me, whether I return, or am left in the Baltic seeing I have done all in my power for you. And if dead, you will find I have done the same; therefore my only wish is, to be left to myself; and wishing you every happiness, believe that I am, your affectionate Nelson and Bronte.

Only two days later he was concluding a letter to Emma : 'Kiss my dear, dear godchild for me, and be assured I am for ever, ever, ever, your, your, more than ever yours yours, your only, only your, &c.'

Arriving at Yarmouth Roads on 6 March, Nelson found little to his liking. Expedition was, as he saw it, the order of the day, and here was Sir Hyde Parker more concerned with the arrangements for a forthcoming ball than with getting the fleet to sea. The weather was terrible, cold, foggy, and dank with that bone-chilling miasma of the North Sea. Nelson could only too easily forget how he himself had happily lingered inactive in Naples and Palermo, and was full of indignation at finding Sir Hyde preoccupied with his young bride. Troubridge had recently been appointed to the Board of Admiralty and he, as well as St Vincent, received letters requesting that urgent orders be sent to get the fleet to sea. To Troubridge, Nelson wrote : 'Consider how nice it must be laying in bed with a young wife, compared to a damned cold raw wind. But, my dear Troubridge, pack us off. I am interested, as I want to return.' The result of this gadfly approach was that orders came for the fleet to proceed to sea immediately. Lady Parker's ball never took place. Sir Hyde for his part must have been well aware that this flurry of activity had followed hard on the heels of the arrival of his second-in-command. Relations between him and Nelson were not unnaturally strained, and the latter complained that he seemed unable to get any hard information as to Parker's intentions. He was aware that negotiations with the Danes were to be attempted first of all, with force being used only as a last resort. He disapproved strongly – 'A fleet of British men-of-war are the best negotiators in Europe.' Nelson was certainly right in his desire for immediate action, for the sooner the British moved, the less chance was there of the Danes, the Swedes, and the Russians effecting a juncture of the fleets. Although their quality, and particularly that of the Russians, was not up to the British, they would nevertheless have far outnumbered the fleet assembled under Sir Hyde Parker. This consisted of eighteen sail-of-the-line, eleven frigates, and attendant sloops, fireships and bomb vessels, to the total number of fifty-three ships.

March is no season for the North Sea – that mud-coloured tract of water which can be inhospitable even in midsummer – and this year was no exception. As the fleet headed north the weather grew steadily colder and fog gave place to sleet, and then to snow and ice. Nelson had ended his letter to Emma, 'I am wet through and cold', and so was everyone else. Not having worked together before, the fleet had not had time to shake down into a disciplined unit like that miracle-squadron which Nelson had commanded at the Nile. He commented sourly that : 'Although the Commander-in-Chief made the signal for close order of sailing, yet scarcely one have kept their stations and in particular the good going ships.' He need not have worried unduly, for the calibre of the officers and men was such that, as they would soon prove, it only needed the stimulus of action for them to become an exceptional fighting force. The quality of the captains alone should have encouraged him, for he had his trusted Foley from the Nile in command of the *Elephant*, Sir Thomas Thompson in the *Bellona*, and Fremantle in the *Ganges*. Among other equally distinguished captains was William Bligh in the 54-gun *Glatton*, who twelve years earlier had survived the famous mutiny in the *Bounty* to complete one of the longest small-boat voyages on record, 4,000 miles in an open boat. Bligh – though much-maligned in later centuries – was one of the finest seamen and navigators of his time.

As they neared the Dogger Bank a certain Lieutenant Layman who was aboard the *St George* remarked that he had once before caught a fine turbot in that area. Nelson was interested, knowing that Hyde Parker was fond of the pleasures of the table, and asked the lieutenant to have a try again. In due course to Nelson's delight a small turbot was caught and the Admiral immediately said : 'Send it across to Sir Hyde.' Although it was near nightfall with a rising sea, and there was some disquiet at sending a boat across under such conditions, Nelson was determined to make this small gesture – a turbot rather than an olive branch – towards his chief. The action was appreciated, the ice between the two men thawed, and Parker sent back a friendly note of thanks. Layman later maintained that the victory that was to follow was won by the turbot, for if Nelson had not made this gesture he would not have been taken into his chief's confidence, and would not have been given the detached squadron which ensured the triumph of British arms at Copenhagen.

On 18 March, after a severe gale and dismal weather conditions, the British sighted the northernmost part of Jutland, the long arm known as the Skaw. On the twentieth, the wind being fair for Copenhagen, they anchored some eighteen miles above Hamlet's Elsinore. A Foreign Office official had already been sent on ahead with instructions that gave Denmark forty-eight hours to withdraw from the coalition of Armed Neutrality, or else face the consequences represented by this fleet that now lay poised against her shores. The Crown Prince of Denmark, who acted as Regent to his father (who was even more insane than Tsar Paul), would probably have been willing to accede to this request but he was far too frightened of offending the Russians

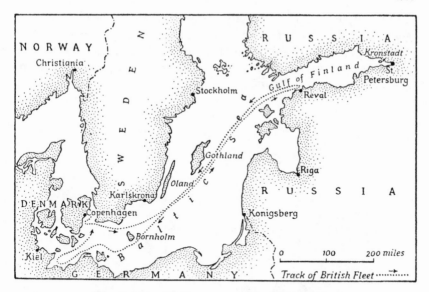

The Baltic with the route of the British Fleet

to do so. Three days passed before the British diplomat returned with the answer that Denmark refused the offer. Nelson, who had already paid a visit to Sir Hyde but had been unable to get any satisfactory statement as to his intentions, was delighted when a message reached him to join a general council aboard the *London*. Affairs clearly were to be settled by action – and not by pen and ink. He wrote a brief line to Emma : 'Now we are sure of fighting, I am sent for. When it was a joke I was kept in the background; tomorrow will, I hope, be a proud day for England.'

Lieutenant Layman, who accompanied Nelson, noted the gloomy atmosphere as the council opened. Nicholas Vansittart of the Foreign Office had painted a gloomy picture of the strength of the defences of Copenhagen, while the accepted viewpoint of the period that ships could not prevail against strong and well-sited shore batteries had had a depressing effect upon Parker and his assembled captains. Nelson was immediately determined to inject some fire and enthusiasm into this assembly and began questioning Vansittart about the disposition of the Danish fleet. Having learned that they had placed their strongest ships at the head of the line, he immediately suggested that the British should take them by surprise by attacking their rear. The drawback to this was that it would necessitate their entering the Baltic by the Great Belt – a difficult passage – rather than by the Sound.

But in any event, as he quickly made clear, the sooner the ships got into action the better. Every moment that they delayed gave the Danes further opportunity for strengthening their defences and bringing their ships to readiness 'Let it be by the Sound, by the Belt, or any how, only lose not an hour.'

CHAPTER TWENTY-NINE

Copenhagen

NELSON'S genius in his hard trade never showed itself more clearly than at Copenhagen. Immediately upon returning to the *St George* he sat down and composed a letter to Sir Hyde Parker which set out explicitly the options that lay before him. Not only does it reveal his grasp of overall strategy and his appreciation of the tactical options, but at the same time it tactfully manages to put the necessary fire into an indecisive Commander-in-Chief. Whatever Nelson may have felt about Sir Hyde Parker, it is clear from the whole attitude towards his senior that he had more regard for him than he had ever entertained towards Lord Keith in the Mediterranean.

'My Dear Sir Hyde,' he wrote :

The conversation we had yesterday has naturally, from its importance, been the subject of my thoughts; and the more I have reflected, the more I am confirmed in opinion, that not a moment should be lost in attacking the Enemy : they will every day and hour be stronger; we shall never be so good a match for them as at this moment. The only consideration in my mind, is how to get at them with the least risk to our Ships. By Mr Vansittart's account, the Danes have taken every means in their power to prevent our getting to attack Copenhagen by the Passage of the Sound. Cronenburg has been strengthened, the Crown Islands fortified, on the outermost of which are twenty guns pointed mostly downwards, and only eight hundred yards from very formidable batteries placed under the Citadel, supported by five Sail of the Line, seven Floating batteries of fifty guns each, besides Small-craft, Gun-boats, &c. &c.; and that the Revel Squadron [in the Gulf of Finland] of twelve or fourteen Sail of the Line are soon expected, as also five Sail of Swedes. It would appear by what you have told me of your instructions, that Government took for granted you would find no difficulty in getting off Copenhagen, and in the event of a failure of negotiation, you might instantly attack; and that there would be scarcely a doubt but the Danish Fleet would be destroyed, and the Capital made so hot that Denmark would listen to reason and its true interest. By Mr Vansittart's account, their state of preparation exceeds what he conceives our Government thought possible, and that the Danish Government is hostile to us in the greatest possible degree. Therefore here you are, with almost the safety, certainly with the honour of England more intrusted to you, than ever yet fell to the lot of any British Officer. On your decision depends, whether our Country shall be degraded in the eyes of Europe, or whether she shall rear her head higher than ever: again do I repeat, never did our Country depend so much on the success of any Fleet as on this. How best to honour our Country and abate the pride of her Enemies, by defeating their schemes, must be the subject of your deepest consideration as Commander-in-Chief; and if what I have to offer can be the least useful in forming your decision, you are most heartily welcome.

I shall begin with supposing you are determined to enter by the Passage of the Sound, as there are those who think, if you leave that Passage open, that the Danish Fleet may sail from Copenhagen, and join the Dutch or French. I own I have no fears on that subject; for it is not likely that whilst their Capital is menaced with an attack, 9,000 of her best men should be sent out of the Kingdom. I suppose that some damage may arise amongst our masts and yards; yet perhaps there will not be one of them but could be made serviceable again. You are now about Cronenburg; if the wind be fair, and you determine to attack the Ships and Crown Islands, you must expect the natural issue of such a battle – Ships crippled, and perhaps one or two lost; for the wind which carries you in, will most probably not bring out a crippled Ship. This mode I call taking the bull by the horns. It, however, will not prevent the Revel Ships, or Swedes, from joining the Danes; and to prevent this from taking effect, is, in my humble opinion, a measure absolutely necessary – and still to attack Copenhagen.

Two modes are in my view; one to pass Cronenberg, taking the risk of damage, and to pass up the deepest and straightest Channel above the Middle Grounds, and coming down the Garbar or King's Channel, to attack their Floating batteries &c. &c., as we find it convenient. It must have the effect of preventing a junction between the Russians, Swedes, and Danes, and may give us an opportunity of bombarding Copenhagen. I am also pretty certain that a passage could be found to the northernward of Southholm for all our Ships; perhaps it might be necessary to warp a short distance in the very narrow part. Should this mode of attack be ineligible, the passage of the Belt, I have no doubt, would be accomplished in four or five days, and then the attack by Draco could be carried into effect, and the junction of the Russians prevented, with every probability of success against the Danish Floating batteries. What effect a bombardment might have, I am not called upon to give an opinion; but think the way would be cleared for the trial.

Supposing us through the Belt with the wind first westerly, would it not be possible to either go with the Fleet, or detach ten ships of three and two decks, with one Bomb and two Fire-ships, to Revel, to destroy the Russian Squadron at that place? I do not see the great risk of such a detachment, and with the remainder to attempt the business at Copenhagen. The measure may be thought bold, but I am of the opinion the boldest measures are the safest; and our Country demands a most vigorous exertion of her force, directed with judgement. In supporting you, my dear Sir Hyde, through the arduous and important task you have undertaken, no exertion of head or heart shall be wanting from your most obedient and faithful servant,

Nelson and Bronte.

There can be no doubt that Nelson's advice had a salutary effect. On 26 March the fleet was ordered to weigh, and the same evening they anchored again about six miles above Cronenburg. Nelson now received orders from Parker to take ten sail-of-the-line under his command, together with four frigates, seven bomb vessels, two fire-ships, and twelve brigs. He was to be despatched on special service to carry out the assault against the Danish defences, while his chief in the heavier ships held the ring outside in case the Danish men-of-war should make a sortie out of Copenhagen. Parker still hoped that all could be resolved without action and a messenger was sent to the Governor of Elsinore castle inquiring his intentions if the British should stand on, to which the reply came back that he could not under any circumstances permit a fleet with unknown intentions to pass the fortress of Cronenburg. Patience, it is said, is a virtue learned at sea. For the next three days even the fiery second-in-command had to exercise it, for calms, coupled with head-winds, held the fleet immobile. It was not until 30 March that they were able to weigh and attempt the passage of the Sound. Only three miles wide, the strait was dominated on the Danish side by Cronenburg and on the Swedish side by the fort at Helsingborg. Fortunately for the British, the Swedes had given no instruction for their gunners to fire on this impressive fleet as it held on its way into the Baltic. Keeping to the Swedish side of the channel, then, Parker's ships moved on with a favourable north-west wind towards the island of Hveen. The Danes for their part blazed away, but quite ineffectually. Later the same day Nelson was to write to Emma :

> We this morning passed the fancied tremendous fortress of Cronen-burg, mounted with 270 pieces of cannon. More powder and shot, I believe, never were thrown away, for not one shot struck a single ship of the British fleet. Some of our ships fired; but the *Elephant* did not return a single shot. I hope to reserve them for a better occasion. I have just been reconnoitring the Danish line of defence. It looks formidable to those who are children at war, but to my judgement, with ten Sail of the Line I think I can annihilate them; at all events, I hope to be allowed to try.

Nelson had transferred his flag for the second time, on this occasion from the *St George* to the *Elephant* and for the same reason as before, that his new ship had an even shallower draught. The reconnaissance to which he referred in his letter to Emma was made that evening in a schooner in company with Sir Hyde Parker and other senior officers. What it revealed more than confirmed Vansittart's previous gloomy prognostications. The Danes had taken good advantage of the British delay and had even further strengthened their defences. As Colonel Stewart commented : '[They] had lined the northern edge of the shoals near the Crown batteries, and the front of the harbour and arsenal, with a formidable flotilla. The Trekroner, or Three Crowns, battery appeared in particular to have been strengthened. . . .' It was also observed that they had removed all the buoys marking the Northern and the King's Channel. Later, under Nelson's supervision, these were efficiently replaced by British pilots, to serve as markers to his squadron when it went into the attack.

On 31 March, after a further examination of the Danish positions, carried out in the frigate *Amazon*, commanded by one of the finest officers in the Navy, Captain Riou, a council of war was called. Such councils were everything that Nelson detested (he had never needed one before the Nile), for he held that they tended to promote indecision. As he was to write on another occasion : 'If a man consults whether he is to fight, when he has the power in his own hands, *it is certain that his opinion is against fighting.*' Nelson sensed at once, as on the previous occasion, that there was hesitancy and even pessimism in the air. He proceeded to dispel it, and Colonel Stewart, who was present, left a vivid record of the occasion. In it one seems to feel that electric quality in Nelson which could change the whole atmosphere around him. 'During this Council of War,' Stewart wrote:

the energy of Lord Nelson's character was remarked: certain difficulties had been started by some of the members, relative to each of the three powers we should have to engage, in succession or united, in those seas. The number of the Russians was, in particular, represented as formidable. Lord Nelson kept pacing the cabin, mortified at everything which savoured of alarm or irresolution. When the above remark was applied to the Swedes, he sharply observed, 'The more numerous the better'; and when to the Russians, he repeatedly said; 'So much the better, I wish they were twice as many; the easier the victory, depend on it.' [One seems to hear the voice of his old master John Jervis in those moments before the Battle of Cape St Vincent.] He alluded as he afterwards explained in private, to the total want of tactique among the Northern Fleets; and to his intention, whenever he should bring either the Swedes or Russians to action, of attacking the head of their Line, and confusing their movements as much as possible. He used to say: 'Close with a Frenchman, but out-manoeuvre a Russian.'

The conclusion of the conference was that Nelson's plan of passing 'up the deepest and straightest Channel above the Middle Grounds, and coming down the Garbar or King's Channel, to attack their Floating batteries' was the one adopted. It must at once be said of Sir Hyde Parker that he acted more than handsomely towards his junior by allocating to Nelson's squadron two additional ships-of-the-line, giving him twelve in all for his assault from the south upon the Danish ships moored in their protective line as the outer defences of Copenhagen. This defence, consisting of hulks and floating batteries (all of which could be reinforced by men and munitions from the shore), possessed a fire-power, an invulnerability almost, which had never been available to Brueys in Aboukir Bay. For one thing, they were moored fore and aft on shoal ground, so that there could be absolutely no chance of getting inshore of them. At the northern end was the massive Trekroner Fort, to attack which would certainly result in grave losses among the British men-of-war. Nelson's plan was for his squadron to come down the Outer Sound with a northerly wind, a difficult enough feat of pilotage in itself, and then to drop anchor beyond the shoals of the Middle Ground. There he would have to wait until the wind shifted to the south and enabled him to run down the line of hulks and floating batteries, the weaker part of Copenhagen's defences. At the same time he would, by this evolution, be placing his squadron in such a position that neither the Swedes nor the Russians would be able to come to the aid of their allies. The fact that the Danes had placed their weakest ships at this tail end of the line gave him every hope that, as at the Nile, his squadron could annihilate them one by one.

On the morning of 1 April, the wind set fair from the north and Parker ordered the fleet to weigh. A towering cloud of sail advanced inexorably towards Copenhagen, bringing up in a fresh anchorage only six miles from the threatened city. Nelson now boarded Captain Riou's frigate the *Amazon* and sailed down the Outer Deep to make a final examination of the Channel. Satisfied with what he found, he returned to the *Elephant* and the signal was hoisted for the squadron to get under way. It was already agreed that, while Sir Hyde Parker should lie to the north of Copenhagen threatening the Trekroner Fort, and preventing the exit of any of the Danish fleet moored within the harbour, Nelson would strike from the south the moment that he had a fair wind. His ships would then sail down the enemy defences, the first anchoring by the stern opposite a designated vessel, the second passing outboard of her and placing herself against another, and so on all down the Danish line until each of the men-of-war had brought up abreast one of the enemy. To Edward Riou was assigned the hazardous place of taking his *Amazon* and four other frigates to attack the northern end of the Danish line, while Captain Rose in the frigate *Jamaica* was to engage their southern flank in company with six gun-brigs.

Early that afternoon Nelson's squadron got under way and, piloted by the *Amazon*, passed safely down the Outer Channel, coming to anchor at the southern end of the Middle Ground. Here they must stay of necessity until a shift of wind into the south could boost them up the King's Channel and bring them abreast of the Danes. The hard core of the column chosen for this attack was composed of seven 74s with Nelson flying his flag in the *Elephant* commanded by Captain Foley (Hardy was also with him as a volunteer), three 64s, Bligh's *Glatton* of 54 guns, and Walker's 50-gun *Isis*. The 74 *Bellona* had Captain Sir Thomas Thompson, a Nile veteran, in command, while an old friend of Nelson's, Captain Murray, commanded the *Edgar* and another, Rear-Admiral Graves, flew his flag in Captain Retalick's

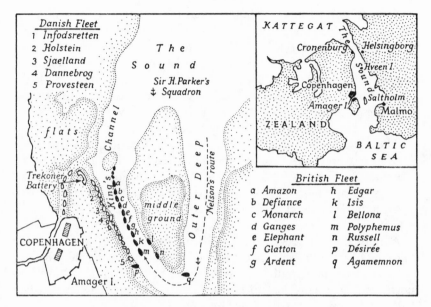

The Battle of Copenhagen, April 2, 1801

Defiance. Counting the smaller ships of under 50 guns, he had a force of 21 ships with which to attack the carefully prepared defences of Copenhagen. It was little enough perhaps, but Nelson was in a good humour when he sat down to dine that night in the cabin of Foley's ship with a party of his comrades-in-arms. As Colonel Stewart recorded: 'He was in the highest spirits, and drank to a leading wind, and to the success of the ensuing day.' Nevertheless circumstances were very different from at the Nile: not only were the enemy far more securely entrenched and completely prepared for the forthcoming attack, but Nelson had not had the opportunity to work with this squadron in the same way as he had with his 'Band of Brothers'. This necessitated the preparation of elaborate orders, and, supper completed, a large part of the night was occupied with writing instructions to be issued to each ship on the following day.

Colonel Stewart left a memorable account of the scene in Foley's cabin:

From the previous fatigue of this day, and of the two preceding, Lord Nelson was so much exhausted while dictating his instructions, that it was recommended to him by us all, and indeed, insisted upon by his old servant, Allen, who assumed much command on these occasions, that he should go to his cot. It was placed on the floor, but from it he still continued to dictate. The orders were completed about one o'clock, when half a dozen Clerks in the foremost cabin proceeded to transcribe them. Lord Nelson's impatience again showed itself; for instead of sleeping undisturbedly, as he might have done, he was every half hour calling from his cot to these Clerks to hasten their work, for that the wind was becoming fair : he was constantly receiving a report of this during the night. The work being finished about six in the morning, his Lordship, who was previously up and dressed, breakfasted, and about seven made the Signal for all captains. The instructions were delivered to each by eight o'clock; and a special command was given to Captain Riou to act as circumstances might require.

Admiral Mahan has the comment that 'It was characteristic of the "heaven-born" admiral, that the wind which had been fair the day before to take him south, changed by the hour of battle to take him north; but it is only just to notice also that he himself never trifled with a fair wind, nor with time.'

He had also, it must be added, superb captains and seamen to help him. During the night Captain Hardy had made a further survey of the enemy disposition, something that called for extreme skill under those conditions. He had taken a small boat down from the British anchorage, and had sounded around the rearmost enemy ships. So that the splash of lead and line should not be heard by sentries aboard the Danes, he had used a quant, or long pole, to discover exactly what depths lay around them. Hardy, Nelson's invaluable Hardy, was the only captain to be present at all of Nelson's great victories – the Nile, now at Copenhagen, and finally at Trafalgar.

The wind was now settled in the south-east, ideal for the enterprise, and at 9.30 the order was made to weigh in succession. The first thing to go wrong with the events of the day was the reluctance of the pilots to take the ships up the Channel. They were merchant-marine mates and navigators, accustomed to the Baltic trade, but alarmed at the draught of the vessels they were now expected to con as closely as possible to the Danish defence vessels – which they well knew were moored on shoal ground. Nelson later noted how he suffered 'the misery of having the honour of our Country intrusted to pilots who had no other thought than to keep the ships clear of danger, and their own silly heads clear of shot'. The solution was found when Mr Briarly, a veteran of the Nile and the Master of the *Bellona*, offered to lead the ships in. He was accordingly transferred to Captain

Murray's 74, the *Edgar*, which was followed by the *Agamemnon*, Nelson's beloved old ship. Under a fine swell of sail the *Edgar* successfully rounded the end of the Middle Ground shoal and headed for the Danish line. But disaster struck, for the *Agamemnon* found herself so placed that she could not weather the shoal and, although not running aground, had to re-anchor. In the event she never managed to clear the shoal and get into action throughout the course of the day. The *Polyphemus* was now ordered to take up the place previously assigned to the *Agamemnon*. Both these first two ships to come into action inevitably received a very heavy weight of fire, and Murray was forced to anchor opposite the Danish *Jylland* at a distance of about 500 yards, whereas Nelson's instructions had been that all ships should try to bring up at 250 yards range. The result of this was that the *Polyphemus* and the other ships following, in order to maintain the line, all anchored at this less effective range, instead of point-blank as had been intended.

Worse was now to follow. The *Bellona* and the *Russell*, coming too close to the western edge of the Middle Ground, ran aground. It was true that even from this position they were throughout the day able to maintain a reasonably heavy fire on the southern tail of the enemy, but it was naturally nowhere near as effective as it would have been had they been anchored at close quarters. The situation thus was that, at the opening of the battle, Nelson found himself deprived of three ships out of his squadron. Nevertheless, he managed to bring his remaining nine into close action, each anchored opposite an enemy – even though at twice the intended range. Nelson, who was following in the *Elephant*, passed down the centre of the channel with the grounded ships to starboard and the enemy batteries to port. He took up his berth opposite the Danish Admiral's flagship, the *Dannebrog*, the position which had originally been assigned to the *Bellona*. Captain Bertie in the *Ardent* and Bligh in the *Glatton* skilfully anchored between the *Edgar* and the *Elephant*. Captain James Mosse of the *Monarch* was killed within a few moments of his ship's getting into action, just as the last man-of-war, the *Defiance*, flying the flag of Rear-Admiral Graves, anchored ahead of him. From now on, in that grey northern light, the adversaries settled down like old-fashioned pugilists to a sheer slogging match. To quote Nelson, 'Here was no manoeuvring. It was downright fighting.' Furthermore, since the British line was shortened by the absence of three ships, it meant that most of those engaged had to deal with two adversaries at the same time.

The first shot had been fired at five minutes past ten and a little over an hour later all the ships were engaged, the last to come into action being the bomb-vessels which opened fire on the town, dock-yard and enemy ships by quarter to twelve. In terms of the number of guns involved, the two sides were fairly evenly matched, it having been calculated that the Danes had about 380 (including those of the Trekroner Fort) and the British a little over 400. Southey, whose information stemmed from his brother Thomas who was present at the battle, describes Nelson's agitation when he saw at the very beginning that he had lost a fourth part of his ships to the dangers of the Middle Ground, 'but no sooner was he in battle . . . than, as if that artillery, like music, had driven away all care and painful thoughts, his countenance brightened; and, as a bystander describes him, his conversation became joyous, animated, elevated, and delight-ful'. While the heavier units were all actively engaged, Captain Riou's small craft had taken on the formidable Trekroner Fort itself. The absence of the *Agamemnon*, the *Russell* and the *Bellona* now made itself sadly felt.

Meanwhile, Sir Hyde Parker was beating up from the north but was unable to add the weight of the firepower of his division against the Trekroner, for the same wind that had favoured Nelson's approach inevitably blew dead in the teeth of his Commander-in-Chief. Parker could easily tell, however, as the gunfire raged on uninterrupted right up to one o'clock, that the Danes were putting up a far fiercer resistance than had ever been expected. Tom Southey recalled the following: ' "I will make the signal of recall," ' said he to his captain, ' "for Nelson's sake. If he is in a condition to continue the action suc-cessfully, he will disregard it; if he is not, it will be an excuse for his retreat, and no blame can be imputed to him." ' Captain Domett urged him at least to delay the signal till he could communicate with Nelson; but in Sir Hyde's opinion the danger was too pressing for delay. ' "The fire," he said, "was too hot for Nelson to oppose; a retreat he thought must be made; he was aware of the consequences to his own personal reputation, but it would be cowardly in him to leave Nelson to bear the whole shame of the failure, if shame it should be deemed." Under a mistaken judgement therefore, with this disinterested and generous feeling, he made the signal for retreat.' The famous recall, then, was not made – as has sometimes been suggested – out of trepidation on Sir Hyde Parker's part, but out of a generous desire to save his junior from 'the shame of failure' and to take some part of it upon his own shoulders. Furthermore, as he clearly put it to Domett, Nelson could always disregard the signal if he so wished.

Signal 39, the recall, was accordingly made from the Commander-in-Chief's *London*. Nelson's signal lieutenant immediately reported it to him, asking whether he should repeat it for the benefit of the rest of the squadron. The moments that followed have passed into history, for Colonel Stewart, who was with Nelson as he paced the quarter-deck, left us his vivid recollections :

'He continued his walk, and did not appear to take notice of it. The Lieutenant, meeting his Lordship at the next turn, asked "whether he should repeat it?" Lord Nelson answered, "No, acknowledge it." On the officer returning to the poop, his Lordship called after him, "Is No. 16, for close action, still hoisted?" The lieutenant answering in the affirmative, Lord Nelson said, "Mind you keep it so." He now walked the deck considerably agitated, which was always known by his moving the stump of his right arm. After a turn or two he said to me, in a quick manner, "Do you know what's shown on board of the Commander-in-Chief? No. 39!" On asking him what that meant, he answered, "Why, to leave off action." "Leave off action!" he repeated, and then added with a shrug, "Now damn me if I do!" He also observed, I believe to Captain Foley, "You know, Foley, I have only one eye – I have a right to be blind sometimes;" and then, with an archness peculiar to his character, putting his glass to his blind eye, he exclaimed, "I really do not see the signal!" '

Rear-Admiral Graves at the head of the column also saw fit to disregard the recall, and later commented, 'if we had discontinued the action before the enemy struck, we should all have gone aground and been destroyed'. Only Captain Riou and his division, who were heavily engaged by the Trekroner Fort, and were far closer to Parker's flagship, obeyed signal No. 39. Riou had already been wounded by a splinter in the head but, on obeying his Commander-in-Chief, he is said to have remarked : 'What will Nelson think of us?' As the *Amazon* and those with her turned her stern to the Trekroner Fort, the Danes, exhilarated at this British retreat, redoubled their fire. Several more men aboard Riou's ship were killed and her captain exclaimed : 'Come, then, my boys, let us all die together!' A few seconds later he was cut in two. Stewart commented of him that his death deprived the British Navy 'of one of its greatest ornaments, and society of a character of singular worth, resembling the heroes of romance'.

The battle was finally decided by the British superiority in gunnery. Although, in theory at least, the floating batteries combined with the fire of the fort should have wrought havoc among such sitting targets as Nelson's ships-of-the-line, the British rate of fire far exceeded that of the Danes. Many of the latter were volunteers and inexperienced, and they could not compete in sheer iron-hard efficiency with those semi-naked man who toiled, with their sweat rags clamped around their ears, in the thunder and fury of the British gun-decks. By about two o'clock in the afternoon, the bulk of the Danish line was silenced – all the ships astern of the *Elephant* having been reduced to ruined hulks; many of the other ships being on fire. Even the great *Dannebrog*, the Danish flagship, had struck her Commodore's colours, and was drifting in a mass of flames down the anchored line of Copenhagen's defences. (She blew up later in the afternoon.) Nelson considered moving his ships further down the Danish line to come into action against those at the northern end which had not yet been engaged, but Fremantle wisely advised against this, pointing out that they were already short of three of their number, and that those which had been engaged were nearly all severely damaged.

Southey comments that :

Between one and two the fire of the Danes slackened; about two it ceased from the greater part of the line; and some of their lighter ships were adrift. It was, however, difficult to take possession of those which struck, because the batteries on Amager Island protected them, and because an irregular fire was kept up from the ships themselves as the boats approached. This arose from the nature of the action : the crews were continually reinforced from the shore : and fresh men coming aboard did not inquire whether the flag had been struck, or perhaps did not heed it, many or most of them never having been engaged in war before. . . .

This was the crux of the matter. The Danish floating batteries, battered though they were, were steadily fed by boatloads of men coming fresh from Copenhagen. The fact that nearly all their guns were silenced, their ships on fire, and the destruction of the tail of their line complete, did not alter the situation. Nelson himself was so upset at the failure of his boats to reach the *Dannebrog* and rescue the survivors – being prevented from doing so by a steady fire from the shore – that he was heard to remark : 'Either I must send on shore, and stop this irregular proceeding, or send in our fire ships and burn them.' To Fremantle who, as has been said, was against any further proceeding down the enemy line to take on the as yet unengaged Danish vessels, he proposed the following message and asked for his opinion on it :

To the Brothers of Englishmen, the Danes.
Lord Nelson has directions to spare Denmark, when no longer
resisting; but if the firing is continued on the part of Denmark,
Lord Nelson will be obliged to set on fire all the Floating-batteries
he has taken, without having the power of saving the brave Danes
who have defended them. Dated on board his Britannic Majesty's
ship Elephant, Copenhagen Roads, April 2nd, 1801.

Captain Sir Frederick Thesiger, a Danish-and-Russian speaker, and
a member of Nelson's staff, was sent ashore under a flag of truce to
convey this message to the Prince Regent of Denmark, who was in
overall command of the action. It is significant of Nelson's temperament, and his application to detail, that even at this moment, in the
hardest fought battle of his life up to date, he did not forget a certain
psychological finesse which may have had some effect in turning the
issue of the day. He had written his note carefully on the rudderhead
of the *Elephant*, and the Purser, who stood by taking a copy of it,
recalled, when it came to putting it in an envelope, 'At first I was
going to seal it with a wafer, but he would not allow this to be done,
observing that it must be sealed properly, or the Enemy would think
it was written and sent in a hurry.'
   By about four o'clock in the afternoon the action was almost over.
The Prince Regent had sent back a message 'to ask the particular
meaning of sending his flag of truce', and had received the reply that
'Lord Nelson's object in sending on shore a flag of truce is humanity.
He therefore consents that hostilities shall cease, and that the wounded
Danes may be taken ashore. . . .' He went on to say that he hoped that
'this flag of truce may be the happy forerunner of a lasting and happy
Union between my most Gracious Sovereign and His Majesty the
King of Denmark'. Shortly after this all firing ceased, and the Danish
Adjutant-General, Lindholm, came out with a flag of truce and went
aboard the *London* to see Sir Hyde Parker. The signal was now made
for the five ships at the head of the British line, *Defiance*, *Monarch*,
Ganges, *Elephant*, and *Glatton* to weigh anchor in succession and
proceed on down the channel – the wind still blowing fair. Of the
five of them, only the *Glatton* avoided running aground at one point
or another. Nelson's *Elephant*, within a mile of the formidable but
now silent Trekroner Fort, took the ground so hard that she could not
be got off until the following day. If the truce, which Nelson had
initiated at what was just the right moment, had spared many Danish
lives, it had also saved the British from what might possibly have
turned into a disaster. As he embarked in his gig, to make his way

to the conference aboard the *London*, Nelson remarked, 'Well, I have fought contrary to order, and perhaps I shall be hanged. Never mind, let them!'

He need never have doubted. His reception by Parker was somewhat similar to that which he had received from St Vincent on the occasion of that first famous indiscretion. There could be absolutely no doubt that his action in taking his squadron round the Middle Ground and attacking the Danes from the south, falling upon the weaker end of their defences (which they had thought secure since they had envisaged that any attack must be made from the north), had won the day. Now began the long process of bargaining, ultimately to result in Adjutant-General Lindholm's conceding that the Danish ships which had not already been captured should be formally surrendered, and that the armistice should be continued. That night, after the conference was over, Nelson slept aboard his own ship, the *St George*. Nodding over his journal, he made the following entry : 'April 2. Moderate breezes southerly, at 9 [10 in fact] made the signal to engage the Danish line; the action began at 5 min, and lasted about 4 hours, when 17 out of 18 of the Danish line were taken, burnt or sunk. Our ships suffered a great deal. At night went on board the *St George* very unwell.' It was hardly surprising. He was forty-two years old, approaching blindness, and had slept little for six days. He had brought his ships through shoals and narrow passages that would have taxed the nerve, ability and energy of a far younger man and, after fighting the hardest action of his life, had then proved himself a master of diplomacy. He deserved his rest.

CHAPTER THIRTY

Victory – and after

THE battle of Copenhagen had been unnecessary. On 24 March 1801, the Tsar of Russia, Paul I, had been murdered by a party of Russian noblemen who had become increasingly dissatisfied with his policies and fearful of the growing evidence of his insanity. It was only the influence of the Tsar upon his smaller neighbours that had provoked the Northern Federation, and it was very largely fear of Russia that had led the Danes to act in open hostility to the British. But, so slow were communications in those days, the news of the Tsar's assassination did not reach Copenhagen until 9 April, over two weeks after the event, and after the final arrangements had been made with the Danes for an Armistice designed to last fourteen weeks. Southey's comment admirably sums up Nelson's own feelings about this battle (at a time when it was unknown to him that the principal enemy was already dead, or that his successor would reverse Paul I's pro-French policy):

> The fate of these men [the crew of the flagship *Dannebrog*], after the gallantry which they had displayed, particularly affected Nelson: for there was nothing in this action of that indignation against the enemy and that impression of retributive justice, which at the Nile had given a sterner temper to his mind, and a sense of austere delight in beholding the vengeance of which he was the appointed minister. The Danes were an honourable foe; they were of English mould as well as English blood; and now that the battle had ceased, he regarded them rather as brethren than as enemies.

It was undoubtedly the saddest battle in Nelson's life, but it was certainly, as he was later to say to the Prince of Denmark, the hardest-fought of all to date. 'The French fought bravely, but they could not have stood for one hour the fight which the Danes had supported for four.' The British had lost nearly 1,000 men, the Danes nearly 2,000, but the wounded and captured brought their losses up to double this amount. Although the British ships had been badly cut up in the action, not one had been so disabled as to be put out of the fight. The Danes on the other hand had lost seventeen ships out of eighteen in their line of battle, some burnt, some sunk, and the others taken as prizes. Like the Nile it was a battle of annihilation, and at this point one may interpose Joseph Conrad's assessment of the change which Nelson brought into naval warfare : 'In a few short years he revolutionised, not the strategy or tactics of sea-warfare, but the *very conception of victory itself*. [My italics.] And this is genius. In that alone, through the fidelity of his fortune and the power of his inspiration, he stands unique among the leaders of fleets and sailors. He brought heroism into the line of duty. Verily he is a terrible ancestor.'

It was the undeniable fact of his own recognised heroism that, on the morning after the battle, brought within the British grasp the 74-gun *Syaelland*. Nelson had already been aboard his own ship, the *Elephant* (delighted to find that she was no longer aground but anchored securely in Copenhagen Roads), and had been informed that the *Syaelland*, lying under the guns of the Trekroner Fort, refused to surrender to anyone except Lord Nelson. After a visit to the Danish Commodore aboard his ship, the similarly named *Elephanten*, Nelson swiftly boarded his gig and went alongside the recalcitrant Dane. On stepping aboard, he threw back his salt-stained boat-cloak to reveal his orders and the pinned-back sleeve – those evidences of his identity which were as well known to the Danes as to everyone else in Europe. The *Syaelland* surrendered, and was towed away as a prize, although her Captain, game to the last, would still have preferred the guns of Trekroner to have broken their silence and destroy his ship where she lay.

It was a very cold day, Nelson had only had a brief sleep, and yet his extraordinary vitality was never more in evidence than on the morning of that Good Friday, 1801. He went on to inspect the ships that had been in action with him the day before, learning to his great grief that his old companion of the Nile, Captain Thompson, who had commanded the *Bellona* in the recent action, had lost a leg, while Captain Riou and Captain Mosse of the *Edgar* were dead. Meanwhile the British were actively engaged in refitting their ships, splicing their spars, mending standing- and running-rigging, and preparing, if it were necessary, to continue the action should the armistice not be renewed. Prizes were being secured, prize crews put aboard, and Danish prisoners were being transferred to the victors. At the same time the sad procession of boats carrying the wounded and the dead to the shores of Denmark carried on ceaselessly.

It would hardly have seemed the right moment for Nelson himself to go ashore to meet the Crown Prince and to discuss the terms of the armistice. But one of the most astonishing events of the Battle of Copenhagen is that Sir Hyde Parker, who had been through no fault of his own inactive throughout the battle, should now have asked his junior to undertake the negotiations with the Danes, which surely should have been his own contribution as Commander-in-Chief of the victorious fleet. The only possible reason, one can suppose, that Parker now asked the tired and battle-weary Nelson to do so was that he recognised Nelson's fame was infinitely greater than his own. Since the Crown Prince must know that Nelson had really been the driving force behind the attack, he would be more respected for his opinions than would his senior officer. But, if the Admiralty's original intention in sending Parker as senior officer was that he should act the diplomat – while to Nelson was left the business of action should it be necessary – their estimation of Parker was gravely at fault.

It was hardly surprising that a strong military guard had been placed upon the route that Nelson, suitably dressed for the occasion, had to take for his interview with the Crown Prince. Curiosity, a little admiration even, or – more likely – downright hostility might well have been expected from the citizens of Copenhagen, who had had the unenviable front-row seat at the spectacle of Nelson and the navy of Britain in action against their fleet and their city. But, says a Danish report, 'The people did not degrade themselves with the former, nor disgrace themselves with the latter : the admiral was received as one brave enemy ever ought to receive another – he was received with respect.' After a State Dinner, where all eyes inevitably were fixed upon this slight, somewhat undistinguished-looking, one-armed man who had just humbled the pride of their country, there was a formal meeting between Nelson, the Crown Prince and the Adjutant-General Hans Lindholm. The odds were two to one, and they had the further advantage over him that, though both spoke fluent English, Nelson had not a word of Danish.

From an account which Nelson later gave to Addington, who had succeeded Pitt as Prime Minister, it becomes clear that the Danes were as open-minded and honest with their temporary guest as was he with them :

His Royal Highness began the conversation by saying how happy he was to see me, and thanked me for my humanity to the wounded Danes. I then said it was to me, and would be the greatest affliction to every man in England, from the King to the lowest person, to think that Denmark had fired on the British flag, and become leagued with her enemies. His Royal Highness stopped me by saying that Admiral Parker had declared war against Denmark. This I denied, and requested His Royal Highness to send for the papers, and he would find the direct contrary, and that it was furthest from the thoughts of the British Admiral.

This in effect was true, for the guns of Cronenburg fortress had been the first to open fire upon the approaching British fleet. The fact remains that, whatever Sir Hyde Parker's pacific and diplomatic intentions had been, Nelson had never entertained any other thought but of coming immediately to grips with the Danes unless they withdrew from their coalition with Russia. He was now given permission to speak his mind openly, which he did to no mean effect, pointing out that it was the unnatural alliance of Britain's old friends the Danes with their enemies the Russians which had provoked the whole issue. The Prince for his part replied that Denmark would never be the enemy of England, but that his country could not tolerate interference with its lawful commerce such as the British had been practising, since Denmark was above all a trading nation.

The discussion went on in some depth over the whole matter of trading rights, freedom of navigation, and that perennially tricky question as to whether the commander of a convoy could be in a position to know whether there were contraband goods among the articles aboard the ships which came under his protection. The Prince then put the direct question : 'For what is the British Fleet come into the Baltic ?' to which Nelson replied : 'To crush a most formidable and unprovoked Coalition against Great Britain.' In further conversation the Prince made it quite clear that it was fear of Russia which had provoked him into the coalition, adding that, 'When all Europe is in such a dreadful state of confusion, it is absolutely necessary that States should be on their guard.' Nelson requested a free entry of the British Fleet into Copenhagen, and access to such stores and materials as they might require. This was readily granted and the two men parted, after both had apologised for everything overheated that they might have said in the course of the argument. Everything was now set for a further discussion in which the whole matter of a formal Armistice might be settled. Although throughout this meeting the Crown Prince was necessarily acting under the duress of knowing that his capital was at that very moment under threat from the guns of the British Fleet, it was Nelson's conduct of the whole affair which clinched matters. His evident appreciation of the Danish position vis-à-vis

Russia, but his determination that he would yield nothing when his country's life was at stake, coupled also with that vital charm which not even his detractors could ever gainsay, produced a satisfactory end to the day's talks.

In the subsequent negotiations, at which Colonel Stewart was present, the point which caused most debate was the duration of the Armistice. Nelson argued for sixteen weeks, but the Danes would have preferred to make it much shorter, calculating possibly that a combined Russo-Swedish fleet would soon arrive and drive the British out of the Baltic. In the end, according to Stewart, 'The point not being acceded to on either side, one of the Danish Commissioners hinted at the renewal of hostilities. Upon which Lord Nelson, who understood French sufficiently to make out what the Commissioner said (for the parley was conducted in this tongue), turned to one of his friends with warmth, and said : "Renew hostilities! Tell him that we are ready in a moment; ready to bombard this very night." ' The Commissioner apologised with politeness, and the business went on more amicably. The duration of the Armistice could not, however, be adjusted, and the conference broke up for reference to the Prince.

A levée was consequently held in one of the State Rooms, the whole of which were without furniture, from the apprehension of a bombardment. His Lordship then proceeded to a grand dinner upstairs, the Prince leading the way. Nelson, leaning on the arm of a friend, whispered, 'Though I have only one eye, I see all this will burn very well !'

There was fortunately never any need for his threat to be implemented, for an Armistice was agreed upon to last fourteen weeks, 'at the expiration of which time, it shall be in the power of either to declare a cessation of the same, and to recommence hostilities, upon giving fourteen days' previous notice'. During the period of the Armistice Denmark was to suspend her part in the Armed Neutrality, while Copenhagen was to be left unharmed by the British, who might at the same time buy from the Danes what ships' stores and other materials they required. News of the negotiations was taken home by Colonel Stewart and once again – as with Drinkwater – Nelson found in a military officer not only a fervent admirer but one who was eager to spread the word as to Nelson's exhilarating spirit and unquestioned genius in the art of war. He took with him also official despatches, together with a letter from Nelson which exculpated the captains whose ships had run aground, and paid generous tribute to all who had been engaged in action. Captain Bligh of the *Glatton*, aware no doubt that since the *Bounty* affair his reputation was still somewhat suspect, had asked Nelson for a testimony to his good conduct. It was unnecessary, as Nelson well knew, for the *Glatton* had fought superbly throughout the action, but nevertheless he happily endorsed it in a letter to St Vincent: 'His behaviour on this occasion can reap no additional credit from my testimony. He was my second, and the moment the Action ceased, I sent for him, on board the *Elephant*, to thank him for his support.' At the same time he called attention to the case of Captain Thompson, who had sadly remarked: 'I am now totally disabled and my career is run through, only at the age of 35.' In those harsh days, whether officer or man (unless the officer had private means), it was often better to die in battle than to be left an unemployable wreck on England's shores. On 9 April he also wrote to Emma Hamilton, a letter full of concern about the mythical Thompson's child (Horatia's wet-nurse had suffered from some disorder), and in a passing reference to his wife added that he did not, 'nor cannot care about her'. At the same time his anguished jealousy had not abated, and he begged Emma not to 'let your uncle [Sir William] persuade you to receive bad company. When you do your friend hopes he may be killed.'

The delay occasioned by the discussions and ratification of the Armistice, which was not finally signed until 9 April, was not at all to Nelson's liking. He was eager to be off to Reval, to deal with the Russians. Although Danish resistance was now at an end, he rightly commented that: 'I look upon the Northern League to be like a tree, of which Paul was the trunk, and Sweden and Denmark the branches.' His desire was to 'get at the trunk, and hew it down . . .'. While he waited impatiently, Parker happily reverted to the inactivity which seems to have suited his nature. Before he left with the despatches for England Colonel Stewart carefully noted the behaviour of his hero when not in action, observing that he never left the ship except for his necessary formal visits to the Crown Prince:

His hour of rising was four or five o'clock, and of going to rest about ten; breakfast was never later than six, and generally nearer to five o'clock. A midshipman or two were always of the party; and I have known him send during the middle watch to invite the little fellows to breakfast with him when relieved. At table with them he would enter into their boyish jokes and be the most youthful of the party. At dinner he invariably had every officer of the ship in their turn, and was both a polite and hospitable host. The whole ordinary business of the fleet was invariably despatched, as it had been by Earl St Vincent, before eight o'clock.

Unlike the Nile, feelings about the Battle of Copenhagen were varied, and the honours accruing were parsimonious. Nelson himself was made a viscount, and he was privileged to invest Rear-Admiral Graves with the Order of the Bath on the quarter-deck of the *St George.* For the rest there was nothing. The sovereign's gold medal, which Nelson had said he valued more than a Dukedom, and which he had been awarded for the battles of St Vincent and the Nile, was withheld from him and from all his captains. Two of the latter had been killed, Thompson had lost a leg, and all of them had fought their ships throughout a longer and harder action than that at Aboukir Bay. No vote of thanks was accorded by the City of London to the very men who had saved Britain's trade and, in doing so, had saved the country from what might well have turned out to be economic defeat in the war. As for the seamen, the men who in the thunder of the guns had died in their hundreds, there was nothing at all − not even the small amount of prize money that might have come their way. Sir Hyde Parker ('for he is rich and does not want it' as Nelson wrote to St Vincent) had ordered that, with the exception of one 74 to be used as a hospital ship for conveying the wounded to England, all the prizes were to be burned. This was due not only to indifference on Parker's account towards the money, but to his apprehension that the Russians and the Swedes might combine their fleets. In the event of their approach, and his putting out to meet them, he thought it would be folly to leave so many Danish ships behind them. His thinking, here as in every other aspect of the campaign, was not only hesitant but timorous. Nelson in his letter to St Vincent put the matter in its right terms :

[It is] not from any desire to get a few hundred pounds that actuates me to address this letter to you; but, my dear Lord, justice to the brave officers and men who fought on that day. . . . I think the King should send a gracious Message to the House of Commons as a gift to this Fleet; for what must be the natural feelings of the Officers and men belonging to it, to see their rich Commander-in-Chief burn all the fruits of their victory, which, if fitted up and sent to England, as many of them might have been by dismantling part of our Fleet, would have sold for a good round sum?

The Battle of Copenhagen proved a political embarrassment to the Government and to the Admiralty. They had always hoped that the Danes could be brought to withdraw from the Northern Alliance without the application of force; the two countries had not technically

been at war at the time; and no one could be found in England who
had any hatred towards the Danes. The war was against France, and
Denmark had been drawn into the alliance with Russia out of fear,
as had the other signatories. The battle had achieved its object but,
now that all was over, those in authority almost seemed as if they
wished to forget all about it. George III's own indifference, possibly
feigned, towards the recent events in the Baltic was borne home to
Nelson when, upon his return, the King asked him, 'Lord Nelson, do
you get out?' – meaning, in the parlance of the time, did circumstances and his health permit Nelson to take part in the social world.
Nelson was so infuriated that he is recorded as having been tempted
to say: 'Sir, I have been out and am come in again. Your Majesty
perhaps has not heard of the Battle of Copenhagen!'

It was not until 12 April that Sir Hyde Parker saw fit to take his
fleet, now reduced to seventeen sail-of-the-line (two had been sent
home) further into the Baltic. Three days before, Nelson, who had
been fuming over the delay caused by the Armistice talks, had written
to St Vincent: 'I make no scruple in saying that I would have been
at Revel fourteen days ago. . . . I wanted Sir Hyde to let me at least
go and cruise off Carlscrona to prevent the Revel ships from getting
in to join them [the Swedes].' The passage was extremely difficult:
all the ships had had to be lightened to get through, and Nelson's
St George had to have some of her guns removed. This meant that she
was twenty miles astern of the fleet when the news came through that
a Swedish squadron had been sighted at sea. Nelson was so eager not
to miss what he imagined to be an impending battle that he ordered
a boat lowered, and expressed his intention of catching up with the
Elephant and shifting his flag to her. The weather was bitterly cold
and, Tom Allen having forgotten to have his boat-cloak ready, Nelson
got into the boat without it. He refused the offer of a coat from
another officer aboard – saying, 'No, I am not cold; my anxiety for
my country will keep me warm' – and made the five-hour journey to
join the fleet in plain uniform, so anxious was he that they might
already have weighed and sailed for action. As it turned out, the
Swedes, on seeing the approach of Parker's ships, had wisely returned
to Karlskrona. It was not until midnight that Nelson stepped aboard
the *Elephant*, to be greeted by his old friend Foley, and by that time
the Baltic air had set its mark on his weakened frame. He was later
to tell Emma how 'A cold struck me to the heart. On the 27th I had
one of my terrible spasms of heart-stroke. . . . From that time to the
end of May I brought up what everyone thought was my lungs, and
I was emaciated more than you can conceive.'

Nelson was still as eager as ever to get the ships into the Gulf of Finland to prevent the junction of the Russian fleets from Kronstadt and Reval, which would be possible as soon as the ice melted at the latter port. Parker, true to his nature, preferred to wait off Karlskrona, and thus immobilise the relatively unimportant Swedish squadron at anchor there. As events turned out, the Tsar Alexander I now ordered his fleet to abstain from all hostilities. His father's pro-French policy was at an end, and so to all effects and purposes was the necessity for a British presence in the Baltic. St Vincent meanwhile had received the despatches from Copenhagen and had made up his mind: Sir Hyde Parker must be recalled, and Nelson was to take over the command (Parker was never employed again). Nelson immediately took the fleet east – determined, even though he knew that the Russians were no longer hostile, to prevent the junction of their two fleets until such a time as the Armed Neutrality had been disbanded. The Tsar remonstrated when Nelson's ships appeared off Reval, asking for 'the prompt withdrawal of the fleet under your command'. Nelson was quick to see that tact and diplomacy, not arms, were what was now required. He sent a letter to the Tsar stating that his arrival at Reval was intended as no more than a desire to pay his respects to the new ruler of Russia, and that he would be sailing immediately for the Baltic. On 19 May the Armed Neutrality was dissolved. The threat to Britain from the North, the threat to her trade and to her maritime requirements, was over. On 14 June, Nelson's repeated requests for relief from his command were answered. His old friend Sir Charles Pole, another one of Locker's pupils and now a vice-admiral, arrived to relieve Nelson. Once again, his mission accomplished by the annihilation of an opposing fleet, Nelson sailed for Yarmouth. This time, more befittingly than on the previous occasion, he was without civilian accompaniment, and aboard a small naval brig. He had made it clear that he did not want to deprive the fleet of a larger vessel. In much the same vein as he had so often written to Fanny, he now wrote to Emma: 'I am fixed to live a country life, and to have many (I hope) years of comfort. . . .'

CHAPTER THIRTY-ONE

Narrow Seas and Country Home

NELSON'S first action upon arrival in Yarmouth was to visit the wounded from Copenhagen in the naval hospital. No one knew better than he the price that was paid for such victories and, while the press and the public might write fulsome articles or cheer him in the streets, they little knew the roar of battle, the scream and whimper of jagged wooden splinters, or the crash and confusion as masts and yards came tumbling down. Like most men of action – much though he adored adulation – he may have reserved in some corner of his heart a feeling of distaste, or even perhaps contempt, for the fat burghers, bechained mayors, simpering ladies and elegant gentlemen (it was the age of the dandy) who celebrated the result of events which they did not understand. The word 'Victory', so dear to him, implied not only many dead, but also legless and armless seamen, young men part-destroyed before they had hardly shaken hands with life, and limitless suffering among women and children for whom there would be no providers. He was soon to see, as news of Napoleon's invasion plans were carefully leaked to demoralise his countrymen, how the southern counties of England would be temporarily evacuated by all those who could afford to leave their homes and travel north.

Meanwhile he hoped for nothing more than a long rest, a holiday with Emma and inevitably of course, for the sake of appearances, Sir William. He longed to see Horatia again – his one pledge to the future. She would inherit neither his name nor his titles. . . . When his peerage was gazetted in the August of that year, the succession was remaindered first upon his old father, should he outlive him, and then upon his male heirs and, in default, to the male heirs of his sisters. He now joined the Hamiltons at Burford Bridge in Surrey and, for a few weeks only, enjoyed the peace of the quiet posting-inn where they were staying, lodged in the shadow of Box Hill. East Anglia seemed to call him no longer and, after his landing at Yarmouth and proceeding to London, he never again revisited his home county. The associations were now perhaps somewhat uncomfortable – childhood at the parsonage, his long years on the beach, Fanny, Round Wood, and the failure of his marriage. Surrey, so gentle and romantic a county, was Emma and the future. It is significant that the house which he was soon to buy, Merton Place, was also in Surrey, and that it would prove a far call from the humble cottage which he had long ago envisaged as the home to which he and Fanny would finally retire.

While he and Sir William went fishing in the company of his brother the Reverend William and his wife and daughter, Emma, and a young captain, Edward Parker, who was acting as Nelson's aide-de-camp, the post-chaises rumbled past the inn. Their route lay between Portsmouth and London; they carried the news from the Channel and the directives from the capital. Nelson's holiday was to be all too brief. On 20 July he was summoned to Whitehall. With the Treaty of Luneville, which had been signed in February that year, Bonaparte had been relieved of all his foreign enemies with the exception of Portugal and Britain. He dealt with the former by inducing Spain to declare war upon her neighbour. Now, with the whole of the Continent secure behind him, he could afford to devote his undivided attention to Britain. It was only her sea power which still held out against him, which had recaptured Malta, was on the point of compelling his Army of the East to abandon Egypt, and which had just been instrumental in causing the dissolution of the Armed Neutrality of the North by Nelson's victory at Copenhagen. The only way to strike at Britain was across the Channel.

Those 'Narrow Seas', which Drake had helped secure for his country over two centuries before, were still her defensive moat. As Jacques Bainville put it in his biography:

Napoleon had to seize England by the throat and overcome her; anything else could only postpone the day of reckoning. . . . If he had not realised that, he would not deserve his fame as an extraordinary man, and there would be a vast lacuna in his genius. And it is a poor tribute to his intelligence to suppose that the camp at Boulogne, the building of a whole fleet for transporting his army across the Channel, were mere feints. Actually, it was Napoleon himself who, by prolonging his sojourn in Italy after the coronation in Milan, strove to delude the English into the belief that his projects against them were a blind. . . . If a crossing of the Channel at last succeeded and a French army landed, that would be the end of England as surely as the day when William the Conqueror set foot on the island. It was a decisive game that was in play.

It was because the threat was so serious that Nelson was now summoned to London. Among the numerous measures being taken by the Government was the formation of a 'Squadron on a Particular Service'. This consisted of a large squadron of light craft, consisting of frigates, gun- and bomb-vessels, floating batteries and numerous other small craft, for the defence of the coast from Beachy Head to Orfordness. Although it was hardly the kind of command that under normal circumstances would have been given to an admiral of Nelson's rank and renown, Addington and St Vincent had concluded that no one less than Nelson would serve to take charge of it. His name alone, it was felt, would inspire his countrymen with confidence and would instil into the enemy, if not fear, the knowledge that Britain was sending against them the finest of her seamen – the men who had already destroyed the flower of their fleet at Aboukir Bay. It has been suggested that another reason why St Vincent was anxious to appoint Nelson to this command was that he wished at all costs to remove him from the company of Emma, and a relationship which had already become a public scandal and was making a laughing-stock of a man whose worth he well knew and admired so much. There may have been something of that behind the reasons for his choice. Certainly Nelson, who had returned from the Baltic largely on grounds of ill-health, would have hardly seemed the appropriate man to be appointed to a command which would involve great physical activity, constant exposure to Channel weather, and a berth aboard a ship no larger than a frigate. His proneness to seasickness in small ships was well known and he was – at any rate during this period of his life – always at his best in command of large ships-of-the-line. A man like Captain Riou, had he had the rank and had he survived Copenhagen, would have been ideally suited to this type of service.

Nelson's brother Maurice had recently died and he took time off to see his 'widow', a lady whom Maurice in fact had never married, and he also made sure of paying a visit to little Horatia. It was during this period of his life that Nelson received a letter from his wife, who was staying at Bath, as was his father whom she lovingly and conscientiously looked after in his old age:

My Dear Husband, I cannot be silent in the general joy throughout the Kingdom, I must express my thankfulness and happiness it hath pleased God to spare your life. All greet you with every testimony of gratitude and praise. This victory is said to surpass Aboukir. What my feelings are your own good heart will tell you. Let me beg, nay intreat you, to believe no wife ever felt greater affection for a husband than I do. And to the best of my knowledge I have invariably done everything you desired. If I have omitted anything I am sorry for it.

On receiving a letter from our father written in a melancholy and distressing manner, I offered to go to him if I could in the least contribute to ease his mind. By return of post he desired to see me immediately but I was to stop a few days in town to see for a house. I will do every thing in my power to alleviate the many infirmities which bear him down.

What more can I do to convince you that I am truly your affectionate wife?

Fanny's letter went unanswered. But, on 27 July, already arrived at Sheerness to take over his command, he was writing to Emma in jocular tone: 'Tonight I dine with Adl. Graeme, who has also lost his right arm, and as the Commander of the Troops has lost his leg, I expect we shall be caricatured as the *lame* defenders of England.' He had already written a long memorandum to St Vincent, analysing the enemy's object, possible method and means of transporting his forces across the Channel, and his suggested dispositions of the forces available. He concluded: 'The moment the enemy touch our coast, they are to be attacked by every man afloat and on shore: this must be perfectly understood. *Never fear the event.*' He hoisted his flag in the frigate *Medusa* of 32 guns and by 3 August was off Boulogne in company with a number of bomb-ketches. This was not a raid of any great moment, but rather an opportunity for him to take a first look at the enemy's defences and the preparations for the invasion. Two or three floating batteries were sunk and a brig was forced to run aground. The action achieved little else, for it was not Nelson's intention to harm civilians ('The town is spared as much as the nature of the service will admit'). But the very fact that it was aggressive, as opposed to all the *defensive* works by which they were surrounded, put heart into the coastal dwellers of England. Crowds of people collected at Dover, gazing seaward as their ancestors had so often gazed before, and took heart as they listened to the distant rumble of gunfire, and heard 'Nelson speaking to the French'.

Encouraged by this first encounter, he planned an elaborate raid on Boulogne, to be carried out in a surprise assault by boats in the small hours of the morning. It was Santa Cruz de Tenerife all over again. If the Spaniards on that occasion had not been expected to put up much of a resistance, what did he expect of the French, in the flower of military self-confidence and masters of the Continent? The raid proved a costly failure. Despite covering fire from mortars and gun-vessels, this forerunner of a commando raid in the style of the Second World War did little more than anticipate, though in a smaller way, the twentieth-century disaster of Dieppe. Twelve British boats were lost, no French craft sunk or taken, and 44 of his men were killed and 128 wounded. 'I am sorry to tell you', he wrote to St Vincent, 'that I have not succeeded in bringing out or destroying the Enemy's Flotilla moored in the mouth of the harbour of Boulogne.' He praised the bravery of his men and – rightly – took the blame entirely upon himself. 'All behaved well, and it was their misfortune to be sent on a service which the precautions of the enemy rendered impossible.' He had already come to the conclusion (which proved to be quite accurate) that the invasion scare had been over-emphasised. Peace was in the air and Bonaparte, however much he may at one time have thought invasion feasible, had changed his mind. In any case, all his preparations, and the sight of the Grand Army that had conquered all others in Europe encamped opposite Britain across those narrow seas, had sufficiently alarmed the British politicians to desire the peace that Napoleon now sought.

While Nelson was planning yet another attempt upon Boulogne, he received instructions from the Admiralty that on no account should any further hostile action at sea be made against France. Addington and his colleagues had come to the conclusion that a peace treaty should be signed – something which was finally ratified on 25 March 1802, and which occasioned Nelson's anger, as well as his accurate diagnosis of the future. Whatever the politicians might think, the sailor knew well enough that a France under Napoleon could never be trusted: 'We have made peace with the French despotism, and we will, I hope, adhere to it whilst the French continue in due bounds; but whenever they overstep that and usurp a power that would degrade Europe, then I trust we shall trust Europe in crushing her ambition. . . .' Meanwhile inactive, not 'in a foreign court' but on his own shores, he had much else to distress him. His aide-de-camp Edward Parker, whom he had come to love like a son, had had a thigh shattered in the ill-judged attempt against Boulogne, and died of his wounds. Nelson had also come to consider that his old and tried friend Troubridge, now 'one of my Lords and Masters' at the Admiralty, was against him. The latter had written to him with the advice that he should take long healthy walks ashore and wear flannel vests – fine words to a man who was permanently seasick aboard a small ship like a frigate, whose one good eye was failing him, who suffered from chronic toothache, and who was without a right arm. The fact was that Troubridge, like so many others among his real friends, was prepared to do almost anything to stop Nelson from resuming his relationship with Emma Hamilton.

This was something that was beyond all their powers to prevent. Even before the peace was signed, when the Admiralty would not grant him any leave – even though he was fulfilling no useful function – the Hamiltons had come down to stay in Deal, and the *tria juncta in uno* were reunited for a fortnight. When they left, however, to return to London, Nelson was completely desolate and in a letter to Emma which was addressed to 'Mrs Thomson, care of Lady Hamilton' he wrote : 'My dearest wife, how can I bear our separation? Good God, what a change! I am so low I cannot hold up my head. When I reflect on the many happy scenes we have passed together, the being separated is terrible, but better times *will* come, *shall* come if it pleases God. And to make one worse, the fate of poor Parker! But God's will be done. Love my Horatia, and prepare for me the farm. . . .'

This reference was to the house at Merton, which could hardly have been referred to as a 'farm', but Nelson still persisted in writing, if not indeed in thinking, in simple country terms. Merton Place was in fact a gentleman's residence even if rather small, built about a century earlier. It was one hour's drive from Hyde Park, and had pleasant grounds that included a moat and a pond, where he and Sir William later intended to fish. It had cost Nelson £9,000, a considerable sum in those days and one which Nelson could ill afford. It was his friend and prize agent Alexander Davison who helped to make the purchase possible and Nelson wrote expressing his thanks in a letter of 14 September 1801. He went on to say :

> It is true, it will take every farthing I have in the world, and leave me in your debt . . . but I hope in a little time to be able at least to pay my debts. Should I really want your help, and now that I have enough in the world to pay you, I shall ask no one else. The Baltic expedition cost me full £2,000. Since I left London it has cost me, for Nelson cannot be like others, near £1,000 in six weeks. If I am continued here, ruin to my finances must be the consequence, for everyone knows that Lord Nelson is *amazingly rich*!

The fact was that at no time in his life had he been lucky with prize money (something that had been the good fortune of other far less distinguished sea-officers). His numerous sea engagements, his two great victories even, had yielded little, yet in the fashion of the time he was still expected to live as befitted a great admiral, England's hero, and a Lord. In the matter of Merton Place he was determined that the property should be entirely his. He could not bring himself to ask for any money from Sir William, and he wanted no money at all from the Hamiltons, even though they were to live at Merton along with him. At his station off the Downs, seasick and very low in health and spirits, he envisaged this fitting home which his beloved Emma was preparing for him and where he could retire and leave the sea for ever.

On 16 October Sir William wrote him a letter from Merton which must have cheered the Admiral's heart :

> We have now inhabited your Lordship's premises some days, & I can now speak with some certainty. I have lived with our dear Emma several years. I know her merit, have a great opinion of the head and heart that God Almighty has been pleased to give her; but a seaman alone could have given a fine woman full power to chuse & fit up a residence for him without seeing it for himself. You are in luck, for in my conscience I verily believe that a place so suitable to your views could not be found. . . . The proximity to the capital, and the perfect retirement of this place are, for your Lordship, two points beyond estimation; but the house is so comfortable, the furniture clean and good, and I never saw so many conveniences united in so small a compass. You have nothing but to come and enjoy immediately; you have a good mile of pleasant dry walk around your own farm. It would make you laugh to see Emma & her mother fitting up pig-sties and hen-coops, & already the Canal is enlivened with ducks, & the cock is strutting with his hen about the walks.

It was to this idyllic world that Nelson finally came on 23 October 1801, having at last been given leave by St Vincent. (His flag, in fact, continued to fly until April of the following year, but to all intents and purposes he was no longer required to remain in command of that 'Squadron on a Particular Service' whose purpose was at an end now that the threatened invasion seemed to be over.) Nelson's real delight in Merton and its surrounds exceeded even his dreams. Here, for a year and a half, he was to live a life of peace and tranquillity such as he had not known since all those years ago at Burnham Thorpe. But then he had been no more than a captain on half-pay – and then he had been with Fanny. Now he was with the great love of his life, he could regularly visit his daughter in London, and he still enjoyed the company of his mistress's husband with whom he could go fishing. Sir William was long used to accepting the position with equanimity, though at times Emma's extravagances upset him. But, taken all in all, this strange ménage seems to have co-existed extremely happily. It was ironical perhaps, if no more, that Nelson and the Hamiltons regularly attended the local church for Sunday services. Earlier he had written: 'Have we a nice church at Merton? We will set an example of goodness to the under-parishioners. . . .'

But not all who visited Nelson during this period of his life were as prepared to tolerate the irregularity of the situation, nor even to admire the house that Emma had furnished for her lover. Lord Minto, who had met them together in Vienna and whose personal friendship for Nelson had never slackened over the years, wrote to his wife after a visit in March 1802 :

The whole establishment and way of life are such as to make me angry, as well as melancholy; but I cannot alter it, and I do not think myself obliged, or at liberty, to quarrel with him for his weakness, though nothing shall ever induce me to give the smallest countenance to Lady Hamilton. She looks ultimately to the chance of marriage, as Sir William will not be long in her way, and she probably indulges a hope that she may survive Lady Nelson. . . . She is in high looks, but more immense than ever. The love she makes to Nelson is not only ridiculous, but disgusting : not only the rooms, but the whole house, staircase and all, are covered with nothing but pictures of her and him, of all sizes and sorts, and representations of his naval actions, coats-of-arms, pieces of plate in his honour, the flagstaff of *L'Orient*, &c. – an excess of vanity which counteracts its own purpose.

The fact was that Nelson, like many great men, was without a sense of humour. He could in no way see that all this paraphernalia by which he was surrounded at Merton made him painfully absurd in the eyes of the world, and particularly in the eyes of his friends.

George Matcham, his nephew, later came to Nelson's defence, though admitting to 'his one great error', in an account which describes the man himself as living unostentatiously, enjoying quiet conversation, and 'so far from being the hero of his own tale, I never heard him voluntarily refer to any of the great actions of his life'. The daughter of the Vicar of Merton also later confirmed that : 'His residence at Merton was a continued course of charity and goodness, setting such an example of propriety and regularity that there are few who could not be benefited by following it.' All men are strange mixtures and contradictions, and it would be surprising if Nelson had been any exception to this rule. It was only in his treatment of his wife Fanny that he could be definitely faulted, and in his cruelty to her one senses his own deep feelings of guilt being transferred upon the guiltless. Those who liked and respected his wife could never forgive or forget his treatment of her, and accordingly they could never see any good in Emma. Sir William, the other injured party, had long expected – and now long accepted – that with increasing age he would be supplanted in Emma's affections. He wrote to her in the last year of his life what amounts to a mild directive, pointing out that he sought peace and quiet, whereas she was always filling the house with visitors and giving large dinner parties. With the polished euphemistic manner of an eighteenth-century gentleman he stated that he well knew 'the purity of Ld. N's friendship for Emma', but he also pointed out that if she was going to persist in having alter-cations with him (Sir William), then a separation would really be necessary. He concluded, 'But I think, considering the probability of my not troubling any party long in this world, the best for us all would be to bear those ills we have rather than flie to those we know not of. . . . I know and admire your talents and many excellent qualities, but I am not blind to your defects, and confess having many myself; therefore let us bear and forbear for God's sake.'

While the rest of Nelson's relations had long since deserted Fanny and made their cause with her successor, the Reverend Edmund had constantly regretted his son's treatment of his wife. Fanny had always been good to him, had looked after him as if he had been her own father, and in his simplicity of mind he could not understand how Nelson could have come to have abandoned her. But even he, in the end, was almost on the point of joining Nelson at Merton, Emma prevailing upon him how well looked after he would be, and how he would have a companion in Sir William. While he was still hesi-tating during the winter of 1801 at Bath, where he still went to escape the rigours of the winter, he fell seriously ill and died in the following April. It might have been expected that Nelson would at least attend the funeral of his father, a man whose old-fashioned and upright character had been a model of what a clergyman's should be, but he declined. His own ill-health was given as a reason, but it is more likely that he could not bear to meet Fanny, who would certainly be in attendance. The double reproach of meeting his wife at the grave of his seventy-nine-year-old father (whose principles he had betrayed) was more than he could contemplate. In his last letter to his son, written in the March of that year, the Reverend Edmund had said : 'Amongst many other may your lott be cast where there is not only a goodly Heritage but also abundance of internal *peace* such as you have never yet enjoyed much of, but are now of age to enjoy.'

CHAPTER THIRTY-TWO

Return to the Mediterranean

ON 6 APRIL 1803, Nelson wrote to Alexander Davison: 'Our dear Sir William died at ten minutes past ten, this morning, in Lady Hamilton's and my arms, without a sigh or a struggle. Poor Lady Hamilton is, as you may expect, desolate. I hope she will be left properly, but I doubt.' The last remark was an unfair reflection on Sir William. He left Emma three hundred pounds to be paid immediately after his death, a hundred to her mother, and an annuity of eight hundred pounds which was to be paid to Emma quarterly, the sum of one hundred pounds again being assigned to Mrs Cadogan during her lifetime. Charles Greville received the residue of the estate. A special codicil mentioned Nelson: 'The copy of Madame Le Brun's picture of Emma, in enamel, by Bone, I give to my dearest friend Lord Nelson, Duke of Bronte, a very small token of the great regard I have for his Lordship, the most virtuous, loyal, and truly brave character I ever met with. God bless him, and shame fall on those who do not say Amen.' The *tria juncta in uno* was finally and forever at an end. Within a month of Sir William's death Nelson had also left the happy territory of Merton. He had been appointed Commander-in-Chief of the Mediterranean fleet. Emma, who was again pregnant, was in London.

The war with France had been resumed on 18 May 1803. Napoleon, who had only wished for a breathing space by the Treaty of Amiens, now felt himself ready to crush Britain, his last and eternal enemy. On the very same day that war was declared the blue ensign was hoisted at the stern of the 100-gun *Victory*, lying at Portsmouth, and Nelson's flag as Vice-Admiral of the Red lifted in the wind at the fore. Two days later the *Victory* was under full sail to rendezvous with the Channel fleet, where Nelson transferred his flag to the frigate *Amphion* under Captain Hardy for a swift passage to Gibraltar. Before leaving, he found time to write a last letter to Emma: 'You will believe that although I am glad to leave that horrid place, Portsmouth, yet the being afloat makes me now feel that we do not tread the same element.' But already 'the great embraces of the sea' held him rather than those of the shore. It would be over two years before he would see Emma again in the garden of Merton.

Meantime he was happy as the frigate struck down the Biscay swell. It was good to have Hardy with him as Captain. In the short space of time that he had been aboard the *Victory* under her Captain, Samuel Sutton, he had recorded, 'A good man but not so active as Hardy.' As on previous occasions, Nelson was optimistic that it would only be a short war, 'long enough to make me independent in pecuniary matters'. He viewed his return to the Mediterranean as a time when he could at last clear the French from the sea, capture many of their merchantmen, and ensure that peaceful retirement which for a moment he had thought to have already found. It seemed a good augury that after a sparkling run from Cape St Vincent to the Straits the *Amphion* seized a French brig shortly before bringing up in Rosia Bay. The Rock, where he had first set foot ashore so many years before as a young lieutenant, was to see little of him now. Within twenty-four hours he was under way again – 'I am anxious to get to the Fleet.' His orders from St Vincent were that, while Cornwallis held the Channel against the massive French preparations which were under way there, Nelson's duty was to watch Toulon. He was also, as before, to keep an eye on the East, for Napoleon's dreams of a vast Oriental empire had far from diminished now that, as Consul for life, he had an entire Continental empire behind him. Nelson was, of course, 'to take, sink, burn, or otherwise destroy' any French shipping of whatsoever description that his ships might encounter.

His first concern was for Malta, where he expected to find the Mediterranean Fleet under Rear-Admiral Sir Richard Bickerton awaiting him. But he found the blue waters of that superlative harbour empty, for Bickerton had wisely taken the fleet to sea to cruise between Sicily and Naples. This was an intelligent but purely precautionary measure, for Nelson found that in Malta, as in Gibraltar, the news that the war had reopened had not yet arrived. After a brief visit to Sir Alexander Ball, that old friend, whom he had years ago in France designated a 'coxcomb' for wearing epaulettes, and who was now Governor of Malta, Nelson sailed for Sicily and the Straits of Messina. Every mile of sea that the *Amphion* covered was full of memories – even for a man who lived as much in the present as he did. Malta itself, limestone-golden, and with the great battlements of Valetta now securely in British hands – where he had found the Maltese 'in the highest spirits, and sincerely hope that they will now never be separated from England' – must have reminded him of that cruise in the *Foudroyant* during which young Horatia had been conceived.

In a long letter to the Prime Minister Addington, which was begun on 28 June, 'between Sardinia and Naples', he analysed the whole Mediterranean situation as he saw it – and who could know it better than the 'Old Mediterranean Man'? After touching on the composition of the troops in Gibraltar, he commented on the situation at Algiers, agreeing with the British Consul's statement that, if the Dey were given way to in the slightest, his insolence would increase. He was happy with the situation in Malta, but was convinced that the island was useless, being so remote, for keeping a watch on Toulon. Of Sicily he remarked that its state was 'as bad as a civilized country can be'. Its troops were demoralised, the nobility oppressors, the middle classes looking for a change, and the peasantry starving. Sardinia was declared neutral, but he doubted if this neutrality could be maintained if the French were determined on invasion. Tuscany was in an invidious state, with the French besieging Leghorn, so he suggested that the Government should consider placing it under blockade. As for Genoa, it was as much French as the Republic itself. He recalled from his earlier experience how Genoa had proved the granary of southern France, and suggested that it should be blockaded immediately. On the subject of the Morea, he had no doubt that French agents were at work there, either inducing the Greeks to revolt against the Porte, or preparing them for the reception of a French army. This undoubtedly pointed to a further French attempt against Egypt and the East. All in all, it was not a very happy picture. He concluded the letter on 9 July, 'I joined our Fleet yesterday. With the casual absence of one or two Ships, we shall always be seven Sail of the Line; and as the French have at least seven – I believe nine – nearly ready, we are in hopes that Buonaparte may be angry, and order them out, which, I have no doubt, will put our Ships in high feather; for I never knew any wants after a Victory, although we are always full of them before.'

The British fleet consisting of nine sail-of-the-line, a frigate and two sloops was to be augmented on 30 July by the arrival of the *Victory.* Nelson immediately transferred his flag to her, while Hardy went with him, superseding Captain Sutton. Now he could really feel happy that, despite the immense supply and maintenance problems attendant upon keeping the fleet at sea so far from a home port, he had the measure of his enemy. The French fleet at Toulon was commanded by Rear-Admiral Latouche-Tréville, one of the finest officers to serve in

Napoleon's fleet, an aristocrat turned Republican who had already given proof of his ability by his repulse of Nelson's attack on Boulogne. One of Nelson's first actions on taking command was to withdraw the fleet from its position of close watch-and-ward off Toulon to a position thirty miles or more to the west of the harbour. Sir Richard Bickerton, who had already happily greeted Nelson's arrival, and asked him to inform the Admiralty that he was very happy to stay on service in the Mediterranean, will have quickly appreciated his chief's reasons for this change. The first was that the French from their positions ashore, or by sending out a frigate, could readily enough establish that the great topsails were still passing and repassing along their patrol line. The second was that it was easier for the British to withdraw one or two ships at a time for repairs, watering or revictualling, without the fact being obvious to the enemy. When they were on inshore patrol, their numbers were readily apparent. 'It is not my intention', Nelson wrote, 'to close-watch Toulon, even with frigates.'

He hoped, indeed, that one day when the visibility was down, or his fleet out of sight at the far extent of its patrol-line, Latouche-Tréville might be tempted to think the British gone, and sally out from the harbour. This technique of distant patrol also enabled him to make use of the Maddalena islands to the north-east of Sardinia. Here he had found 'one of the best anchorages I have met with', and here individual ships could be sent to water and buy livestock, as well as fresh fruit and vegetables. Of Maddalena he wrote : 'It is twenty-four hours' sail from Toulon; it covers Italy; it is a position that the wind which carries the French to the westward is fair for you to follow. In short, it covers Egypt, Italy, and Turkey.' He urged the Government to take possession of Sardinia before the French. Meanwhile, for week after week, month after month, exceeding in sea-time even those ships of the Second World War in the Pacific with all their modern lines of communication and fleet-trains in attendance, the British men-of-war maintained their ceaseless watch off Toulon. 'The fleet put to sea', Nelson wrote, 'on 18 May [1803], and is still at sea; not a ship has been refitted, or recruited, excepting what has been done at sea.' This was dated nearly a year later, in March 1804.

As during his previous watch over Toulon and the French coast, the routine aboard his flagship and the others in the fleet followed much the same pattern. His Chaplain, the Reverend Alexander Scott, whom Nelson designated 'Doctor' to distinguish him from his official Secretary Mr John Scott, left his *Recollections of Life in the Victory*, while Dr Gillespie, who was Physician to the Fleet and Surgeon aboard the flagship, also recorded his impressions of life on board.

There was an almost amazing regularity – like a perfect chronometer – only to be broken on the few occasions when the French ventured out of harbour, or when the ship changed her station. Dr Gillespie, like Nelson himself, was called at 6 a.m. and informed of the state of the weather and the ship's course. About half an hour afterwards, along with Murray, the Captain of the Fleet, Hardy, the two Scotts, and other ship's officers chosen in rotation, he breakfasted with the Admiral. The menu was inevitably the same: tea, hot rolls, toast, and tongue. '. . . When finished we repair upon deck to enjoy the majestic sight of the rising sun (scarcely ever obscured by clouds in this fine climate) surmounting the smooth and placid waves of the Mediterranean, which supports the lofty and tremendous bulwarks of Britain. . . .' Dr Gillespie clearly picked his weather, for Nelson in a letter to Emma (who had suggested she would like to join the fleet) was more accurate when he wrote: 'Even in summer-time we have a hard gale every week, and two days heavy swell.'

Professional duties occupied everybody aboard from seven until two in the afternoon at which time a band struck up and would play until quarter to three. Then 'the drum beats the tune called "The Roast Beef of Old England", to announce the Admiral's dinner, which is served up at exactly three o'clock, and which generally consists of three courses and a dessert of the choicest fruit, together with three or four of the best wines, champagne and claret not excepted. If a person does not feel himself perfectly at his ease it must be his own fault, such is the urbanity and hospitality which reign here. . . .' After coffee and liqueurs the company usually walked the deck while the band played for nearly an hour. Between six and seven o'clock tea was served and, continues the doctor:

> the party continue to converse with his lordship, who at this time generally unbends himself, though he is at all times as free from stiffness and pomp as a regard to proper dignity will admit, and is very communicative. At 8 o'clock a rummer of punch with cake or biscuit is served up, soon after which we wish the Admiral a good night (who is generally in bed before 9 o'clock). Such is the journal of a day at sea in fine or at least moderate weather, in which this floating castle goes through the water with the greatest imaginable steadiness.

The 'floating castle' which bore Nelson's flag was of course the same as he had seen as a small boy of twelve when he had first joined the *Raisonable* at Chatham. The description was not inaccurate for, although designed to be a little over 2,000 tons, it has been estimated that in fact she displaced over 3,000. Launched from Old Single Dock in Chatham in 1765, she was the fifth ship of the Navy to bear the name *Victory* – the first having been the flagship of Sir John Hawkins during the Spanish Armada campaign. It was William Pitt the Elder, later the first Earl of Chatham, who had been responsible for the Bill of 1758 which had ensured the laying down of twelve ships of the line, the list being headed by a 'First Rate of 100 Guns'. This was the *Victory*, over 200 feet long (226 from her figurehead to her taffrail), with a hull made of English oak over two feet thick. Completed in 1778, she had first been the flagship of Admiral Keppel and subsequently of Lord Hood, Lord Hotham, and of Lord St Vincent. Painted with black bands between the varnish-yellow of the gun-decks, she presented a chequered look when the dark gun-ports were down. This style of painting was soon to be followed by most other first-rates in the Navy, and was to be known as *à la Nelson*. A floating fortress, with a crew of 850 men (Nelson, unlike some commanders, would tolerate no women on board), she mounted thirty 32-pounders on her lower gun-deck, twenty-eight 24-pounders on her middle deck, thirty 12-pounders on the upper deck, ten 12-pounders on the half-deck, and two 12-pounders on the fo'c'sle deck as well as two massive 68-pounder carronades (for close-quarter work, and called after Carron in Scotland where such guns were first made).

'Dreadfully sea-sick,' as he wrote, 'always tossed-about and always seasick', but he had worse physical problems: 'A few years must, as I have always predicted, render me blind, . . .' Yet his attention to his fleet and to the men themselves was unremitting. This was the Nelson that men loved, the Nelson whose shadow looms so much longer than those of the other great sea-captains or commanders. 'He governed men', as Southey wrote, 'by their reason and their affections; they knew that he was incapable of caprice or tyranny; and they obeyed him with alacrity and joy, because he possessed their confidence as well as their love.' His concern about the men's clothing, their quarters, and above all their victualling would not have been unusual in the twentieth century but, at the time when he lived, it was so rare as to be almost eccentric. He had never forgotten what the squirearchy of Norfolk had never even noticed – the condition of the working man upon whom, in the final analysis, the country depended. There, in those long acres of chocolate-brown earth, it was the agricultural labourer who carried the burden through the seasons of the year – dank autumn, piercing winter, uncertain spring and (sometimes) hot and gnat-ridden summer. Here it was the seamen, unknown to the fops of Bath or the merchants of London, who furled the sails in high-rising wind, lived in cramped quarters where only a short man could stand erect, and – when the enemy's topsails were sighted – ran out the guns and tied their sweaty handkerchiefs round their ears. He cared for them : 'The great thing in all military service is health, and you will agree with me, that it is easier for an officer to keep men healthy, than for a physician to cure them.' So he wrote to his old friend Dr Moseley whom he had known since 1780, in his days on the Mosquito coast :

Situated as this fleet has been, without a friendly port, where we could get all the things so necessary to us, yet I have, by changing the cruising ground, not allowed the sameness of prospect to satiate the mind – sometimes by looking at Toulon, Ville Franche, Barcelona, and Rosas; then running round Minorca, Majorca, Sardinia and Corsica; and two or three times anchoring for a few days, and sending a ship to the last place for *onions*, which I find the best thing that can be given to seamen; having always good mutton for the sick, cattle when we can get them, and plenty of fresh water. In the winter it is the best plan to give half the allowance of grog, instead of all wine.

Later, in December 1804, he wrote in a letter to the Admiralty : 'The Fleet is in perfect good health and good humour, unequalled by anything which has ever come within my knowledge, and equal to the most active service which the times may call for.' He had the perfect instrument to his hand, and now all that was required was the opportunity to use it.

The quarters from which his correspondence was conducted – innumerable private letters, quite apart from the dictated letters to the Prime Minister, the Admiralty, the Fleet, and British consuls and representatives around the Mediterranean – were comfortable enough for a man who had grown up in a simple Norfolk parsonage and known the rigours of a midshipman's berth. They lay immediately beneath those of Captain Hardy, which in their turn were immediately below the poop deck. There were three rooms in all : the stateroom at the stern with its nine windows, where he worked with his secretaries and attended to formal business; the dining-room from which a staircase led to the upper deck; and his sleeping-cabin – the latter twelve foot by twenty, whereas the dining-room was thirty-five foot wide. Personal attendants, including Chevalier, his Italian steward, occupied adjacent cabins. Mahogany furniture of provincial

Georgian design, handsome but without especial elegance, stood out against a canvas-covered floor painted in black and white chequers. Emma's portrait, caught sometimes by flashing sun or illuminated by candlelight at night, watched over the prematurely ageing, seasick man who directed from these ever-moving quarters the innumerable affairs of the whole Mediterranean command. William Beatty, a doctor who was later to record Nelson's dying hours and to perform the autopsy on his body, recorded how Nelson generally walked on deck for six or seven hours of the day:

He ate very sparingly, the liver and wing of a fowl and small plate of macaroni in general composing his meal, during which he occasionally took a glass of champagne. . . . He possessed such a wonderful activity of wind, as even prevented him from taking ordinary repose, seldom enjoying two hours of uninterrupted sleep; and on several occasions he did not quit the deck the whole night. At these times he took no pains to protect himself from the wet, or the night air; wearing only a thin coat; and he has frequently, after having his clothes wet through with rain, refused to have them changed, saying that the leather waistcoat which he wore over his flannel one would secure him from complaint. He seldom wore boots, and was consequently very liable to have his feet wet. When this occurred he has often been known to go down to his cabin, throw off his clothes, and walk on the carpet in his stockings for the purpose of drying the feet on them. He chose to adopt this uncomfortable expedient, rather than to give his servants the trouble of assisting him to put on fresh stockings, which, from his having only one hand, he could not himself conveniently effect.

Frigates, or rather the lack of them, were his constant source of concern. Without enough of these eyes of the fleet it was almost impossible to keep an adequate watch on the French coastline, while at the same time permitting his ships-of-the-line to patrol out of sight below the horizon, or be withdrawn for necessary victualling, repairs, and watering. 'From Cape St Vincent to the Adriatic, I have only eight . . .' and, 'I want ten more than I have in order to watch that the French do not escape me.' His problems were considerably heightened by the fact that the Spaniards had once again indicated that their interests were linked with France, and subsequent to a treaty of friendship signed in October 1803 were allowing a French 74, *Aigle*, to operate out of Cadiz. Nelson had no equivalent ship to spare out of his small force in Gibraltar, and was compelled to order his frigate commander in the area not to attempt to attack her. He was convinced that no two or even three frigates were a match for a 74, and he could in no way afford to have his small force of fast lookouts sunk, or put out of commission. While he dealt with all these affairs he never for a moment forgot Emma, Horatia, and Merton.

In the lash of gales, as the mistral roared down into the Gulf of Lions, or in hot sultry days of autumn when the sirocco pushed up a swell from the south and the ships sweated with humidity – he dreamed of his home. 'For the winter, the carriage can be put in the barn. The new building, the chamber over the dining-room, you must consider. The stair window, we settled, was not to be stopped up.' Mail was very irregular, brought only by the arrival of a new ship in the Mediterranean, and it was not until March 1804 that he received the painful letter that told him that Emma had borne him a second daughter who had died within a few weeks. There were to be no sons, then; the name and title would in any case go elsewhere, his 'wife' could not be acknowledged, and his only daughter would grow up as 'Miss Horatia Nelson Thomson'. None of his intimates, none of his captains, suspected that the Admiral had any personal concerns or worries. His life was devoted to the fleet. On St George's Day, 1804, he was gazetted Vice-Admiral of the White (the rank in which he died).

Early in 1804 Latouche-Tréville began to exercise his ships out of the harbour of Toulon. He had need to, for, however well his fleet might be equipped and prepared, he knew well enough that the men could not be exercised in harbour – and that the enemy whose topsails fringed the horizon was as familiar as a fish with the environment upon which the issue must one day be decided. 'My friend Monsieur La Touche', wrote Nelson, 'sometimes plays bo-peep in and out of Toulon, like a mouse at the edge of a hole.' On 9 April, 'a rear admiral and seven sail, including frigates, put their nose outside the harbour. If they go on playing this game, some day we shall lay salt upon their tails, and so end the campaign.' He was far less amused when, later that summer, a sortie made by Latouche-Tréville in person – to which Nelson responded by standing towards him – was interpreted by the latter as a refusal by the British fleet to give battle. 'You will have seen Monsieur La Touche's letter,' he wrote in fury to his brother William, 'of how he chased me, and how I *ran*. I keep it; and, by God, if I take him, he shall *eat* it!' There is no doubt he meant what he said, but the encounter was never to take place. In August 1804 Latouche-Tréville died, his place being taken by Vice-Admiral Villeneuve. 'He has given me the slip,' wrote Nelson. 'The

French papers say he died of walking so often up to the signal-post to watch us : I always pronounced that would be his death.' His new adversary, Villeneuve, had also given Nelson the slip once before – at Aboukir Bay. He was destined to do so again, and to cause Nelson the greatest anguish of his professional life, only to be brought to bay in the scarred waters off Cape Trafalgar.

CHAPTER THIRTY-THREE

The Chase

By the midsummer of 1804 Nelson's health was so bad that he had applied to be sent home. It was not only his failing eyesight that plagued him, but also a flare-up of that internal injury which he had suffered during the Battle of St Vincent. He had a bad cough, and he found that his coughing bouts triggered off the pain in his stomach. There is no doubt that on this occasion his desire to return home was very genuinely on health grounds, for he went on to say: 'No officer could be placed in a more agreeable Command, and no Command ever produced so much happiness to a Commander-in-Chief.' In one sense, however, he was not happy with what had happened to his Command, for a part of it – and the most lucrative – had been taken away from him and given to Sir John Orde. It was Orde who had quarrelled with St Vincent about the latter's appointment of Nelson to lead the squadron which had broken into the Mediterranean in the spring of 1798. Now, so ill with gout that he could not leave his cabin, he had been given the section of the Mediterranean command which lay to the west of Gibraltar and extended to Cape Finisterre. This was the very area in which most prize-money was to be made and Nelson, permanently worried about money, could hardly help complaining that: 'He is sent off Cadiz to reap the golden harvest. . . . But never mind: I am superior to those who could treat me so. I believe I attach more to the French fleet than making captures.'

On 11 January 1805 Nelson's ships anchored in Maddalena roadstead to take on water. Before leaving the patrol line off Toulon he had satisfied himself that it did not look as if Villeneuve was likely to proceed to sea, but he had left behind two frigates to maintain the watch in the event of his doing so. On the nineteenth the frigates H.M.S. *Active* and *Seahorse* came bustling down to the anchorage. Telescopes flashed to read the flags at their yards, and immediately the fleet was suffused with joy and activity. The signal for which the British had waited for so many long months was flying: 'The Enemy

314

is at sea.' Within three hours of the news being received the *Victory* led out through the rocky, narrow passage to the east. It was difficult for large vessels at any time, but with the wind that was blowing Nelson could not pass through the Bonifacio Straits. The only news the frigates could give him was that Villeneuve seemed to be headed for the southern end of Sardinia. He concluded from this that their destination was either Naples, Sicily, or the eastern Mediterranean. Unfortunately, no sooner was the British fleet out than it ran into a full southerly gale and for three days could make no headway, or gain any news of the enemy's course. It was not until the twenty-sixth that Nelson learned that the French *Indomptable* of 80 guns had been dismasted in the gale and had taken refuge in Ajaccio. Nothing was known about the rest of the fleet except that it had not attempted Sardinia, and had not been seen off Cagliari. If they had been bound for Sicily they would certainly have been sighted.

He could only assume that they were headed, as they had been in 1798, for Egypt and the East. Napoleon's original plan had been exactly this: for Villeneuve's fleet to draw Nelson into the eastern Mediterranean, while the main body from Brest and Rochefort sailed up Channel, covering the invasion fleet which was scheduled to cross with four army corps (150,000 men) on the night of 29 February. This plan had been changed more than once, and Villeneuve's current orders were to evade Nelson and leave the Mediterranean. Having crossed the Atlantic, he was to rendezvous with Admiral Ganteaume and the Brest Squadron, and cause the utmost damage to Britain's Caribbean colonies. The French fleet from Brest and Rochefort and the Spanish out of Cadiz would finally combine off Ushant, gain command of the Channel, and in the early summer of 1805 cover the passage of the Grande Armée. On paper, and as Napoleon envisaged things, this plan, and even the other which had already been scrapped, looked perfectly feasible. Unfortunately the Emperor (as he became in May that year) could never understand the difficulties of the sea service, nor the fact that the winds and weather called the tune – not captains, admirals, or even emperors. Such was the case at this moment. Villeneuve having left Toulon had run straight into a gale in the Gulf of Lions. Although his ships were well-equipped, his captains and his men had not had the British experience of that ever-treacherous area. Their small sallies out of harbour had hardly provided sufficient training or proving ground, and they suffered so much damage to masts, yards and sails that they were forced to run for safety. While Nelson was heading south towards Sicily, the French were limping back to the safety of Toulon.

Once again the British fleet drove through the Messina Straits. Unlike that occasion seven years before, they were not in pursuit of Brueys, Napoleon, and the Army of the East, but, as Nelson thought, of Villeneuve and the Toulon squadron. His reasoning was sound, he was indeed anticipating what had been Napoleon's original plan, but he was not to know that all had been changed again – and that the French fleet was licking its wounds in harbour. On 29 January, off the Faro of Messina, he wrote to the Admiralty explaining the circumstances that had prompted his course; 'One of two things must have happened, that either the French Fleet must have put back crippled [after the gale] or that they are gone to the Eastward, probably to Egypt. . . .' Viscount Melville was now First Lord of the Admiralty, and over a fortnight later Nelson was writing to him, as he had once written sadly to St Vincent, that he had been unable to find the French : 'I considered the character of Buonaparte; and that the orders given by him, on the banks of the Seine, would not take into consideration winds and weather. . . .' He had been to the Morea and then to Alexandria. He returned in anguish of spirits to Malta, where he finally learned the truth.

In the meantime Napoleon had yet again changed his plans. Villeneuve's delay meant that there was now no time for him to make a rendezvous with Rear-Admiral Missiessy in the West Indies. The latter, who had managed to elude the blockading British off Rochefort, had failed in his attempts against the British-held islands in the Caribbean. Summoned back to Rochefort he had been dismissed his command by Napoleon for failing to capture Diamond Rock, that islet off Martinique which had been seized by the British in 1804 and which menaced Port Royal, capital of the French West Indies. Villeneuve, now that his ships were repaired, was ordered to sail from Toulon to Cadiz. Here he was to collect whatever Spanish ships were ready, and proceed to Martinique where he was to be joined by Ganteaume. The latter was to evade the British blockade of Brest with his twenty-one ships-of-the-line, pick up whatever French and Spanish ships could escape from Rochefort and Ferrol, and sail for his rendezvous with Villeneuve. Having alarmed the British for the safety of their Caribbean possessions – no doubt provoking Nelson to follow them across the Atlantic – the combined French fleet was to avoid major action and return to the Channel. Here they would, it was assumed, defeat Cornwallis's ships and secure the safe crossing of the invasion army. On paper, all – at least to the military mind of the Emperor – looked relatively simple. But what Napoleon could never understand was that the movements of ships upon seas and oceans were so very different from the movement of armies upon the land. The juncture of fleets could not be easily correlated; frigates sent with despatches failed to find the admiral for whom they were destined; above all, the vagaries of wind and weather could never be calculated.

Following his new orders, Villeneuve slipped out of Toulon on 30 March, at a moment when Nelson and his ships were in the Gulf of Palmas at the south-western end of Sardinia. It was not until 4 April, when Nelson was at sea beating westward against a foul wind, that the frigate *Phoebe* came running down from the north with the news that Villeneuve's fleet was out, and that the frigate *Active* was keeping contact with the French. Nelson was in a terrible state of anxiety, 'very, very miserable', for he still could not know whether they were coming south towards him, bound round Sardinia for Sicily and the East, or whether they were heading for the western end of the Mediterranean. As always, the shortage of frigates tortured him. Once more he was playing blind man's buff in the blue acres of the Mediterranean. He decided to stay on cruise between Sardinia and the Barbary Coast in the hope of catching Villeneuve, if he should turn eastward. The *Active* meanwhile had lost contact, for Villeneuve, having heard by chance that Nelson was to the south of him, had altered course overnight to pass west of the Balearics towards the Straits of Gibraltar. It was not until 18 April that a passing merchantman brought Nelson the news that the French fleet had been sighted ten days before, off Cape Gata in southern Spain, heading westward. Nelson realised that his concern about the eastern Mediterranean, stemming from his previously correct assumption before the Battle of the Nile, had allowed the Frenchman to outwit him. 'I am going out of the Mediterranean,' he wrote. 'It may be thought that I have protected too well Sardinia, Naples, Sicily, the Morea and Egypt; but I feel I have done right and am, therefore, easy about any fate which may await me for having missed the French fleet.'

Villeneuve, having found that the Spanish ships which were supposed to join him at Cartagena were unready, had wasted no time. On 8 April he had passed Gibraltar, his ships being sighted and immediately reported to Sir John Orde, who was stationed off Cadiz. Orde with his four sail-of-the-line accordingly withdrew, in accordance with normal strategy, to join the British fleet off Ushant. When the enemy's intentions were unknown, it was always wisest to concentrate forces so as to guard the approaches to the Channel. Nelson toiled westward against light head winds – 'Dead foul! Dead foul!' – longing for the Levanter that might boost him out of the Mediterranean. Fortune favoured the French. In the saga of the Long Watch that turned into the Long Chase it must be seen that Nelson's strategy of keeping a distant watch in order to lure the French out of Toulon had proved successful. But Villeneuve's ability in escaping – principally by going west of the Balearics instead of east as had been expected – must not be underestimated. At the moment he was ahead of Nelson, not only in fact, but in the strategical game that had been played out in the Mediterranean over so many long months. It was not until 5 May that Nelson dropped anchor off Gibraltar, by which time Villeneuve was well on his way across the Atlantic, cramming on all sail to reach the West Indies and fulfil his mission.

Nelson, after debating the other options – Ireland or the Channel – had come to the conclusion that the French were bound for the West Indies. His judgement was based not so much on rumours or considered speculation as on a private visit from Rear-Admiral Donald Campbell, a British officer in the Portuguese Navy, who had assured him that this was indeed their destination. (Campbell by this action was contravening his neutrality and was later dismissed his command at the instigation of the French Ambassador in Lisbon.) 'If they are not gone to the West Indies,' Nelson told Dr Scott, 'I shall be blamed. To be burnt in effigy or Westminster Abbey is my alternative.' After so many months at sea it was hardly surprising that all officers and men who could be spared from the duties of watering and victualling the ships hastened ashore to enjoy such pleasures as the Rock afforded. The fleet's linen had also been landed. Nelson, having come to his decision, was naturally all eagerness to be under way as soon as possible, but for the moment the wind was still foul. Scott provides the following anecdote about him at this salient moment in his life, just before the Atlantic chase that was the forerunner of the drama of Trafalgar:

Lord Nelson, however, observing and weatherwise as he was, perceived an indication of a probable change of wind. Off went a gun from the *Victory*, and up went the Blue Peter, whilst the Admiral paced the deck in a hurry, with anxious steps and impatient of a moment's delay. The officers said, 'Here is one of Nelson's mad pranks.' But he was nevertheless right, the wind did become favourable, the linen was left on shore, the fleet cleared the Gut, and way they steered for the West Indies.

Villeneuve's passage across the Atlantic took thirty-four days in a fleet fresh out of Toulon; Nelson took twenty-four in a fleet that had been at sea for many months and which, without the benefit of a

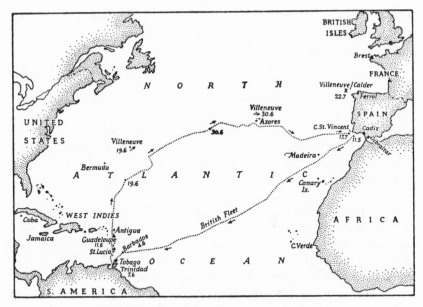

Nelson's course to and from the West Indies in search of Villeneuve

friendly port, had been entirely self-maintained. Yet, at this very moment, Napoleon was of the opinion that Nelson 'must have gone back to England to revictual, and to turn over his crews to other ships; for his vessels require docking, and his squadron may be supposed to be in a very bad condition'. These vessels, which were indeed in need of docking, were meanwhile running down the north-east trades with their studding-sails set and a bone between their teeth. Even so the French, with their long start on them, were at Martinique by mid-May, when Nelson was only off Madeira. Villeneuve had eighteen sail-of-the-line (six of them Spaniards under an able Spanish admiral, Don Federigo Gravina) and six frigates. Nelson in pursuit had only ten sail-of-the-line and three frigates. If Ganteaume had effected his escape from Brest and rendezvoused with Villeneuve the combination of their fleets would have been more than the British, even under Nelson and aided by the West Indies ships, could have withstood. But Ganteaume was still locked up in port by Cornwallis when Villeneuve's ships were waiting in Martinique. The instructions were for him to stay there for forty days until Ganteaume arrived (he never did) and during that time to employ himself by seizing whatever British possessions he could. He started with Diamond Rock – determined not to make the mistake of

Missiessy – and compelled its surrender. This relieved the situation at Port Royal but did little else, and his main achievement during this period was the capture of a British homeward-bound convoy. He had now been reinforced by Rear-Admiral Magon from Rochefort with two eighty-gun ships, and further orders for him to wait thirty days for Ganteaume. The Emperor's numerous orders, orders of a type which might have been explicit on the chessboard of Europe, had a habit of confusing his admirals. As E. H. Jenkins points out in his *History of the French Navy*: 'Villeneuve objected with justice, that he could not both sail in sufficient force to capture British islands and yet be ready at Martinique to weigh at once when Ganteaume arrived. . . .'

On 4 June 1805, Nelson stood into Carlisle Bay, the open anchorage off the capital of Barbados. The last time he had been in Caribbean waters was in 1787, but he had known them since he was a midshipman, and he could well recall all the vexation he had experienced in them as a young captain. He had also, but perhaps he deliberately discarded the memory, married Fanny in the Caribbean. His presence in the area was quickly learned by Villeneuve who, in the course of standing south to attack Antigua, had captured the British convoy and learned at the same time that Nelson was in Barbados. He was told that the British consisted of fourteen sail-of-the-line, not ten, but the very name of Nelson was enough to dissuade him from any further activity. The object of his coming to the West Indies in the first place had been to draw Nelson away from the Continent and the approaches to the Channel. It seemed that his purpose was fulfilled and, although he had only been waiting for Ganteaume for twenty-six days, he was confident that the latter had not managed to slip out of Brest. In this he was correct, for Cornwallis kept so tight a watch that the French Admiral, who had been ordered only to slip out if he could do so without a battle, had never been able to make a move. On 9 June, Villeneuve made sail for Europe. Nelson had been distracted from heading for Martinique by information from General Brereton, who commanded the troops at St Lucia, that the enemy had gone south to attack Trinidad and Tobago. He wasted several days running south to Trinidad in the expectation of a battle that would prove as annihilating as the Nile. On finding that no French had passed in that direction, he bitterly retraced his course. As he later wrote : 'But for false information I should have been off Port Royal as they were putting to sea; and our battle, most probably, would have been fought on the spot where brave Rodney beat de Grasse.' He was now convinced that the enemy had left for Europe and that no further purpose could be served by staying in the West Indies. 'Nelson,' Napoleon said, 'when he learns that Villeneuve is not at the Windward Islands, will go to Jamaica, and during the time he is wasting there in getting provisions and waiting for news, the great blows will be struck.' Of course Nelson was well aware of the grave threat to Jamaica and indeed all the West Indian colonies. If they were lost it would be a disaster for Britain, but the greatest disaster of all would be if, in his absence, the threatened invasion of Britain itself took place.

On 13 June, taking with him from the West Indies squadron the *Spartiate* of 74 guns, which brought his numbers up to eleven, he set sail in pursuit of Villeneuve to Europe. His mood was black. Though it seemed that no more than his presence in the area had been enough to save the British colonies and, with the exception of one convoy, to protect the rich lifeline of shipping upon which much of the country's wealth depended, yet he had once again failed to bring the French to battle. On 21 June he recorded in his diary: 'Midnight, very nearly calm, saw three planks, which I think came from the French Fleet. Very miserable, which is very foolish.' So far everything he had done seemed ineffectual. Villeneuve had got out of the Mediterranean scot-free; he had then escaped without being brought to battle in the West Indies; and now, elusive as ever, he was away into the Atlantic, miles ahead of his pursuer. Ireland was a possible destination, so equally was the Channel. But these areas were covered by Cornwallis, and Nelson's duty now was once more to protect the Mediterranean. He swung south to pass through the Azores and headed direct for the approaches to Gibraltar. On 17 July, Cape St Vincent loomed ahead, that formidable outrider of Europe where he had first been sealed with fame. Throughout all these long months of endless sea-time his kindness and consideration for his officers and men had never faltered. The *Superb* was a slow sailor and had delayed the fleet's progress on the way out, but Nelson had written to her captain, Richard Keats, '. . . I know and feel that the *Superb* does all that which is possible for a ship to accomplish; and I desire that you will not fret upon the occasion'. We know from a letter written by one of his captains what they thought about him: 'We are all half-starved, and otherwise inconvenienced by being so long away from a port, but our full recompense is that we are with Nelson.'

On 20 July, at Gibraltar, he recorded in his private diary: 'I went on shore for the first time since the 16th of June, 1803; and from having my foot out of the *Victory*, two years, wanting ten days.'

CHAPTER THIRTY-FOUR

The Last of England

Two days after Nelson set foot ashore in Gibraltar, the battle which he had been seeking for so long was fought off Cape Finisterre. Captain Bettesworth, a veteran of twenty-five who had been wounded in action even more times than Nelson, had been despatched in the brig *Curieux* in advance of the fleet to tell the Admiralty that Nelson was returning to Europe, and to convey his assessment of the French fleet's movements. Bettesworth, sailing fast and direct for England, had come up with Villeneuve in the Atlantic, had stayed in the vicinity of the French long enough to ascertain their numbers and course, and had then made course to get this all-important information home.

On 9 July, Lord Barham, the First Lord of the Admiralty, was given the news by Bettesworth in person. Although he was nearly eighty, Barham showed that he had lost none of the activity which had made his career in the Navy so remarkable. He immediately sent orders for Cornwallis to despatch the five ships-of-the-line which were on watch off Rochefort to join the ten with which Sir Robert Calder was blockading Ferrol. Calder, with these fifteen under his command, was ordered to intercept Villeneuve one hundred miles west of Cape Finisterre. On 22 July the two fleets were in contact. The wind was very light, a fog came down, and an indecisive action was fought in which, although the French and Spanish ships outnumbered the British by five ships-of-the-line, the victory went to Calder – two Spaniards striking their colours. Unfortunately, when dawn broke the next day, the two fleets were about seventeen miles apart and Calder, rather than following up the attack, contented himself with securing his two prizes and attending to the damage among his own ships.

Calder, who had been critical of Nelson's famous indiscipline at the Battle of Cape St Vincent, showed that he did not possess that instinctive feeling for the moment of opportunity which is the hallmark of a great naval commander. It seemed to him that he had fought a satisfactory action under difficult circumstances and had driven the enemy away from the Biscayan approaches to the Channel. He did not feel that he had done anything but his best under the conditions obtaining at the time. Indeed, Nelson himself, writing to his old friend Thomas Fremantle on 16 August in acknowledgement of a letter and a large packet of newspapers, was surprised by their contents:

> I was in truth bewildered by the account of Sir Robert Calder's Victory, and the joy of the event; together with the hearing that John Bull was not content, which I am sorry for. Who can, my dear Fremantle, command all the success which our Country may wish? We have fought together, and therefore well know what it is. I have had the best disposed Fleet of friends, but who can say what will be the event of a Battle : and it most sincerely grieves me, that in any of the papers it should be insinuated, that Lord Nelson could have done better.

This was fair and generous, but the fact remained that Nelson had given men a new concept of victory. The old days, when a fleet engagement was considered satisfactory – even glorious – if the other side withdrew and prizes were taken, were over. Annihilation was now expected.

Villeneuve, having first put into Vigo, where he left three ships, had slipped round into Ferrol, the best and largest harbour in Spain. Calder, having lost touch with his opponent after the battle, had joined Cornwallis off Ushant. Nelson also joined Cornwallis on 14 August, adding ten ships to the fleet that secured the approaches to England. Cornwallis excused him the normal courtesy visit and allowed him to make his way on to Spithead in the *Victory*, taking with him also the *Superb*, which was badly in need of dockyard hands. On 19 August, Nelson's flag was hauled down and he was free to go on a leave which had in fact been granted him nine months before. He had been away from home for two years and three months, and it may have seemed, on looking back, as if he had achieved nothing. The many months of waiting and watching had ended with Villeneuve's escape; the chase across the Atlantic had proved fruitless; and the battle that should have been his had fallen to Calder. If he felt sympathy for the latter, he may well have expected to find that he was equally subject to criticism. This was far from the case, as is made clear by the words of Lord Minto: 'I met Nelson, today, in a mob in Piccadilly, and got hold of his arm, so that I was mobbed too. It is really quite affecting to see the wonder and admiration and love and respect of the whole world; and the general expression of all these sentiments at once, from gentle and simple, the moment he is seen. It is beyond anything represented in a play or poem.' Lord Minto's brother, Hugh Elliot, writing from Naples, summed up precisely what it was that everyone in England felt about him :

Either the distances between the different quarters of the globe are diminished, or you have extended the powers of human action. After an unremitting cruise of two long years in the stormy Gulf of Lions, to have proceeded without going into port to Alexandria, from Alexandria to the West Indies, from the West Indies back again to Gibraltar; to have kept your ships afloat, your rigging standing, and your crews in health and spirits – is an effort such as never was realised in former times, nor, I doubt, will ever again be repeated by any other admiral. You have protected us for two long years, and you have saved the West Indies.

On 20 August the moment for which he had longed all those many months in his cabin in the *Victory* took place. He saw Emma, Horatia and his home at Merton once more. The idyll was resumed, but this time on even happier terms, since Sir William's death had removed the necessity for keeping Horatia concealed, and she now lived with her mother as an adopted daughter. She was four and a half, an intelligent child, able to write, and already being taught French and Italian. Nelson sat down to dine in the company of his child, the woman he loved (and whom he regarded as his wife), in the presence of his brother and his wife, his sister and her husband, 'Mother Cadogan', Emma's mother, and, as he put it, 'people that do care for us'. He had after all, and despite a permanent concern about money, achieved that conservative English ideal of happiness – to relax with family and friends in his own home, his mini-castle protected by the stream known as 'the Nile'. 'He looks remarkably well,' wrote Lord Minto, 'and full of spirits', and of Emma he had finally had to concede that 'She is a clever woman after all : the passion is as hot as ever.' In these, his last days in England, Nelson found a secure happiness such as he had never known before in all his life.

Since Merton was only an hour's journey from London it was natural that he should often visit the capital to see Lord Barham at the Admiralty, as well as other ministers and friends. The threat to the country had in no way diminished, and Napoleon was eagerly awaiting his expected fleet which would clear the Channel for his invasion forces. Instructions had been sent to Villeneuve to 'sweep all before you, come boldly down on the enemy; if you give us control [of the Channel] for three days, nay, even for twenty-four hours, your task will be done; all is ready, Europe waits breathless on this great event; I put my trust in your bravery and skill'. It was under these circumstances, when England was threatened as never before, that the two men who played so decisive a part in the history of those days met in London. The cool and patrician Arthur Wellesley, the future Duke of Wellington, was already a man whom those who served with him could respect and admire for his iron-clad qualities of prevision, sagacity and endurance. The writer and politician John Wilson Croker tells of the incident :

We were talking of Lord Nelson, and some instances were mentioned of the egotism and vanity that derogated from his character. 'Why,' said the Duke, 'I am not surprised at such instances, for Lord Nelson was, in different circumstances, two quite different men, as I myself can vouch, though I only saw him once in my life, and for, perhaps, an hour. It was soon after I returned from India. I went to the Colonial Office in Downing Street, and there I was shown into the little waiting room on the right hand, where I found, also waiting to see the Secretary of State, a gentleman, whom, from his likeness to his pictures and the loss of an arm, I immediately recognised as Lord Nelson. He could not know who I was, but he entered at once into conversation with me, if I can call it conversation, for it was almost all on his side and all about himself, and, in, really, a style so vain and silly as to surprise and almost disgust me. I suppose something that I happened to say may have made him guess that I was *somebody*, and he went out of the room for a moment, I have no doubt to ask the office-keeper who I was, for when he came back he was altogether a different man, both in style and matter. All that I had thought a charlatan style had vanished, and he talked of the state of this country and of the aspect and probabilities of affairs on the Continent with good sense, and a knowledge of subjects both at home and abroad, that surprised me equally and more agreeably than the first part of our interview had done; in fact, he talked like an officer and a statesman. The Secretary of State kept us long waiting, and certainly, for the last half or three quarters of an hour, I don't know that I ever had a conversation that interested me more. Now, if the Secretary of State had been punctual, and admitted Lord Nelson in the first quarter of an hour, I should have had the same impression of a light and trivial character that other people have had; but luckily I saw enough to be satisfied that he was really a very superior man; but certainly a more sudden and complete metamorphosis I never saw.

Nelson *was* 'two quite different men'. The one that his wife Fanny knew (or had known) was much the same as the one that all the officers and men who served under him loved and respected. The other side of his nature, never strongly in evidence until after the Battle of the Nile, was a strange by-product of his desire for fame coupled with his passionate love for Emma Hamilton. Vanity had long been his weakness, but if Emma had not made so great a play upon this aspect of his character it is more than probable that it would have remained under control. It was, however, this curious duality that gave him his irresistible appeal to the great mass of people; seeing in him, as they did, not only an embodiment of all their hopes and aspirations, but a touching evidence of those weaknesses which each could recognise in himself. Wellington, as his life was to demonstrate, was a man whom people could admire and even reverence, but Nelson, as an officer who knew them both remarked, 'was the man to love'.

His days at Merton were constantly interrupted by the demands of the time. 'God knows I want rest,' he wrote, 'but self is entirely out of the question.' Austria and Russia had now joined Britain in a coalition against France, and on 24 August, Napoleon, despairing of ever getting his admirals to execute his orders efficiently, had decided to march against Germany. On 2 September, Nelson learned from Captain Blackwood of the frigate *Euryalus* that Villeneuve had retired to Cadiz. Blackwood was an old friend who had been largely responsible, when in command of the *Penelope*, for the capture of the *Guillaume Tell* off Malta, and Nelson listened to his news with close attention. 'I think I shall yet have to beat them,' he said. It was clear that the concentration of the French and Spanish forces – over thirty ships-of-the-line – could only mean a major movement against England and her allies. It could be into the field of the Mediterranean, or it could be once again northward to the Channel, to cover Napoleon's invasion fleet. One thing was clear, Cadiz itself could not maintain for very long the provisioning of so many ships and men. Nelson, from his long experience of blockading, knew well that 'we have a better chance of forcing them out by want of provisions: it is said hunger will break through stone walls – ours is only a wall of wood'. Jenkins comments in his *History of the French Navy*: 'Villeneuve had been having a difficult time in Cadiz. He was, in all, two thousand men short (seventeen hundred sick and three hundred deserters – but he had troops who could serve the guns): he had also great difficulty in supplying his fleet and in making good damages, for the arsenal of Cadiz had exhausted itself in fitting out the Spanish ships.'

It was clear to the British Government that the combined fleets of France and Spain must be held within Cadiz. Pitt, who was once again Prime Minister (for so long Nelson's favourite politician), had no hesitation in selecting him to lead the force which would undertake this task. Nelson had given great thought to the best way in which a major fleet engagement could be fought and, as he had put in a discussion at the Cabinet, achieve the total destruction of the enemy. The formal line of battle, under which actions had been fought in the eighteenth century, he had long ago decided was a thing of the past. At the Nile he had fallen upon the van of the enemy and at Copenhagen upon the rear, but both these actions had been against vessels at anchor. What must now be fought was an engagement between great fleets at sea. He outlined his plans in a conversation he had with Captain Keats at Merton during these last days in England:

'No day can be long enough to arrange a couple of fleets, and fight a decisive Battle, according to the old system. When *we* meet them, (for meet them we shall), I'll tell you how I shall fight them. I shall form the Fleet into three Divisions in three Lines. One Division shall be composed of twelve or fourteen of the fastest two-decked Ships, which I shall always keep to windward, or in a situation of advantage; and I shall put them under an Officer, who, I am sure, will employ them in the manner I wish, if possible. I consider it will always be in my power to throw them into Battle in any part I may choose; but if circumstances prevent their being carried against the Enemy where I desire, I shall feel certain he will employ them effectually, and, perhaps, in a more advantageous manner than if he could have followed orders.' He went on to say: 'With the remaining part of the Fleet formed in two Lines, I shall go at them at once, if I can, about one-third of their Line from their leading Ship.' He asked Keats what he thought of the plan, and the latter paused as he considered something so audacious and quite unlike any sea-battle before. Nelson swept on: 'I'll tell you what *I* think of it. I think it will surprise and confound the enemy. They won't know what I am about. It will bring forward a pell-mell battle, and that is what I want.'

What was startling, and immediately clear to Keats, was that the ships in the van of the two spearhead columns would have to endure an almost intolerable weight of fire from the enemy in their conventional line-ahead formation. Nelson, it seemed, was prepared to risk this. He would accept heavy casualties in the foremost ships so long as he could break the enemy line and bring on an action at close quarters, in which he felt confident that his officers and men would be more than a match for a combined French–Spanish fleet. He knew that the morale in some of their ships was low, he envisaged confusion of intentions between ships of different calibre and construction, and manned by officers and men of different nations. In this he was to be amply confirmed in his judgement. The only basic difference between the plan as he told it at Merton and the actuality of Trafalgar was that he did not have the fast squadron for which he had hoped.

Nelson had arrived at Merton on 20 August 1805, and on the night of 13 September he left for ever. 'I am again broken hearted,' Emma told Lady Bolton, 'as our dear Nelson is immediately going. It seems as though I have had a fortnight's dream, and am awoke to all the misery of this cruel separation. But what can I do? His powerful arm is of so much consequence to his country.' Lord Minto records that on the day before he left Emma would neither eat nor drink but sat in a kind of swoon at the table. But suggestions that she tried to prevail on him not to go can be discounted: Emma knew her man as gentle, nervous Fanny had never done. One of his very last acts before taking leave of Emma was to go up to Horatia's bedside where the child of their Mediterranean passion lay asleep. He prayed, kneeling beside her bed, that her life might be happy – a prayer that was to be granted. In his private diary for Friday night, 13th September, he made the entry:

At half-past ten drove from dear dear Merton, where I left all which I hold dear in this world, to go to serve my King and Country. May the Great God whom I adore enable me to fulfill the expectations of my Country; and if it is His good pleasure that I should return, my thanks will never cease being offered up to the Throne of His Mercy. If it is His good providence to cut short my days upon earth, I bow with the greatest submission, relying that He will protect those so dear to me, that I may leave behind. – His will be done: Amen, Amen, Amen.

Next morning he arrived at Portsmouth, transacted his shore business, and embarked at Southsea beach with George Canning, the

Treasurer of the Navy, and George Rose, from the Board of Trade, both of whom were to dine with him in the *Victory*. 'Nelson', wrote Southey, 'endeavoured to take a by-way to the beach; but a crowd collected in his train, pressing forward to obtain a sight of his face: many were in tears, and many knelt down before him and blessed him as he passed. England has had many heroes; but never one who so entirely possessed the love of his countrymen as Nelson.' As ever he was in a fever of impatience to be gone. Hearing that the *Agamemnon*, the *Defiance*, and the *Royal Sovereign* were not yet ready, he gave orders for them to follow as soon as possible. On the morning of 15 September the *Victory* weighed anchor. She was accompanied only by Blackwood in the *Euryalus*. Light airs from the south-south-east hardly disturbed the water as, her giant sides dwarfing the dancing frigate, the *Victory* set course down Channel, bound for Cadiz and Cape Trafalgar.

CHAPTER THIRTY-FIVE

Cape Trafalgar

On 17 September the *Victory* was off Plymouth and Blackwood was sent into harbour with orders for the *Ajax* and the *Thunderer* to join. At nine o'clock in the morning, 'Blowing fresh at W.S.W., dead foul wind', Nelson wrote to Emma: 'I intreat, my dear Emma, that you will cheer up; and we will look forward to many, many happy years, and be surrounded by our children's children. God Almighty can, when he pleases, remove the impediment. My heart and soul is with you and Horatia.' Two days later, south-west of the Scillies, a frigate was sighted which proved to be the *Decade* from the fleet off Cadiz. She was bearing home Nelson's old second-in-command, Sir Richard Bickerton, who was sick; she also conveyed the cheering news that the French were still within Cadiz and that no battle had yet been fought by Admiral Collingwood. The *Euryalus* was now despatched with letters to the British Consul at Lisbon, to Captain Sutton of the *Amphion* off the Tagus, and to Collingwood, urging them to secure 'every man, in every way, for the Fleet under my command'. Instructions were also sent that Nelson's arrival was in no way to be made known and no salutes to be paid when he joined the fleet. Villeneuve's lookouts would thus be aware of nothing more than that a further first-rate had joined the blockading fleet. Nelson, as far as was known at Cadiz, was on leave in England. He had no wish for the awe-inspiring quality of his name to give Villeneuve any further excuse for not coming out and giving battle.

On 28 September, the *Victory* sauntering along – 'we have very little wind' – Nelson sighted the fleet of which he was to take command. There they were – eighteen sail-of-the-line maintaining their watch and ward, and there in Cadiz harbour were the masts and yards of the combined Franco-Spanish fleets. It was reckoned that there were thirty-six sail-of-the-line, against which Nelson, as soon as he received expected reinforcements, would be able to muster thirty-three. The odds would not be too unequal and, if he had but known the dissension that existed in Cadiz between Frenchman and Spaniard, admirals, officers, and men alike, he would rightly have judged that they were on his side. Nor need he have worried that Villeneuve would fail to be drawn out, for the latter had only recently received orders to take the fleets to sea, enter the Mediterranean, land the troops they carried in the Kingdom of Naples, and then proceed to destroy all British trade. Villeneuve was further to be spurred into action by hearing unofficially that he was shortly to be relieved of his command by Vice-Admiral Rosily, and that Napoleon himself had castigated Villeneuve as a scoundrel and a traitor.

On taking command of the fleet Nelson's first duty was an unhappy one. He had orders to tell Sir Robert Calder that he was to return home at once to stand trial by court-martial for his conduct of the recent engagement against the French. Nelson, as has been seen, had every sympathy with Calder and it was probably because he felt so strongly towards him that he accepted his plea to be allowed to return home to face the charges in his 90-gun the *Prince of Wales*. This was misplaced sentiment on Nelson's part, to deprive the fleet of so powerful a vessel at the very moment when a major engagement was to be expected. It was, however, just this kind of tenderness towards worthy men in distress which had been evident throughout his career, that had made him the man whom all the fleet loved. He was also quickly to find out that, before the engagement took place, a new spirit had to be breathed into the blockading British ships. It was not that there had been anything basically wrong with Collingwood's command, but he was an austere man whose attitude towards discipline was reminiscent of St Vincent's, but who did not have the capacity to inspire affection among those who served under him. While on blockade, for instance, he had allowed no social visiting between ship and ship, and no boats to be hoisted out to buy fresh food from passing coasters, with the result that the fleet had settled down to an iron-bound routine. 'For Charity's sake,' wrote Captain Codrington of the *Orion*, 'send us Lord Nelson, ye men of power!'

At once all was to change and, with the news that Nelson was now in command, an almost tangible feeling of good cheer and, indeed, joy spread throughout the fleet. Nelson himself was pleasantly sensible of it: 'The reception I met with on joining the Fleet caused the sweetest sensation of my life. The officers who came on board to welcome my return forgot my rank as Commander-in-Chief in the enthusiasm with which they greeted me. As soon as these emotions were passed, I laid before them the Plan I had previously arranged for attacking the Enemy; and it was not only my pleasure to find it generally approved, but clearly perceived and understood.' A tactical memorandum to the same effect, and still assuming that he would have enough ships for three columns, was issued a few days later. Meanwhile, in contradistinction to Collingwood's grave rule, captains were invited aboard to dine with the Admiral, the buying of fresh provisions was encouraged, and as Captain Duff of the *Mars* put it : 'He is so good and pleasant that we all wish to do what he likes, without any kind of orders.' The day after the *Victory* had joined the fleet had been Nelson's forty-seventh birthday and he had half the commanding officers to dine with him, and the other half the following day. 'He certainly is the pleasantest Admiral I ever served under,' wrote Captain Duff. The dinner parties were also what would today be called briefings and as Nelson wrote in a letter to Emma : 'When I came to explain to them the "Nelson touch", it was like an electric shock. Some shed tears, all approved – "It was new – it was singular – it was simple !"; and, from Admirals downwards, it was repeated – "It must succeed, if ever they will allow us to get at them. You are, my Lord, surrounded by friends whom you inspire with confidence." ' Already, and within so short a time, he had infused into his commanders the spirit of 'the Band of Brothers' who had fought the Nile.

Collingwood may have been unpopular with the other officers but Nelson knew his value. He was brave and efficient, naturally enough, but he was also entirely dependable and he and Nelson had a rapport, the latter referring to him as 'my dear Coll. as perfect as could be expected'. One change in Collingwood's disposition of the fleet was quickly made, and this followed upon Nelson's thinking in the blockade of Toulon. Collingwood had maintained a close blockade, which was natural enough since this had been the policy which he had rightly followed at Brest. Furthermore, until he had received additional ships into the fleet he had only been in a position to keep the enemy bottled up, not being strong enough to lure them out to fight. Nelson's fleet soon being brought up to thirty-three ships-of-the-line, he felt that he could now give Villeneuve the feeling that at the right moment he could make a dash for it. After all, he had beaten the British at this very game before. Accordingly, Rear-Admiral Louis was recalled from his inshore station and the body of the British fleet withdrew to a position fifty miles west-south-west of Cadiz. The frigates were sent inshore to watch the enemy, other ships acting as relaying stations to Nelson and the fleet. On 3 October, Nelson despatched five ships from the fleet to Gibraltar for stores and water, and to Tetuan where they could embark beef. It was his intention to keep a movement like this in constant rota so that the fleet would at all times be in good health and condition. (The blockaded enemy of course always had this advantage that, while the British must of necessity despatch ships to water and provision, the fleet within the harbour could always sally out with its full complement.) Admiral Louis, who was in command of the ships detached, and who had been at the Nile as Captain of the *Minotaur*, was reluctant to leave : 'You are sending us away, my Lord – the Enemy will come out, and we shall have no share in the Battle.' Nelson reassured him, saying that he was sending him away first so as to be sure that he would be back in time. But Louis was to be proved right.

A welcome addition to the fleet hove in sight on Sunday, 13 October, Nelson's favourite old ship the *Agamemnon*, and in command of her none other than Sir Edward Berry. Nelson was delighted. 'Here comes that damned fool Berry!' he exclaimed. '*Now* we shall have a battle.'

Throughout these anxious days Nelson had also to deal with all the routine administration of his command, which ranged from correspondence with the Consul at Lisbon, and the Dey of Algiers (his old adversary), to dockyard affairs in Gibraltar, and even to personal matters such as a young lieutenant who had run away with a ballet dancer. Furthermore his right hand, the indomitable Hardy, was ill, with the result that much of the work and routine business which he would have normally taken off Nelson's shoulders had now to be borne by the Admiral. The day after Berry's arrival the signal was made that the enemy was seen at the harbour mouth. This could only mean one thing, that they would come out at the first suitable moment. At six in the morning on 19 October, the frigate *Sirius* reported 'Enemy have their topsails hoisted.' The *Sirius* was standing close inshore and, even with the admirable signal system devised by Admiral Popham and introduced into the Navy two years before, it took some time for the news to spread down the line of reporting ships to reach Nelson nearly fifty miles away. He himself had also made a signal that morning inviting several captains to dine with him, and had sent a letter across to Collingwood : 'What a beautiful day! Will you be tempted out of your ship? If you will, hoist the Assent and *Victory*'s pendants.' At nine-thirty that morning the news from Cadiz reached him, the dinner invitations were cancelled, and Nelson signalled : 'General chase south-east.' He was placing the fleet between Villeneuve and the Straits of Gibraltar.

With a light south-westerly wind scarce filling her sails, the *Victory* settled easily on to her course. In his sun-barred cabin the Admiral sat down to write a letter : 'My dearest beloved Emma, the dear friend of my bosom,' it read,

the signal has been made that the Enemy's Combined fleet are coming out of Port. We have very little wind, so that I have no hopes of seeing them before tomorrow. May the God of Battles crown my endeavours with success at all events, I will take care that my name shall ever be most dear to you and Horatia, both of whom I love as much as my own life, and as my last writing before the battle will be to you, so I hope in God I shall live to finish my letter after the Battle. May Heaven bless you prays your *Nelson and Bronte*.

The following day he added a further paragraph :

October 20th. In the morning we were close to the Mouth of the straights, but the Wind had not come far enough to the Westward to allow the Combined fleets to weather the Shoals off Trafalgar; but they were counted as far as forty Sails of Ships of War, which I suppose to be 34 of the Line and six Frigates, a group of them was seen off the Lighthouse of Cadiz this morning but it blows so very fresh and thick weather that I rather believe they will go into the Harbour before night. May God Almighty give us success over these fellows, and enable us to get a Peace.

'Peace' was the last word he wrote to the woman he loved with all his heart. His assessment that the enemy would put back to harbour was wrong. Soon after daybreak on that Sunday of 20 October, Villeneuve ordered the rest of his fleet to leave Cadiz. His intention was to stand to the westward so that, as soon as all the ships were out and clear, he could with a favourable wind make a quick run for the entrance to the Straits. It was not until noon that all the ships were at sea, and it was a further four hours before they were formed up in line of battle. This was composed of three divisions under Villeneuve's command, with a further twelve ships under Admiral Gravina taking the windward station, to act as a scouting squadron and to try to drive off the shadowing British frigates. There was no question of the allied fleet fighting as two separate national bodies. They had quite deliberately been mixed with one another in such a way as to form a composite force and – it must be added – so that the French, who mistrusted the Spaniards, could keep an eye on them and see that they did not slink away in action back to the haven of Cadiz.

On Sunday morning the British fleet lay guarding the entrance to the Straits. There was as yet no sign of the enemy and there was time for Collingwood and some of the other captains to come aboard *Victory* for a last discussion with Nelson. It was thick weather and rainy, and Nelson was still concerned that the enemy would evade action and return to port. Reassuring news reached him in the afternoon from Blackwood that the whole enemy fleet was at sea and appeared to be headed in a westerly direction. Nelson sent a message back that he relied on Blackwood and his frigates not to lose touch with them. He was concerned lest their destination might not be the Mediterranean after all, but the Channel approaches. He now issued his orders for communications during the coming night. If the enemy were standing to the southward, or towards the Straits, two blue lights were to be burned, but if on the other hand they were headed west 'three guns, quick, every hour'. Collingwood had suggested that they should press for action that same day, but Nelson had rejected the idea. Although Villeneuve was only about twenty miles away, it would have meant an engagement that would have started too late for any conclusive result, and a night action involving so many ships, and in the confused mêlée that Nelson intended to provoke, would have involved far too great a risk of friend firing upon friend. The Atlantic was not Aboukir Bay. He intended to keep away from the enemy throughout the night so that the dawn of the twenty-first would see Villeneuve too far committed to be able to turn back and would leave the British with all the daylight hours to execute their task. His private diary reads: 'At 8 [PM] we wore, and stood to the S.W., and at four AM wore, and stood to the N.E.' Nelson was quite convinced that the morrow would bring the battle so long desired over so many months. October 21 was the forty-sixth anniversary of his uncle Maurice Suckling's defeat of de Kersaint in the West Indies, something that had inspired Nelson to join the Navy all those years ago.

'Cabo Trafalgar,' reads the Admiralty Pilot, 'called by the Romans Promontorium Junonis, and by the Arabs Taraf el agar (promontory of caves) is a small peninsula, about 66 feet high, and is uneven and sandy.' Dangerous rocky ridges and shallows extend off it, and between Cape Trafalgar and Bajo Aceitera there is a tidal race 'about half a mile in extent, caused by the unevenness of the bottom'. On the morning of 21 October, Villeneuve lay half-way between Cape Trafalgar and the British. The *Victory* was some twenty miles from the Cape. There was a light westerly wind and good visibility, but an ominous slow swell indicated to old hands that somewhere out in the Atlantic a westerly gale was blowing up. By steering on a parallel

course to Villeneuve for most of the night, and then by standing to
the north-east from four o'clock onward, Nelson had so positioned the
fleet that he had reduced Villeneuve's chances of returning to Cadiz.
He had ensured that he must either maintain his course to the Straits
(and be brought to battle) or must turn about – and still be brought
to battle. His movements had also placed the British fleet at daybreak
some nine miles to windward of the enemy – an excellent position for
a commander intent on forcing an action. Furthermore, the fact that
the Combined Fleet lay to the east of him meant that their ships were
silhouetted against the dawn, whereas it was nearly a quarter of an
hour before the French and Spaniards became aware of the cumulus
clouds of sails glowing in the early light to the west.

On sighting the enemy Nelson bore away. One ship, Captain
Digby's 64-gun *Africa*, had got out of touch during the night and
was some ten miles to the north of the fleet at dawn. This meant that
Nelson was coming into action with only twenty-six ships against
thirty-three, but it was a battle that he had carefully planned and it
was taking place according to his design. Villeneuve was in a far
different situation : either way he was being compelled to fight when
he did not wish to do so, and when he was in command of a mixed
fleet of indifferent morale which had never worked together as a unit.
He decided, as Nelson had anticipated that he would, to turn his ships
to the north and stand back for Cadiz. At six a.m. Nelson signalled,
'Form the order of sailing in two columns.' Everyone knew what this
meant, for it was the order of battle which they had discussed with
Nelson. They were to cut the enemy line in two places, concentrating
their forces against their rear and centre.

Villeneuve in the meantime had signalled his fleet to get into line,
prior to reversing course for Cadiz. It is possible that, even at this
late hour, he had considered carrying on into the Mediterranean : he
might always escape overnight. But one thought must have restrained
him. He knew that Rear-Admiral Louis and his squadron had been
down off Gibraltar so, if he pressed on, he would not only have Nelson
behind him but Louis barring the gate. On the other hand, the nearer
he was to Cadiz when the clearly unavoidable action took place the
better, for he would have shelter to hand and the British would have
none. It took the Combined Fleet over two hours before they were
headed northward, and then in anything but good order, for the wind
was so light, and the approaching swell so long, that the ships were
very difficult to handle. (It should always be remembered that there
is no man alive in the world today who could handle a fleet of ships
under sail, and precious few even a single ship-of-the-line.)

The British had now scrambled into their two columns, Colling-wood in the *Royal Sovereign* leading the lee line of fifteen ships, and Nelson in the *Victory* leading the weather line of eleven (the *Africa* was coming down slowly from the north to rejoin them). It would take six hours for the attackers to close on Villeneuve's long 'crescent, convexing to leeward', as Collingwood described it. At 6.45 the course, which had originally been east-north-east, was amended to east, to close the angle of approach. All were repeatedly enjoined to make more sail. But, even with studding-sails set – something never before known when a fleet was going into action – the rate of approach was never more than two knots, a leisurely walking pace.

Nelson had been on the quarter-deck of the *Victory* since first light. He was wearing his old undress uniform, with the stars of his four Orders of Knighthood, but was without his sword which had been left on a table below. It had been suggested by several officers that it might be wise if the Admiral was to wear a plain uniform coat as his present one would only call him to the attention of enemy riflemen, but no one had dared to take the liberty of approaching him on this score. Mr Beatty, the surgeon, had finally elected to do so, but was unable to find any opportunity as Nelson was busy conferring with his frigate captains, Blackwood, Dundas, Capel, and Prowse. Then the Admiral went below with Blackwood and Hardy, so once again he could not get a word with him. The reason for the last two accompanying Nelson to his quarters was that he wanted them to witness a document which he had already prepared. It gave an account of Emma Hamilton's services to the nation during her resi-dence in Naples at the time of the Nile campaign and it concluded:

Could I have rewarded these services I would not now call upon my Country; but as that has not been in my power, I leave Emma Lady Hamilton, therefore, a Legacy to my King and Country, that they will give her an ample provision to maintain her rank in life. I also leave to the beneficence of my Country my adopted daughter, Horatia Nelson Thompson; and I desire she will use in the future the name of Nelson only. These are the only favours I ask of my King and Country at this moment when I am going to fight their battle.

The day wore on. The ships lounged forward, a rolling swell of sail that shook, came back, then filled again with a flacker as the long ocean poured beneath their keels. All was ready. The slow-matches, which were still carried in case the flint-locks missed fire, sizzled around the forked linstocks. On upper decks the bands played the traditional tunes: 'Rule Britannia', 'Hearts of Oak', and 'Britons, Strike Home'. (Many were not Britons. The *Victory* alone was manned by a composite crew that included Americans, Scandinavians, Dutch, Swiss, Germans and Portuguese.) The bulkheads were all struck down, Nelson's cabin was almost as bare as everywhere else, even his 'Guardian Angel' had been carefully taken below. Only his desk with his private diary upon it remained. In it he wrote his last words:

At daylight saw the Enemy's Combined Fleet from East to E.S.E.; bore away; made the signal for Order of Sailing, and to prepare for Battle; the Enemy with their heads to the Southward; at seven the Enemy wearing in succession. May the Great God, whom I worship, grant to my Country, and for the benefit of Europe in general, a great and glorious Victory, and may no misconduct in any one tarnish it; and may humanity after Victory be the predominant feature in the British Fleet. For myself, individually, I commit my life to Him, who made me, and may his blessing light upon my endeavours for serving my Country faithfully. To him I resign myself and the just cause which is entrusted to me to defend. Amen. Amen. Amen.

At 11 a.m. Lieutenant Pasco, who was acting as Signal Lieutenant, entered Nelson's cabin. He was smarting from the fact that his seniority entitled him to be the executive officer and he wished to mention it to the Admiral. He stopped on entering, seeing Nelson on his knees, and 'could not at such a moment disturb his mind with any grievance of mine'. Earlier Captain Blackwood had suggested to Nelson that he should shift his flag to the *Euryalus*, but 'he would not hear of it, and gave as his reason the force of example'. Blackwood was as concerned as all were that the enemy would make a dead set at Nelson, and it was known that the French had special sharpshooters instructed to pick off officers visible on the quarter-decks, something which is confirmed by the fiery little Captain Lucas of the *Redoubtable*: 'I also had on board a hundred muskets fitted with long bayonets. These were issued to picked men who were specially trained as musketeers and stationed in the rigging.' Nelson did agree, however, to a suggestion made by Blackwood and Hardy that the *Téméraire*, which was second in the line, should be allowed to precede the *Victory* and lead into battle. It is very doubtful if he meant what he said. His agreement, in fact, was almost certainly designed to get both ships sailing as fast as possible, for when at one moment the

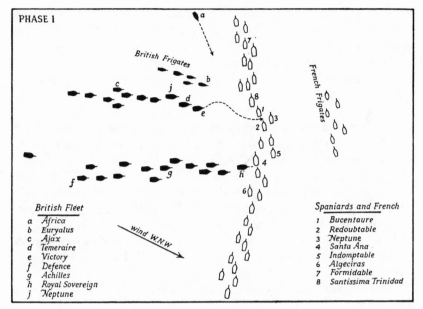

PHASE 1

British Frigates

French Frigates

British Fleet

a   *Africa*
b   *Euryalus*
c   *Ajax*
d   *Temeraire*
e   *Victory*
f   *Defence*
g   *Achilles*
h   *Royal Sovereign*
j   *Neptune*

Wind W.N.W

Spaniards and French

1   *Bucentaure*
2   *Redoubtable*
3   *Neptune*
4   *Santa Ana*
5   *Indomptable*
6   *Algeciras*
7   *Formidable*
8   *Santissima Trinidad*

The Battle of Trafalgar

Téméraire did begin to range up on the flagship's quarter Nelson called out: 'I'll thank you, Captain Harvey, to keep in your proper station, which is astern of the *Victory.*'

The swell was growing steadily more pronounced. The wind would be close on its heels. Nelson no doubt remembered how Hawke had saved the British fleet by anchoring after the action at Quiberon Bay, in which the French had suffered such a disaster from the gale that followed. He instructed Pasco to hoist the signal, 'Prepare to anchor after the close of day.' Previous to this he had signalled to Colling-wood: 'I intend to push or go through the end of the enemy's line to prevent them getting into Cadiz.' It was only as an afterthought that he remarked: 'I'll now amuse the Fleet,' adding, 'Mr Pasco, I want to say to the fleet, ENGLAND CONFIDES THAT EVERY MAN WILL DO HIS DUTY. You must be quick, for I have one more to add, which is for close action.' Pasco asked if he might substitute 'expects' for 'confides' because the first was in the signal book whereas the second would have to be spelled out, involving seven more flag hoists. Nelson agreed: 'That will do; make it directly.' Collingwood's reaction was typical of the dour old Northumbrian: 'What *is* Nelson signalling about? We all know what we have to do.' The gap between the fleets was closing very slowly, for the wind had fallen even further, and the rate of approach was now only about one and a half knots. *Victory* now made Signal No. 16 to the Fleet, 'Close Action'. The flag remained at her top-gallant masthead until it was shot away.

Two eyewitnesses set the scene as the twin arrowheads bore down on the extended curve of the Combined Fleet. A midshipman in the *Neptune* wrote:

> It was a beautiful sight when their line was completed, their broadsides turned towards us, showing their iron teeth. Some of the enemy's ships were painted like ourselves with double yellow streaks, some with a broad single red or yellow streak, others all black, and the noble *Santissima Trinidad* with four distinct lines of red, with a white ribbon between them, made her seem to be a superb man-of-war, which, indeed, she was. Her appearance was imposing, her head splendidly ornamented with a colossal group of figures, painted white, representing the Holy Trinity from which she took her name.

Aboard the *Ajax* Second-Lieutenant Ellis of the Marines remembered how

> I was sent below with orders and was much struck with the preparations made by the bluejackets, the majority of whom were stripped to the waist; a handkerchief was tightly bound round their heads and over the ears, to deaden the noise of the cannon, many men being deaf for days after an action. The men were variously occupied – some were sharpening their cutlasses, others polishing the guns, as though an inspection were about to take place instead of mortal combat, whilst three or four, as if in mere bravado, were dancing a hornpipe. Occasionally they would look out of the ports and speculate as to the various ships of the enemy, many of which had been on former occasions engaged by our vessels.

Collingwood in the *Royal Sovereign*, which had recently been coppered, was drawing ahead and, though Nelson had hoped to bring the *Victory* in the van of the windward column into action first, it was clear the honour would go to his second-in-command. 'See how that noble fellow Collingwood takes his ship into action!' he commented as the *Royal Sovereign* came under fire from the huge, dark *Santa Anna*, the second largest warship in the world, mounting 122 guns. Collingwood, for his part, remarked to his captain: 'Rotherham, what would Nelson give to be here!' A few minutes later the *Victory* herself came under fire, long ranging shots, the first falling short, the second almost alongside, and the third over – good gunnery. At this point Nelson despatched his frigate captains, and Blackwood, as he left the man he admired above all others in the world, crossed the *Victory*'s side 'with a heart very sad'. The last words he heard from Nelson were clear and distinct: 'God bless you, Blackwood; I shall never speak to you again.'

The sixth shot fired at the *Victory* went through her main top-gallant sail. The enemy now had her range and six ships or more opened a concentrated fire on her. A round shot screaming across her quarter-deck almost cut in half the Admiral's secretary as he was talking to Hardy. Captain Adair of the Marines ordered some seamen to throw the body overboard. 'Is that poor Scott?' asked Nelson, adding 'Poor fellow!' A few minutes later Mr Whipple, the Captain's clerk, was killed and then a shot struck a group of marines stationed on the quarter-deck, killing eight of them. Nelson ordered Adair to disperse his men around the ship. Another shot now hit the forebrace bitts and a splinter struck the buckle of Hardy's shoe and bruised his foot. The two men were pacing the quarter-deck together and both stopped instinctively and looked to see if the other was hurt. 'This is too warm work to last long,' Nelson commented and they resumed their walk. Nelson was making a feint of attacking the enemy van so that Collingwood should be 'as little interrupted as possible' and, the objective now attained, the order was given to port the helm. She had been at least twenty minutes under concentrated fire without being able to return a single shot. Many men were dead, her rigging had been damaged, and her main topmast, with studding-sail and booms still set, had been shot away. The wheel had been hit and shattered so that she had to be steered by tackles from below. Now it was her turn. As the poet Thomas Campbell wrote:

> . . . When each gun
> From its adamantine lips
> Spread a death-shade round the ships
> Like a hurricane-eclipse
> Of the sun.

The *Victory* passed close under the stern of Villeneuve's flagship the *Bucentaure*, firing first her fo'c'sle carronade and then discharging a ripple broadside double-shotted. It was as if a hurricane had hit the Frenchman as the shot tore through the entire length of the ship, putting twenty guns out of action and, according to the French estimate, killing or wounding four hundred men. Collingwood had already broken the line, and now it was Nelson's turn. Hardy had

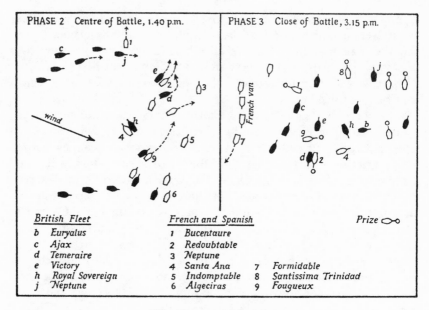

British Fleet		French and Spanish		Prize ○—○
b	Euryalus	1	Bucentaure	
c	Ajax	2	Redoubtable	
d	Temeraire	3	Neptune	
e	Victory	4	Santa Ana	7 Formidable
h	Royal Sovereign	5	Indomptable	8 Santissima Trinidad
j	Neptune	6	Algeciras	9 Fougueux

The Battle of Trafalgar

told him that he could not get through without running on board one of the enemy ships, to which he had replied: 'Take your choice, it does not signify which.' Hardy accordingly chose Captain Lucas' *Redoutable*, which happened to be the most efficient and best-manned ship in the Combined Fleet, and ran on board her, the *Victory*'s main yard catching in the Frenchman's rigging and locking the two vessels together. *Victory*'s starboard guns were now pouring round upon round into the *Redoutable*'s side while her port batteries engaged the enormous *Santissima Trinidad* which lay ahead of her. Lucas' men, who had been specially trained in marksmanship and the use of hand grenades, several times nearly cleared the *Victory*'s decks and at one moment were on the point of boarding her. The *Téméraire* ranging up on the starboard side came to the aid of her flagship and inflicted such a devastating fire on the *Redoutable* that she sank on the following day. Everywhere the smoke of battle covered the slowly heaving sea as ship after ship came up, picked an opponent, and went into action. The enemy's backbone was broken, and now the mêlée which Nelson had wanted to bring about was developing all over the battle arena.

The *Victory* had been in action for an hour when, at about a quarter past one, Hardy turned in his walk and suddenly realised that he was alone. He looked back and saw the Admiral on his knees, with the fingertips of his left hand just touching the deck. Then Nelson's arm gave way and he fell on his left side. He collapsed on the very spot where Scott had been killed.

Sergeant-Major Secker of the Marines and two seamen ran to the Admiral's assistance and gently raised him up. Hardy too was at his side and, bending his tall frame over the frail figure, caught the words, 'They have done for me at last,' and, when he made a protestation, Nelson answered, 'Yes, my backbone is shot through.' Hardy told the men to carry the Admiral below to the cockpit and resumed his pacing of the quarter-deck. As far as all the other engaged ships knew, Nelson still directed the battle. Hardy, as his Captain, was his Admiral's representative. As long as Nelson lived, the *Victory* remained the flagship.

CHAPTER THIRTY-SIX

Death and Storm

THE three men passed through the middle deck, as they carried the Admiral down to the red cockpit below the waterline. Nelson, alert even at this moment, noticed that the tiller ropes needed to be re-rove and ordered that this should be attended to immediately. He then drew a handkerchief out of his pocket and covered his face as well as his Orders, so that he might not be noticed by the crew. Dr Scott, the chaplain, was hastening out of the cockpit, overcome by his first sight of the 'butcher's shambles' that it became in action, when his attention was drawn to the Admiral. Although his only wish had been to get away for a few minutes from the horror below, he at once turned back, and stayed with Nelson to the end. The surgeon, Mr William Beatty, who wrote an admirable account, *The Authentic Narrative of the Death of Lord Nelson* in 1807, is the best witness of his last hours. He also tells the circumstances of his wounding:

It is by no means certain, though highly probable, that Lord Nelson was particularly aimed at by the Enemy. There were only two Frenchmen left alive in the mizen-top of the *Redoutable* at the time of His Lordship's being wounded, and by the hands of one of these he fell. These men continued firing at Captains Hardy and Adair, Lieutenant Roteley of the Marines, and some of the Midshipmen on the *Victory*'s poop, for some time afterwards. At length one of them was killed by a musket-ball : and on the other's then attempting to make his escape, Mr Pollard (Midshipman) fired his musket at him, and shot him in the back; when he fell dead from the shrouds, on the *Redoutable*'s poop.

The Admiral was now put in a midshipman's berth, the marine and two sailors went back to their duties, and Mr Burke, the purser, helped to undress him. Under his shirt Nelson was wearing a miniature depicting Lady Hamilton as a Bacchante. Beatty took Nelson's pulse and, after examining him, concluded that the musket ball had gone deep into the chest. (It had in fact entered through Nelson's left epaulette, taking some of the cloth and the gold with it, broken two ribs, severed a main branch of the left pulmonary artery, and then fractured the sixth and seventh dorsal vertebrae.) 'Ah, Mr Beatty!' Nelson murmured, 'You can do nothing for me. I have but a short time to live : my back is shot through.' While he was being undressed he had said in an urgent and agitated manner to Dr Scott, 'Doctor, I told you so, Doctor, I am gone!' and then, after a pause, 'Remember me to Lady Hamilton! Remember me to Horatia!' Beatty's account states that he added in a low voice, 'I have to leave Lady Hamilton, and my adopted daughter Horatia, as a legacy to my country.' On Beatty's asking him what were his sensations, Nelson answered that 'he felt a gush of blood every minute within his breast : that he had no feeling in the lower part of his body : and that his breathing was difficult, and attended with very severe pain about that part of the spine where he was confident that the ball had struck'.

Beatty realised that the case was hopeless, but concealed his condition from all but Hardy, who had of necessity to be informed. Although Nelson repeatedly asked for him, Hardy was too busy on the upper deck to come below until nearly three o'clock. The *Victory* had for a time been one of a group of four ships, all foul of one another, the *Redoutable*, the *Téméraire* and the *Fougueux*. The two Frenchmen had finally been subdued, after an action in which Lucas' *Redoutable* had been fought with astonishing courage, and had lost the greater part of her crew. The *Victory*, which by now had come clear on her own, was in imminent danger of being attacked by five of the French van. When Hardy finally came below Nelson had passed his initial agitation and was cool and lucid. Beatty recalled the dialogue :

' "Well, Hardy, how goes the battle? How goes the day with us?"

' "Very well, my Lord. We have got twelve or fourteen of the Enemy's ships in our possession; but five of their van have tacked, and shew an intention of bearing down upon the *Victory*. I have, therefore, called two or three of our fresh ships round us, and have no doubt of giving them a drubbing."

' "I hope none of *our* ships have struck, Hardy?"

' "No, my Lord, there is no fear of that."

' "I am a dead man, Hardy. I am going fast : it will be all over with me soon. Come nearer to me. Pray let my dear Lady Hamilton have my hair, and all other things belonging to me." '

Shortly afterwards Hardy shook his hand and took his leave. He could no longer conceal from Collingwood the condition of his chief and sent a message across to tell him that the Admiral was mortally wounded. Beatty, who was still attending him, was told by Nelson to return to his other patients for 'you can do nothing for me'. Finally he complied and Dr Scott, Mr Burke, Nelson's steward Chevalier, and another of his personal servants stayed in attendance on the dying man. It was hot and airless in the evil-smelling cockpit and Nelson felt a hunger for air and a great thirst due to his severe haemorrhage. A paper fan was constructed and he was constantly fanned while lemonade was brought to him. Every now and then the whole area would shake and the lights in the horn lanterns would dance and shiver as the *Victory* opened fire. Then there was a great noise of cheering and, on Nelson inquiring what was the cause, Lieutenant Pasco, who was lying wounded nearby, explained that the men were cheering because yet another ship had struck. Beatty, who had been away attending to the other wounded, among them a midshipman who had lost a leg, came back again to see the Admiral. Upon his inquiring whether the pain was still intense, he was told that, 'it continued so very severe, that he wished he was dead'. Then he added in a low voice, 'One would like to live a little longer, too,' and after a pause, 'What would become of poor Lady Hamilton, if she knew my situation!'

Hardy came down again about fifty minutes after his first visit and shook Nelson's hand. Beatty noted that this time he did not relinquish it, as 'he congratulated him even in the arms of Death on his brilliant victory; which, he said, was complete; though he did not know how many of the enemy were captured, as it was impossible to perceive every ship distinctly. He was certain however of fourteen or fifteen having surrendered. His Lordship answered, "That is well, but I bargained for twenty:" and then emphatically exclaimed, "*Anchor*, Hardy, *anchor*!" To this the Captain replied: "I suppose, my Lord, Admiral Collingwood will now take upon himself the direction of affairs." "Not while I live, I hope, Hardy!" cried the dying Chief; and at that moment endeavoured ineffectually to raise himself from the bed. "No," added he; "do *you* anchor, Hardy." Upon Hardy's asking whether *Victory* should make the signal Nelson answered, "Yes, for if I live, I'll anchor."

'He was determined to retain command until his last breath which, indeed, he felt was imminent for he added in a low tone: "Don't throw me overboard, Hardy." Never a man of words, all that the tall West Country man could find to say was: "Oh no, certainly not."

' "Then you know what to do," Nelson replied. "And take care of my dear Lady Hamilton, Hardy. Take care of poor Lady Hamilton. Kiss me Hardy." '

The Captain, Beatty recorded, 'now knelt down and kissed his cheek, when his Lordship said: "Now I am satisfied; thank God, I have done my duty." Captain Hardy stood for a minute or two in silent contemplation: he then knelt down again, and kissed His Lordship's forehead. His Lordship said: "Who is that?" The Captain answered: "It is Hardy", to which his Lordship replied, "God bless you, Hardy!" '

Hardy returned to the quarter-deck, having been about eight minutes below with his dying friend. Blackwood was one of the few others who learned that Nelson was dying. He desperately wanted to see him, but the *Euryalus* had Collingwood's *Royal Sovereign* under tow. (Her masts had been badly damaged in the action with the *Santa Anna*, the latter having finally struck her colours.) Upon the tow being accidentally cut by a shot, Blackwood, instead of trying to pass another, hauled off and made for the *Victory*. He got aboard and was told that the Admiral was still alive, but on reaching the cockpit he found him already dead. During his last moments Nelson had asked his steward, Chevalier, to turn him on his right side, saying, 'I wish I had not left the deck, for I shall soon be gone.' He pined for that sea air which he had known all his life, even heavy as now with gun-smoke, blowing over the open spaces of the planking where in his time he had walked so very many miles. He said little after Hardy had gone, only brief requests such as 'Drink, drink', 'Fan, fan' and 'Rub, rub' – the latter addressed to Doctor Scott who had been massaging his chest, which seemed to give him some relief. At one moment he said to Scott in a faint voice, 'Doctor, I have *not* been a *great* sinner,' and then, '*Remember* that I leave Lady Hamilton and my daughter as a legacy to my Country – never forget Horatia.' His last words, several times repeated, were: 'Thank God, I have done my duty.' At length he was silent. Doctor Scott and Mr Burke, who all this time had held up the cot at an angle that seemed to give Nelson some relief, said no more to the dying man. Chevalier tiptoed from the scene and went to Mr Beatty who came at once and knelt by his side. He took up the Admiral's hand and found no pulse discernible in the wrist. The Log of the *Victory* written in pencil by the Midshipman of the Watch records: 'Partial firing continued until 4.30, when a victory having been reported to the Right Hon. Lord Viscount Nelson, K.B., and Commander-in-Chief, he died of his wound.'

Half an hour later, as if to set the seal upon the awesome scene of disabled ships, struggling men and floating wreckage – all varnished with a haze of smoke – there came a tremendous explosion. The *Achilles*, which had been dismasted and had then caught fire, had blown up. An officer in the *Defence* remembered : 'It was a sight the most awful and grand that can be conceived. In a moment the hull burst into a cloud of smoke and fire. A column of vivid flame shot up to an enormous height in the atmosphere and terminated by expanding into an immense globe, representing, for a few seconds, a prodigious tree in flames, speckled with many dark spots, which the pieces of timber and bodies of men occasioned while they were suspended in the clouds.' The whole incident was reminiscent of that other occasion when, on the dark waters of Aboukir Bay, the explosion of *L'Orient* had signalled the first of Nelson's great victories.

Trafalgar was the fitting culmination of Nelson's life-work. As Chaucer wrote :

> The lyf so short, the craft so long to lerne,
> Th'assay so hard, so sharp the conquerynge.

Eighteen of the Combined Fleet had either been taken as prizes or destroyed while the British, although many of them badly mauled, had lost only a single ship. The ruin of Napoleon's ambitions at sea was complete. Of the ships that escaped from the holocaust of Trafalgar, eleven which reached Cadiz never put to sea again, while Rear-Admiral Dumanoir's squadron, which had run to the southward, was captured by Sir Richard Strachan later in the year.

Three things were responsible for the British victory at Cape Trafalgar : Nelson's genius in devising an unorthodox, risky, but brilliant manner of attack; the superiority of British seamanship, honed by the long months of blockading duties, while the enemy had grown stale in harbour; and, above all, by the marked superiority of British gunnery. Nelson was a master in the harsh art of war, a personally gentle man who was a genius in administering death. His own death, at the climax of his greatest battle, laid a classical laurel on his brow. He did not die too soon. Beatty, who later conducted the autopsy on his body, remarked that 'all the vital parts were so perfectly healthy in appearance, and so small, that they resembled more those of a youth, than of a man who had attained his forty-seventh year'. He concluded that, in view of Nelson's temperate habits, there was every reason to believe that he might have lived to a ripe old age. But there was another and darker side to the surgeon's report: 'Had he lived a few years longer, and continued at sea, he would have lost his sight totally.'

The expected gale came up from the south-west. Collingwood did not anchor, for he considered it better for the fleet to wear and stand out westward into the open sea. In this he may well have been right, although partisans of Nelson maintain that not so many of the prizes would have been lost if the Admiral's last order had been transmitted and obeyed. It is somewhat doubtful, in view of the condition of the ships after one of the hardest fought battles on record, if any more would have survived had they anchored. Indeed, in some cases it would have been impossible to do so, for either their anchors had been lost or their anchor cables had been too badly damaged to be serviceable. Storm, heavy rain and all-obscuring nimbus clouds followed on the death of the Sea-King, and for four days neither sun, moon, nor stars were seen. The savaged ships clawed their way off shore, while to their lee the shoals and rocks off-lying Cape Trafalgar roared to the boom and thunder of the westerly. Logs of the ships all tell the same tale. The *Spartiate*: 'Fresh gales with hard rain – fleet and prizes much scattered.' The *Phoebe*: 'Lost three whole hawsers and 100 fathoms of rope endeavouring to take *L'Aigle* and *Fougueux* in tow.' Midshipman Barker of the *Swiftsure* recalled: 'On the 22nd it came on a most Violent Gale of wind. The Prize in Tow, the *Redoutable*, seemed to weather it out tolerable well notwithstanding her shattered state until about three in the afternoon, when from her rolling so violently in a heavy sea, she carried away her fore Mast, the only mast she had standing.' Here, as in many other cases, Nelson's last prayer that 'humanity after Victory [should] be the predominant feature in the British fleet' was answered. Barker continues: 'Towards the evening she repeatedly made signals of distress to us: we now hoisted out our boats, and sent them on board of her although there was a very high Sea, and we were afraid the boats would be swampt alongside the Prize, but they happily succeeded in saving a great number.' Lieutenant Edwards of the *Prince* described the fate of the ship which the midshipman of the *Neptune* had earlier admired as a 'superb man-of-war':

We had the *Santissima Trinidad*, the largest ship in the world in tow. 'Tis impossible to describe the horrors the morning presented, nothing but signals of distress flying in every direction. The signal was made to destroy the prizes. We had no time before to remove the prisoners; but what a sight when we came to remove the wounded, of which there were between three and four hundred.

We had to tie the poor mangled wretches round their waists, and lower them down into a tumbling boat, some without arms, others no legs, and lacerated all over in the most dreadful manner.

The news of Nelson's death became swiftly known throughout the fleet and an immense sadness followed hard on the heels of the exhilaration of victory. (When the news of Trafalgar reached London on 6 November, the triumph of the event was almost overshadowed by the sense of loss that his death inspired.) Far away in Naples the poet Coleridge, who was passing through the city on his way home after a period of being Private Secretary to Sir Alexander Ball in Malta, wrote how, 'When Nelson died, it seemed as if no man was a stranger to another : for all were made acquaintances in the rights of a common anguish. . . . Numbers stopped and shook hands with me, because they had seen the tears on my cheek, and conjectured that I was an Englishman; and some, as they held my hand, burst, themselves, into tears.' Blackwood writing to his wife on the day after the battle could not conceal his grief : 'A Victory, such a one as has never been achieved, yesterday took place in the course of five hours; but at such an expense, in the loss of the most gallant man, and best of friends, as renders it to me a Victory I never wished to have witnessed – at least on such terms.' He did not fail to pay tribute to the enemy :

They waited the attack of the British with a coolness I was sorry to witness. And they fought in a way that must do them honour. As a spectator, who saw the faults, or rather mistakes, on both sides, I shall ever do them the justice to say so. They are, however, beat. . . . Buonaparte, I firmly believe, forced them to sea to try his luck, and what it might procure him in a pitched battle. They had the flower of the Combined Fleet, and I hope it will convince Europe at large that he has not yet learnt enough to cope with the English at sea.

A humble sailor in a letter home summed up the feelings of all the battle-weary, storm-tossed men whose discipline, courage and endurance had made the victory possible. 'I never set eyes on him,' he wrote, 'for which I am both sorry and glad, for to be sure I should like to have seen him, but then, all the men in our ship are such soft toads, they have done nothing but Blast their Eyes and cry ever since he was killed. God bless you ! chaps that fought like the Devil sit down and cry like a wench.'

Napoleon's only official comment on the battle read : 'Gales have caused the loss of several vessels after a battle which had been entered upon imprudently.' The fact remained that the British ships, which had also taken heavy punishment in the engagement, did not run ashore or founder – although many, including the badly damaged *Victory*, had a very hard time in weathering the storm. Collingwood, commenting in a letter that only four of the prizes had been saved to be towed to Gibraltar, remarked : 'I can only say that in my life I never saw such exertions as were made to save those Ships. It more astonished the Spaniards than the beating they got; and one of them said, when I assured him that none of our Ships were lost, "How can we contend with such a people, on whom the utmost violence of the elements has no effect?" '

Collingwood's list of the fate of the flag-officers of the Combined Fleet tells the story of Trafalgar quite as clearly as any detailed account of the damage suffered by the individual ships. The Commander-in-Chief, Admiral Villeneuve, aboard the *Bucentaure* was taken prisoner. (Later, repatriated from England to his native land, this unfortunate but far from cowardly admiral took his own life.) The Spanish Admiral Don Federico Gravina aboard the *Principe de Asturias* managed to escape to Cadiz, although badly wounded in the right arm. The Spanish Vice-Admiral Don Ignatio Maria d'Alava aboard the *Santa Anna* suffered a severe head wound, was captured, but then during the chaos of the storm escaped into Cadiz in his devastated ship. Rear-Admiral Cisneros of the *Santissima Trinidad* was captured, the French Rear-Admiral Magon of the *Algéciras* was killed. Rear-Admiral Dumanoir on board the *Formidable* escaped and, as we know, together with his squadron of four ships, was later captured by Sir Richard Strachan.

Nelson's body was put into a leaguer, one of the largest casks carried aboard ship, after his hair had been cut off and he had been stripped of all his clothes save a shirt. The cask was then filled with brandy – not rum as is often said (hence the inaccurate navy slang for rum, 'Nelson's blood') – brandy being the purest type of spirit on board. At Gibraltar the body was transferred into spirits of wine, the best preservative available. Beatty records the macabre story of how the admiral's body made its last journey to Gibraltar :

In the evening after this melancholy task had been accomplished, the gale came on with violence from the South-west, and continued that night and the succeeding day without any abatement. During this boisterous weather, Lord Nelson's body remained under the charge of a sentinel on the middle deck. The cask was placed on its end, having a closed aperture at its top and another below; the object of which was, that as a frequent renewal of the spirit was thought necessary, the old could thus be drawn off below and fresh quantity introduced above, without moving the cask, or occasioning the least agitation of the Body. On the 24th there was a disengagement of air from the Body to such a degree, that the sentinel became alarmed on seeing the head of the cask raised : he therefore applied to the Officers, who were under the necessity of having the cask spiled to give the air a discharge.

On 28 October, the *Victory*, under tow from the *Neptune*, came in under the shadow of the great Rock. Gibraltar, the symbol of the sea-power of Britain, to which Nelson had devoted his life, frowned with guns and the half-masted British flag flew over all. Ships surged and swayed in the anchorage, and all the while the never-ceasing current poured from the grey Atlantic into the Mediterranean. 'The Keel of a Ship', said the ancients, 'leaves no trace', but Nelson had signed his name for ever upon the great tumbled ocean as well as upon the ancient inland sea.

CHAPTER THIRTY-SEVEN

Time and the Survivors

A SOUTH-WEST gale hurled down the Thames on 8 January 1806, the day that Nelson's body was conveyed up river from Greenwich to Whitehall. It had lain in state in Wren's magnificent Painted Hall, and over 30,000 people had filed past the coffin of the man whom they had come to love not only as the heroic defender of their country but as a beloved son. Dr Scott, his devoted chaplain, had stayed by the coffin in a vigil to which he had clearly committed himself in those last hours when he had rubbed Nelson's breast, heard his final words, and watched him die. Now the body was destined for the full pomp and ceremony of a state funeral, a funeral surpassing any other within living memory, a funeral indeed such as he would have planned for himself. What would further have pleased him was that he was to be buried in St Paul's and not in Westminster Abbey. It was true that in earlier days he had more than once expressed the wish to reach the Valhalla of the Abbey if he were to die in battle, but more recently he had remarked that if he were 'to be interred at the public expense, I wish to be buried in St Paul's rather than in Westminster Abbey. I heard an old tradition when I was a boy that Westminster Abbey is built on a spot where once existed a deep morass, and I think it likely that the lapse of time will reduce the ground on which it now stands to its primitive state of a swamp, without leaving a trace of the Abbey.'

Following hard on the heels of the south-westerly a hailstorm struck the capital as the coffin was being landed at Whitehall Stairs. The next day, as if to celebrate the famous unpredictability of the British climate, dawned clear and cold. The sky was as cloudless and blue as it is in East Anglia when the wind cries off the North Sea. Admiral Sir Peter Parker, who all those long years ago had first promoted Nelson to Captain in the West Indies, was foremost of the mourners, together with thirty other flag-officers and one hundred captains. The Prince of Wales, the Duke of Clarence, later to be the 'Sailor King'

353

William IV (who had occasioned Nelson so much trouble in the West Indies), the Duke of York, the nobility, and all the notables of gentry and city were present to pay their last respects to a man who had risen from the obscurity of a Norfolk parsonage to a sphere of immortality whither he had been beckoned by that 'radiant orb'. George Matcham, Nelson's nephew, recalled : 'The procession moved on slowly, the sailors lining the streets, and the Band playing the Dead March in Saul. At Temple Bar it was joined by the Mayor and suite, who took their place after the Prince of Wales. At St Pauls we got out, and walked in procession up the Passage. It was the most aweful sight I ever saw. All the Bands played. The Colours were all carried by the Sailors and a Canopy was held over the Coffin, supported by Admirals.' For sadly obvious reasons Nelson's 'bequest to the nation', the woman whose name had been on his lips in his last hour, could not be present. Dr Scott, as thoughtful as he was faithful, afterwards wrote to Emma that 'the very beggars left their stands, neglected the passing crowd, and seemed to pay tribute to his memory by a look. Many did I see, tattered and on crutches, shaking their heads with plain signs of sorrow. This must be truly unbought affection of the heart.' As the cortège passed through the streets of London, the city which he had defended against the aggression of Napoleon, the vast crowd lining the route bared their heads, and in this sound and in their sighs could be detected the long susurrus of the sea.

His body had been placed within that coffin which Ben Hallowell had had made for him out of the mainmast of L'Orient, and this was now lowered into a sarcophagus of black marble which had been originally intended for Cardinal Wolsey. It rests exactly beneath the cupola of St Paul's, simple and austere, surmounted by a viscount's coronet, and inscribed only with his name and the dates of his birth and death. Nearby rest Cooke of the Bellerophon and Duff of the Mars, two captains who were also killed at Trafalgar, as well as the faithful Collingwood who joined him five years later, worn out by his subsequent years as Nelson's successor as Commander-in-Chief of the Mediterranean. Not far away, in the full flower of high Victorian pomp and splendour, rises the great tomb in which rest the remains of Arthur Wellesley, first Duke of Wellington, that other giant who completed upon the land the task that Nelson had begun upon the sea.

Just as the Battle of the Nile had occurred at a moment when the nation's spirits were at a low ebb as it faced the new Napoleonic Europe and the threat to India, so Trafalgar put fresh heart into a Britain that was confronted by disaster upon the Continent. Napoleon's forces had overwhelmed the Austrians at Ulm. The Third

Coalition was shattered, and once more Britain faced the land mass of Europe totally dominated by the Corsican genius. Lord Auckland remarked that, 'The news from Cadiz came like a cordial to a fainting man.' Thus, two out of Nelson's three great victories acquired an additional significance in British history because of their inspirational effect upon morale. The third, Copenhagen, which had been politically embarrassing, had nevertheless been of the utmost importance in economic terms, saving the City of London, and indeed the Navy itself, from what would almost certainly have been ruin. Those who were in the know acknowledged Copenhagen as the triumph that it was, but it could not be given the public acknowledgement that it deserved. Trafalgar on the other hand was celebrated then, as it has been ever since, as the crowning glory of British naval achievement. It has never been equalled.

Nelson's relatives, as he had accurately surmised, were well looked after by those in authority. His brother William, a cleric very unlike his father in being neither simple nor without worldly aspirations, was made an earl. A pension of £5,000 a year was attached to the new title, while Nelson's sisters each received £15,000. Fanny received a pension of £2,000 a year for life. The new earl also received a large grant from Parliament to enable him to purchase an estate. All those, then, who legitimately had a claim upon their country's gratitude for the services which their dead relative had rendered were taken care of in a handsome manner. But Emma? There was little or nothing that could be done for her, even in an age when many public men kept mistresses quite openly, and when the profligate behaviour of George III's sons was common knowledge. The fact remained that Emma could still only be acknowledged as the widow of Sir William Hamilton, former envoy to the court of Naples. On the surface of it she might have seemed well enough provided for, with the annuities left her by her husband and her lover, together with the possession of Merton Place. It is true that if she had lived very quietly like a widow she might have stayed on at Merton with Horatia, but if she had been temperamentally suited to such a life she would never have risen to become Sir William's wife, nor Nelson's adored mistress. It was not only her financial imprudence that caused her downfall but also her open heart, for after the splendours of Naples and Palermo – and even, in a quieter way, of Merton in its brief heyday – she could never understand that she could neither afford to entertain largely, look after poor relatives, nor, above all, to indulge in gambling. In 1808 a meeting of her friends managed between them to raise enough money to cope with her more immediate debts, but they could not hold back for ever the increasing pressure of her creditors. In the following year the banker Abraham Goldsmid bought Merton and she subsequently lived at various addresses in the heart of London, all within a short distance of Piccadilly and the fashionable world where once she had shone on the arm of her husband in the company of the Victor of the Nile. Her last years are tragic to contemplate. Her Nelson relics were gradually sold off, while in 1810 the death of her mother, Mrs Cadogan, left Emma without that shrewd old counsellor who had been largely responsible for making her fortune in the world although in her last years she had been unable to check its decline. Emma was imprisoned for debt, she suffered from jaundice with all its debilitating and depressing effects, and in July 1814, taking Horatia with her, she fled to Calais. Her last days are best described by her daughter :

> At the time of her death she was in great distress, and had I not, unknown to her, written to Lord Nelson to ask the loan of £10, and to another kind friend of hers, who immediately sent her £20, she would not literally have had one shilling till her next allowance became due. Latterly she was scarcely sensible. I imagine that her illness originally began by being bled whilst labouring under an attack of jaundice whilst she lived at Richmond. From that time she was never well, and added to this, the baneful habit she had of taking wine and spirits to a fearful degree, brought on water on the chest. She died in January, 1815, and was buried in the burying ground attached to the town.

The site of her grave is unknown. A few months later the Battle of Waterloo brought Napoleon's career to an end.

Horatia grew up never knowing that Emma was her mother, although she happily acknowledged that Nelson was her father. She had a vague suspicion that her mother might have been the Queen of Naples. She found a home with Nelson's favourite sister, her aunt, Mrs Matcham, and in 1822 married the Reverend Philip Ward. So the Nelson blood returned to the church, and Horatia's subsequent life followed the pattern of her paternal grandmother. As wife to a clergyman, mother of many sons, she lived in the quiet countryside, far from the roar of guns, affairs of state, or the ever-expanding imperial and industrial world of a Britain which Nelson had helped to make mistress of the seas. She died aged eighty-one. Nelson's prayer that her life should be a happy one had been answered.

Fanny Nelson, like so many who suffer from delicate health, also reached a ripe age, dying at seventy-three, having outlived her son

Josiah Nisbet. The latter, for whom Nelson had once striven so much, and who had occasioned him such trouble and concern, never made a success in the Navy. Ashore he did much better, had an instinct for business, married well, and left his wife and children comfortably off when he died at the age of fifty. His was a life not untypical of thousands of others and, indeed, so many names have only survived into posterity because in one way or another they were at some time connected with Nelson. This can never be said of Hardy, who, like others of Nelson's close friends and 'Band of Brothers', went on to prove that their leader was not a strange freak of nature but merely one who grew from the same stock, but happened to have the touch of genius added. He was made a baronet the year after Trafalgar, later became First Sea Lord, and died as Governor of Greenwich Hospital in 1831.

The most decisive naval engagement of the nineteenth century after Trafalgar was fought by Vice-Admiral Sir Edward Codrington at Navarino in 1827 when, in command of an allied fleet that included those former enemies the French and the Russians, he annihilated the Turko-Egyptian navies. It was a victory in the Nelson tradition and led in due course to the liberation of Greece. Codrington had been Captain of the *Orion* at Trafalgar. In his instructions to his senior officers and allies prior to the battle he had – somewhat tactlessly perhaps in view of the French presence – quoted Nelson's words before Trafalgar : 'No captain can do very wrong who places his ship alongside that of an enemy.'

Nelson needs no further epitaph.

Index

359